THE MACARTHUR NEW TESTAMENT COMMENTARY

ACTS 13-28

John MacArthur, Jr.

MOODY PRESS/CHICAGO

*To Bill Koptis, whose friendship,
service, leadership, and generosity
have made him an instrument of
God's grace to me.*

ISBN: 0-8024-0760-9

1 3 5 7 9 10 8 6 4 2

Printed in the United States of America

Contents

Preface

It continues to be a rewarding, divine communion for me to preach expositionally through the New Testament. My goal is always to have deep fellowship with the Lord in the understanding of His Word and out of that experience to explain to His people what a passage means. In the words of Nehemiah 8:8, I strive "to give the sense" of it so they may truly hear God speak and, in so doing, may respond to Him.

Obviously, God's people need to understand Him, which demands knowing His Word of Truth (2 Tim. 2:15) and allowing that Word to dwell in them richly (Col. 3:16). The dominant thrust of my ministry, therefore, is to help make God's living Word alive to His people. It is a refreshing adventure.

This New Testament commentary series reflects this objective of explaining and applying Scripture. Some commentaries are primarily linguistic, others are mostly theological, and some are mainly homiletical. This one is basically explanatory, or expository. It is not linguistically technical but deals with linguistics when that seems helpful to proper interpretation. It is not theologically expansive but focuses on the major doctrines in each text and how they relate to the whole of Scripture. It is not primarily homiletical, although each unit of thought is generally treated as one chapter, with a clear outline and logical flow of thought.

Most truths are illustrated and applied with other Scripture. After establishing the context of a passage, I have tried to follow closely the writer's development and reasoning.

My prayer is that each reader will fully understand what the Holy Spirit is saying through this part of His Word, so that His revelation may lodge in the mind of believers and bring greater obedience and faithfulness—to the glory of our great God.

OUTLINE

The Character of an Effective Church (Acts 13:1–13)

Now there were at Antioch, in the church that was there, prophets and teachers: Barnabas, and Simeon who was called Niger, and Lucius of Cyrene, and Manaen who had been brought up with Herod the tetrarch, and Saul. And while they were ministering to the Lord and fasting, the Holy Spirit said, "Set apart for Me Barnabas and Saul for the work to which I have called them." Then, when they had fasted and prayed and laid their hands on them, they sent them away. So, being sent out by the Holy Spirit, they went down to Seleucia and from there they sailed to Cyprus. And when they reached Salamis, they began to proclaim the word of God in the synagogues of the Jews; and they also had John as their helper. And when they had gone through the whole island as far as Paphos, they found a certain magician, a Jewish false prophet whose name was Bar-Jesus, who was with the proconsul, Sergius Paulus, a man of intelligence. This man summoned Barnabas and Saul and sought to hear the word of God. But Elymas the magician (for thus his name is translated) was opposing them, seeking to turn the proconsul away from the faith. But Saul, who was also known as Paul, filled with the Holy Spirit, fixed his gaze upon him, and said, "You who are full of all deceit and fraud, you son of the

devil, you enemy of all righteousness, will you not cease to make crooked the straight ways of the Lord? And now, behold, the hand of the Lord is upon you, and you will be blind and not see the sun for a time." And immediately a mist and a darkness fell upon him, and he went about seeking those who would lead him by the hand. Then the proconsul believed when he saw what had happened, being amazed at the teaching of the Lord. Now Paul and his companions put out to sea from Paphos and came to Perga in Pamphylia; and John left them and returned to Jerusalem. (13:1–13)

There is much truth in the humorous adage that some people make things happen, others watch things happen, while still others are left wondering what happened. What is true of individuals is also true of churches. Some churches are dynamic, aggressively reaching out with the gospel to make an impact on the world. Some know God is moving in other churches and wonder why they aren't experiencing that power. Still others just barely exist, languishing while the spiritual (and maybe even physical) weeds grow. They make an impact only on their members' social lives.

Acts 11 introduced a leadership and a congregation that God used to make things happen—the Antioch church, the first beachhead of Christianity in the pagan world. That church had an impressive beginning. Acts 11:21 records that "a large number who believed turned to the Lord" under the ministry of Hellenistic Jews who fled Jerusalem following Stephen's martyrdom (11:19–20). The Antioch church grew dramatically under the capable leadership of Barnabas and Saul (11:26). It was in Antioch that the name *Christians* was first given to the followers of Jesus Christ (11:26). Although it was intended as a derisive term, the believers wore it as a badge of honor. Members of this largely Gentile church showed their love for their Jewish brethren by sending them famine relief (11:27–30).

But of all the factors that made the Antioch church strong, the most significant was its submission to the Holy Spirit. Both the leaders (cf. 11:24; 13:9) and the congregation (cf. 13:2, 4) of the Antioch church were Spirit-filled. They were utterly dependent on the Spirit, who energized every phase of their ministry.

What marks a Spirit-filled church? A Spirit-filled church may be defined simply as one whose members walk in obedience to the will of God. Since God reveals His will in Scripture, a Spirit-filled church must be deeply committed to the Word of God. Indeed, a comparison of Ephesians 5 and Colossians 3 reveals that being filled with the Spirit and letting the Word richly dwell in one's life produce the same effects. Therefore they are the two sides of the same spiritual reality.

Chapter 13 marks a turning point in Acts. The first twelve chapters have focused on the ministry of Peter; the remaining chapters focus on Paul. Until now the emphasis has been on the Jewish church in Jerusalem and Judea; chapters 13–28 describe the spread of the Gentile church throughout the Roman world. And it was from the dynamic, doctrinally sound, growing, Spirit-controlled church at Antioch that the flag of Gentile missions was unfurled. It had spiritual leaders, with a spiritual ministry, who went on a spiritual mission, faced spiritual opposition, and experienced spiritual victory.

Spiritual Leaders

Now there were at Antioch, in the church that was there, prophets and teachers: Barnabas, and Simeon who was called Niger, and Lucius of Cyrene, and Manaen who had been brought up with Herod the tetrarch, and Saul. (13:1)

Effective, strong churches inevitably have godly leaders, and the church **at Antioch** was no exception. God has always put a premium on spiritual leadership (Acts 6:3; 1 Tim. 3:1–13; Titus 1:5–9; cf. Hos. 4:9; Matt. 9:36). These five men were the heart of the ministry at Antioch.

Luke describes them as **prophets and teachers,** two important New Testament terms. **Prophets** played a significant role in the apostolic church (cf. 1 Cor. 12:28; Eph. 2:20; 3:5; 4:11). Like the apostles, they were preachers of God's Word and were responsible in the early years of the church to instruct the local congregations. Sometimes they received new revelation from God, as in Acts 11:28 and 21:10–11. Both of those incidents record that the prophets, in contrast to the apostles, received practical, not doctrinal revelation. The prophets' function as receivers of divine revelation ended with the cessation of the temporary sign gifts. Even their office, like that of the apostles, was replaced by pastor-teachers and evangelists (cf. Eph. 4:11–12), who were the elders and overseers (1 Tim. 3:1ff.; Titus 1:5–9). (For a discussion of the cessation of the sign gifts, see John MacArthur, *Charismatic Chaos* [Grand Rapids: Zondervan, 1992] and *1 Corinthians*, MacArthur New Testament Commentary [Chicago: Moody, 1984].)

The prophets edified the saints by preaching expositions of existing revelation (cf. 1 Thess. 5:20). Although prophets of that unique kind no longer exist, the similar gift for preaching the Word of God remains. It is given to pastors and evangelists, who proclaim what Peter called "the prophetic word" (2 Pet. 1:19) and is still vital to the spiritual health of the church (cf. Rom. 10:14–18). All the way to the return of the Lord, the "spirit of prophecy" continues to be "the testimony of Jesus" (Rev. 19:10).

Teachers are critical in today's church (cf. 1 Cor. 12:28; Eph. 4:11; James 3:1). Theirs is the ministry of giving others a clear understanding of biblical truth. The distinctive of the ministry of teachers is its emphasis on pedagogy rather than on proclamation. That they are somewhat different from preachers seems apparent in texts that discuss both, though the same gifted man can sometimes perform both functions, as Acts 15:35 indicates.

Antioch had five men who were both preachers and teachers of God's Word. It was through their ministry that the church was built up in the faith.

Barnabas has already appeared several times in Acts. From 4:36 we learn he was a Levite from the island of Cyprus. His birth name was Joseph, but the apostles named him **Barnabas,** which means "Son of Encouragement"—an apt description of this gentle, loving man. It was Barnabas who convinced the skeptical and suspicious believers at Jerusalem that Saul's conversion was genuine (9:27). The Jerusalem fellowship sent him to investigate the rumors that Gentiles had been saved in Antioch (11:22)—a sign of the high esteem in which the Jerusalem church held him. He brought Saul from Tarsus and got him involved in the ministry in Antioch (11:25–26). Barnabas, along with Saul, carried the Antioch church's contributions for the relief of the Judean church to Jerusalem (11:30).

Little is known about **Simeon, Lucius,** and **Manaen.** Luke's note that **Simeon was called Niger** (which means "black") may suggest that he was a dark–skinned man, an African, or both. While some identify him with Simon of Cyrene, who carried Jesus' cross (Mark 15:21), there is no direct evidence for that identification. **Lucius,** but not Simeon, is identified with the city of **Cyrene** in North Africa. There is nothing to link him with the Lucius whom Paul greets in Romans 16:21 and certainly no evidence to identify him (as some have argued) as Luke the physician. **Manaen** was notable, Luke records, because he **had been brought up with Herod the tetrarch** (Herod Antipas, the Herod of the gospels). *Suntrophos* (**had been brought up with**) can be translated "foster-brother." He had been reared in Herod the Great's household along with Herod Antipas. **Saul,** or Paul, needs no introduction. Through his tireless efforts the gospel spread throughout the Gentile world. These were the shepherds who led the flock to effectiveness and impact.

SPIRITUAL MINISTRY

And while they were ministering to the Lord and fasting, (13:2*a*)

The responsibility of spiritual shepherds is spiritual ministry.

Unlike many in the ministry today who are busy with shallow activities and programs, the leaders at Antioch understood their spiritual mandate clearly. They patterned themselves after the apostles, who, according to Acts 6:4, devoted themselves to prayer and the ministry of the Word. Those are ever the priorities for the man of God.

Ministering is from *leitourgeō*, a word that originally meant "to discharge a public office." It was "used of the Attic orators who served the state at their own cost" (A. T. Robertson, *Word Pictures in the New Testament* [Grand Rapids: Baker's reprint of the 1930 edition], 3:177). The leaders of the Antioch church faithfully discharged the office God called them to and fulfilled their ministry (cf. 2 Tim. 4:5).

In Scripture, however, *leitourgeō* means more than public service; it describes priestly service. In the Septuagint it described the priests who ministered in the tabernacle (Ex. 28:41). Serving in a leadership role in the church must be viewed as an act of worship to God. Such service consists of offering spiritual sacrifices to Him (cf. Heb. 13:15–16), including prayer, oversight of the flock, studying, and preaching and teaching the Word.

Their **ministering** was not to the congregation but to **the Lord.** It is crucial to understand that God is the audience for all spiritual ministry (cf. Acts 20:19–20). Those whose goal is ministering to people will be tempted to compromise to achieve that end. Making the Lord the object of ministry obviates the need for compromise.

Like the Macedonian believers, those in ministry must give themselves first to the Lord and only then to other believers (cf. 2 Cor. 8:5). They are to "be diligent to present [themselves] approved to God," not to men (2 Tim. 2:15). The man of God, like every believer, does his "work heartily, as for the Lord rather than for men," because "it is the Lord Christ whom [he serves]" (Col. 3:23–24).

The Bible frequently connects **fasting** with times of vigilant, passionate prayer (cf. Neh. 1:4; Ps. 35:13; Dan. 9:3; Matt. 17:21; Luke 2:37; 5:33; Acts 14:23). Believers may become so concerned with spiritual issues that they lose the desire to eat, or they set aside food to concentrate on intense intercession. Those who know little of fasting perhaps know little about such concern. Scripture nowhere commands believers to fast, but Jesus assumed His followers would do so (Matt. 6:17; Luke 5:33–35). In sharp contrast to the showy, hypocritical fasting of the Pharisees, believers' fasting is for God's eyes only (Matt. 6:16–18). (For a further discussion of fasting, see *Matthew 1–7*, MacArthur New Testament Commentary [Chicago: Moody, 1985], 399ff.)

SPIRITUAL MISSION

the Holy Spirit said, "Set apart for Me Barnabas and Saul for the work to which I have called them." Then, when they had fasted and prayed and laid their hands on them, they sent them away. So, being sent out by the Holy Spirit, they went down to Seleucia and from there they sailed to Cyprus. And when they reached Salamis, they began to proclaim the word of God in the synagogues of the Jews; and they also had John as their helper. (13:2b–5)

Spiritual men with effective spiritual ministry will see God extend their spiritual mission. God chooses for further ministry those already actively serving Him. He is not likely to take idle Christians down from the shelf, dust them off, and entrust them with important work. Saul and Barnabas were deeply involved in ministering to the Lord when their call to further service came. God chose experienced, proven men for the vitally important mission to the Gentiles.

The truth that all ministry is to be done for the Lord is here reinforced by the Spirit's command to **set apart** Barnabas and Saul **for** Himself. They were His men, to use as He would and send wherever He desired.

Another principle that flows out of this text is that God sovereignly calls men to the ministry. The church did not choose Saul and Barnabas. Indeed, they would probably have been the last two chosen, since they were the best the church had. Nor did Saul and Barnabas volunteer. Instead, the Spirit sovereignly **called them** to full-time missionary service.

A final principle to be gleaned from this text is the importance of waiting for God's timing. The Antioch church did not concoct schemes or map out strategies to reach the Gentile world. Instead, it concentrated on carrying out the ministries God had already entrusted to it. An important feature in discerning God's will for the future is to do His will in the present.

How **the Holy Spirit** communicated to the church is not revealed. Presumably He spoke through one of the prophets. However the message was communicated, the church's response was instant obedience. There was no grumbling or resentment; the Holy Spirit demanded the church's best, and Antioch joyously provided Saul and Barnabas.

After **they had fasted and prayed,** no doubt for the success of Saul and Barnabas's ministry, the leaders **laid their hands on them.** The laying on of hands neither granted Saul and Barnabas the Holy Spirit nor ordained them to ministry. Both had already received the Spirit

(Acts 9:17; 11:24) and had been serving in the ministry for many years. The laying on of hands simply signified identification, confirmation, and unity in their upcoming mission (cf. Num. 8:10; 27:18–23).

Having prayed for Saul and Barnabas and having publicly identified with them, the Antioch church **sent them away.** A better translation of *apoluō* (**sent them away**) might be "they let them go," or "they released them." It is clear from verse 1 that the Spirit, not the church, sent out the two missionaries. Since He had already sent them, all the church could do was cut the cord and let them go. That truth is repeated in verse 4, where Luke relates that the missionaries were **sent out by the Holy Spirit.**

Leaving Antioch to begin the mission, **they went down to Seleucia.** Located some sixteen miles away, near the mouth of the Orontes River, **Seleucia** served as the port of Antioch. Whether the missionaries took the road to Seleucia or traveled by boat down the Orontes is not stated. Once in Seleucia, they took passage on a ship and **sailed to Cyprus.**

Cyprus is the third largest island in the Mediterranean, after Sicily and Sardinia. It is about 60 miles off the Syrian coast and would have been visible from Seleucia on a clear day. The main part of the island is 90 to 100 miles long and up to 60 miles wide. In New Testament times its two major cities were Salamis, the chief port and commercial center, and Paphos, the capital.

Saul and Barnabas no doubt chose to begin their missionary outreach on Cyprus for several reasons. According to Acts 4:36, it was Barnabas's home and thus familiar territory. Also, it was close to Antioch, probably two days' journey at most. Further, Cyprus had a large Jewish population. All those reasons made it an ideal starting point for outreach to the Gentile world.

Arriving at the main port city, **Salamis, they began to proclaim the word of God in the synagogues of the Jews.** To preach the gospel first to the Jews was Paul's custom throughout his missionary journeys. Cyprus had a Jewish settlement large enough to support several synagogues in Salamis. As they traveled from synagogue to synagogue, Saul and Barnabas **had John** Mark **as their helper.** He was a native of Jerusalem (Acts 12:12) and was Barnabas's cousin (Col. 4:10). When Saul and Barnabas returned to Antioch from Jerusalem after delivering relief aid, John Mark came with them (Acts 12:25). He had undoubtedly left Antioch along with Saul and Barnabas. Although he was soon to desert them and return to Jerusalem, for now he was a member of the team, helping Saul and Barnabas carry out their spiritual mission.

SPIRITUAL OPPOSITION

And when they had gone through the whole island as far as Paphos, they found a certain magician, a Jewish false prophet whose name was Bar-Jesus, who was with the proconsul, Sergius Paulus, a man of intelligence. This man summoned Barnabas and Saul and sought to hear the word of God. But Elymas the magician (for thus his name is translated) was opposing them, seeking to turn the proconsul away from the faith. . . . Now Paul and his companions put out to sea from Paphos and came to Perga in Pamphylia; and John left them and returned to Jerusalem. (13:6–8, 13)

When God's people seek to advance His purposes, satanic opposition is unavoidable. The missionary team had by now traversed **the whole island** from Salamis in the northeast corner **as far as Paphos** on the southwest coast. Besides being the seat of the Roman government, **Paphos** was

> a great center for the worship of Aphrodite [Venus]. . . . The greatest festival in Cyprus in honor of Aphrodite was the Aphrodisia, held for three days each spring. It was attended by great crowds not only from all parts of Cyprus but also from surrounding countries. (Charles F. Pfeiffer and Howard F. Vos, *The Wycliffe Historical Geography of Bible Lands* [Chicago: Moody, 1967], 305–6)

It was a city rife with immorality: "Extensive religious prostitution accompanied [Aphrodite's] rites at Paphos" (Pfeiffer and Vos, 306).

Here, in the capital, **they found a certain magician.** As happened when Peter and John brought the gospel to Samaria, Saul and Barnabas were confronted by a **magician.** *Magos* (**magician**) does not necessarily have an evil connotation. It is used, for example, in Matthew 2:1 to describe the wise men who visited the infant Jesus and His family. The term originally referred to the hereditary priestly tribe within the Median nation. They were well-versed in astronomy and astrology, agriculture, mathematics, and history. They were involved in various occult practices and were famous for their ability to interpret dreams (cf. Dan. 2:1ff.). Such was their political power and influence that no Persian ruler came to power without their approval. (For further information, see *Matthew 1–7*, MacArthur New Testament Commentary [Chicago: Moody, 1985], 26–28.) Later, however, the term **magician** was used to describe all sorts of practitioners of magic and dabblers in the occult. **Bar-Jesus,** being **Jewish,** obviously was not one of the Medo-Persian magi. Like

Simon (Acts 8:9–11), he was a deceiver who put his knowledge to evil use.

Bar-Jesus was not only a magician; Luke further describes him as a **false prophet.** His name, ironically, means "son of salvation"—a strange name indeed for a deceiving false prophet. It was no accident that this man had attached himself to the Roman **proconsul.** The kingdom of darkness is eager to influence those who rule. Much of the evil in this world can be traced ultimately to such baleful influence by "the spiritual forces of wickedness in the heavenly places" (Eph. 6:12; cf. Dan. 10:13–11:1).

The Roman governor of Cyprus was **Sergius Paulus,** whom Luke describes as **a man of intelligence.** The accuracy of Luke's account is verified by an inscription found at Soloi, on the north coast of Cyprus. That inscription dates itself "in the proconsulship of Paulus" (Sir William M. Ramsay, *St. Paul the Traveller and the Roman Citizen* [reprint; Grand Rapids: Baker, 1975], 74).

As an intelligent Roman, the governor no doubt had a keen interest in new philosophies and religious beliefs. That he had in his entourage a Jewish teacher (albeit a renegade one) showed he had some interest in Judaism. Saul and Barnabas appeared to him to be two more Jewish teachers from whom he could learn more about the Jewish faith. Further, his duties as governor prompted him to investigate this new teaching that was sweeping Cyprus. Accordingly, he **summoned Barnabas and Saul and sought to hear the word of God.**

Alarmed at the prospect of Sergius Paulus's conversion, and his own subsequent loss of status, **Elymas the magician (for thus his name is translated) was opposing them, seeking to turn the proconsul away from the faith.** He was doing the bidding of his evil master, Satan. Like many Jewish people at this time, Bar-Jesus also had a Greek name, **Elymas,** by which he was known at the court of Sergius Paulus. Luke's parenthetical note that **thus his name is translated** does not mean **Elymas** translates Bar-Jesus. Instead, **Elymas** was apparently the Greek transliteration of an Arabic word for "magician" (Simon J. Kistemaker, *New Testament Commentary: Acts* [Grand Rapids: Baker, 1990], 462).

It is well to remember the lesson of these verses. Leading someone to Christ is not merely an academic exercise, nor is it a matter of making a successful sales pitch. Rather, it involves all-out war against the forces of hell. Saul and Barnabas battled Bar-Jesus for the soul of Sergius Paulus.

But such external attacks are not Satan's only strategy. Even more deadly over the centuries have been his attacks on the church from within. It is hardly surprising, then, that he sought to derail the mission to the Gentiles with internal pressure as well. That pressure came in John

Mark's desertion. Having completed their work on Cyprus, **Paul and his companions put out to sea from Paphos and came to Perga in Pamphylia; and John left them and returned to Jerusalem. Perga** was a major city in the Roman province of **Pamphylia,** in Asia Minor.

What specifically was the reason **John left them and returned to Jerusalem** is not clear. Some have suggested that he was afraid to travel in the dangerous mountains of Pamphylia, a region infested with bands of robbers (cf. 2 Cor. 11:26). Others think he resented Paul's taking the ascendancy over his cousin, Barnabas; others that he disapproved of Paul's emphasis on preaching the gospel to the Gentiles; and still others that he feared persecution. Whatever the reason, Paul did not consider it valid (Acts 15:38). And, tragically, although John Mark's desertion did not stop the mission to the Gentiles, it did split the successful team of Paul and Barnabas (Acts 15:36–40). Internal dissension, division, and disunity continue to disrupt works of God that have stood fast against the storms of external opposition.

SPIRITUAL VICTORY

But Saul, who was also known as Paul, filled with the Holy Spirit, fixed his gaze upon him, and said, "You who are full of all deceit and fraud, you son of the devil, you enemy of all righteousness, will you not cease to make crooked the straight ways of the Lord? And now, behold, the hand of the Lord is upon you, and you will be blind and not see the sun for a time." And immediately a mist and a darkness fell upon him, and he went about seeking those who would lead him by the hand. Then the proconsul believed when he saw what had happened, being amazed at the teaching of the Lord. (13:9–12)

The battle for the soul of Sergius Paulus now reached its climax. **Saul,** who, Luke notes, **was also known** by his Roman name **Paul,** had had enough of the magician's interference. Being **filled with the Holy Spirit,** Paul **fixed his gaze upon** that false prophet. As with all those who dabble in the occult and demonic doctrine, Bar-Jesus was **full of all deceit and fraud.** *Dolos* (**deceit**) is the Greek word for "a snare." Like a cleverly disguised snare, Bar-Jesus was not what he appeared to be to his unsuspecting victims. *Radiourgias* (**fraud**) appears only here in the New Testament. It meant originally, "ease or facility in doing; hence readiness in turning the hand to anything, bad or good; and so recklessness, unscrupulousness, wickedness" (Marvin R. Vincent, *Word Studies in the New Testament* [Grand Rapids: Eerdmans, 1946], 1:516). Far from being a "son of salvation," Bar-Jesus was accused by Paul as being in reality a **son of the devil.** Bar-Jesus fancied himself a righteous prophet, but Paul denounced him as the **enemy of all righteousness.** He constantly twisted and perverted God's truth, leading to Paul's withering question, **"will you not cease to make crooked the straight ways of the Lord?"**

Bar-Jesus was not to escape with a mere tongue lashing, however. As he had made others spiritually blind, he was now to suffer physical blindness. Paul informed him, **"the hand of the Lord is upon you, and you will be blind and not see the sun for a time."** That Bar-Jesus' blindness was to be temporary was an indication of God's mercy. One can only hope that he recovered from his spiritual blindness as well.

The missionaries' spiritual victory was not only negative, as seen in the defeat of Bar-Jesus, but also positive. Satan's emissary had been defeated and silenced; and now Paul and Barnabas were about to win the battle for Sergius Paulus's soul: **Then the proconsul believed when he saw what had happened, being amazed at the teaching of the Lord.** As so often is related in Acts, God used a miracle to confirm the authenticity of His messengers and the truth of His Word. Significantly, it was **the teaching of the Lord,** not the stunning miracle he had just witnessed, that prompted **the proconsul** to believe. He was **amazed at the teaching of the Lord,** not at the miracle.

There is no reason to doubt the genuineness of Sergius Paulus's belief. That he became a true Christian is suggested by some extrabiblical sources. The great nineteenth–century archaeologist Sir William Ramsay "argued from other literary sources that Sergia Paulla, the proconsul's daughter, was a Christian, as was her son Gaius Caristanius Fronto, the first citizen of Pisidian Antioch to enter the Roman senate" (Richard N. Longenecker, "The Acts of the Apostles," in Frank E. Gaebelein, ed. *The Expositor's Bible Commentary* [Grand Rapids: Zondervan, 1981], 9:421; cf. E. M. Blaiklock, *The Archaeology of the New Testament* [Grand Rapids: Zondervan, 1977], 107; J. A. Thompson, *The Bible and Archaeology* [Grand Rapids: Eerdmans, 1987], 392). But apart from such external evidence, Luke's account is clear. The conversion of Sergius Paulus "has been the main point of the whole Cyprus narrative" (John B. Polhill, *The New American Commentary: Acts* [Nashville: Broadman, 1992], 295). As his erstwhile counselor was plunged into physical darkness, the proconsul emerged from spiritual darkness into the gospel's glorious light.

The church at Antioch stands for all time as an example of an effective church. The successful mission to evangelize the Gentile world that it initiated was a turning point in history. The true church of Jesus Christ on earth today is the spiritual legacy of that outreach.

Paul
Preaches Jesus
(Acts 13:14–41)

2

But going on from Perga, they arrived at Pisidian Antioch, and on the Sabbath day they went into the synagogue and sat down. And after the reading of the Law and the Prophets the synagogue officials sent to them, saying, "Brethren, if you have any word of exhortation for the people, say it." And Paul stood up, and motioning with his hand, he said, "Men of Israel, and you who fear God, listen: The God of this people Israel chose our fathers, and made the people great during their stay in the land of Egypt, and with an uplifted arm He led them out from it. And for a period of about forty years He put up with them in the wilderness. And when He had destroyed seven nations in the land of Canaan, He distributed their land as an inheritance—all of which took about four hundred and fifty years. And after these things He gave them judges until Samuel the prophet. And then they asked for a king, and God gave them Saul the son of Kish, a man of the tribe of Benjamin, for forty years. And after He had removed him, He raised up David to be their king, concerning whom He also testified and said, 'I have found David the son of Jesse, a man after My heart, who will do all My will.' From the offspring of this man, according to promise, God has brought to Israel a Savior, Jesus, after John had proclaimed before His coming a baptism of repentance to all the people of Israel. And while John was completing his course, he kept saying, 'What do you suppose that I am? I am not He. But behold, one is coming after me the sandals of whose feet I am not worthy to untie.' Brethren, sons of Abraham's family, and those among you who fear God, to us the word of this salvation is sent out. For those who live in Jerusalem, and their rulers, recognizing neither Him nor the utterances of the prophets which are read every Sabbath, fulfilled these by condemning Him. And though they found no ground for putting Him to death, they asked Pilate that He be executed. And when they had carried out all that was written concerning Him, they took Him down from the cross and laid Him in a tomb. But God raised Him from the dead; and for many days He appeared to those who came up with Him from Galilee to Jerusalem, the very ones who are now His witnesses to the people. And we preach to you the good news of the promise made to the fathers, that God has fulfilled this promise to our children in that He raised up Jesus, as it is also written in the second Psalm, 'Thou art My Son; today I have begotten Thee.' And as for the fact that He raised Him up from the dead, no more to return to decay, He has spoken in this way: 'I will give you the holy and sure blessings of David.' Therefore He also says in another Psalm, 'Thou wilt not allow Thy Holy One to undergo decay.' For David, after he had served the purpose of God in his own generation, fell asleep, and was laid among his fathers, and underwent decay; but He whom God raised did not undergo decay. Therefore let it be known to you, brethren, that through Him forgiveness of sins is proclaimed to you, and through Him everyone who believes is freed from all things, from which you could not be freed through the Law of Moses. Take heed therefore, so that the thing spoken of in the Prophets may not come upon you: 'Behold, you scoffers, and marvel, and perish; for I am accomplishing a work in your days, a work which you will never believe, though someone should describe it to you.'" (13:14–41)

"If some homiletically inclined archangel were to permit me to select another time and place in which to live," writes Warren Wiersbe, "I immediately would ask to be transported to Great Britain during the reign of Queen Victoria" (*Walking with the Giants* [Grand Rapids: Baker, 1980], 51). Among the great preachers who flourished during that era, notes Wiersbe, were Charles Spurgeon, Canon Henry Liddon, Alexander Maclaren, R. W. Dale, Alexander Whyte, and Joseph Parker.

But for those, like Warren Wiersbe, who love great preaching (as all Christians should), an even more exciting time to be alive was during the early years of the church. It was then that the greatest preaching in the church's history took place. Already in Acts, Luke has presented such masterful preachers as Peter, Philip, and Stephen. Acts 13 contains the first (and longest) recorded sermon of the greatest preacher of them all—Paul the apostle.

Although this is the first of his sermons recorded in Acts, Paul was hardly a novice preacher. He had preached in Damascus immediately after his conversion (Acts 9:20), during his three years in Arabia (Gal. 1:15–18), and while serving as a pastor at Antioch (Acts 13:1). Indeed, he could not help but preach (1 Cor. 9:16), since it was for that purpose that the Lord had called him (Acts 26:15–20; 1 Cor. 1:17, 21–23; 2 Cor. 5:19–20; Rom. 15:19; Eph. 3:8; Col. 1:25, 28; 1 Tim. 2:7; 2 Tim. 1:11). Paul's words to the believers at Rome reflect the importance he placed on preaching: "How then shall they call upon Him in whom they have not believed? And how shall they believe in Him whom they have not heard? And how shall they hear without a preacher" (Rom. 10:14)? His words to Timothy are the classic call to this responsibility: "Preach the word." (2 Tun, 4:2) To Titus he said, "Speak the things which are fitting for sound doctrine," and, "Speak ... with all authority" (Titus 2:1, 15), emphasizing that preaching is to be doctrinal and authoritative.

Sadly, many in the church today do not share Paul's commitment to preaching the Word. There is a dearth of biblically sound preaching, creating "a famine on the land, not a famine for bread or a thirst for water, but rather for hearing the words of the Lord" (Amos 8:11). From today's pulpits come the uncertain sounds of psychology, relational chitchat, social commentary, storytelling, shallow homilies, and political rhetoric. Many view preaching as an anachronism in today's era of user-friendly, entertainment-oriented churches. Programs, intractable church members, and administrative details eat away at the preparation time of those pastors who do want to preach.

While many downplay the significance of biblical preaching, it is nonetheless vital to a spiritually strong church. The preacher represents Christ to his people, reinforcing the concept of authority and submission within the Body of Christ. Turning the church into a therapy group or entertainment center undermines that authority. Strong biblical preaching also upholds the authority of God's Word. How strange it is that many who affirm the inerrancy of the Bible fail to preach it expositionally (cf. John MacArthur, "The Mandate of Biblical Inerrancy: Expository Preaching," *The Master's Seminary Journal* 1 [Spring 1990]: 3–15).

The New Testament repeatedly stresses the importance of preaching. Jesus told a prospective follower to "go and proclaim everywhere the kingdom of God" (Luke 9:60), even as He Himself did (Luke 4:18–19, 43). Paul, in charging his young protégé Timothy to "preach the word; be ready in season and out of season; reprove, rebuke, exhort, with great patience and instruction" (2 Tim. 4:2), stressed the singularity and comprehensiveness of this duty. "Let the elders who rule well be considered worthy of double honor," Paul commanded, "especially those who work hard at preaching and teaching" (1 Tim. 5:17). Paul's own passion and calling was to preach the Word.

Biblical preaching has been the catalyst of every great revival in church history. The church Fathers took the baton from the apostles, and through their preaching Christianity conquered the Roman Empire. The preaching of the great Reformers Luther, Calvin, Knox, Zwingli, and Latimer brought the light of truth to the church after centuries of darkness. The powerful preaching of John Owen, John Bunyan, Richard Baxter, Thomas Manton, Thomas Brooks, Thomas Watson, and Jeremiah Burroughs, among many others, fired the Puritan revival in seventeenth-century England. John Wesley, George Whitefield, and Jonathan Edwards led the eighteenth-century Great Awakening. The nineteenth century, as already noted, was blessed with the preaching of Spurgeon, Parker, Maclaren, and Whyte. Perhaps the church today knows little of revival because it knows little of strong, biblical, doctrinal preaching.

The church was born on the Day of Pentecost when Peter preached (Acts 2:14ff.). The gospel spread to Samaria through Philip's preaching (Acts 8:4–5, 12). As the gospel spread to the Gentile world, the catalyst was again powerful preaching by God's chosen messengers.

Having first visited Barnabas's home island of Cyprus, the missionary team next visited Paul's home region, Asia Minor. Leaving Cyprus, they sailed north nearly 200 miles across the Mediterranean Sea and landed at Attalia, the port of **Perga.** At that point, John Mark deserted Paul and Barnabas and returned to Jerusalem.

Paul and Barnabas apparently did not preach in **Perga** at this time, although they did on their return journey (Acts 14:25). Some have speculated that Paul was ill (cf. Gal. 4:13), possibly with malaria, and needed to leave the coastal lowlands for the cooler mountain regions (Pisidian Antioch was 3,600 feet above sea level). In any case, they did not remain there, but **going on from Perga, they arrived at Pisidian Antioch.** This city was located in Asia Minor and is not to be confused with Antioch in Syria, from which the missionaries set out on their journey.

Luke's terse statement passes over in silence what must have been an arduous journey (especially if Paul was ill with malaria). The road from **Perga** to **Pisidian Antioch,** some one hundred miles away, was difficult and dangerous. It wound its way through the rugged Taurus mountains, clinging to cliffs that ascended to dizzying heights. Travelers also had to cross the turbulent and flood-prone Cestrus and Eurymedon rivers. The Taurus mountains were notorious for the robber bands who infested them. Those brigands, who had plagued Alexander the Great and Augustus Caesar, were still unsubdued in Paul's time. When Paul wrote, "I have been on frequent journeys, in dangers from rivers, dangers from robbers" (2 Cor. 11:26), he may well have had this journey in mind.

After their difficult trip was over, Paul and Barnabas arrived in Antioch. In what became the pattern for Paul's ministry, **on the Sabbath day they went into the synagogue and sat down.**. In the synagogues Paul found a ready audience of people interested in religious truth. Further, it was customary to grant visiting rabbis, such as Paul, the right to address the synagogue. Both he and the synagogue audience shared the common ground of the Old Testament. Paul could and did make use of that common pool of knowledge as a departure point when he presented the gospel. Finally, his great love for his Jewish countrymen and burning desire to see them saved (Rom. 10:1) led the apostle to preach the gospel in the synagogues.

Verse 15 suggests the liturgy common to first-century synagogues. The service opened with the recitation of the *shema* (Deut. 6:4ff.)—the Jewish profession of faith. Following further prayers came **the reading of the Law and the Prophets.** Then came the teaching, usually based on that week's Scripture reading. Since it was customary to invite prominent visitors to deliver the teaching—and all the more so since Paul was a student of the celebrated rabbi Gamaliel—**the synagogue officials sent to them, saying, "Brethren, if you have any word of exhortation for the people, say it."**

The Holy Spirit sovereignly arranged the circumstances, opening wide the door for Paul to proclaim the gospel. He **stood up, and motioning with his hand** to get the audience's attention (cf. Acts 12:17; 19:33; 21:40; 26:1), he launched into his message. The **men of Israel** were the Jews present, whereas the phrase **you who fear God** refers to Gentile proselytes. Paul commanded them to **listen,** for what he was about to say contained the most important message they would ever hear.

Two main characters dominated Paul's sermon: God the Father (vv. 17, 18, 19, 20, 21, 22, 23, 30, 33, 37) and the Lord Jesus Christ. Although He is mentioned by name only in verse 23, Jesus' life, death, and resurrection were the major theme.

Paul's evangelistic message falls logically into three parts. He presents Jesus as the culmination of history, the fulfillment of prophecy, and the justifier of sinners.

JESUS: THE CULMINATION OF HISTORY

The God of this people Israel chose our fathers, and made the

people great during their stay in the land of Egypt, and with an uplifted arm He led them out from it. And for a period of about forty years He put up with them in the wilderness. And when He had destroyed seven nations in the land of Canaan, He distributed their land as an inheritance—all of which took about four hundred and fifty years. And after these things He gave them judges until Samuel the prophet. And then they asked for a king, and God gave them Saul the son of Kish, a man of the tribe of Benjamin, for forty years. And after He had removed him, He raised up David to be their king, concerning whom He also testified and said, "I have found David the son of Jesse, a man after My heart, who will do all My will." (13:17–22)

Men have long wrestled with the question of where (if anywhere) history is going. Is there a purpose, goal, or culmination to history? Or is it merely a succession of sunrises and sunsets, a meaningless series of swiftly flowing years leading nowhere? Is history, as the Stoic philosophers of Paul's day taught and Eastern religions of today teach, an endless series of cycles?

The French existentialist philosopher Jean-Paul Sartre expresses the bleak hopelessness of such a view in his novel *Nausea.* In it one character comments, "While you live, nothing happens. The scenery changes, people come in and go out, that's all. There are no beginnings. Days add on to days without rhyme or reason, an interminable and monotonous addition" (Robert Denoon Cumming, ed., *The Philosophy of Jean-Paul Sartre* [New York: Random House, 1965], 58). Later in the novel he adds, "'I was just thinking,' I tell him laughing, 'that here we sit, all of us, eating and drinking to preserve our precious existence, and really there is nothing, nothing, absolutely no reason for existing'" (cited in C. Stephen Evans, *Existentialism: The Philosophy of Despair and the Quest for Hope* [Grand Rapids: Zondervan, 1984], 47).

Viewing history as purposeless appeals to sinful people, since it grants them freedom to do as they want with no fear of accountability to a divine moral judge. As one of the brothers in Dostoyevsky's novel *The Brothers Karamazov* expressed it, "If there is no God, then everything is permitted" (cited in Evans, *Existentialism*, 17). Such "freedom" is in reality, however, a crushing burden of despair and hopelessness. For removing God from the picture reduces man to "a chance configuration of atoms in the slipstream of meaningless chance history" (Francis A. Schaeffer, *Death in the City* [Downers Grove, Ill.: InterVarsity, 1972], 18).

But despite such cynicism and despair, history *is* going somewhere. And every Jew and Gentile proselyte in Paul's audience knew exactly where: to its culmination in the coming kingdom of Messiah. Man's fellowship with God, shattered by the Fall, would be restored when

Messiah came and delivered men from the bondage of sin. History would ultimately resolve itself in the redeemed being back in full fellowship with God and giving Him glory. Jesus' incarnation and sacrificial death, His second coming to set up His earthly, millennial reign, and His eternal rule over the new heavens and new earth are the climax of history.

Paul intended to present Jesus as the long-awaited Messiah. But being a skillful communicator, he knew he must first get his audience's attention. So he began by addressing a topic dear to the hearts of his countrymen, God's providential care for Israel.

The history of that care began when **the God of this people Israel chose** their **fathers. God** is in total control of history. He sovereignly **chose** the **fathers** (Abraham, Isaac, Jacob, Joseph) of the nation, and made His covenant with them. After the patriarchal age, God **made the people great during their stay in the land of Egypt.** That phrase refers to His sovereign purpose effected in their increase in number and influence.

Eventually, "a new king arose over Egypt, who did not know Joseph" (Ex. 1:8). Fearing the power of the growing numbers of Israelites, he enslaved and cruelly mistreated them. God did not forget His people, however, **and with an uplifted arm He led them out from** Egypt. The phrase **with an uplifted arm,** denoting His power (Ps. 89:10, 13, 21; 136:12; Isa. 40:10; 51:9; 62:8; Jer. 21:5; 27:5; 32:17, 21; Ezek. 20:33–34), became the common expression of God's deliverance of the nation from Egyptian bondage (Ex. 6:6; Deut. 4:34; 5:15; 7:19; 9:29; 26:8; 2 Kings 17:36; Ps. 44:3).

After the Exodus, God continued to care for the nation, as **for a period of about forty years He put up with them in the wilderness.** The manuscript evidence is evenly divided between *etropophorāsen* (**He put up with them**) and *etrophophorāsān* ("He cared for them") (Bruce M. Metzger, *A Textual Commentary on the Greek New Testament* [London: United Bible Societies, 1975], 405). Both statements are true. God cared for the nation during the forty years of wilderness wandering (Deut. 1:31; 2:7; 8:2, 4; 29:5; Neh. 9:21) and **put up with** their sin and rebellion (Neh. 9:16–19; Ps. 95:7–11; Amos 5:25–26; Heb. 3:7–11, 17–18). God cared for His people in spite of their rebellion, enduring their sin because they had a key role to play in His plan for history.

After their forty years of wilderness wandering, God brought a new generation of Israel into the promised land. **And when He had destroyed seven nations in the land of Canaan, He distributed their land as an inheritance—all of which took about four hundred and fifty years.** Deuteronomy 7:1 lists the seven nations that were destroyed. Following their destruction, God **distributed their land as an inheritance** to His people. From the captivity in Egypt to the distribution of the land, noted Paul, **about four hundred and fifty years** elapsed—four hundred years of captivity in Egypt, forty years of wilderness wandering, and about ten years from the crossing of the Jordan to the division of the land in Joshua 14:1ff. Throughout that entire period, God showed His power, care, and faithfulness toward Israel.

After they took possession of the land, the people of Israel continued to be unfaithful, but God continued to be faithful. When they were oppressed by their enemies, **He gave them judges** (deliverers) **until Samuel the prophet. Samuel** links the period of the judges and that of the kings. He was the last judge, and he anointed the first king, Saul. Samuel was both a judge and a **prophet.**

Falling prey to their lack of trust in God and desire to be like the other nations, Israel **asked for a king**. In 1 Samuel 8:5, "they said to [Samuel], 'Behold, you have grown old, and your sons do not walk in your ways. Now appoint a king for us to judge us like all the nations.'" Although their request was a rejection of the Lord (1 Sam. 8:7), **God gave them Saul the son of Kish, a man of the tribe of Benjamin, for forty years.** Paul's Jewish name, Saul, was undoubtedly given him in honor of Israel's first king. And like Paul (Rom. 11:1; Phil. 3:5), **Saul** was **a man of the tribe of Benjamin.** There, however, the similarity ended. For whereas Paul was an obedient servant of God, Saul was proud, self-willed, and disobedient. His defiance of God's explicit instructions led to his removal as king (1 Sam. 15:1ff.), though God graciously allowed him to reign **for forty years.** That is the only direct statement of the length of Saul's reign in Scripture, and it agrees with the length of his reign given by Josephus (David J. Williams, *New International Biblical Commentary: Acts* [Peabody, Mass.: Hendrickson, 1990], 232–33). The Hebrew text of 1 Sam. 13:1 omits the number for Saul's age at the beginning of his reign. Accordingly, the NASB gives his age as "forty," and adds "thirty" later in the verse to make the length of Saul's reign thirty-two years. That, however, is pure conjecture and contradicts Paul's explicit words here. Gleason Archer notes that 1 Samuel 13:1–2 should be translated,"He had ruled for two years in Israel when . . . Saul chose out for himself three thousand from Israel" (*Encyclopedia of Bible Difficulties* [Grand Rapids: Zondervan, 1982], 171–72).

After God **had removed** Saul from the kingship, **He raised up David to be their king.** In sharp contrast to Saul, David was obedient, so much so that **concerning** him God **testified and said, 'I have found David the son of Jesse, a man after My heart, who will do all My will.'** Some may question the designation of David as a man after God's heart. After all, he was guilty of cowardice (1 Sam. 21:10–22:1), adultery (2 Sam. 11:1–4), and murder (2 Sam. 12:9). A man after God's heart, however, is not a perfect man. He is a man who sees his sin for what it is and repents of it. That David did (Pss. 32, 38, 51); divine chastening had a perfecting work. David may justly be termed a man after God's heart because (unlike Saul) his greatest desire came to be the doing of God's will. It was from his line that Messiah came.

JESUS: THE FULFILLMENT OF PROPHECY

From the offspring of this man, according to promise, God has brought to Israel a Savior, Jesus, after John had proclaimed before His coming a baptism of repentance to all the people of Israel. And while John was completing his course, he kept saying, 'What do you suppose that I am? I am not He. But behold, one is coming after me the sandals of whose feet I am not worthy to untie.' Brethren, sons of Abraham's family, and those among you who fear God, to us the word of this salvation is sent out. For those who live in Jerusalem, and their rulers, recognizing neither Him nor the utterances of the prophets which are read every Sabbath, fulfilled these by condemning Him. And though they found no ground for putting Him to death, they asked Pilate that He be executed. And when they had carried out all that was written concerning Him, they took Him down from the cross and laid Him in a tomb. But God raised Him from the dead; and for many days He appeared to those who came up with Him from Galilee to Jerusalem, the very ones who are now His witnesses to the people. And we preach to you the good news of the promise made to the fathers, that God has fulfilled this promise to our children in that He raised up Jesus, as it is also written in the second Psalm, 'Thou art My Son; today I have begotten Thee.' And as for the fact that He raised Him up from the dead, no more to return to decay, He has spoken in this way: 'I will give you the holy and sure blessings of David.' Therefore He also says in another Psalm, 'Thou wilt not allow Thy Holy One to undergo decay.' For David, after he had served the purpose of God in his own generation, fell asleep, and was laid among his fathers, and underwent decay; but He whom God raised did not undergo decay. (13:23–37)

Not only does Old Testament history point to Jesus Christ, but so also does Old Testament prophecy (Rev. 19:10). He was the Seed of the woman who bruised the serpent's head (Gen. 3:15). He was the virgin-born Son whose name was "God with us" (Isa. 7:14). He was the Wonderful Counselor, the Mighty God of Isaiah 9:6. Micah 5:2 foretold that Messiah would be born in Bethlehem, and Jesus was (Matt. 2:1). Messiah was to be a descendant of Abraham (Gen. 12:2–3), Jacob (Num.

24:17), and Jesse (Isa. 11:1), and Jesus was (Matt. 1:1; Gal. 3:16; Luke 3:32). He was to be a descendant of David (Jer. 23:5; 2 Sam. 7), and Jesus was (Matt. 1:1). Psalm 110:4 predicted Messiah would be a priest after the order of Melchizedek, and Jesus was (Heb. 6:20). Centuries before Jesus rode into Jerusalem on a donkey, Zechariah 9:9 predicted Messiah would do just that. Psalm 41:9 predicted Judas's betrayal, and Zechariah 11:12 the exact amount of money he would receive for doing it. The fulfillment of those prophecies and dozens more provide overwhelming proof that Jesus of Nazareth was indeed Israel's prophesied and long–awaited Messiah.

Verse 23 ties together Paul's first two points. Historically, Jesus was **the offspring of** David. Prophetically, He was the One whom, **according to promise, God brought to Israel** as **a Savior.** He was the fulfillment of the Old Testament prophecies of the coming Messiah. In Him God's **promise** in the Old Testament was realized.

The first prophecy Paul mentioned was that of the forerunner to Messiah. Isaiah 40:3–5 describes his ministry:

> A voice is calling, "Clear the way for the Lord in the wilderness; make smooth in the desert a highway for our God. Let every valley be lifted up, and every mountain and hill be made low; and let the rough ground become a plain, and the rugged terrain a broad valley; then the glory of the Lord will be revealed, and all flesh will see it together; for the mouth of the Lord has spoken."

In Malachi 3:1 God said of him, "Behold, I am going to send My messenger, and he will clear the way before Me." Those prophecies were fulfilled in **John** the Baptist, who **proclaimed before His coming a baptism of repentance to all the people of Israel.** John's **baptism** was not, of course, Christian baptism, which had not yet been instituted. It was a Jewish ceremonial cleansing, symbolizing true, heartfelt **repentance.** John called upon **all the people of Israel** to repent and prepare their hearts for the coming of Messiah. Repentance has always been a necessary element of salvation.

John was not the Messiah, for **while** he **was completing his course, he kept saying, 'What do you suppose that I am? I am not He. But behold, one is coming after me the sandals of whose feet I am not worthy to untie.'** His remarkable humility, although he was the greatest man who had lived up to his time (Matt. 11:11), kept him from any such pretensions. When confronted by the Jewish authorities, John clearly distinguished himself from the yet-to-be-revealed Messiah:

And this is the witness of John, when the Jews sent to him priests and
Levites from Jerusalem to ask him, "Who are you?" And he confessed,
and did not deny, and he confessed, "I am not the Christ." And they
asked him, "What then? Are you Elijah?" And he said, "I am not." "Are you
the Prophet?" And he answered, "No." They said then to him, "Who are
you, so that we may give an answer to those who sent us? What do you
say about yourself?" He said, "I am a voice of one crying in the wilderness, 'Make straight the way of the Lord,' as Isaiah the prophet said."
(John 1:19–23)

John did not even consider himself **worthy to untie** the **sandals of**
Messiah's **feet**—the task of the lowliest slave.

John's ministry was well known to Paul's hearers, since he had
followers in Asia Minor then (Acts 19:1–3). All in the audience must
have known of John's identification of Jesus of Nazareth as the Messiah
(John 1:29, 36).

Paul had reached an important point in his sermon, and he
paused to emphasize it. Readdressing the two groups in the audience as
**brethren, sons of Abraham's family, and those among you who
fear God,** Paul declared that **to us the word of this salvation**
announced by John **is sent out.** It was proclaimed and thus made available "to everyone who believes, to the Jew first and also to the Greek"
(Rom. 1:16).

Paul now anticipated and answered two questions that might
have arisen in the minds of his hearers, a technique he employed frequently in his writings (Rom. 3:3, 7–9, 21; 6:1, 15; 7:7, 13; 9:14; 11:1, 11; 1
Cor. 15:35; Gal. 3:21).

The first question was one Jewish people have wrestled with
from apostolic times until now: If Jesus is the Messiah, why did the
Jewish leaders fail to recognize Him as such? Paul gave the same answer
Stephen did: because of their hardened, sin-darkened hearts. He
explained that **those who live in Jerusalem, and their rulers, recognizing neither Him nor the utterances of the prophets which
are read every Sabbath, fulfilled these by condemning Him.** The
so-called experts in the Old Testament (scribes, Pharisees, Sadducees,
priests) failed completely to understand its teaching (cf. Matt. 22:29;
John 5:39). Had they done so, they would have recognized Jesus as the
Messiah. Those who are ignorant of the written Word will inevitably be
ignorant of the living Word. Ignorance had become a way of life for
them, as they substituted ritualism for the truth. Ironically, they then **fulfilled** the very prophecies of the Scriptures they didn't understand **by
condemning** Jesus.

Paul then answered a second question that would have arisen: If
Messiah was rejected, does that nullify God's plan? Far from it, replied

Paul. Isaiah 53:3 foresaw that Messiah would be "despised and forsaken of men." They hated Jesus without cause, so that even **though they found no ground for putting Him to death, they asked Pilate that He be executed.** They thus unwittingly fulfilled Psalm 69:4, "Those who hate me without a cause are more than the hairs of my head" (cf. John 15:25).

Even the heinous crime of the crucifixion fulfilled prophecy. Paul declares in verse 29 that **when they had carried out all that was written concerning Him, they took Him down from the cross.** Among the prophecies fulfilled on the cross were that Messiah would be a reproach, one at whom the people wagged their heads (Ps. 109:25; cf. Matt. 27:39); that the crowds at the crucifixion site would stare at Him (Ps. 22:17; cf. Luke 23:35); and that His executioners would divide His clothing among themselves by lot (Ps. 22:18; cf. John 19:23–24). Psalm 69:21 predicted He would be given vinegar and gall for His thirst, Matthew 27:34 records the fulfillment of that prediction. Jesus' cry from the cross "My God, My God, why hast Thou forsaken Me?" (Matt. 27:46) was the fulfillment of Psalm 22:1, and His words "Father, into Thy hands I commit My spirit" (Luke 23:46) were foretold in Psalm 31:5. His executioners did not break any of His bones (John 19:33), just as Psalm 34:20 predicted would happen. Zechariah 12:10 foretold the piercing of His side with a spear, recorded in John 19:34.

Beside those prophecies, the very fact that the Old Testament predicted that Messiah would be *crucified* is amazing. Crucifixion was not a Jewish form of execution, if indeed it was even known to them in Old Testament times. Yet Psalm 22 and Numbers 21 picture such a death (cf. John 3:14).

Christ's burial also fulfilled prophecy. Victims of crucifixion were commonly thrown into mass graves, since such an execution was normally reserved for the lowest classes of criminals. Yet after Jesus' death, they **laid Him in a tomb.** That seemingly insignificant detail was a fulfillment of Isaiah 53:9, which says, "His grave was assigned with wicked men, yet He was with a rich man in His death."

In verse 30 Paul comes to the climactic truth of his sermon when he sounds the keynote of apostolic preaching by declaring that **God raised** Jesus **from the dead** (cf. Acts 2:24, 32; 3:15; 4:10; 5:30; 10:40). Of all the proofs that Jesus is the Messiah, that is the greatest. As Paul was later to write in Romans 1:4, Jesus "was declared the Son of God with power by the resurrection from the dead."

As evidence for the resurrection, Paul cited the fact that **for many days He appeared to those who came up with Him from Galilee to Jerusalem, the very ones who are now His witnesses to the people.** There were more than 500 of those witnesses (1 Cor. 15:6), including Paul himself (1 Cor. 15:8). Nor is there any credible explanation for the events of the first Easter morning other than that Jesus rose from the dead. (For a discussion and refutation of the various alternative theories, see *Matthew 24–28*, MacArthur New Testament Commentary [Chicago: Moody, 1989], 317ff.; Josh McDowell, *Evidence That Demands a Verdict* [San Bernardino, Calif.: Here's Life, 1986], 1:232ff.; Frank Morison, *Who Moved the Stone?* [Grand Rapids: Zondervan, 1958], 88ff.; George Eldon Ladd, *I Believe in the Resurrection of Jesus* [Grand Rapids: Eerdmans, 1976], 132ff.)

Paul concludes this section on the resurrection by showing that by it **the good news of the promise** God **made to the fathers has** been **fulfilled.** In verses 33–37, Paul lists three of those promises.

The first promise was fulfilled when God **raised up Jesus, as it is also written in the second Psalm, 'Thou art My Son; today I have begotten Thee.'** Psalm 2:7, quoted here by Paul, predicts not only Christ's incarnation but also His resurrection. The resurrection magnified and glorified Christ's sonship.

A second promise, from Isaiah 55:3, came true when God **raised** Jesus **up from the dead, no more to return to decay. He has spoken in this way: 'I will give you the holy and sure blessings of David.'** A dead Messiah could not have been the channel for the **holy and sure blessings** God promised to David and his posterity.

The last, and greatest, promise comes from **another Psalm**, Psalm 16. David writes in verse 10, **'Thou wilt not allow Thy Holy One to undergo decay.'** That David had Messiah, not himself, in view is obvious, **for David, after he had served the purpose of God in his own generation, fell asleep, and was laid among his fathers, and underwent decay.** That David's body remained in his grave after his death is also obvious, since no one believed that he had already been resurrected. In sharp contrast to David, however, the One **whom God raised did not undergo decay.**

All those promises, and countless others, required the resurrection of Jesus for their fulfillment. A dead Messiah fulfills nothing. Thus those promises are also powerful Old Testament proofs that Jesus is the Messiah.

JESUS: THE JUSTIFIER OF SINNERS

Therefore let it be known to you, brethren, that through Him forgiveness of sins is proclaimed to you, and through Him everyone who believes is freed from all things, from which you could not be freed through the Law of Moses. Take heed therefore, so that the thing spoken of in the Prophets may not come upon you: 'Behold, you scoffers, and marvel, and perish; for I am accom-

plishing a work in your days, a work which you will never believe, though someone should describe it to you.'" (13:38–41)

The Jewish people were profoundly aware of the ravages of sin and its consequences. They had clung to sin individually and nationally throughout their existence. All the people could echo the plaintive cries of David for forgiveness, which were expressed in the penitential Psalms (32, 38, 51). Solomon succinctly summed up their dilemma when he said, "There is no man who does not sin" (1 Kings 8:46).

The critical issue for the Jewish people was what to do about sin. As the ancient book of Job expressed it, "How can a man be in the right before God? . . . How then can a man be just with God? Or how can he be clean who is born of woman" (Job 9:2; 25:4)? The most common answer, adhered to above all by the Pharisees, was rigid external conformity to the law. But such legalism, being mere human effort, was powerless to restrain the sinful tendencies of man's fallen nature. And it imposed a crushing burden that no one could bear (Matt. 23:2–4; Luke 11:46; Acts 15:10), since "cursed is everyone who does not abide by all things written in the book of the law, to perform them" (Gal. 3:10).

To those laboring in vain to earn their salvation through keeping the law Paul dramatically proclaimed the most glorious, liberating truth imaginable: **through** Jesus **forgiveness of sins is proclaimed to you, and through Him everyone who believes is freed from all things, from which you could not be freed through the Law of Moses.** The atoning death of Jesus the Messiah fully satisfied the demands of God's law (Gal. 3:13), making **forgiveness of sins** available to **everyone who believes** in Him. That forgiveness is **from all things,** that is, it brings complete pardon for all sins (Col. 2:13–14). How astonishing that the very sin of murdering the Messiah provided the sacrifice for all sin and the path to glory through the complete forgiveness of the sins of all who repent and believe.

As Paul the ex-Pharisee well knew, keeping the law freed no one from his sins. To the Romans he wrote, "For we maintain that a man is justified by faith apart from works of the Law" (Rom. 3:28; cf. 1 Cor. 1:30; Gal. 2:16; 3:11; Phil. 3:9). The forgiveness offered in Christ frees sinners **from** that which they **could not be freed through the Law of Moses.** Paul affirms that truth in Romans 3:20–22:

> By the works of the Law no flesh will be justified in His sight; for through the Law comes the knowledge of sin. But now apart from the Law the righteousness of God has been manifested, being witnessed by the Law and the Prophets, even the righteousness of God through faith in Jesus Christ for all those who believe; for there is no distinction.

Paul closed his sermon with a warning against rejecting the salvation offered in Jesus Christ. He solemnly charged his hearers to **take heed therefore, so that the thing spoken of in the Prophets may not come upon you,** namely judgment on impenitent and unbelieving sinners. The Old Testament warned against rejecting the Messiah (cf. Ps. 2:12). Paul concluded his sermon by quoting one of those many judgment passages, Habakkuk 1:5: **Behold, you scoffers, and marvel, and perish; for I am accomplishing a work in your days, a work which you will never believe, though someone should describe it to you.** Those words were spoken about God's judgment that was coming on Judah. God was going to use the wicked Chaldeans as His instrument to bring severe judgment on wicked Judah. Paul used it to illustrate the destruction that the Old Testament pledges to sinners who refuse to repent and submit to the Lord.

The choice with which Paul left his audience is the choice every person faces. Accepting the salvation offered in Jesus Christ brings forgiveness of sin and eternal bliss. Rejecting it brings judgment and eternal damnation. God's grace and love do not cancel His justice and holy hatred of sin. The sober words of the writer of Hebrews stand for all time as a warning to those who reject the gospel:

> For this reason we must pay much closer attention to what we have heard, lest we drift away from it. For if the word spoken through angels proved unalterable, and every transgression and disobedience received a just recompense, how shall we escape if we neglect so great a salvation? (Heb. 2:1–3)

The Troubling Gospel (Acts 13:42–52)

3

And as Paul and Barnabas were going out, the people kept begging that these things might be spoken to them the next Sabbath. Now when the meeting of the synagogue had broken up, many of the Jews and of the God-fearing proselytes followed Paul and Barnabas, who, speaking to them, were urging them to continue in the grace of God. And the next Sabbath nearly the whole city assembled to hear the word of God. But when the Jews saw the crowds, they were filled with jealousy, and began contradicting the things spoken by Paul, and were blaspheming. And Paul and Barnabas spoke out boldly and said, "It was necessary that the word of God should be spoken to you first; since you repudiate it, and judge yourselves unworthy of eternal life, behold, we are turning to the Gentiles. For thus the Lord has commanded us, 'I have placed You as a light for the Gentiles, that You should bring salvation to the end of the earth.'" And when the Gentiles heard this, they began rejoicing and glorifying the word of the Lord; and as many as had been appointed to eternal life believed. And the word of the Lord was being spread through the whole region. But the Jews aroused the devout women of prominence and the leading men of the city, and instigated a persecution against Paul and Barnabas, and drove them out of their district. But they shook off the dust of their feet in protest against them and went

to Iconium. And the disciples were continually filled with joy and with the Holy Spirit. (13:42–52)

In Romans 1:16 Paul describes the gospel as "the power of God for salvation." The Greek word translated "power" is *dunamis,* from which our English word "dynamite" derives. It refers to the positively dramatic transformation of those who believe. When the gospel is preached with power and conviction, the results can also be negatively explosive. For the gospel first confronts sinners with the law and judgment, then the grace of God in Christ. Such a confrontation and exposure of guilt, shame, and doom, along with the offer of salvation by grace, demands a response; it often forces people to rather passionate rejection. It exposes them as the helpless sinners they are and strips them of their self-righteous pretenses and aspirations. And that stripping often infuriates those who reject the message.

From the first preacher of the New Testament on, this has been the case. John the Baptist's preaching aroused the opposition of the Jewish authorities to such a level that they sent representatives to him demanding to know who he was (John 1:19–22) and, by implication, what right he had to preach such confrontational calls to repentance.

The Lord Jesus Christ was the most troubling preacher who ever spoke. His life and message so infuriated the rejecting Jewish authorities that they finally demanded His execution. He Himself stated the divisiveness of the gospel in Matthew 10:34–36:

> Do not think that I came to bring peace on the earth; I did not come to bring peace, but a sword. For I came to set a man against his father, and a daughter against her mother, and a daughter-in-law against her mother-in-law; and a man's enemies will be the members of his household.

The apostles also preached a divisive message that led to hostility. Peter's sermons in Jerusalem set the city in an uproar and resulted in the persecution of the apostles. Stephen's sermon caused such a stir that not only was he stoned to death, but also persecution broke out against the church as a whole. Throughout Acts, the gospel continued to cause divisions wherever it was preached, as the record of conflict to the end of the book demonstrates.

Conflict will often occur when the true gospel is preached today. The gospel does not gather everyone together, nor is it a generally tolerable opinion that nonbelievers can take or leave. Instead it splits people, dividing the penitent from the hardhearted, the saved from the unsaved, the righteous from the reprobate, those who love its truth from those who reject it.

Most of the opposition to the gospel in the early years came from the Jewish people—a tragic corollary to their rejection of their Messiah, Jesus Christ (John 1:11). In Jerusalem, the persecution came from the Jewish leaders (Acts 4, 5, 7). In Samaria, the opposition came from Simon the magician, who likely was either fully or partly Jewish. Paul faced bitter opposition from the Jews in Damascus (Acts 9:20–23). In Acts 12, Herod, attempting to please the Jewish leaders, murdered James and imprisoned Peter. On the first stop of their current journey, Paul and Barnabas encountered the Jewish false prophet Bar-Jesus (Acts 13:6–8). Acts 14:2 records that "the Jews who disbelieved stirred up the minds of the Gentiles, and embittered them against the brethren." Verse 19 of that same chapter describes how "Jews came from Antioch and Iconium, and having won over the multitudes, they stoned Paul and dragged him out of the city, supposing him to be dead." Similar opposition appears in Acts 17:5, 13; 18:6; 19:9; 20:3; 21:27ff.; 23:12ff. That the very hope of Israel, so long awaited, did not arouse their faith and love, but their anger, is the greatest tragedy of redemptive history.

Acts 13:42–52 finds Paul and Barnabas in Pisidian Antioch. Here, too, the gospel would prove divisive. Like a giant boulder cast into a tiny pond, it shattered the surface calm between the city's various ethnic groups. The passage describes the differing reactions to the sermon Paul had just preached (13:16–41). The initial reaction seemed positive; the subsequent response was mixed.

THE INITIAL REACTION

And as Paul and Barnabas were going out, the people kept begging that these things might be spoken to them the next Sabbath. Now when the meeting of the synagogue had broken up, many of the Jews and of the God-fearing proselytes followed Paul and Barnabas, who, speaking to them, were urging them to continue in the grace of God. And the next Sabbath nearly the whole city assembled to hear the word of God. (13:42–44)

The preliminary response to Paul's sermon by the synagogue audience was favorable, though that attitude would soon change. Four features of their initial positive response stand out.

THEY WERE PLEASED

And as Paul and Barnabas were going out, the people kept begging that these things might be spoken to them the next Sabbath. (13:42)

Intrigued by what they had heard, **as Paul and Barnabas were going out, the people kept begging that these things might be spoken to them the next Sabbath.** Paul's dynamic, powerful preaching about the Messiah had piqued their interest, and they wanted to hear more. His message was steeped in the Old Testament. Paul had spoken of God's sovereign choice of and care for Israel. He had referred to Israel's greatest king, David, and the prophets. There was nothing objectionable in Paul's message, except his naming Jesus of Nazareth as the Messiah. If not convinced of that truth, the people at Antioch at least did not manifest the violent opposition to it rampant in Jerusalem.

The ability to arouse people's interest is the mark of a good preacher. In Acts 17, Paul again displayed that ability:

> And the brethren immediately sent Paul and Silas away by night to Berea; and when they arrived, they went into the synagogue of the Jews. Now these were more noble-minded than those in Thessalonica, for they received the word with great eagerness, examining the Scriptures daily, to see whether these things were so. (vv. 10–11)

Paul's persuasive preaching drove the Bereans back into the Old Testament to verify for themselves that what he preached was true. Paul's speech on Mars Hill to the pagan Athenians so stirred their interest that some said to him, "We shall hear you again concerning this" (Acts 17:32).

For a preacher to so fascinate his listeners that they demand to hear him again is a testimony to the effectiveness of his preaching. For them to delay a conclusion about Jesus Christ, however, is dangerous. To the Corinthians, Paul wrote, "For He says, 'At the acceptable time I listened to you, and on the day of salvation I helped you'; behold, now is 'the acceptable time,' behold, now is 'the day of salvation'" (2 Cor. 6:2). The writer of Hebrews, echoing the psalmist, wrote, "Therefore, just as the Holy Spirit says, 'Today if you hear His voice, do not harden your hearts as when they provoked Me, as in the day of trial in the wilderness'" (Heb. 3:7–8; cf. Ps. 95:7–11).

THEY WERE PERSISTENT

Now when the meeting of the synagogue had broken up, many of the Jews and of the God-fearing proselytes followed Paul and Barnabas, (13:43a)

Some in the audience were so affected by Paul's message that they could not wait until the next Sabbath to hear more. Accordingly,

when the meeting of the synagogue had broken up, many of them, including both **Jews** and **God-fearing proselytes** (full converts to Judaism who had been circumcised) **followed Paul and Barnabas** out of the synagogue. They kept up a running dialogue with the missionaries through the streets of Antioch. Their openness to the message and desire for more knowledge about it were encouraging signs.

THEY WERE PROFESSING

[Paul and Barnabas] **speaking to them, were urging them to continue in the grace of God.** (13:43b)

Some in the crowd who heard Paul's sermon apparently professed to believe. As they continued **speaking to them,** Paul and Barnabas **were urging them to continue in the grace of God.** Whether the faith of those listeners was genuine was not immediately apparent; they needed to validate their confession by continuing **in the grace of God.** Perseverance is a mark of saving faith. The apostle John describes those whose faith was not genuine as those who "went out from us, but they were not really of us; for if they had been of us, they would have remained with us; but they went out, in order that it might be shown that they all are not of us" (1 John 2:19). Our Lord also stressed perseverance as the mark of true saving faith: "Jesus therefore was saying to those Jews who had believed Him, 'If you abide in My word, then you are truly disciples of Mine'" (John 8:31). It is the sign of true branches that they abide in the Vine:

> I am the true vine, and My Father is the vinedresser. Every branch in Me that does not bear fruit, He takes away; and every branch that bears fruit, He prunes it, that it may bear more fruit. You are already clean because of the word which I have spoken to you. Abide in Me, and I in you. As the branch cannot bear fruit of itself, unless it abides in the vine, so neither can you, unless you abide in Me. I am the vine, you are the branches; he who abides in Me, and I in him, he bears much fruit; for apart from Me you can do nothing. If anyone does not abide in Me, he is thrown away as a branch, and dries up; and they gather them, and cast them into the fire, and they are burned. (John 15:1–6)

Compare also Colossians 1:21–23:

> And although you were formerly alienated and hostile in mind,

engaged in evil deeds, yet He has now reconciled you in His fleshly body through death, in order to present you before Him holy and blameless and beyond reproach—if indeed you continue in the faith firmly established and steadfast, and not moved away from the hope of the gospel that you have heard, which was proclaimed in all creation under heaven, and of which I, Paul, was made a minister.

The key is the phrase "if indeed you continue." The writer of Hebrews makes the same point: "For we have become partakers of Christ, if we hold fast the beginning of our assurance firm until the end" (Heb. 3:14).

A tragic defect in much contemporary evangelism is the reliance on syllogistic assurance. A person making a profession of faith in Jesus Christ is presented with the following syllogism, designed to provide assurance of salvation: "Those who put their faith in Jesus Christ will be saved. You have put your faith in Him. Therefore, you are saved." Unfortunately, the second premise presupposes that the individual's faith is genuine, which cannot be proven at that moment but can be proven by his perseverance.

The result of such defective evangelistic methodology is that many who do not have genuine faith are given a false psychological assurance. Genuine biblical assurance is God's gift through the Holy Spirit to obedient believers. (For more information on the doctrine of assurance, see John MacArthur, *Saved Without a Doubt* [Wheaton, Ill.: Victor, 1992]; Thomas Brooks, *Heaven on Earth* [reprint; Edinburgh: Banner of Truth], 1982.)

A special temptation faced by Paul and Barnabas's Jewish listeners was to fall back into legalism. Many who were intellectually convinced that the gospel was true stopped short of saving faith, because they could not let go of their traditional works-righteousness system. They faced and succumbed to societal and cultural pressures and held onto legalism and ritualism, eventually falling back from the message of grace.

The book of Hebrews contains several warning passages aimed at those in that perilous position. They are summed up in chapter 10: "But My righteous one shall live by faith; and if he shrinks back, My soul has no pleasure in him. But we are not of those who shrink back to destruction, but of those who have faith to the preserving of the soul" (vv. 38–39).

Paul addressed the following warning to those Galatians seeking to be justified by keeping the law: "You have been severed from Christ, you who are seeking to be justified by law; you have fallen from grace" (Gal. 5:4). Law-keeping and faith in Jesus Christ are mutually exclusive ways of seeking salvation. To the Romans Paul wrote, "If it is by grace, it is no longer on the basis of works, otherwise grace is no longer grace" (Rom. 11:6). Those who seek salvation through works righteousness forfeit God's grace and Jesus Christ and are eternally damned.

THEY WERE PRESENT

And the next Sabbath nearly the whole city assembled to hear the word of God. (13:44)

The interest shown by Paul's listeners was somewhat sustained. They were not like many who profess only momentary interest in the gospel. On **the next Sabbath** they were back, anxiously awaiting the message Paul had for them. And because of their contagious enthusiasm, **nearly the whole city assembled to hear the word of God** proclaimed by Paul and Barnabas.

THE SUBSEQUENT RESPONSE

But when the Jews saw the crowds, they were filled with jealousy, and began contradicting the things spoken by Paul, and were blaspheming. And Paul and Barnabas spoke out boldly and said, "It was necessary that the word of God should be spoken to you first; since you repudiate it, and judge yourselves unworthy of eternal life, behold, we are turning to the Gentiles. For thus the Lord has commanded us, 'I have placed You as a light for the Gentiles, that You should bring salvation to the end of the earth.'" And when the Gentiles heard this, they began rejoicing and glorifying the word of the Lord; and as many as had been appointed to eternal life believed. And the word of the Lord was being spread through the whole region. (13:45–49)

After the initial positive response to Paul's sermon, the subsequent reaction split along racial lines. The response of the Jewish people was negative; that of the Gentiles positive.

THE NEGATIVE RESPONSE

But when the Jews saw the crowds, they were filled with jealousy, and began contradicting the things spoken by Paul, and were blaspheming. And Paul and Barnabas spoke out boldly and said, "It was necessary that the word of God should be spoken to you first; since you repudiate it, and judge yourselves unworthy of eternal life, behold, we are turning to the Gentiles. For thus the Lord has commanded us, 'I have placed You as a light for the Gentiles, that You should bring salvation to the end of the earth.'" (13:45–47)

In an amazing reversal from the previous Sabbath, **when the Jews saw the crowds, they were filled with jealousy.** What caused their vehement reverse reaction? It was really prejudice; they resented that salvation was made available to Jew and Gentile alike. The attitude of the prophet Jonah is the classic case that illustrates that provincial attitude. When sent to preach to the Gentiles at Nineveh, he promptly fled in the opposite direction because he feared they would repent and turn to God. And when the city did repent, Jonah was so angry that he wanted to die (Jonah 4:1–3).

Nothing so infuriated **the Jews** as the thought that the blessings of salvation might be extended to the despised Gentiles. That thought **filled** them **with jealousy**, as it had previously the Sanhedrin (Acts 5:17). Not only that, it stirred them to action. They **began contradicting the things spoken by Paul.** The imperfect tense of *antilegō* (**contradicting**) indicates they were continually speaking against Paul's message, attempting to refute him.

Not content with engaging in a furious debate with the apostle, his opponents **were** also **blaspheming** (cf. Acts 18:6). By speaking evil of God and Christ, they rejected their only hope for salvation and made clear that their initial profession of faith (see the discussion of v. 13 above) was shallow and false. No true believer could ever be guilty of such blasphemy (cf. 1 Cor. 12:3). Blind, unreasoning prejudice against the Gentiles cost them their Messiah, their kingdom, and heaven.

Far from being intimidated, **Paul and Barnabas spoke out boldly** in reply. As the crowd's fury intensified, so did the missionaries' courage. Finally, Paul and Barnabas brought the debate to a close by informing their adversaries, **"It was necessary that the word of God should be spoken to you first."** God's plan was that salvation should be first offered to the Jewish people. In Matthew 15:24 Jesus "answered [a Canaanite woman] and said, 'I was sent only to the lost sheep of the house of Israel.'" When He sent the twelve out on a preaching tour, Jesus commanded them, "Do not go in the way of the Gentiles, and do not enter any city of the Samaritans; but rather go to the lost sheep of the house of Israel" (Matt. 10:5–6). The resurrected Christ said that "repentance for forgiveness of sins should be proclaimed in His name to all the nations, beginning from Jerusalem" (Luke 24:47). Peter told the Jews in Jerusalem, "For you first, God raised up His Servant, and sent Him to bless you by turning every one of you from your wicked ways" (Acts 3:26). Paul would later write that the gospel "is the power of God for salvation to everyone who believes, to the Jew first and also to the Greek" (Rom. 1:16). Although known as the apostle to the Gentiles (Rom. 11:13), Paul nonetheless placed a high priority on Jewish evangelism. He normally began his evangelism in Gentile cities by preaching to the Jews, thus gathering some believers to assist in the witness to the Gentiles.

Tragically, Paul's hearers chose to **repudiate** the gospel, **and** by so doing **judge** themselves **unworthy of eternal life.** They brought the verdict on themselves by their own choice. After centuries of waiting for Messiah, His own people rejected Him and the salvation He brought (John 1:11). They would pay a fearful price for such nationalistic pride and love of self–righteousness.

This passage teaches the important biblical truth of human responsibility. Like all who go to hell, the unbelieving Jews at Antioch judged themselves unworthy of eternal life by their unbelief. John 3:18 reads, "He who believes in Him is not judged; he who does not believe has been judged already, because he has not believed in the name of the only begotten Son of God." People perish because they choose to reject and refuse to believe, and their choice shuts them out of eternal life. Jesus once said to the unbelieving Jews, "You are unwilling to come to Me, that you may have life" (John 5:40). Later He said, "Unless you believe that I am He, you shall die in your sins (John 8:24). Damnation is the result of rejection and unbelief, for which each faithless soul is utterly responsible. That truth of personal volition must be held in tandem with the equally biblical truth that God is absolutely sovereign in salvation and saves whomever He wills to save (see the discussion of v. 48 below). The resulting antinomy (an apparent incompatibility between two undeniable truths) is beyond the ability of our finite minds to resolve. J. I. Packer writes:

> The particular antinomy which concerns us here is the apparent opposition between divine sovereignty and human responsibility, or (putting it more biblically) between what God does as King and what He does as Judge. Scripture teaches that, as King, He orders and controls all things, human actions among them, in accordance with His own eternal purpose. Scripture also teaches that, as Judge, He holds every man responsible for the choices he makes and the courses of action he pursues. Thus, hearers of the gospel are responsible for their reaction; if they reject the good news, they are guilty of unbelief.

> Man without Christ is a guilty sinner, answerable to God for breaking His law. That is why he needs the gospel. When he hears the gospel, he is responsible for the decision that he makes about it. It sets before him a choice between life and death, the most momentous choice that any man can ever face. ... When we preach the promises and invitations of the gospel, and offer Christ to sinful men and women, it is part of our task to emphasize and re-emphasize that they are responsible to God for the way in which they react to the good news of His grace. (*Evangelism and the Sovereignty of God* [Downers Grove, Ill.: InterVarsity, 1978], 22, 25–26)

Faced with rejection by the Jewish community, Paul and Barnabas announced that they were **turning to the Gentiles**, as the **Lord** had **commanded** them. To support that decision, they quoted from Isaiah 49:6, a well-known messianic prophecy. In that passage God says of Messiah, **"I have placed You as a light for the Gentiles, that You should bring salvation to the end of the earth."** The narrow-minded view of salvation as an exclusively Jewish possession is even foreign to the Old Testament, which clearly taught that Messiah would be sent to the Gentiles as well (see also Isa. 42:1, 6; cf. Acts 26:22–23). There was no justification for the hostile, negative response of the Jewish people to Gentile salvation.

THE POSITIVE RESPONSE

And when the Gentiles heard this, they began rejoicing and glorifying the word of the Lord; and as many as had been appointed to eternal life believed. And the word of the Lord was being spread through the whole region. (13:48–49)

In contrast to the Jewish animosity, **when the Gentiles heard** the good news that salvation was offered to them, **they began rejoicing and glorifying the word of the Lord.** The news that proved a stumbling block to the Jews resulted in **rejoicing** among the Gentiles. They were **glorifying the word of the Lord; and as many** of them **as had been appointed to eternal life believed.**

That last phrase is one of the clearest statements in all of Scripture concerning God's sovereignty in salvation. As such, it is the balancing truth to the doctrine of human responsibility discussed earlier. The Bible unhesitatingly affirms that in salvation man does not choose God, but God chooses man. "No one," Jesus stated plainly, "can come to Me, unless it has been granted him from the Father" (John 6:65). Paul described Christians as "those who have been chosen of God" (Col. 3:12; cf. 2 Tim. 2:10; Titus 1:1). To the Thessalonians he wrote, "We should always give thanks to God for you, brethren beloved by the Lord, because God has chosen you from the beginning for salvation through sanctification by the Spirit and faith in the truth" (2 Thess. 2:13). In fact, the term *elect* is used as a title for believers in such passages as Matthew 24:22, 24, 31; Luke 18:7; and Romans 8:33. Peter calls believers "those . . . who are chosen" (1 Pet. 1:1). This choice by God was made before the world began (Eph. 1:4), when their names were actually written in the book of life (Rev. 13:8). The matter of human will and divine election is so inscrutable, so incomprehensible to our minds, as to demand that we believe both without being able to comprehend how they fit together in God's mind.

Appointed is from *tassō*, which is used in some ancient documents in the sense of "to inscribe" or "to enroll" (F. F. Bruce, *The Book of the Acts*, The New International Commentary on the New Testament [Grand Rapids: Eerdmans, 1971], 283 n. 72). The list on which the elect are enrolled is described as "the book of life" (Ps. 69:28; Phil. 4:3; Rev. 3:5; 13:8; 17:8; 20:12, 15; 21:27; 22:19; cf. Ex. 32:32–33; Dan. 12:1).

Scripture affirms that those who go to hell do so because they judge themselves unworthy of eternal life (v. 46). Conversely, the elect are saved because God appointed them for eternal life (v. 48). Those truths form a narrow causeway between two deep chasms. To emphasize either truth at the expense of the other is to plunge oneself into the abyss of doctrinal error.

Evangelism always follows true salvation, as those who are saved naturally desire to share their faith. The converts in Antioch were no exception. Through their enthusiastic testimony, **the word of the Lord was being spread through the whole region.** As always, the agent through which salvation came was **the word of the Lord** (cf. vv. 44, 46, 48). Antioch was turned upside down not because Paul discoursed on self-esteem, politics, or social issues, but because he proclaimed God's Word.

THE RESULTS

But the Jews aroused the devout women of prominence and the leading men of the city, and instigated a persecution against Paul and Barnabas, and drove them out of their district. But they shook off the dust of their feet in protest against them and went to Iconium. And the disciples were continually filled with joy and with the Holy Spirit. (13:50–52)

Unable to best the missionaries in debate, **the Jews aroused the devout women of prominence and the leading men of the city, and instigated a persecution against Paul and Barnabas, and drove them out of their district.** They cleverly used the religious and respected women of the city and the prominent men to persuade the authorities to expel Paul and Barnabas. Paul refers to this persecution in 2 Timothy 3:11; possibly he and Barnabas were beaten with rods or whips (cf. 2 Cor. 11:24–25).

Verse 51 describes the sad, fearful result for the unbelieving Jews, as Paul and Barnabas **shook off the dust of their feet in protest against them and went to Iconium.** That act was one of ominous symbolism. When Jesus sent out the seventy, He charged them:

> Whatever city you enter and they do not receive you, go out into its streets and say, "Even the dust of your city which clings to our feet, we wipe off in protest against you; yet be sure of this, that the kingdom of God has come near." I say to you, it will be more tolerable in that day for Sodom, than for that city. (Luke 10:10–12)

The Jews of Paul's day were scrupulous not to bring Gentile dust back into Israel. By their act, Paul and Barnabas were saying in effect that they considered the Jews at Antioch no better than pagans. There could be no stronger condemnation. Those Jews were left in their obstinate unbelief.

On the contrary, **the disciples were continually filled with joy and with the Holy Spirit.** As the missionaries started for Iconium (about eight miles away), they left behind them two completely different groups: the rejecting, prejudiced, hate-filled Jews; and the joyous, Spirit-filled believers.

This brief passage paints in stark relief the choice facing every man. All men either trust in Jesus and are saved or reject Him and are damned. As He Himself put it, "He who is not with Me is against Me; and he who does not gather with Me scatters" (Matt. 12:30). He left us no third alternative.

Qualities of an Effective Servant of Jesus Christ (Acts 14:1–28)

4

And it came about that in Iconium they entered the synagogue of the Jews together, and spoke in such a manner that a great multitude believed, both of Jews and of Greeks. But the Jews who disbelieved stirred up the minds of the Gentiles, and embittered them against the brethren. Therefore they spent a long time there speaking boldly with reliance upon the Lord, who was bearing witness to the word of His grace, granting that signs and wonders be done by their hands. But the multitude of the city was divided; and some sided with the Jews, and some with the apostles. And when an attempt was made by both the Gentiles and the Jews with their rulers, to mistreat and to stone them, they became aware of it and fled to the cities of Lycaonia, Lystra and Derbe, and the surrounding region; and there they continued to preach the gospel. And at Lystra there was sitting a certain man, without strength in his feet, lame from his mother's womb, who had never walked. This man was listening to Paul as he spoke, who, when he had fixed his gaze upon him, and had seen that he had faith to be made well, said with a loud voice, "Stand upright on your feet." And he leaped up and began to walk. And when the multitudes saw what Paul had done, they raised their voice, saying in the Lycaonian language, "The gods have become like men and have come down to us." And they began calling Barnabas, Zeus, and Paul, Hermes, because he was the chief speaker. And the priest of Zeus, whose temple was just outside the city, brought oxen and garlands to the gates, and wanted to offer sacrifice with the crowds. But when the apostles, Barnabas and Paul, heard of it, they tore their robes and rushed out into the crowd, crying out and saying, "Men, why are you doing these things? We are also men of the same nature as you, and preach the gospel to you in order that you should turn from these vain things to a living God, who made the heaven and the earth and the sea, and all that is in them. And in the generations gone by He permitted all the nations to go their own ways; and yet He did not leave Himself without witness, in that He did good and gave you rains from heaven and fruitful seasons, satisfying your hearts with food and gladness." And even saying these things, they with difficulty restrained the crowds from offering sacrifice to them. But Jews came from Antioch and Iconium, and having won over the multitudes, they stoned Paul and dragged him out of the city, supposing him to be dead. But while the disciples stood around him, he arose and entered the city. And the next day he went away with Barnabas to Derbe. And after they had preached the gospel to that city and had made many disciples, they returned to Lystra and to Iconium and to Antioch, strengthening the souls of the disciples, encouraging them to continue in the faith, and saying, "Through many tribulations we must enter the kingdom of God." And when they had appointed elders for them in every church, having prayed with fasting, they commended them to the Lord in whom they had believed. And they passed through Pisidia and came into Pamphylia. And when they had spoken the word in Perga, they went down to Attalia; and from there they sailed to Antioch, from which they had been commended to the grace of God for the work that they had accomplished. And when they had arrived and gathered the church together, they began to report all things that God had done with them and how He had opened a door of faith to the Gentiles. And they spent a long time with the disciples. (14:1–28)

Admittedly, this lengthy narrative passage contains no explicit teaching on God's requirements for effective service. It does, however, present two highly qualified and effective servants who modeled the qualifications necessary for all who would proclaim the good news through the Lord Jesus Christ. The many diverse and unique features of this inspired record of the further extension of the gospel into the Gentile world can be tied together by focusing on the two constants in the diversity—Paul and Barnabas. Through the flow of this narrative, these two servants of God manifest examples of seven qualities that make for effective spiritual ministry: Spirit-giftedness, boldness, humility, persistence, caring, commitment, and reverence.

SPIRIT-GIFTEDNESS

The characteristic of Spirit-giftedness is evident throughout the chapter. As Paul and Barnabas ministered, they employed the gifts the Spirit had given them.

A spiritual gift is not a natural human ability or talent but a bestowment by the grace of God on believers that provides a channel through which the Holy Spirit's power flows in ministry (1 Cor. 12:7). The mutual exercise of those enablements is thus vital to the proper functioning and building of the Body of Christ (1 Cor. 12:14ff.).

In this chapter, four of these gifts can be seen in operation. The first is prophecy (1 Cor. 12:10), the Spirit-given ability to proclaim the Word of God with clarity and power. Verse 1 notes that **it came about that in Iconium they entered the synagogue of the Jews together, and spoke in such a manner that a great multitude believed, both of Jews and of Greeks.** Verse 21 says that **after they had preached the gospel** in Derbe **and had made many disciples, they returned to Lystra and to Iconium and to Antioch.** Verse 25 relates that **when** Paul and Barnabas **had spoken the word in Perga, they went down to Attalia.**

A second grace gift exhibited by the missionaries was teaching (Rom. 12:7). Verse 22 describes their ministry of **strengthening the souls of the disciples.** Such strengthening was a result of teaching them the Word (cf. Acts 2:42).

Paul and Barnabas also manifested the gift of exhortation (Rom. 12:8)—the spiritual encouragement that leads the one encouraged to pursue a righteous course of action. Verse 22 finds them **encouraging** the believers **to continue in the faith.**

A final gift evident in this chapter is that of leadership (Rom. 12:8). As part of their duties, Paul and Barnabas **appointed elders for them in every church** (v. 23). They did not leave their new converts to fend for themselves. Their leadership gifts enabled them to bring structure to the newly formed congregations and install appropriate leaders.

Those four gifts are at the heart of all spiritual ministry in building the church. They are still vital today for pastor-teachers and evangelists. Besides those permanent edifying gifts, the apostles also possessed temporary sign gifts unique to their Lord and to them (2 Cor. 12:12). This passage mentions two of those apostolic gifts: miracles (v. 3) and healing (v. 8). Those unique gifts confirmed that the apostles spoke for God (Heb. 2:3–4). Such supernatural confirmation is unnecessary today. Whether a man speaks for God can and must now be determined by whether his message conforms to the only standard, which is Scripture.

Since effective ministry demands the collective functioning of spiritual gifts, in Romans 12:6–8 Paul exhorts the church:

> Since we have gifts that differ according to the grace given to us, let each exercise them accordingly: if prophecy, according to the proportion of his faith; if service, in his serving; or he who teaches, in his teaching; or he who exhorts, in his exhortation; he who gives, with liberality; he who leads, with diligence; he who shows mercy, with cheerfulness.

Peter also wrote of the urgent need for each individual to minister his particular gift: "As each one has received a special gift, employ it in serving one another, as good stewards of the manifold grace of God" (1 Pet. 4:10). The singularity of the term *gift* does not preclude the reality that the one gift we possess may be a combination of the various categories of giftedness, blended uniquely for each believer.

It was because Paul and Barnabas had ministered their gifts effectively in their local church (cf. Acts 13:1–3) that God chose them for the challenge of missionary service. They had proven their faithfulness and were ready for a wider scope of ministry.

BOLDNESS

And it came about that in Iconium they entered the synagogue of the Jews together, and spoke in such a manner that a great multitude believed, both of Jews and of Greeks. But the Jews who disbelieved stirred up the minds of the Gentiles, and embittered them against the brethren. Therefore they spent a long time there speaking boldly with reliance upon the Lord, who was bearing witness to the word of His grace, granting that signs and wonders be done by their hands. But the multitude of the city was divided; and some sided with the Jews, and some with the apostles. And when an attempt was made by both the Gentiles and the Jews with their rulers, to mistreat and to stone them, they became aware of it and fled to the cities of Lycaonia, Lystra and Derbe, and the surrounding region; and there they continued to preach the gospel. (14:1–7)

Having been driven out of Pisidian Antioch (Acts 13:50), Paul and Barnabas went to **Iconium,** about eighty miles to the southeast. **Iconium** was a cultural melting pot—native Phrygians whose ancestors had occupied the area from ancient times, Greeks and Jews who dated back to the Seleucid period (312–65 B. C.), and Roman colonists who had arrived more recently.

When Paul and Barnabas arrived in **Iconium** they, as was their custom in evangelizing a new city, immediately **entered the synagogue of the Jews.** If they went to Gentiles first, they would not be able to go to the synagogue. There they **spoke in such a manner that a great multitude believed, both of Jews and of Greeks.** The missionaries' preaching was no doubt premised on the Old Testament and aimed at proving that Jesus was the Christ. It bore much fruit because it was done in the power of the Holy Spirit.

As at Pisidian Antioch, however, jealousy rapidly appeared in all its ugliness. Those **Jews who disbelieved stirred up the minds of the** unbelieving **Gentiles, and embittered them against the brethren. Disbelieved** is from *apeitheō* and could be translated "disobeyed." The New Testament equates unbelief in the gospel with disobedience (John 3:36; Rom. 2:8; 15:31; Eph. 2:2; 5:6; 2 Thess. 1:8; Titus 3:3; 1 Pet. 4:17), since "God is now declaring to men that all everywhere should repent" and believe in the Lord Jesus Christ (Acts 17:30–31). Those who refuse to do so are disobedient to God's command.

Embittered translates *kakoō*, which can mean "to poison." While Paul and Barnabas **spent a long time** at Iconium **speaking boldly with reliance upon the Lord**, their enemies slowly poisoned public opinion against them. As it had at Pisidian Antioch, the missionaries' preaching gradually polarized the population of Iconium. That is the expected result when the gospel is properly presented (cf. the discussion of Acts 13:42-52 in chapter 3 of this volume).

Luke's use of the term **therefore** to begin verse 3 appears puzzling at first glance. The word implies a logical connection with what precedes it, yet the connection with verse 2 is not immediately apparent. Because of that, some have argued that verse 2 was not part of the original text of Acts, or that it belongs in another location. In their view, it interrupts the logical flow of the text from verses 1 to 3. Such a view is shortsighted, however, as John Polhill explains:

> Verse 3 is in deliberate tension with the preceding and emphasizes the power of the Christian witness and the divine enabling behind it. Even though there was strong resistance to the Christians (v. 2), still they were able to maintain their witness. The two apostles were not about to back down. They had the power of the Holy Spirit to speak "boldly" for the Lord (cf. 4:29–31). Far from being intimidated, they were inspired

to even bolder witness. (*The New American Commentary: Acts* [Nashville: Broadman, 1992], 311)

The mounting opposition did not intimidate Paul and Barnabas but energized them to speak out **boldly.** Nor did it deter them from spending **a long time** ministering at Iconium.

Boldness is that essential quality without which nothing significant can be accomplished for the gospel. Boldness is what enables believers to persist in the face of opposition.

Boldness certainly defined the apostle Paul. To the Thessalonians he wrote, "After we had already suffered and been mistreated in Philippi, as you know, we had the boldness in our God to speak to you the gospel of God amid much opposition" (1 Thess. 2:2; cf. Acts 9:27–28; 13:46; 19:8). That he would continue to speak boldly was his constant concern (Eph. 6:19–20; Phil. 1:19–20).

Boldness also marked the other early preachers. Sternly warned by the Sanhedrin to stop preaching in the name of Jesus, "Peter and John answered and said to them, 'Whether it is right in the sight of God to give heed to you rather than to God, you be the judge; for we cannot stop speaking what we have seen and heard'" (Acts 4:19–20). Peter and John then reported the Sanhedrin's threats to the rest of the church. The church's response was to pray for even greater boldness: "Now, Lord, take note of their threats, and grant that Thy bond-servants may speak Thy word with all confidence" (Acts 4:29). Such boldness has been basic to effective Christian service throughout the centuries.

As the missionaries continued to courageously and faithfully proclaim the gospel, **the Lord was bearing witness to the word of His grace, granting that signs and wonders be done by their hands.** These amazing acts of divine power through them affirmed that they spoke for God. The designation **the word of His grace** is appropriate, since the message of the gospel is about God's grace granted to unworthy sinners so that they might be reconciled to Him. That grace is the heart of the gospel. Miraculous **signs and wonders** were the confirmation that the message of grace for sinners that Paul and Barnabas spoke was truly from God.

As marvelous as the message was, and as powerful the confirmation, there was opposition again from the unbelieving Jews. As a result, **the multitude of the city was divided; and some sided with the Jews, and some with the apostles.** Like Pisidian Antioch, Iconium had become a polarized, smoldering cauldron. It was not long before the city erupted in response to the confrontational preaching of the two men.

Luke refers to both Paul and Barnabas as **apostles.** In what sense was Barnabas an apostle? He obviously was not an apostle in the same sense as the twelve and Paul. They were eyewitnesses of the resurrected Christ and were personally called by Him. Barnabas qualified on neither count. He was commissioned not by Jesus Christ directly, but by the church (cf. 2 Cor. 8:19). He was therefore an apostle only in the general sense of the word. Because of that, it is best to translate **apostles** here not as an official title but as "messengers" (cf. 2 Cor. 8:23; Phil. 2:25). The verb *apostellō*, from which *apostolos* ("apostle") derives, means "to send." Paul and Barnabas were both apostles, or sent ones, of the church at Antioch. In addition, Paul was officially an apostle of Jesus Christ (Rom. 1:1, 5; 1 Cor. 1:1; 9:1; 2 Cor. 1:1; Gal. 1:1; Eph. 1:1; Col. 1:1; 1 Tim. 1:1; 2:7; 2 Tim. 1:1, 11; Titus 1:1), and Barnabas, by serving with him, came under the shadow of Paul's apostolic authority.

The smoldering opposition to Paul and Barnabas eventually burst into flame. At the instigation of their Jewish opponents, **an attempt was made by both the Gentiles and the Jews with their rulers to mistreat and to stone them. Attempt** translates *hormē*, which literally means "a rush" or "an assault." The verb form of *hormē* appears in Acts 19:29, where it describes the assault on Paul's companions by the mob at Ephesus. No doubt a similar scene of mob violence took place at Iconium, as the unruly crowd sought **to mistreat and to stone** the two missionaries. The attempt to **stone** Paul and Barnabas proves that their Jewish opponents were the instigators. Stoning was a Jewish form of execution, usually for blasphemy.

Paul and Barnabas were bold, but not foolish. When **they became aware of** what was happening, in sensible self-preservation they **fled to the cities of Lycaonia, Lystra and Derbe, and the surrounding region.** Their flight was an act of prudence, not cowardice (cf. Matt. 10:23). There was obviously nothing more they could accomplish by remaining at Iconium, so it was time to move on to new territory where the gospel was needed. As it had done earlier in Acts (8:1–4), persecution merely pushed the good news of forgiveness and salvation into new regions.

Paul made a profound impression during his stay at Iconium. That impression

> is reflected in the description of him preserved in the second-century *Acts of Paul*—a description so vigorous and unconventional that it must surely rest upon a good local tradition of what Paul looked like. One Onesiphorus, a resident in Iconium, sets out to meet Paul, who is on his way to the city. "And he saw Paul approaching, a man small in size, with meeting eyebrows, with a rather large nose, bald-headed, bowlegged, strongly built, full of grace, for at times he looked like a man, and at times he had the face of an angel" (F. F. Bruce, *The Book of*

the *Acts*, The New International Commentary on the New Testament [Grand Rapids: Eerdmans, 1971], 288).

As this tradition shows, the believers at Iconium did not think any less of him for his flight.

The **cities of** the region of **Lycaonia**, **Lystra and Derbe,** to which Paul and Barnabas fled, were quiet, provincial towns, well off the beaten path. Both were located in the Roman province of Galatia. **Lystra** was about eighteen miles from Iconium and was the home of Lois, Eunice, and Timothy (Acts 16:1; 2 Tim. 1:5), who may have been saved during this visit by the apostle. **Derbe** was forty miles southeast of **Lystra.** Since no synagogue is mentioned in **Lystra,** it probably had a very small Jewish population. That did not deter the missionaries, however, and they immediately proclaimed the gospel. From this effort in Lystra, Luke records three remarkable events: the healing of the man who had never walked, the bizarre incident of pagans worshiping the preachers, and the stoning of Paul.

HUMILITY

And at Lystra there was sitting a certain man, without strength in his feet, lame from his mother's womb, who had never walked. This man was listening to Paul as he spoke, who, when he had fixed his gaze upon him, and had seen that he had faith to be made well, said with a loud voice, "Stand upright on your feet." And he leaped up and began to walk. And when the multitudes saw what Paul had done, they raised their voice, saying in the Lycaonian language, "The gods have become like men and have come down to us." And they began calling Barnabas, Zeus, and Paul, Hermes, because he was the chief speaker. And the priest of Zeus, whose temple was just outside the city, brought oxen and garlands to the gates, and wanted to offer sacrifice with the crowds. But when the apostles, Barnabas and Paul, heard of it, they tore their robes and rushed out into the crowd, crying out and saying, "Men, why are you doing these things? We are also men of the same nature as you, and preach the gospel to you in order that you should turn from these vain things to a living God, who made the heaven and the earth and the sea, and all that is in them. And in the generations gone by He permitted all the nations to go their own ways; and yet He did not leave Himself without witness, in that He did good and gave you rains from heaven and fruitful seasons, satisfying your hearts with food and

gladness." And even saying these things, they with difficulty restrained the crowds from offering sacrifice to them. (14:8–18)

Paul, of course, ministered as the Spirit's power flowed freely through him. While preaching **at Lystra,** probably in the marketplace, he noticed **sitting** there **a certain man, without strength in his feet, lame from his mother's womb, who had never walked.** Luke's three-fold description emphasizes the hopelessness of the man's condition. He was congenitally crippled, and everyone in town knew it. **This man was** in the habit of **listening to Paul as he spoke,** as the imperfect tense of the verb translated **listening** indicates.

Out of the dozens of people in the crowd, Paul **fixed his gaze upon him. Having seen that he had faith to be made well**, Paul **said with a loud voice, "Stand upright on your feet."** The apostle saw an opportunity to confirm his message with a miraculous sign. This man who had never taken a step in his life promptly **leaped up and began to walk.** The unhindered flow of the Holy Spirit's power through Paul resulted in a dramatic miracle.

Although today's believers do not possess miraculous healing power as Paul did, the principle is instructive—God's power is absolutely necessary if His work is to be accomplished (Eph. 6:10; 1 Pet. 4:11). The power "to do exceeding abundantly beyond all that we ask or think" (Eph. 3:20) comes to all believers at salvation. The power of the Holy Spirit is released in believers' lives as they walk moment by moment in obedience to the truth. That enables them to be used as agents through whom no physical healing occurs, but rather the transformation of the soul in salvation and sanctification.

Along with power and results in service for Christ comes the temptation of pride. It is often difficult to acknowledge that the results stem from God's power, not human ingenuity and ability.

Peter wrote of the centrality of humility in 1 Peter 5:5–6:

> You younger men, likewise, be subject to your elders; and all of you, clothe yourselves with humility toward one another, for God is opposed to the proud, but gives grace to the humble. Humble yourselves, therefore, under the mighty hand of God, that He may exalt you at the proper time.

James echoed those thoughts in James 4:6, 10: "God is opposed to the proud, but gives grace to the humble. . . . Humble yourselves in the presence of the Lord, and He will exalt you." Humility is the supreme spiritual virtue because it gives God His rightful place. Paul's understanding of the reality of humility is best seen in his words to the Corinthians:

And He has said to me, "My grace is sufficient for you, for power is perfected in weakness." Most gladly, therefore, I will rather boast about my weaknesses, that the power of Christ may dwell in me. Therefore I am well content with weaknesses, with insults, with distresses, with persecutions, with difficulties, for Christ's sake; for when I am weak, then I am strong. (2 Cor. 12:9–10)

After God performed through Paul the spectacular miracle of healing the crippled man, a bizarre reaction ensued. **When the multitudes saw what Paul had done, they raised their voice, saying in the Lycaonian language, "The gods have become like men and have come down to us."** This strange and surprising turn of events had its roots in local folklore. There was a tradition in Lystra (recorded by the Roman poet Ovid, who died in A. D. 17) that the gods Zeus and Hermes once came to earth incognito. When they arrived at Lystra and asked for food and lodging, everyone refused them. Finally, an old peasant named Philemon and his wife, Baucis, took them in. Their inhospitable neighbors were drowned in a flood sent by the vengeful gods. Philemon and Baucis, however, saw their humble cottage turned into a magnificent temple, where they served as priest and priestess. After their deaths, they were turned into two stately trees.

Determined not to repeat their ancestors' mistake, the people of Lystra **began calling Barnabas, Zeus, and Paul, Hermes, because he was the chief speaker.** The identifications are intriguing. That they identified **Barnabas** with **Zeus** suggests he presented a more distinguished and imposing appearance than Paul. Paul's identification with **Hermes**, the messenger of the gods, is perfectly logical, since **he was the chief speaker.** Because the crowds spoke **in the Lycaonian language,** neither Paul nor Barnabas could comprehend what was going on.

Not to be outdone, **the priest of Zeus, whose temple was just outside the city, brought oxen and garlands to the gates, and wanted to offer sacrifice with the crowds.** If Zeus had indeed come down to earth in the form of this preacher, he had to lead the people in offering him worship.

Luke then describes the reaction of Paul and Barnabas when they finally became aware of what was transpiring: **when the apostles, Barnabas and Paul, heard of it, they tore their robes** (a Jewish expression of horror and revulsion at blasphemy; cf. Matt. 26:65) **and rushed out into the crowd.** Determined to put a stop to the unwanted exaltation, the missionaries began **crying out and saying, "Men, why are you doing these things? We are also men of the same nature as you, and preach the gospel to you in order that you should turn from these vain things."** They were not gods, Paul and

Barnabas insisted, but **men of the same nature** as the Lyconians. Far from seeking their worship, the missionaries had come to Lystra to **preach the gospel to** them **in order that** they **should turn from these vain things.** That last phrase aptly describes not only the idolatry of Lystra, but also all false religion. All religion apart from the worship of the one true God is futile, hopeless, and in **vain**.

The crowd at Lystra was a pagan crowd, unversed in the Old Testament Scriptures. Accordingly, Paul's message was very different from the ones he preached in the Jewish synagogues at Iconium and Pisidian Antioch. Instead of proclaiming the God of Abraham, Isaac, and Jacob from the Scriptures, he proclaimed the **living God, who made the heaven and the earth and the sea, and all that is in them.** Since they did not know the Old Testament, he appealed to the universal, rational knowledge of the Creator, the first cause in a cause-and-effect world. As he was later to write to the Romans:

> The wrath of God is revealed from heaven against all ungodliness and unrighteousness of men, who suppress the truth in unrighteousness, because that which is known about God is evident within them; for God made it evident to them. For since the creation of the world His invisible attributes, His eternal power and divine nature, have been clearly seen, being understood through what has been made, so that they are without excuse. (Rom. 1:18–20; cf. Ps. 19:1–6)

Paul later evangelized the pagans on Mars Hill in Athens from the same starting point—the need to explain the ultimate cause for the world and everything in it (cf. the discussion of 17:22–31 in chapter 10 of this volume).

Although He had revealed Himself in general revelation through reason and conscience, God **in the generations gone by permitted all the nations to go their own ways.** There was a tolerance on God's part toward sinners who did not have the full revelation of His holy will.

It is important to realize at this point that nothing has ravaged gospel preaching to the untaught world more than the theory of evolution. Because it poses an explanation of the existence of everything without a Creator or moral lawgiver, people who accept it fail to see any need for God or a first cause. Thus they cut themselves off from all that creation, reason, conscience, and providence are designed to do—namely lead them to God. (For further discussion of the theory of evolution, see chapter 10 of this volume.)

Special revelation came only in the Old Testament Scriptures, entrusted to Israel. The pagan nations, in their ignorance, were left **to go**

their own ways, having only general revelation. As commentator Albert Barnes explains, that meant God allowed them

> to conduct themselves without the restraints and instructions of a written law. They were permitted to follow their own reason and passions, and their own system of religion. God gave them no written laws, and sent to them no messengers. (*Notes on the New Testament: Acts–Romans* [reprint of the 1884–85 edition; Grand Rapids: Baker], 219–20)

Those times ended with the coming of Christ (cf. Acts 4:12). Since then, although "having overlooked the times of ignorance, God is now declaring to men that all everywhere should repent" (Acts 17:30), and the gospel is to be preached to every creature (Mark 16:15; Luke 24:47).

Although the Gentile nations had no written, special revelation, God **did not leave Himself without witness, in that He did good and gave** them **rains from heaven and fruitful seasons, satisfying** their **hearts with food and gladness.** God's providence, as theologians call this unlimited goodness, as well as a rational response to His creative power, testify to all men of His existence. So also do their own consciences, which contain moral law (Rom. 2:13–15). Because of such provisions, those who reject Him are without excuse (Rom. 1:20).

So intent was the pagan crowd on honoring the two "gods" that **even saying these things,** it was only **with difficulty** that Paul and Barnabas **restrained the crowds from offering sacrifice to them.** At length they managed to make themselves understood, and the ceremony came to a halt.

This incident reveals the humility of Paul and Barnabas. To be acclaimed a god was the highest honor imaginable in the Greco-Roman world, and was much sought after (cf. Acts 12:22). Yet they disavowed any such notions about themselves and instead pointed the pagan crowd to the Creator God. They successfully handled the temptation to succumb to pride. Had Paul and Barnabas yielded to that temptation, it would have destroyed their usefulness. Those who seek glory for themselves are on the path to spiritual weakness and impotence.

PERSISTENCE

But Jews came from Antioch and Iconium, and having won over the multitudes, they stoned Paul and dragged him out of the city, supposing him to be dead. But while the disciples stood around him, he arose and entered the city. And the next day he went away with Barnabas to Derbe. And after they had preached the

gospel to that city and had made many disciples, they returned to Lystra and to Iconium and to Antioch, (14:19- 21)

Whether the **Jews** who came to Lystra **from Antioch and Iconium** were hunting for Paul and Barnabas, or were simply traveling on business, is unknown. In any case, they were outraged at finding the two missionaries again proclaiming the gospel. They took immediate action and, **having won over the multitudes, they stoned Paul and dragged him out of the city, supposing him to be dead.** Luke does not record what arguments these Jews used to turn the pagan crowd against Paul and Barnabas, but they were obviously effective. Some of the same people who had wanted to worship Paul as a god now turned savagely on him. Their fickleness is reminiscent of the people of Jerusalem who hailed Jesus as the Messiah at the triumphal entry, then a few days later called for His execution. In an act of mob violence the crowd stoned Paul—an act to which he refers in 2 Corinthians 11:25 (cf. Gal. 6:17). Luke does not record why Barnabas was not also attacked. Perhaps he managed to escape, or the crowd focused its fury on Paul because he was the chief spokesman (v. 12).

The question arises as to whether Paul died from the stoning and was resurrected. Some argue that he was, and they link this incident with his third-heaven experience recorded in 2 Corinthians 12. That view is unlikely, however, for several reasons.

Supposing is from *nomizō*, which usually means "to suppose something that is not true." *Nomizō* appears in Acts 7:25, where Moses wrongly supposed the Israelites would understand that God had sent him to deliver them. In Acts 8:20, it describes Simon's false assumption that he could buy the Holy Spirit's power. *Nomizō* is used in Acts 16:27 to describe the Philippian jailer's nearly fatal supposition that the prisoners had escaped (cf. Acts 17:29; 21:29; Matt. 5:17; 10:34; 20:10; Luke 2:44; 1 Tim. 6:5). The predominant New Testament usage of *nomizō* argues that Paul was not dead, and the crowd's supposition was incorrect.

Further, if Paul had died and been resurrected, why would Luke insert the word **supposing?** That would undermine the credibility of the miracle, since skeptics could argue that the crowd wrongly assumed that Paul was dead.

Nor are miracles, especially resurrections, minimized in Acts. The resurrections of Dorcas (Acts 9:36–42) and Eutychus (Acts 20:9–12) are clearly and unambiguously presented as the raising of a dead person to life. If Paul had died and been resurrected, why relate the incident in such a vague, uncertain way? Throughout Acts, miracles are supernatural signs pointing men to the truth. A confusing sign, however, points nowhere.

Finally, in 2 Corinthians 12:2, Paul states that his third-heaven experience took place fourteen years before he wrote 2 Corinthians (A.D. 56 or 57). That dates the third-heaven experience at A.D. 42 or 43—an impossibly early date for Paul's stoning at Lystra on the first missionary journey.

His would-be executioners, however, believed Paul to be dead. They hauled his body out of the city and contemptuously dumped it, not even deigning to give him a decent burial. The missionaries' ministry at Lystra had not been without fruit, and some of the **disciples** they had made now **stood around** the battered, unconscious body of their fallen leader. They came either to take his body away for burial or to protect him from further harm. Possibly among them were Timothy, a native of Lystra (Acts 16:1), his mother, Eunice, and grandmother, Lois (cf. 2 Tim. 1:5). To the believers' joy and amazement, Paul regained consciousness, **arose and** courageously **entered the city.**

Most would have taken some time off to recuperate, but not Paul. **The** very **next day he went away with Barnabas to Derbe,** a forty-mile walk. The trip, for one in Paul's condition, must have been excruciatingly painful. Paul never willingly lost a day, however. Since the door for ministry was temporarily closed at Lystra, he simply moved on to minister somewhere else. Nothing daunted him, not even being stoned nearly to death (cf. Phil. 4:11). He was persistent, committed to "making the most of [his] time, because the days are evil" (Eph. 5:16).

CARING

And after they had preached the gospel to that city and had made many disciples, they returned to Lystra and to Iconium and to Antioch, strengthening the souls of the disciples, encouraging them to continue in the faith, and saying, "Through many tribulations we must enter the kingdom of God." And when they had appointed elders for them in every church, having prayed with fasting, they commended them to the Lord in whom they had believed. (14:21–23)

Paul and Barnabas expressed their care and concern for the new believers. An effective servant of God knows the Great Commission is not merely to gain professions of faith but to nurture that faith to maturity. **After** the missionaries **had preached the gospel** at Derbe **and had made many disciples, they returned to Lystra and to Iconium and to Antioch.** When they had completed the work in Derbe, Paul and Barnabas revisited the three cities they had just come from. Such visits were fraught with danger. Some have speculated that by this time new Roman magistrates were in office. Even if that were true, the Jewish communities in all three cities remained implacably opposed to the gospel. Paul and Barnabas knew, however, that it was far more dangerous to the gospel cause for those new flocks not to be strengthened.

Paul and Barnabas's nurture of their children in the faith involved at least four elements. Their first task was **strengthening the souls of the disciples. Strengthening** is from *epistērizō*, a word used elsewhere in Acts to speak of strengthening believers (15:32, 41; 18:23). That should be the goal of every pastor (cf. Eph. 4:11–16; Col. 4:12–13), and is done by the teaching of the Word (Acts 20:31–32; 1 John 2:14).

Besides their teaching, Paul and Barnabas were **encouraging,** or coming alongside, the disciples to exhort them to obedience. Believers must not only be taught sound biblical truths but also exhorted to practice them. Paul reminded the Thessalonians that "we were exhorting and encouraging and imploring each one of you as a father would his own children" (1 Thess. 2:11). Exhortation is teaching's inseparable companion.

Paul and Barnabas's exhortation was twofold. First, they exhorted the believers to **continue in the faith.** Perseverance is an essential mark of saving faith (cf. John 8:31; Col. 1:21–23; Heb. 3:6; and the discussion of Acts 13:42*b* in chapter 3 of this volume). That aspect of exhortation was especially important considering that **through many tribulations we must enter the kingdom of God** (cf. Matt. 11:12; 13:20–21; 16:24–25; 19:27–29; Mark 4:16–17; Luke 14:26–35). Perseverance in the Christian life is a ceaseless warfare against the forces of the kingdom of darkness (cf. Eph. 6:10ff.). Christians therefore need to be reminded to expect hardships and persecution and not be dismayed by them. Jesus promised that "in the world you have tribulation" (John 16:33). "Suffer hardship with me, as a good soldier of Christ Jesus," Paul exhorted Timothy, since "all who desire to live godly in Christ Jesus will be persecuted" (2 Tim. 2:3; 3:12). James gave the good news that such tribulation produces spiritual endurance (James 1:2–4), and Peter confirms that truth in 1 Peter 5:10.

Another key to effective follow-up is organization. Knowing their time with the believers in these cities would be brief, Paul and Barnabas made long-term arrangements for their continued growth. They did that by appointing **elders for them in every church.** Those undershepherds of the Great Shepherd were to faithfully lead and care for the flock long after Paul and Barnabas were gone (cf. 1 Thess. 5:12; 1 Tim. 5:17; Heb. 13:17; 1 Pet. 5:1–3). That some had reached the level of spiritual maturity required of elders in so short a time shows the intensity of Paul and Barnabas's teaching and exhortation. That the elders were chosen only after they had **prayed with fasting** shows the seriousness with which the selection process should be approached.

Having done all that was humanly possible for their converts, the missionaries **commended them to the Lord in whom they had believed** (cf. Acts 20:32). Such an attitude acknowledges the Lord Jesus Christ as the head of the church and the source of all truth and power.

COMMITMENT

And they passed through Pisidia and came into Pamphylia. And when they had spoken the word in Perga, they went down to Attalia; (14:24–25)

Exhausted by their travels and hard work in the proclamation of the gospel, the two missionaries headed home. Having **passed through Pisidia,** they **came into Pamphylia,** to the city of **Perga.** Others may have rested before going **down to** the seaport of **Attalia** and booking passage for home, but not Paul and Barnabas. Such was their commitment to their evangelistic calling that they did not leave until **they had spoken the word in Perga.** As noted in the discussion of Acts 13:14 in chapter 2 of this volume, Paul and Barnabas apparently had not preached in Perga the first time they were there. Leaving nothing undone, they proceeded to do so. They were committed, no matter what their circumstances, to fulfilling their calling.

REVERENCE

and from there they sailed to Antioch, from which they had been commended to the grace of God for the work that they had accomplished. And when they had arrived and gathered the church together, they began to report all things that God had done with them and how He had opened a door of faith to the Gentiles. And they spent a long time with the disciples. (14:26–28)

Their long, arduous journey finally over, Paul and Barnabas left Attalia and **from there they sailed to Antioch, from which they had been commended to the grace of God for the work that they had accomplished.** The church at **Antioch** was no doubt overjoyed at the return of their two beloved pastors. Their work, **commended** at the outset **to the grace of God** (cf. 9:15–16; 13:2–4), had been very successful, as the missionaries **began to report.**

Some may have boasted of all they had done, of the churches they had planted, the number of converts they had made, and the miracles they had performed, but not Paul and Barnabas. They kept all their accomplishments in the proper perspective, noting that **God had done** all those things through **them and** that **He had opened a door of faith to the Gentiles.** They saw themselves as instruments through whom God had accomplished His purposes; and all the glory went to Him. That is an essential perspective for a servant of the Lord.

Through their Spirit-giftedness, boldness, power, humility, persistence, caring, commitment, and reverence for God, Paul and Barnabas had been used to accomplish much for the kingdom. Those qualities still mark those who walk the path to effective Christian service.

The Jerusalem Council: Is Salvation by Law or Grace? (Acts 15:1-35)

And some men came down from Judea and began teaching the brethren, "Unless you are circumcised according to the custom of Moses, you cannot be saved." And when Paul and Barnabas had great dissension and debate with them, the brethren determined that Paul and Barnabas and certain others of them should go up to Jerusalem to the apostles and elders concerning this issue. Therefore, being sent on their way by the church, they were passing through both Phoenicia and Samaria, describing in detail the conversion of the Gentiles, and were bringing great joy to all the brethren. And when they arrived at Jerusalem, they were received by the church and the apostles and the elders, and they reported all that God had done with them. But certain ones of the sect of the Pharisees who had believed, stood up, saying, "It is necessary to circumcise them, and to direct them to observe the Law of Moses." And the apostles and the elders came together to look into this matter. And after there had been much debate, Peter stood up and said to them, "Brethren, you know that in the early days God made a choice among you, that by my mouth the Gentiles should hear the word of the gospel and believe. And God, who knows the heart, bore witness to them, giving them the Holy Spirit, just as He also did to us; and He made no distinction between us and them, cleansing their hearts by faith. Now therefore why do you put God to the test by placing upon the neck of the disciples a yoke which neither our fathers nor we have been able to bear? But we believe that we are saved through the grace of the Lord Jesus, in the same way as they also are." And all the multitude kept silent, and they were listening to Barnabas and Paul as they were relating what signs and wonders God had done through them among the Gentiles. And after they had stopped speaking, James answered, saying, "Brethren, listen to me. Simeon has related how God first concerned Himself about taking from among the Gentiles a people for His name. And with this the words of the Prophets agree, just as it is written, 'After these things I will return, and I will rebuild the tabernacle of David which has fallen, and I will rebuild its ruins, and I will restore it, in order that the rest of mankind may seek the Lord, and all the Gentiles who are called by My name, says the Lord, who makes these things known from of old.' Therefore it is my judgment that we do not trouble those who are turning to God from among the Gentiles, but that we write to them that they abstain from things contaminated by idols and from fornication and from what is strangled and from blood. For Moses from ancient generations has in every city those who preach him, since he is read in the synagogues every Sabbath." Then it seemed good to the apostles and the elders, with the whole church, to choose men from among them to send to Antioch with Paul and Barnabas—Judas called Barsabbas, and Silas, leading men among the brethren, and they sent this letter by them,

The apostles and the brethren who are elders, to the brethren in Antioch and Syria and Cilicia who are from the Gentiles, greetings. Since we have heard that some of our number to whom we gave no instruction have disturbed you with their words, unsettling your souls, it seemed good to us, having become of one mind, to select men to send to you with our beloved Barnabas and Paul, men who have risked their lives for the name of our Lord Jesus Christ. Therefore we have sent Judas and Silas, who themselves will also report the same things by word of mouth. For it seemed good to the Holy Spirit and to us to lay upon you no greater burden than these essentials: that you abstain from things sacrificed to idols and from blood and from things strangled and from fornication; if you keep yourselves free from such things, you will do well. Farewell.

So, when they were sent away, they went down to Antioch; and having gathered the congregation together, they delivered the letter. And when they had read it, they rejoiced because of its encouragement. And Judas and Silas, also being prophets themselves, encouraged and strengthened the brethren with a lengthy message. And after they had spent time there, they were sent away from the brethren in peace to those who had sent them out. [But it seemed good to Silas to remain there.] But Paul and Barnabas stayed in Antioch, teaching and preaching, with many others also, the word of the Lord. (15:1–35)

At various times in its history, the church's leaders have met together to settle doctrinal issues. For example, historians recognize seven ecumenical councils in the first several centuries of the church's existence. Of those seven, perhaps the two most significant were the Councils of Nicea (325), and Chalcedon (451). At those councils, erroneous teaching about the person and nature of our Lord was condemned, and the biblical position carefully defined.

As important as those councils were, the Jerusalem Council, described in this chapter, was the first and the most significant of all. For it fixed the most momentous doctrinal question of all: What must a person do to be saved? The apostles and elders successfully resisted the pressure to impose Jewish legalism and ritualism on the Gentile believers. In other words, they forbade the inclusion of works as a part of salvation. They affirmed for all time the truth that salvation is wholly by God's grace through faith alone, apart from any human efforts.

The wholesale entrance of Gentiles into the church was very disturbing and threatening to some of the Jewish believers. Many believed that Gentiles who wanted to become Christians had to first become Jewish proselytes. They saw Christianity as the culmination of Judaism. That Gentiles were short-circuiting the process and becoming Christians without first becoming Jewish proselytes shocked and overwhelmed them. They could not conceive that pagans could simply enter the church and immediately be on an equal basis with Jewish believers. That seemed unfair to those who had devoted their lives to keeping God's law. They feared, too, that in an increasingly Gentile church, Jewish culture, traditions, and influence would be lost.

Given those concerns, conflict was inevitable. As long as the Gentile converts were few and were already Jewish proselytes (like the Ethiopian eunuch and Cornelius), the issue could be avoided. But by the time of the Jerusalem Council, matters had come to a head. The issue was not whether God wanted to save Gentiles, but how they were to be saved. Could they enter the kingdom of God directly, without coming through the vestibule of Judaism? That was the question the

Jerusalem Council convened to decide. From the inspired record emerge four features: the dissension, the discussion, the decision, and the development.

THE DISSENSION

And some men came down from Judea and began teaching the brethren, "Unless you are circumcised according to the custom of Moses, you cannot be saved." And when Paul and Barnabas had great dissension and debate with them, the brethren determined that Paul and Barnabas and certain others of them should go up to Jerusalem to the apostles and elders concerning this issue. Therefore, being sent on their way by the church, they were passing through both Phoenicia and Samaria, describing in detail the conversion of the Gentiles, and were bringing great joy to all the brethren. And when they arrived at Jerusalem, they were received by the church and the apostles and the elders, and they reported all that God had done with them. But certain ones of the sect of the Pharisees who had believed, stood up, saying, "It is necessary to circumcise them, and to direct them to observe the Law of Moses." (15:1–5)

False teachers have plagued the church throughout its history. They are emissaries of Satan, sent to destroy the church's power and corrupt its proclamation. Two of the apostles at the Jerusalem Council, Peter and Paul, warned of the false teachers' pernicious influence, already being felt in the church. Peter wrote, "But false prophets also arose among the people, just as there will also be false teachers among you, who will secretly introduce destructive heresies, even denying the Master who bought them, bringing swift destruction upon themselves" (2 Pet. 2:1). "I know that after my departure savage wolves will come in among you, not sparing the flock," Paul warned the leaders of the church at Ephesus, "and from among your own selves men will arise, speaking perverse things, to draw away the disciples after them" (Acts 20:29–30).

The most destructive of the "destructive heresies," since it damns men, is the teaching that salvation is by human works, which Peter warned against. That doctrine is the credo of all false religion and the longest-running heresy in the history of the church. The **men** who **came down from Judea** carried this deadly spiritual plague to Antioch, where they **began teaching the brethren, "Unless you are circumcised according to the custom of Moses, you cannot be saved."** Without the authorization of the Jerusalem church (v. 24), these self-appointed guardians of legalism arrived to straighten out the Antioch believers' theology. They no doubt also refused to eat with the Gentiles (cf. Gal. 2:11ff.) and therefore would not fellowship with them in the Lord's Supper. Their teaching and actions posed a grave threat to the truth of the gospel (cf. Gal. 5:2–6), as well as to the unity of the church. The danger of a split between Gentiles and Jews was real.

The Judaizers' pronouncement to the Gentiles, **"unless you are circumcised according to the custom of Moses, you cannot be saved,"** understandably created an uproar in the Antioch church. Gentiles who thought themselves to have been saved already through faith alone in Christ were now informed that their salvation was invalid. Like the good shepherds that they were, **Paul and Barnabas** rallied to the defense of their flock and **had great dissension and debate with** the legalists. They fought furiously for the truth and against the wedge being driven between Jew and Gentile in the church.

Recognizing the far-reaching implications of this issue, **the brethren determined that Paul and Barnabas and certain others** (including Titus, Gal. 2:1, 3) **of them should go up to Jerusalem to the apostles and elders concerning this issue.** The vital issue of how Gentiles were to be saved could not be settled in one local congregation. The decision would have to be made in **Jerusalem** by the God-ordained leaders of the church, **the apostles and elders** (cf. Eph. 2:20).

The delegation of trustworthy men set off for Jerusalem, **being sent on their way by the church** at Antioch. Along the way **they were passing through both Phoenicia and Samaria, describing in detail the conversion of the Gentiles, and were bringing great joy to all the brethren.** Those regions were populated largely by Hellenistic Jews and Samaritans, who were more open to the salvation of Gentiles than the Palestinian Jews were. The news of **the conversion of the Gentiles** brought **great joy to all** these **brethren.** As the spiritual children of Stephen, Philip, Peter, and John, they did not share the views of the legalists troubling the Antioch church. Paul and Barnabas were building support as they went. Not only the Antioch church but also the brethren from Phoenicia and Samaria supported the apostolic doctrine of salvation by faith alone for both Jews and Gentiles.

At length, the delegation from Antioch **arrived at Jerusalem,** where **they were received by the church and the apostles and the elders. They** then **reported all that God had done with them,** acknowledging Him as the source of their accomplishments (cf. 14:27). It must have been a moving scene as the veteran warriors of the cross related their struggles and triumphs for the cause of Christ.

Not all, however, were pleased by Paul and Barnabas's account. Some were appalled at the report that Gentiles were not observing the law of Moses. These **certain ones of the sect of the Pharisees who**

had believed protested, **"It is necessary to circumcise them, and to direct them to observe the Law of Moses."**

Although both groups manifested legalism, these believing Pharisees were different from the Judaizers of verse 1. Clearly, the latter were not true Christians, since they taught that circumcision was required for salvation. By thus mixing human works with faith they nullified grace (Rom. 11:6). Lenski writes:

> To add anything to Christ as being necessary to salvation, say circumcision or any human work of any kind, is to deny that Christ is the complete Savior, is to put something human on a par with him, yea to make it the crowning point. That is fatal. A bridge to heaven that is built of 99/100 of Christ and even only 1/100 of anything human breaks down at the joint and ceases to be a bridge. Even if Christ be thought of as carrying us 999 miles of the way, and something merely human be required for the last mile, this would leave us hanging in the air with heaven being still far away. (R. C. H. Lenski, *The Interpretation of the Acts of the Apostles* [Minneapolis: Augsburg, 1961], 593)

Those who believe that ceremony or ritual plays a part in salvation have denied the truth that "a man is justified by faith apart from works of the law"—including circumcision (Rom. 3:28; cf. Gal. 2:16).

The Pharisees of verse 5 are different, however, since the text describes them as having **believed**. They did not argue that circumcision was necessary for salvation, but that believers were still obligated to keep the law. To them, circumcision and keeping the law were not a means of salvation, but obedience required after salvation. They were still committed to the ceremonial law, which had been set aside in Christ. They were much like the weaker brothers of Romans 14:1–10, who held to dietary laws, rituals, and sabbath codes for conscience's sake. They were convinced that Jesus of Nazareth was the Messiah who died for their sins and rose from the dead. That, however, did not immediately cause them to forsake keeping the Mosaic law as a way of life. They were genuine Christians but had not yet realized the liberating truth that the ceremonial and ritual shadows of the Old Covenant had passed away (Col. 2:16–17; Heb. 8:13).

Pharisees, unlike their arch rivals the Sadducees, could become Christians and retain many of their distinctive beliefs. They believed in the literal interpretation of Scripture, a literal resurrection, life after death, and the existence of angels (cf. Acts 23:8). Thus

> they shared the basic convictions of the Christians. Because of this they are sometimes in Acts found defending the Christians against the

Sadducees, who had much less in common with Christian views (cf. 5:17; 23:8f.). A major barrier between Christians and Pharisees was the extensive use of oral tradition by the Pharisees, which Jesus and Paul both rejected as human tradition. It is not surprising that some Pharisees came to embrace Christ as the Messiah in whom they had hoped. For all their emphasis on law, it is also not surprising that they would be reticent to receive anyone into the fellowship in a manner not in accordance with tradition. That tradition was well-established for proselytes—circumcision and the whole yoke of the law. (John B. Polhill, *The New American Commentary: Acts* [Nashville: Broadman, 1992], 324–25)

New Covenant believers are freed from the unbearable burden (Acts 10:13–15; 15:10) of keeping all the Old Covenant ritual. Yet they are not "without the law of God but under the law of Christ" (1 Cor. 9:21). There is no license to sin in Christian liberty.

THE DISCUSSION

And the apostles and the elders came together to look into this matter. And after there had been much debate, Peter stood up and said to them, "Brethren, you know that in the early days God made a choice among you, that by my mouth the Gentiles should hear the word of the gospel and believe. And God, who knows the heart, bore witness to them, giving them the Holy Spirit, just as He also did to us; and He made no distinction between us and them, cleansing their hearts by faith. Now therefore why do you put God to the test by placing upon the neck of the disciples a yoke which neither our fathers nor we have been able to bear? But we believe that we are saved through the grace of the Lord Jesus, in the same way as they also are." And all the multitude kept silent, and they were listening to Barnabas and Paul as they were relating what signs and wonders God had done through them among the Gentiles. And after they had stopped speaking, James answered, saying, "Brethren, listen to me. Simeon has related how God first concerned Himself about taking from among the Gentiles a people for His name. And with this the words of the Prophets agree, just as it is written, 'After these things I will return, and I will rebuild the tabernacle of David which has fallen, and I will rebuild its ruins, and I will restore it, in order that the rest of mankind may seek the Lord, and all the Gentiles who are called by My name, says the Lord, who makes these things known from of old.' (15:6–18)

After receiving the men from Antioch, **the apostles and the elders came together** privately with them **to look into this matter** of salvation. The leaders, not the congregation, would decide this explosive and potentially divisive issue. And even they were able to arrive at a decision only **after there had been much debate.** Luke does not satisfy our curiosity by giving us an account of that meeting. We can only imagine what it must have been like, with learned and godly men passionately pleading their cases. Luke resumes his account with the entire congregation gathered to hear their leaders' decision. That decision was announced in a series of speeches by Peter, Paul and Barnabas, and James. Each expounded the truth that salvation is wholly by God's sovereign grace through faith, apart from any ritual or law-keeping. Taken together, these speeches constitute one of the strongest defenses of that truth in Scripture. It has well been said that Acts 15 is the Magna Carta of the Christian church.

The speeches of Peter, Paul and Barnabas, and James present six proofs that salvation is solely by grace. Salvation by grace is proven by past revelation, the gift of the Spirit, cleansing from sin, the inability of the law to save, the fact of miracles, and the prophetic promise.

PAST REVELATION PROVES SALVATION IS BY GRACE

Peter stood up and said to them, "Brethren, you know that in the early days God made a choice among you, that by my mouth the Gentiles should hear the word of the gospel and believe. (15:7)

The first speaker was **Peter,** who began by taking the assembled believers back to the **early days** of the church. He reminded them that **God made a choice** that through his ministry **the Gentiles should hear the word of the gospel and believe.** This issue was settled years earlier, Peter asserted, when God saved Cornelius and his household apart from circumcision, law-keeping, and ritual (Acts 10:44–48). His point was simple and direct: the legalists had no right to require of the Gentiles what God had not. The matter was already divinely settled.

THE GIFT OF THE SPIRIT PROVES SALVATION IS BY GRACE

And God, who knows the heart, bore witness to them, giving them the Holy Spirit, just as He also did to us; and He made no distinction between us and them, (15:8–9a)

Peter then skillfully anticipated and refuted a possible objection to his first point. The Judaizers could have argued that since Cornelius and the others did not meet their legalistic requirements for salvation, they could not really have been saved. Peter demolished that potential argument by pointing out that **God, who knows the heart, bore witness** that their salvation was genuine. He did so by **giving them the Holy Spirit, just as He also did to** the Jewish Christians. The gift of the Holy Spirit belongs only to the truly redeemed (Rom. 8:9; 1 Cor. 6:19; 12:13; Gal. 3:14; 4:6). And lest anyone question whether they did receive the Spirit, Peter went on to remind them that God **made no distinction between us and them.** The Gentiles received the same phenomenon, speaking in languages, as had the Jewish believers on Pentecost (Acts 10:44–45; 11:17–18). That proved they had received the Spirit, which in turn affirmed that their salvation was genuine.

CLEANSING FROM SIN PROVES SALVATION IS BY GRACE

cleansing their hearts by faith. (15:9*b*)

The **cleansing** of the Gentile believers' **hearts by faith** alone offers a further proof of salvation by grace (the source of faith—Eph. 2:8–9). Those purified of their sins are obviously saved, and God does not cleanse people who are not truly saved. Such cleansing comes only by God's grace. To the Ephesians Paul wrote, "In Him we have redemption through His blood, the forgiveness of our trespasses, according to the riches of His grace" (Eph. 1:7; cf. Acts 10:43). Since the Gentile believers had already been cleansed of their sins by grace alone, what more could the law and ritual add? The issue of sin had been dealt with, and justification granted.

THE INABILITY OF THE LAW TO SAVE PROVES SALVATION IS BY GRACE

Now therefore why do you put God to the test by placing upon the neck of the disciples a yoke which neither our fathers nor we have been able to bear? But we believe that we are saved through the grace of the Lord Jesus, in the same way as they also are. (15:10–11)

Peter warns the Judaizers not to **put God to the test.** It was not their place to challenge or question God's gracious gospel. He pointed out the folly of **placing upon the neck of the disciples a yoke which neither** their **fathers nor** they had **been able to bear.** The description of the law as a heavy, chafing yoke was an apt one. Describing the legalism of the scribes and Pharisees, Jesus said, "They tie up heavy loads, and lay them on men's shoulders" (Matt. 23:4; cf. Luke 11:46). It was foolish of the legalists to expect Gentiles to shoulder a burden they themselves found too heavy to bear and rejoiced to be freed from.

It was equally fallacious to impose on the Gentiles what had not worked for the Jews. Not one of Peter's Jewish listeners had been saved by the law, purified from their sins by the law, or received the Holy Spirit by keeping the law (cf. Gal. 3:2–3). Since keeping the law could not do any of those vital things for them, why require it of the Gentiles?

Peter closed his speech with a ringing affirmation of the glorious truth that salvation is solely by grace. **We believe,** he declared, **that we are saved through the grace of the Lord Jesus, in the same way as they also are.** Whether for Jews or Gentiles, there has always been and always will be only one way of salvation.

THE FACT OF MIRACLES PROVES THAT SALVATION IS BY GRACE

And all the multitude kept silent, and they were listening to Barnabas and Paul as they were relating what signs and wonders God had done through them among the Gentiles. (15:12)

Unable to contradict Peter's points, **all the multitude kept silent. Barnabas and Paul** then took the stage and began **relating what signs and wonders God had done through them among the Gentiles.** Those miraculous **signs and wonders** confirmed that Paul and Barnabas were God's spokesmen (cf. 2 Cor. 12:12). They taught salvation by grace (Acts 13:38–39), and the miracles God performed through them confirmed the truthfulness of that teaching (Heb. 2:3–4). In contrast, the Judaizers could have produced no miracles to support their teaching. God does not confirm false teaching by granting miracles (a truth applicable in today's church to the many so-called miracle workers with aberrant theology).

Like Peter's arguments, the evidence presented by Paul and Barnabas was irrefutable. Their teaching that salvation was by grace alone was thereby stamped unarguably with God's approval.

PROPHETIC PROMISE PROVES SALVATION IS BY GRACE

And after they had stopped speaking, James answered, saying, "Brethren, listen to me. Simeon has related how God first concerned Himself about taking from among the Gentiles a people

for His name. And with this the words of the Prophets agree, just as it is written, 'After these things I will return, and I will rebuild the tabernacle of David which has fallen, and I will rebuild its ruins, and I will restore it, in order that the rest of mankind may seek the Lord, and all the Gentiles who are called by My name, says the Lord, who makes these things known from of old.'" (15:13–18)

    After Paul and Barnabas **had stopped speaking, James** gave the final speech in defense of salvation by grace. He reminded his listeners that **Simeon** (Peter) had **related how God first concerned Himself about taking from among the Gentiles a people for His name.** James summarized Peter's first point—that God had saved Gentiles by grace years earlier. He then reinforced that point by noting that **with this the words of the Prophets agree.** The Old Testament foretold that God would save Gentiles, and James quoted Amos 9:11–12 to prove it. His quotation differs from the Masoretic Text of the Hebrew Old Testament. Some have speculated that he quoted from the Septuagint, the Greek translation of the Old Testament, yet his quotation does not exactly match the Septuagint either. But the inspired James is certainly giving the sense of the passage as God intended it to be understood, as New Testament writers often do with Old Testament texts.

    The Amos passage speaks of the millennial kingdom. It is then that God **will rebuild the tabernacle of David which has fallen, . . . rebuild its ruins, . . . and restore it.** In the millennial kingdom, **the rest of mankind** will **seek the Lord, and all the Gentiles who are called by My name, says the Lord, who makes these things known from of old.** Gentiles will be saved as Gentiles, without first becoming Jews, or else verse 17 would make no sense. The passage from Amos, quoted in that verse, clearly speaks of those outside the covenant community of Israel being saved, with no mention of their first becoming Jewish proselytes. James reassured his Jewish audience that the inclusion of Gentiles into the church did not abrogate God's plan for Israel. In fact, in the kingdom they will be the messengers to bring Gentiles to God (Zech. 8:20–23).

    James's point is that the prophet said Gentiles will be in the kingdom without becoming Jewish proselytes. Therefore there is no need for them to become proselytes in the present age. His speech is a fitting conclusion to the speeches in defense of salvation by grace. Peter began by stressing that Gentiles in the past were saved by grace alone; James concluded by showing that that will also be the case in the future. Therefore, Gentile salvation in the present must also be by grace alone.

THE DECISION

"Therefore it is my judgment that we do not trouble those who are turning to God from among the Gentiles, but that we write to them that they abstain from things contaminated by idols and from fornication and from what is strangled and from blood. For Moses from ancient generations has in every city those who preach him, since he is read in the synagogues every Sabbath." Then it seemed good to the apostles and the elders, with the whole church, to choose men from among them to send to Antioch with Paul and Barnabas—Judas called Barsabbas, and Silas, leading men among the brethren, and they sent this letter by them,

> **The apostles and the brethren who are elders, to the brethren in Antioch and Syria and Cilicia who are from the Gentiles, greetings. Since we have heard that some of our number to whom we gave no instruction have disturbed you with their words, unsettling your souls, it seemed good to us, having become of one mind, to select men to send to you with our beloved Barnabas and Paul, men who have risked their lives for the name of our Lord Jesus Christ. Therefore we have sent Judas and Silas, who themselves will also report the same things by word of mouth. For it seemed good to the Holy Spirit and to us to lay upon you no greater burden than these essentials: that you abstain from things sacrificed to idols and from blood and from things strangled and from fornication; if you keep yourselves free from such things, you will do well. Farewell.** (15:19–29)

The evidence for salvation by grace presented during the speeches was conclusive. **Therefore,** based on all that had been said, James, as head of the Jerusalem church (cf. Acts 12:17), **gave his judgment that** they **not trouble those who** were **turning to God from among the Gentiles.** Keeping the law and observing rituals were not requirements for salvation. The Judaizers were to be forbidden to **trouble** the **Gentiles** by teaching otherwise.

With the major doctrinal issue resolved, James turned to practical matters of fellowship. He and the other leaders were concerned not only that the Jews not trouble the Gentiles, but also that the Gentiles not trouble the Jews. The danger was that the Gentiles, reveling in their freedom in Christ, would pressure the Jewish believers to exercise that same liberty and violate their consciences. To forestall that, James proposed that they **write** a letter to the Gentiles ordering them to **abstain** from four practices: **things contaminated by idols and from fornication and from what is strangled and from blood.** Those were violations of the law of **Moses,** who **from ancient generations has in every city those who preach him, since he is read in the synagogues every Sabbath.** To needlessly violate the Mosaic sanctions would destroy the church's credibility with unbelieving Jews and also offend believing ones. It would be an abuse of the freedom in Christ believers enjoy (cf. 1 Pet. 2:16).

Things contaminated by idols refers to food offered to pagan gods and then sold in temple butcher shops. Idolatry was a repulsive, blasphemous matter to the Jews. The Old Testament is replete with warnings against it (cf. Ex. 20:3; 34:17; Deut. 5:7). Further, their ancestors' practice of idolatry led to the destruction of the nation (cf. 2 Kings 17:7–18; 2 Chron. 36:14–16). They would naturally seek to avoid any manifestation of it, including eating meat offered to idols. That was a serious issue in the early church, one later dealt with at length by Paul (1 Cor. 8:1–13; 10:14–33).

Fornication describes sexual sin in general, and the orgies associated with the worship of pagan gods in particular. Illicit sex was an integral part of the pagan Gentile worship. Temple priestesses were often little more than prostitutes. Although **fornication** is obviously a moral issue (cf. 1 Cor. 6:15–20), in a broader sense it is also an issue of consideration to Jews. In all their marriage relations and conduct with the opposite sex, the Gentiles were to do nothing offensive to God's law or Jewish sensibilities.

Abstaining from **what is strangled and from blood** involved the dietary laws (Gen. 9:4; Lev. 3:17; 7:26; 17:12–14; 19:26; Deut. 12:16, 23; 15:23; 1 Sam. 14:34; Ezek. 33:25). While certainly not imposing those laws on the Gentile believers (cf. Acts 10:9–16), James set forth these as minimum requirements for fellowship. As noted above, freedom in Christ does not grant the right to sin, or to offend another believer.

Having decided both the doctrinal and practical issues, **it seemed good to the apostles and the elders, with the whole church, to choose men from among them to send to Antioch with Paul and Barnabas—Judas called Barsabbas, and Silas, leading men among the brethren.** The Council's decision needed to be communicated to the church at **Antioch,** the center of Gentile Christianity. That **the apostles and the elders, with the whole church** agreed was yet another manifestation of the unity that marked the early church (cf. Acts 6:5).

It was necessary **to choose men from among them to send to Antioch with Paul and Barnabas,** or else the Judaizers would surely have accused the two missionaries of giving a biased account of the proceedings. Accordingly, they selected **Judas called Barsabbas, and**

Silas, whom Luke describes as **leading men among the brethren.** Nothing more is known of **Judas called Barsabbas,** nor whether he was related to the Joseph Barsabbas mentioned in Acts 1:23. **Silas,** however, played a prominent role in New Testament history. Also known as Silvanus (2 Cor. 1:19; 1 Thess. 1:1; 2 Thess. 1:1; 1 Pet. 5:12), he accompanied Paul on his second missionary journey (15:40; 16:19, 25, 29; 17:4, 10, 14, 15; 18:5). He later served as Peter's amanuensis for his first epistle (1 Pet. 5:12). Luke describes both Judas and Silas as **leading men** in the Jerusalem church. Recognizing the vital importance of the mission, the Jerusalem church sent two of its best. Another indication of how seriously the church leaders viewed the situation is that they sent a **letter** along with the delegation. That letter, **from the apostles and the brethren who are elders** was addressed **to the brethren in Antioch and Syria and Cilicia who are from the Gentiles.** That the Jerusalem church addressed the Gentiles as **brethren** was significant. It affirmed the church's acceptance of them as fellow believers and undermined the Judaizers' position. The salutation *chairein* (**greetings**) appears only here, in Acts 23:26 (where it is used by a Roman, Claudius Lysias), and in James 1:1. That may imply that James wrote the letter on behalf of the others. **Syria and Cilicia** were administered at this time as a single Roman district, of which Antioch was the capital. Many of the churches in **Cilicia** had no doubt been founded by Paul during his stay there after his flight from Jerusalem (Acts 9:30). The Gentile churches on Cyprus and in Galatia were not mentioned. They may have been viewed as extensions of the Antioch church, or the letter may have been addressed only to Antioch because that church had sent the delegation to Jerusalem (Homer A. Kent, Jr., *Jerusalem to Rome* [Grand Rapids: Baker, 1992], 128). In any case, the letter was delivered to the Galatian churches by Paul and Silas (Acts 16:4).

The occasion for the letter is stated. The Jerusalem church had **heard that some of** its **number to whom** it **gave no instruction** had **disturbed** the Antioch believers **with their words, unsettling** their **souls.** The Judaizers who were troubling the Antioch church had no authorization from Jerusalem. *Tarassō* (**disturbed**) is not the same word used in verse 19. It is a strong word, meaning "to deeply upset," "to deeply disturb," "to perplex," or "to create fear." It is used in John 14:1 to describe the disciples' agitated state after Jesus told them of His impending death. It also appears in reference to false teaching in Galatians 1:7 and 5:10. *Anaskeuazō* (**unsettling**) appears only here in the New Testament. In extrabiblical Greek it was used to speak of going bankrupt or of a military force plundering a town (W. E. Vine, *An Expository Dictionary of New Testament Words* [Old Tappan, N. J.: Revell, 1966], 4:88). Taken together, these two words aptly describe the havoc wrought by false teaching.

Having decided to send the letter, **it seemed good to** the leaders of the Jerusalem fellowship, **having become of one mind, to select men to send to** Antioch **with** their **beloved Barnabas and Paul.** That they were **of one mind** about this matter shows again their unity (cf. v. 22). The description of **Barnabas and Paul** as **beloved** shows the affection they felt for these men. The church's commendation of them as **men who have risked their lives for the name of our Lord Jesus Christ** is the noblest anyone could receive. On their first missionary tour, the two had faced persecution (Acts 13:50), and Paul had nearly been killed (Acts 14:19–20). Willingness to suffer for the cause of Christ was the consistent pattern of their lives.

What made them willing to risk their lives? First, they were concerned for others. To the Philippians Paul wrote, "Even if I am being poured out as a drink offering upon the sacrifice and service of your faith, I rejoice and share my joy with you all" (Phil. 2:17). Second, they knew the path of suffering led to a richer provision of God's grace (2 Cor. 12:9–10). Third, they understood the continuity of eternal life. In Romans 14:7–9 Paul wrote:

> For not one of us lives for himself, and not one dies for himself; for if we live, we live for the Lord, or if we die, we die for the Lord; therefore whether we live or die, we are the Lord's. For to this end Christ died and lived again, that He might be Lord both of the dead and of the living.

Knowing that in life or in death they were the Lord's made them fearless. Fourth, they knew that death merely gained them heaven, which they longed for. Paul expressed that hope in Philippians 1:21–23:

> For to me, to live is Christ, and to die is gain. But if I am to live on in the flesh, this will mean fruitful labor for me; and I do not know which to choose. But I am hard-pressed from both directions, having the desire to depart and be with Christ, for that is very much better.

Fifth, they sought to obey Christ at all costs, even when that obedience involved suffering. Peter wrote that believers "have been called for this purpose, since Christ also suffered for you, leaving you an example for you to follow in His steps" (1 Pet. 2:21; cf. 1 Pet. 3:17; 5:10). Finally, and most significant, they were willing to suffer **for the name of our Lord Jesus Christ** (cf. Phil. 3:10). The **name** of Jesus Christ included all He was and purposed, and it motivated Paul's service (Rom. 1:5), as well as the service of others in the early church (3 John 7). When the apostles suffered persecution, they rejoiced "that they had been considered worthy to suffer shame for His name" (Acts 5:41). No cost was too high to pay to protect the honor of the Lord Jesus Christ.

As had been decided earlier (v. 22), **Judas and Silas** would accompany Paul and Barnabas back to Antioch. They could **report the same things by word of mouth,** thus confirming the letter's contents by their firsthand report of the proceedings. Then, reflecting the Council's decision regarding matters of fellowship (vv. 19–21), the letter concluded:

> **For it seemed good to the Holy Spirit and to us to lay upon you no greater burden than these essentials: that you abstain from things sacrificed to idols and from blood and from things strangled and from fornication; if you keep yourselves free from such things, you will do well. Farewell.** (15:28–29)

The letter thus answered the doctrinal question raised by the Antioch church and gave wise instruction on how to avoid rifts in the fellowship.

THE DEVELOPMENT

So, when they were sent away, they went down to Antioch; and having gathered the congregation together, they delivered the letter. And when they had read it, they rejoiced because of its encouragement. And Judas and Silas, also being prophets themselves, encouraged and strengthened the brethren with a lengthy message. And after they had spent time there, they were sent away from the brethren in peace to those who had sent them out. [But it seemed good to Silas to remain there.] But Paul and Barnabas stayed in Antioch, teaching and preaching, with many others also, the word of the Lord. (15:30–35)

Having been **sent away** with the blessings of the Jerusalem fellowship, the messengers **went down to Antioch.** There, **having gathered the congregation together, they delivered the letter.** The entire **congregation,** which had been anxiously awaiting the news of whether their salvation was genuine, gathered **together** to hear the apostles' decision.

The reading of the **letter** and the report of the delegation evoked four responses from the assembled believers. The first was celebration: **they rejoiced.** The confirmation that salvation was indeed by grace alone lifted a tremendous burden of worry from their shoulders. The second response was consolation, **because of** the letter's **encour-**

agement. They no longer needed to fear that their salvation was not genuine. Legalism produces fear, guilt, and pride, while grace alone brings comfort and hope (2 Thess. 2:16). A third response was confirmation, as **Judas and Silas, also being prophets themselves, encouraged and strengthened the brethren with a lengthy message.** The two leaders from Jerusalem added their own heartening words to those of the letter. Then, **after they had spent time there, they were sent away from the brethren in peace to those who had sent them out** and returned to Jerusalem. Legalism produces neither confirmation nor edification; it is "the word of His grace" that is "able to build" up believers (Acts 20:32). The final response was continuation. Verse 34 is not in the best manuscripts, but verse 35 notes that **Paul and Barnabas stayed in Antioch, teaching and preaching, with many others also, the word of the Lord.** Paul and Barnabas picked up where they had left off and continued their ministry of **teaching and preaching . . . the word of the Lord.** Their teaching made clear that salvation is by grace alone. Luke adds that **many others** joined them in proclaiming the liberating truth of salvation by grace.

The apostolic church thus survived the greatest challenge it had yet faced and established the doctrine of salvation by grace. Satan's attempt to inject heretical teaching was thwarted. So also was his attempt to split the church along racial and cultural lines. With the vitally important truth about salvation safeguarded, the church experienced greater days of ministry than ever before.

There has always been, and always will be, only one way to be saved. No one expressed that truth any clearer than the apostle Paul when he penned the familiar words, "For by grace you have been saved through faith; and that not of yourselves, it is the gift of God; not as a result of works, that no one should boast" (Eph. 2:8–9).

Evangelism the Right Way (Acts 15:36–16:10)

6

And after some days Paul said to Barnabas, "Let us return and visit the brethren in every city in which we proclaimed the word of the Lord, and see how they are." And Barnabas was desirous of taking John, called Mark, along with them also. But Paul kept insisting that they should not take him along who had deserted them in Pamphylia and had not gone with them to the work. And there arose such a sharp disagreement that they separated from one another, and Barnabas took Mark with him and sailed away to Cyprus. But Paul chose Silas and departed, being committed by the brethren to the grace of the Lord. And he was traveling through Syria and Cilicia, strengthening the churches. And he came also to Derbe and to Lystra. And behold, a certain disciple was there, named Timothy, the son of a Jewish woman who was a believer, but his father was a Greek, and he was well spoken of by the brethren who were in Lystra and Iconium. Paul wanted this man to go with him; and he took him and circumcised him because of the Jews who were in those parts, for they all knew that his father was a Greek. Now while they were passing through the cities, they were delivering the decrees, which had been decided upon by the apostles and elders who were in Jerusalem, for them to observe. So the churches were being

strengthened in the faith, and were increasing in number daily. And they passed through the Phrygian and Galatian region, having been forbidden by the Holy Spirit to speak the word in Asia; and when they had come to Mysia, they were trying to go into Bithynia, and the Spirit of Jesus did not permit them; and passing by Mysia, they came down to Troas. And a vision appeared to Paul in the night: a certain man of Macedonia was standing and appealing to him, and saying, "Come over to Macedonia and help us." And when he had seen the vision, immediately we sought to go into Macedonia, concluding that God had called us to preach the gospel to them. (15:36–16:10)

The Lord Jesus Christ defined the church's mission when He commanded believers, "Go therefore and make disciples of all the nations, baptizing them in the name of the Father and the Son and the Holy Spirit" (Matt. 28:19). Throughout its history, the church has sought to carry out that mission.

While there is general agreement on the *necessity* of evangelism, there is wide diversity as to methods. There are many different approaches, from simple presentations of a few basic verses to sophisticated multimedia events; from one-on-one encounters to citywide evangelistic crusades. Countless books, tapes, and seminars exist to train Christians in how to share their faith. Schools of evangelism, training centers, Bible colleges, and seminaries all offer courses in evangelism. There is a bewildering plethora of tracts, booklets, and other evangelistic literature, everything from "One Way to Heaven," to "Four Spiritual Laws," to "Six Steps to Peace with God," to "Thirty-nine Steps to Salvation."

What is often overlooked in the emphasis on methodology are the essential, foundational principles undergirding all truly biblical evangelism. This passage illustrates that evangelism calls for the right passion, the right priority, the right personnel, the right precautions, and the right presentation at the right place.

The Right Passion

And after some days Paul said to Barnabas, "Let us return . . ." (15:36a)

After the interlude of the Jerusalem Council, where the crucial issue of salvation by grace was decided, the Antioch church resumed its evangelistic outreach. Specifically, this passage marks the beginning of Paul's second missionary journey. His ministry, too, had been interrupted by the controversy with the legalists and his visit to Jerusalem. With that behind him, he was ready to move ahead with the task of reaching the lost.

The phrase **after some days** denotes an indeterminate period, during which "Paul and Barnabas stayed in Antioch, teaching and preaching, with many others also, the word of the Lord" (15:35). At the end of that time, **Paul said to Barnabas, "Let us return. . . ."** It was not as if Paul was bored in Antioch. Helping pastor a large, growing church is challenge enough for most men. But Paul always felt keenly the call of unevangelized regions. It just was not in him to remain in one place very long when so many thousands still had not heard the gospel and he had been commissioned to reach them. He was a passionate man, driven by a desire to preach the gospel especially where it had yet to be proclaimed (Rom. 15:20). That passion was the result of love for God and commitment to obedience. It led him to write, "I am under compulsion; for woe is me if I do not preach the gospel" (1 Cor. 9:16). No one who lacks that concern for lost souls will ever be effective in evangelism. That lack of internal motivation is something no amount of training or mastery of techniques can overcome.

Everywhere Paul found himself, no matter how long he remained, was merely a step to somewhere else. For many years he longed to visit Rome (Rom. 15:22–23). One would think that Rome would be Paul's ultimate goal, and he would be content to minister there the rest of his life. After all, Rome, capital of the greatest empire the world had ever known, was the most strategic city in the world. It had a vast population and was visited by thousands from every corner of the known world. Yet even mighty Rome was merely another stopping place for Paul. To the church in that city he wrote that he planned to visit them "whenever I go to Spain—for I hope to see you in passing, and to be helped on my way there by you, when I have first enjoyed your company for a while . . . I will go on by way of you to Spain" (Rom. 15:24, 28). He was a man compelled to reach out to the lost, and he could not rest from that burden for long, even in the company of fellow believers.

Paul's passionate concern for those without Christ found an echo in the heart of J. Hudson Taylor, the nineteenth-century English missionary to China. He wrote:

> I have a stronger desire than ever to go to China. That land is ever in my thoughts. Think of it—360 million souls, without God or hope in the world! Think of more than twelve millions of our fellow creatures dying every year without any of the consolations of the Gospel. Barnsley including the Common has only 15,000 inhabitants. Imagine what it would be if all these were to die in twelve months! Yet in China year by year, *hundreds* are dying, for every man, woman and child in Barnsley. Poor, neglected China! Scarcely anyone cares about it. (Dr. and Mrs.

Howard Taylor, *J. Hudson Taylor: A Biography* [Chicago: Moody, 1981], 17. Italics in the original.)

Such passion cannot be learned by studying evangelistic methodology. It comes from knowing and loving Christ so deeply that some of His love for lost sinners becomes our own. And knowing Christ comes from studying His Word. It is through that study that "we all, with unveiled face beholding as in a mirror the glory of the Lord, are being transformed into the same image from glory to glory, just as from the Lord, the Spirit" (2 Cor. 3:18).

THE RIGHT PRIORITY

". . . and visit the brethren in every city in which we proclaimed the word of the Lord, and see how they are." (15:36*b*)

Although Paul was the greatest human evangelist the world has ever known, he certainly did not fit the twentieth-century stereotype. The modern conception of an evangelist is someone who travels from city to city preaching the gospel, leaving his converts to be followed up by others. Paul, however, was a biblical evangelist. He saw his responsibility as not only proclaiming the saving gospel but also establishing churches and maturing the new converts in their faith. It is not surprising, then, that he planned for his second missionary journey to retrace his first one. His goal was to **visit the brethren in every city in which** they had **proclaimed the word of the Lord, and see how they** were. Paul understood clearly that the ultimate priority in evangelism is discipleship—teaching believers to obey all that Christ has commanded (Matt. 28:19–20).

What motivated Paul, apart from his desire for their maturity, to revisit the converts from the first missionary journey? First, he loved them as his spiritual children. He expressed that love to the Philippians when he wrote, "God is my witness, how I long for you all with the affection of Christ Jesus" (Phil. 1:8). He told the Thessalonians, "We, brethren, having been bereft of you for a short while—in person, not in spirit—were all the more eager with great desire to see your face" (1 Thess. 2:17).

That is an element frequently missing in contemporary evangelism. There is too often failure to show enough love to those led to Christ. As a result, the evangelist does not accept responsibility for them. Paul's evangelism suffered from no such lack of love, however. To the Corinthians he wrote, "If you were to have countless tutors in Christ, yet you would not have many fathers; for in Christ Jesus I became your father through the gospel" (1 Cor. 4:15). Paul viewed himself as a loving father, responsible for the spiritual well-being of his children.

A second motive for revisiting his converts was Paul's commitment to the most effective evangelistic strategy of all—building mature believers, not spiritual infants, who are capable of reproducing. Paul's commitment to maturing believers mirrored that of our Lord, who spent most of His time with only twelve men. Paul knew that, as an apostle, he was given to the church

> for the equipping of the saints for the work of service, to the building up of the body of Christ; until we all attain to the unity of the faith, and of the knowledge of the Son of God, to a mature man, to the measure of the stature which belongs to the fulness of Christ. (Eph. 4:12–13)

Paul expressed his philosophy of ministry in Colossians 1:28, where he wrote, "We proclaim Him, admonishing every man and teaching every man with all wisdom, that we may present every man complete in Christ." He was no hit-and-run evangelist. During his ministry at Ephesus, "night and day for a period of three years [he] did not cease to admonish each one with tears" (Acts 20:31).

In the long run, the work of a well-taught, mature, spiritually strong local congregation has a far greater impact than massive evangelistic crusades.

THE RIGHT PERSONNEL

And Barnabas was desirous of taking John, called Mark, along with them also. But Paul kept insisting that they should not take him along who had deserted them in Pamphylia and had not gone with them to the work. And there arose such a sharp disagreement that they separated from one another, and Barnabas took Mark with him and sailed away to Cyprus. But Paul chose Silas and departed, being committed by the brethren to the grace of the Lord. And he was traveling through Syria and Cilicia, strengthening the churches. And he came also to Derbe and to Lystra. And behold, a certain disciple was there, named Timothy, the son of a Jewish woman who was a believer, but his father was a Greek, and he was well spoken of by the brethren who were in Lystra and Iconium. Paul wanted this man to go with him; (15:37–16:3a)

God uses the right people, the people of His choosing, for the tasks He plans for them. To that end, He can and does use even the most negative circumstances to produce the most positive results. He did so in the case detailed in this text.

As they embarked on their renewed journey, Paul and Barnabas stumbled coming out of the gate. **Barnabas was desirous of taking John, called Mark, along with them also.** The imperfect tense of the Greek verb translated **was desirous** shows that Barnabas was persistent. Equally adamant, **Paul kept insisting that they should not take him along who had deserted them in Pamphylia and had not gone with them to the work** (cf. the discussion of Acts 13:13 in chapter 1 of this volume). After John Mark's earlier failure, Paul had no confidence in him. The tough, battle-hardened soldier of Christ had no use for deserters. On the other hand, gentle, encouraging Barnabas insisted on giving his cousin (Col. 4:10) a second chance.

Eventually, **there arose such a sharp disagreement that they separated from one another.** *Paroxusmos* (**sharp disagreement**) is the root of the English word *paroxysm*. Their partnership dissolved not amicably but with violent emotions, and **Barnabas took Mark with him and sailed away to Cyprus** (Barnabas's home—Acts 4:36).

The question arises as to who was right, Barnabas or Paul. Although the Scripture does not explicitly say, the weight of the evidence favors Paul. He was an apostle, Barnabas was not. Therefore, Barnabas should have submitted to Paul's apostolic authority. Also, Paul and Silas, but not Barnabas and Mark, were commended by the church (v. 40). Finally, Barnabas should have realized that it would have been unwise and difficult to have Mark along if Paul did not trust him.

Although they apparently never again ministered together (this is the last mention of Barnabas in Acts), we know Paul and Barnabas eventually reconciled their differences, because Paul later wrote approvingly of Barnabas's ministry (1 Cor. 9:6). Even John Mark, the cause of all the trouble, later became one of Paul's valued co-laborers (Col. 4:10; Philem. 24; 2 Tim. 4:11). He also became a close associate of the apostle Peter (1 Pet. 5:13) and was privileged to write one of the four gospels. Barnabas did a remarkable job in helping to turn around the life and ministry career of his young cousin.

After his split with Barnabas, **Paul chose Silas and departed, being committed by the brethren to the grace of the Lord.** Yet another of Satan's attempts to hinder the spread of the gospel backfired. Now there were two missionary teams where before there had been one. Their impact had doubled.

Paul's new partner, **Silas,** had been one of the leaders of the Jerusalem church (see the discussion of Silas in chapter 5 of this volume). He was in every respect a suitable man for missionary work. As a prophet (Acts 15:32), he was adept at proclaiming and teaching the Word. As a Jew, he had entrance into the synagogues. As a Roman citizen (Acts 16:37), he enjoyed the same protection and benefits as did Paul. And his status as a respected leader of the Jerusalem church reinforced Paul's teaching that Gentile salvation was solely by grace. That was especially significant since part of their ministry involved delivering "the decrees, which had been decided upon by the apostles and elders who were in Jerusalem" (Acts 16:4).

On the first missionary journey, Paul and Barnabas had entered Asia Minor via the island of Cyprus. But with Barnabas and John Mark already there (v. 39), there was no point in Paul and Silas's heading that way. Paul chose instead to travel **through Syria and Cilicia,** thus entering Galatia from the opposite direction. The significance of that will become apparent shortly. **Syria** was the region around Antioch, and the neighboring region of **Cilicia** contained Paul's home city of Tarsus. Many of its churches had no doubt been founded by Paul himself. As Paul and Silas traveled through those areas, they were busy with their priority, **strengthening the churches.**

Having crossed the rugged Taurus Mountains through the Cilician Gates north of Tarsus, the missionaries **came to Derbe and to Lystra.** Paul and Barnabas had visited these cities on the first missionary journey (Acts 14:6ff.), and **Lystra** had been the scene of some remarkable events. It was there that Paul had healed a lame man (14:8–10). In response, the astonished crowd proclaimed the two missionaries gods (14:11–18). Following that, Paul had been stoned nearly to death by jealous Jews from Antioch and Iconium (14:19).

At **Lystra,** the missionaries were joined by **a certain disciple named Timothy.** Just as Silas had replaced Barnabas, so Timothy replaced John Mark. Now the significance of Paul and Silas's entering Asia Minor from the opposite direction becomes apparent. Had they followed the same route as the first missionary journey, they would not have come to Lystra until the end. By adding **Timothy** at the beginning of the journey, they had his help for the entire trip.

Timothy was to play a key role in Paul's life, eventually becoming his right-hand man (1 Cor. 4:17; 1 Thess. 3:2; Phil. 2:19). Timothy was also Paul's "true child in the faith" (1 Tim. 1:2; cf. 1 Cor. 4:17; 2 Tim. 1:2); he had been led to Christ by Paul when the apostle visited Lystra on the first missionary journey.

Timothy was **the son of a Jewish woman** (Eunice) **who was a believer** (as was his grandmother Lois, 2 Tim. 1:5), **but his father was a Greek.** The use of an imperfect tense verb, instead of present tense, to refer to Timothy's father suggests he was dead. Being both Jewish and Gentile, Timothy had access to both cultures—an important qualification for missionary service at that time. He was a young man, probably in his late teens or early twenties, but **he was well spoken of by the brethren who were in Lystra and Iconium.** A key requirement for church leaders is that they be "above reproach" (1 Tim. 3:2, 10). Timothy, even in his youth, was qualified for service on that count.

Recognizing Timothy's value and potential, **Paul wanted this man to go with him.** This was an important step for Timothy and a sacrifice on the part of his family. They knew all too well the dangers he faced as Paul's companion. Eunice and Lois would still vividly recall the events of Paul's last visit to Lystra, when he wound up bloody, battered, and left for dead. It was possible that Timothy might meet a similar fate. Nevertheless, they permitted him to go. After being commissioned by the elders of the local assembly of believers (1 Tim. 4:14; 2 Tim. 1:6), he joined Paul and Silas, and the course of his life was set.

THE RIGHT PRECAUTIONS

and he took him and circumcised him because of the Jews who were in those parts, for they all knew that his father was a Greek. (16:3b)

With Timothy's father likely dead, and having been a Gentile in any case, Paul assumed the role of a father and **took** Timothy **and circumcised him.** Some have sharply criticized Paul for doing so, accusing him of falling into the same heresy he fought at the Jerusalem Council. But such criticism could not be further from the truth. Nowhere is it stated or implied that Paul circumcised Timothy so that he could be saved. The text clearly says that Paul **circumcised him because of the Jews who were in those parts, for they all knew that his father was a Greek.** Circumcision was the *sine qua non* of Judaism. Had Timothy not been circumcised, the **Jews** would have assumed he was renouncing his Jewish heritage and choosing to live as a Gentile. Paul's circumcision of Timothy had nothing to do with salvation; he did it for expediency's sake, to avoid placing an unnecessary stumbling block in the way of Jewish evangelism. Timothy's circumcision granted him full access to the synagogues he would visit with Paul and Silas.

Far from lapsing into legalism, Paul was being consistent with a principle he would later express in 1 Corinthians 9:19–22:

> For though I am free from all men, I have made myself a slave to all, that I might win the more. And to the Jews I became as a Jew, that I might win Jews; to those who are under the Law, as under the Law, though not being myself under the Law, that I might win those who are under the Law; to those who are without law, as without law, though not being

without the law of God but under the law of Christ, that I might win those who are without law. To the weak I became weak, that I might win the weak; I have become all things to all men, that I may by all means save some.

Significantly, Paul refused to circumcise Titus (Gal. 2:3). Titus, unlike Timothy, was a full-blooded Gentile. To have circumcised him would have been to capitulate to legalism.

From Paul's actions concerning his two companions an important principle becomes evident. Missionaries must be sensitive to the unique characteristics of the cultures in which they work. As Paul did in circumcising Timothy, they should avoid giving any unnecessary offense. But like Paul in refusing to circumcise Titus, they must not compromise any of the timeless truths of Scripture.

The Right Presentation

Now while they were passing through the cities, they were delivering the decrees, which had been decided upon by the apostles and elders who were in Jerusalem, for them to observe. So the churches were being strengthened in the faith, and were increasing in number daily. (16:4–5)

Ultimately the key to effective, biblical evangelism is the right message. That message is the truth that salvation is by grace through faith in Jesus Christ, and it was that message Paul, Silas, and Timothy loyally proclaimed. As **they** passed **through the cities** of Galatia, the missionary team was **delivering the decrees, which had been decided upon by the apostles and elders who were in Jerusalem, for them to observe.** They were spreading the liberating truth affirmed at the Jerusalem Council, that salvation was wholly by God's grace. Also, that new believers would not be hindered in their fellowship with their Jewish brothers, the missionaries informed the churches of the regulations imposed on the Gentiles. That is the twofold message of Christianity: salvation by grace and living by love.

Luke's summary statement (cf. 2:41, 47; 4:4; 5:14; 6:7; 9:31) shows the healthy effect of sound biblical evangelism and discipleship. He notes that **the churches were being strengthened in the faith, and were increasing in number daily.** The goal of evangelism is not to rack up huge numbers of converts. Yet it is true that strong churches, established in the faith, will increase in numbers.

THE RIGHT PLACE

And they passed through the Phrygian and Galatian region, having been forbidden by the Holy Spirit to speak the word in Asia; and when they had come to Mysia, they were trying to go into Bithynia, and the Spirit of Jesus did not permit them; and passing by Mysia, they came down to Troas. And a vision appeared to Paul in the night: a certain man of Macedonia was standing and appealing to him, and saying, "Come over to Macedonia and help us." And when he had seen the vision, immediately we sought to go into Macedonia, concluding that God had called us to preach the gospel to them. (16:6–10)

Having **passed through the Phrygian and Galatian region,** Paul decided to move further west into the province of **Asia.** That region was an important one, and there would later be churches in such cities as Ephesus, Smyrna, Philadelphia, Laodicea, Colossae, Sardis, Pergamum, and Thyatira. For now, however, God had other plans for the missionaries, and somehow they were **forbidden by the Holy Spirit to speak the word in Asia.**

With the way west blocked, the missionaries turned north into **Mysia,** the region north of **Asia.** But when they tried **to go** farther north **into Bithynia, the Spirit of Jesus did not permit them.** There is no indication of how they were prevented, but with nowhere else to turn, they **came down to Troas,** a port on the Aegean Sea. They knew God would eventually reveal where He wanted them to go if they kept moving. At last, in dramatic fashion, He did so. **A vision appeared to Paul in the night: a certain man of Macedonia was standing and appealing to him, and saying, "Come over to Macedonia and help us." Macedonia** was across the Aegean Sea on the mainland of Greece. In it were located the important cities of Philippi and Thessalonica. More significant, this would be the first entry of the gospel into the continent of Europe.

Having received the divine summons, Paul did not hesitate. Luke notes that **when he had seen the vision, immediately we sought to go into Macedonia, concluding that God had called us to preach the gospel to them.** The missionary team's experience illustrates a basic principle of knowing God's will: to move ahead and allow Him to close doors until the right opportunity is reached.

Verse 10 is the first of the "we" passages in Acts. Luke, the writer of Acts, has now joined the missionary team. Like Timothy, he was to be Paul's faithful friend and loyal companion for the rest of the apostle's life.

This passage illustrates the foundational principles of evangelism: God uses people with the right passion and the right priority, with the right personnel taking the right precautions, to make the right presentation in the right place. Any evangelistic methodology must be evaluated in the light of such realities.

Portraits of Two Women (Acts 16:11–18)

7

Therefore putting out to sea from Troas, we ran a straight course to Samothrace, and on the day following to Neapolis; and from there to Philippi, which is a leading city of the district of Macedonia, a Roman colony; and we were staying in this city for some days. And on the Sabbath day we went outside the gate to a riverside, where we were supposing that there would be a place of prayer; and we sat down and began speaking to the women who had assembled. And a certain woman named Lydia, from the city of Thyatira, a seller of purple fabrics, a worshiper of God, was listening; and the Lord opened her heart to respond to the things spoken by Paul. And when she and her household had been baptized, she urged us, saying, "If you have judged me to be faithful to the Lord, come into my house and stay." And she prevailed upon us. And it happened that as we were going to the place of prayer, a certain slave-girl having a spirit of divination met us, who was bringing her masters much profit by fortunetelling. Following after Paul and us, she kept crying out, saying, "These men are bond-servants of the Most High God, who are proclaiming to you the way of salvation." And she continued doing this for many days. But Paul was greatly annoyed, and turned and said to the spirit, "I command you in the name of

Jesus Christ to come out of her!" And it came out at that very moment. (16:11–18)

The last few decades have witnessed the rise of many so-called liberation movements. Ostensibly, their goal is to free people from oppression and inequality and elevate them to higher status. Only then, proponents argue, can people be fulfilled.

Like all other such social movements, however, liberation movements ultimately fall far short of their promise. No movement that rearranges people's social status, while leaving their hearts untransformed, is truly liberating. There is only one way to experience genuine freedom, and that is to have a heart set free from the bondage of sin and death. The Lord Jesus Christ expressed that truth in John 8:32 when He said, "You shall know the truth, and the truth shall make you free." Such freedom does not come through human effort. The prophet Jeremiah asked rhetorically, "Can the Ethiopian change his skin or the leopard his spots? Then you also can do good who are accustomed to do evil" (Jer. 13:23). The radical transformation from spiritual death to eternal life, from darkness to light, from Satan's kingdom to God's comes only to those "who were born not of blood, nor of the will of the flesh, nor of the will of man, but of God" (John 1:13). Only through the complete transformation of the new birth does fulfillment come.

There are, therefore, only two types of people in the world: those whom "the law of the Spirit of life in Christ Jesus has set free from the law of sin and of death" (Rom. 8:2) and those "dead in [their] trespasses and sins" (Eph. 2:1). There are only the slaves of unrighteousness and the slaves of righteousness (Rom. 6:16–18).

The women's liberation movement is an example of a social effort that promises freedom and can't deliver anything but bondage to sin. In the portraits of the two women found in Acts 16:11–18, we find examples of both freedom and bondage. Lydia, the first recorded Gentile convert in Europe, was a truly liberated woman. The nameless, demon-possessed slave girl typified those enslaved to sin and Satan.

The Liberated Woman

Therefore putting out to sea from Troas, we ran a straight course to Samothrace, and on the day following to Neapolis; and from there to Philippi, which is a leading city of the district of Macedonia, a Roman colony; and we were staying in this city for some days. And on the Sabbath day we went outside the gate to a riverside, where we were supposing that there would be a place of prayer; and we sat down and began speaking to the

women who had assembled. And a certain woman named Lydia, from the city of Thyatira, a seller of purple fabrics, a worshiper of God, was listening; and the Lord opened her heart to respond to the things spoken by Paul. And when she and her household had been baptized, she urged us, saying, "If you have judged me to be faithful to the Lord, come into my house and stay." And she prevailed upon us. (16:11–15)

The passage opens with the missionary team (Paul, Silas, Timothy, and Luke) in the port city of Troas. Troas was located across the Aegean Sea from Greece, on the western shore of Asia Minor (modern Turkey) near the site of ancient Troy. The missionaries had been directed there by the Holy Spirit, who had closed all other doors of ministry for them (16:6–8). While at Troas, Paul had a vision of a man from Macedonia (on the mainland of Greece), pleading for him to "come over to Macedonia and help us" (16:9). In response to the vision, Luke notes, "immediately we sought to go into Macedonia, concluding that God had called us to preach the gospel to them" (16:10).

Therefore, because of God's call, **putting out to sea from Troas,** they **ran a straight course to Samothrace. Samothrace** is an island in the Aegean Sea, approximately half way between Asia Minor and the Greek mainland. There they stayed overnight (to avoid the hazards of sailing in the dark) **and on the day following** sailed on to **Neapolis,** the port city for Philippi. The winds must have been favorable, for the reverse trip from Philippi to Troas on the third missionary journey took five days (Acts 20:6). When the missionary team landed in **Neapolis,** Paul's ministry finally reached Europe.

The team did not stop to preach in **Neapolis,** but **from there** went on **to Philippi,** about ten miles inland. **Philippi,** as Luke notes, was **a leading city of the district of Macedonia,** and **a Roman colony.** Named after Philip II of Macedon (the father of Alexander the Great), **Philippi** was the eastern terminus for the great Roman highway known as the Egnatian Way. The city was named **a Roman colony** by Octavian, following the battle of Actium in 31 B.C.. As a colony Philippi

> possessed the *ius Italicum*, which carried the right of freedom (*libertas*), that is, they were self–governing, independent of the provincial government; the right of exemption from tax (*immunitas*); and the right of holding land in full ownership, as under Roman law, and of using Italian legal procedures and precedents. In 16:16–40 we have a clear picture of this procedure and one, moreover, that belongs precisely to this time. (David J. Williams, *New International Biblical Commentary: Acts* [Peabody, Mass.: Hendrickson, 1990], 284)

Although eight other cities known to be Roman colonies appear in Acts, Philippi is the only one Luke refers to as a colony.

The missionaries remained in Philippi **for some days,** then **on the Sabbath day went outside the gate to a riverside, where** they **were supposing that there would be a place of prayer.** It was Paul's custom in each city he visited to preach first in the synagogue. As a rabbi and a student of the greatest rabbi of the time, Gamaliel (Acts 22:3), Paul could be assured of getting a hearing there. To form a synagogue, however, required the presence of ten Jewish men who were heads of households. Evidently Philippi's Jewish community was too small to form a synagogue. In such cases, **a place of prayer,** under the open sky and near a river or the sea, was to be arranged for. The one in Philippi was located **outside the gate** by **a riverside,** probably where the road leading out of Philippi crossed the Gangites River. The fact that the group met outside the city probably indicates the meeting place was well beyond the sacred area, within which foreign deities were not permitted.

The missionaries **sat down** (the normal posture for teaching; cf. Matt. 5:1; 13:2; Luke 4:20) **and began speaking to the women who had assembled.** That only **women** are mentioned is further evidence of the small size of the Jewish community at Philippi. Lacking a man to lead them, these women met to pray, read from the Old Testament law, and discuss what they had read. To be taught by a traveling rabbi such as Paul was no doubt a rare privilege.

It is significant that the first people Paul preached to in Europe were women. He is often caricatured as a male chauvinist by those who reject his teaching on the role of women. But he was not prejudiced, as his eagerness to speak with this group shows. Paul's attitude was in sharp contrast to that of his fellow Pharisees. They would not deign to teach a woman, and regularly in their rote prayers they thanked God that they were neither Gentiles, slaves, nor women. It also ran counter to the treatment of women in Greco-Roman society. Paul valued the ministry of women such as Phoebe (Rom. 16:1), the various women among those he greeted in Romans 16:3ff., and even Euodia and Syntyche (Phil. 4:2–3).

Verse 14 introduces **a certain woman named Lydia.** Because her home **city of Thyatira** was located in the Roman province of Lydia, it is possible that "Lydia" was not so much her personal name as her name in business; she may have been known as "the Lydian lady." **Thyatira,** site of one of the seven churches of Revelation (Rev. 2:18–29), was noted for its manufacture of purple dye and dyed goods. Not surprisingly, Lydia herself was **a seller of purple fabrics.** Purple dye, whether made from the glands of the murex shellfish or from the roots of the madder plant, was prohibitively expensive. Purple garments were worn by royalty and the wealthy, and the selling of **purple fabrics** was a very profitable business. That Lydia had a house large enough to accommodate the missionary team (v. 15) and the nascent church at Philippi (v. 40) indicates her wealth.

Three sequential aspects of Lydia's conversion stand out in the narrative. First, she was **a worshiper of God.** Hers was a seeking heart, and she had already turned from pagan idolatry to worship the one true God. The phrase **a worshiper of God** shows that Lydia, like Cornelius (Acts 10:2), was a believer in the God of Israel. She had not yet, however, become a full proselyte to Judaism.

Lydia's seeking was the first step of her spiritual liberation. Yet she, like all sinners, did not seek God on her own until He sought her. In Romans 3:11, Paul wrote, "There is none who understands, there is none who seeks for God." "No one can come to Me," declared the Lord Jesus Christ, "unless the Father who sent Me draws him" (John 6:44).

Her conversion, and those of Cornelius and the Ethiopian eunuch, illustrate an important principle. An often-asked question about evangelism concerns the fate of those who never hear the gospel. Lydia's conversion shows that God will reveal the fullness of the gospel to those whom He causes to honestly seek Him. In John 6:37, Jesus said, "All that the Father gives Me shall come to Me, and the one who comes to Me I will certainly not cast out." God will never turn away the seeking heart.

Not only was Lydia seeking, but she also **was listening** to the gospel proclaimed by Paul. Many hear the sound of the life-giving message preached without really listening to it. They are like Paul's companions on the Damascus Road, who, although they heard its sound, "did not understand the voice of the One who was speaking" (Acts 22:9).

The Lord Jesus Christ condemned those who heard without listening. In response to His disciples' query about why He spoke in parables, He replied:

> To you it has been granted to know the mysteries of the kingdom of heaven, but to them it has not been granted. For whoever has, to him shall more be given, and he shall have an abundance; but whoever does not have, even what he has shall be taken away from him. Therefore I speak to them in parables; because while seeing they do not see, and while hearing they do not hear, nor do they understand. And in their case the prophecy of Isaiah is being fulfilled, which says, "You will keep on hearing, but will not understand; and you will keep on seeing, but will not perceive; for the heart of this people has become dull, and with their ears they scarcely hear, and they have closed their eyes lest they should see with their eyes, and hear with their ears, and understand with their heart and return, and I should heal them." But blessed are your eyes, because they see; and your ears, because they hear. For truly I say to you, that many prophets and right-

eous men desired to see what you see, and did not see it; and to hear what you hear, and did not hear it. (Matt. 13:11–17)

In John 8:43–45, Jesus gave the reason people fail to listen to His Word:

Why do you not understand what I am saying? It is because you cannot hear My word. You are of your father the devil, and you want to do the desires of your father. He was a murderer from the beginning, and does not stand in the truth, because there is no truth in him. Whenever he speaks a lie, he speaks from his own nature; for he is a liar, and the father of lies. But because I speak the truth, you do not believe Me.

Lydia was not like them; she listened with faith to the saving gospel. She did so because **the Lord opened her heart to respond to the things spoken by Paul.** As noted in the discussion of Acts 13:48 in chapter 3 of this volume, God is absolutely sovereign in salvation. Were that not true, no one would be saved. For those "dead in [their] trespasses and sins" (Eph. 2:1) are unable to respond to spiritual truth. God has to open the heart.

Remembering God's sovereignty in salvation is the foundation of a proper perspective on evangelism. Salvation does not depend on clever evangelistic strategies, or the skill of the preacher, or a masterful presentation. It is not a human work at all; it is God's work. "I planted," Paul wrote to the Corinthians, "Apollos watered, but God was causing the growth. So then neither the one who plants nor the one who waters is anything, but God who causes the growth" (1 Cor. 3:6–7).

In 1 Corinthians 2:1–4, Paul described his evangelistic approach to the Corinthians:

When I came to you, brethren, I did not come with superiority of speech or of wisdom, proclaiming to you the testimony of God. For I determined to know nothing among you except Jesus Christ, and Him crucified. And I was with you in weakness and in fear and in much trembling. And my message and my preaching were not in persuasive words of wisdom, but in demonstration of the Spirit and of power.

Although an accomplished scholar, adept at handling the Scriptures, Paul recognized that mere human persuasiveness saves no one. The other early evangelists also knew that truth; one searches the evangelistic messages in Acts in vain for any sort of clever manipulation. Instead, they are filled with interpretation and application of Scripture, and the proclamation of the gospel (cf. 2:14ff., 41; 3:12ff.; 5:42; 8:4–5; 13:15ff.; 16:30–32; 17:10–12).

Many in our day foolishly act as though God were wholly dependent on them to reach the lost. Nothing could be further from the truth. A. W. Tozer points out:

> Probably the hardest thought of all for our natural egotism to entertain is that God does not need our help. We commonly represent Him as a busy, eager, somewhat frustrated Father hurrying about seeking help to carry out His benevolent plan to bring peace and salvation to the world; but as said the Lady Julian, "I saw truly that God doeth all–thing, be it never so little." The God who worketh all things surely needs no help and no helpers.

> Too many missionary appeals are based upon this fancied frustration of Almighty God. An effective speaker can easily excite pity in his hearers, not only for the heathen but for the God who has tried so hard and so long to save them and has failed for want of support. I fear that thousands of young persons enter Christian service from no higher motive than to help deliver God from the embarrassing situation His love has gotten Him into and His limited abilities seem unable to get Him out of. (*The Knowledge of the Holy* [New York: Harper & Row, 1975], 41)

The most important element of any gospel presentation is clarity of content. To present the gospel clearly requires invoking the power of the Spirit and leaving the results to God.

As was customary in the early church, Lydia **and her household** were **baptized** immediately after their conversion, no doubt in the river near the place of prayer. The jailer's household also believed the gospel (Acts 16:33), as God established the church at Philippi. Baptism is the outward sign of the redeemed individual's identification with Jesus Christ. It is an act of obedience by the believer but plays no role in salvation. (For evidence that baptism does not save, see *Acts 1–12*, MacArthur New Testament Commentary [Chicago: Moody, 1994], 73ff.)

After her baptism, Lydia **urged** the missionaries to accept her hospitality **saying, "If you have judged me to be faithful to the Lord, come into my house and stay."** Hospitality is required of all Christians (Rom. 12:13; Heb. 13:2; 1 Pet. 4:9), especially women (1 Tim. 5:10) and church leaders (Titus 1:8). It was critical in the ancient world, where inns were often unsuitable for Christians to stay in. They were filthy, dangerous, expensive, and often little more than brothels. To make a home where travelers could be exposed to Christian love, family life, and fellowship was a high priority for Christian women (cf. 1 Tim.

5:9–10). Lydia's hospitality gave proof that she was a truly liberated woman (cf. John 13:35).

The Enslaved Woman

And it happened that as we were going to the place of prayer, a certain slave-girl having a spirit of divination met us, who was bringing her masters much profit by fortunetelling. Following after Paul and us, she kept crying out, saying, "These men are bond-servants of the Most High God, who are proclaiming to you the way of salvation." And she continued doing this for many days. But Paul was greatly annoyed, and turned and said to the spirit, "I command you in the name of Jesus Christ to come out of her!" And it came out at that very moment. (16:16–18)

As the church took root in Philippi, Satan moved to attack it. Here, as in Samaria (8:9ff.) and Cyprus (13:6ff.), was the clash of light and darkness. He sought to infiltrate the church or to crush it with persecution. Both avenues of attack would prove unsuccessful.

His attempt at infiltration unfolded as the missionaries continued their pattern of **going to the place of prayer** beside the river. They encountered an emissary of the devil, **a certain slave-girl having a spirit of divination.** The Greek text literally reads "a python spirit." That designation derives from Greek mythology, in which the Python was a snake that guarded the famous oracle at Delphi. Eventually, the Python was killed by Apollo, the god of prophecy. Since it was believed that Apollo spoke through the oracle at Delphi, the term "python" came to refer to anyone in contact with Apollo. In modern terms, she was a medium in contact with demons. Luke notes that the demon-possessed girl **was bringing her masters much profit by fortunetelling.** Such people were believed to be able predict the future, a valuable commodity in the Greco-Roman culture:

> Greeks and Romans put great stock on augury and divination. No commander would set out on a major military campaign nor would an emperor make an important decree without first consulting an oracle to see how things might turn out. A slave girl with a clairvoyant gift was thus a veritable gold mine for her owners. (John B. Polhill, *The New American Commentary: Acts* [Nashville: Broadman, 1992], 351)

This hapless tool of Satan kept **following after Paul** and the others, **crying out** at the top of her voice, **"These men are bond-servants of the Most High God, who are proclaiming to you the way of salvation."** This was a subtle and dangerous attack, a bold attempt to infiltrate a deadly tare among the wheat, because what the demon-possessed girl was saying was absolutely true. The demon even used biblical terminology. The term **Most High God** was an Old Testament designation of the God of Israel (Ps. 78:35; Dan. 5:18) She also spoke of **the way of salvation.** The father of lies speaks the truth when it suits his purposes, disguising himself and his emissaries as angels of light (2 Cor. 11:13–14). Some of his most effective and diabolical work is done in the name of Jesus Christ. He often uses a little truth to ensnare people in a false system of religion. Since the demon-possessed girl was agreeing with the Christian preachers, the natural assumption would be that she was part of their group. She would then have been in a position to do unspeakable harm to the cause of Christ.

Like his Lord (Mark 1:34; Luke 4:41), Paul wanted no publicity from Satan. After the girl **continued** her proclamations **for many days, Paul** became **greatly annoyed.** He resented the satanic assault on his ministry and felt sorry for the wretched state of the girl. He ended both when he **turned and said to the spirit, "I command you in the name of Jesus Christ to come out of her!"** In obedience to Paul's apostolic authority, the demon **came out at that very moment.** The ability to cast out demons marked Christ's apostles (Mark 3:15; 2 Cor. 12:12) and passed from the church with them. That and the other miraculous gifts confirmed that the apostles were God's spokesmen. Despite the claims of many today, no believer has direct authority to command demons to obey him. (For further discussion of this point, see John MacArthur, *How to Meet the Enemy* [Wheaton, Ill.: Victor, 1992].) The spiritual battle is now fought with the armor and weapons discussed in Ephesians 6:10ff.

These two women typify all of humanity. Everyone is either liberated by Jesus Christ or enslaved by Satan. The only path to freedom is that followed by Lydia—of seeking God, listening to the gospel, and having a heart opened to respond by the Lord. Those who do so will not be disappointed, for the Lord Himself promises in Jeremiah 29:13, "You will seek Me and find Me, when you search for Me with all your heart."

Turning Persecution into Production (Acts 16:19–40)

8

But when her masters saw that their hope of profit was gone, they seized Paul and Silas and dragged them into the market place before the authorities, and when they had brought them to the chief magistrates, they said, "These men are throwing our city into confusion, being Jews, and are proclaiming customs which it is not lawful for us to accept or to observe, being Romans." And the crowd rose up together against them, and the chief magistrates tore their robes off them, and proceeded to order them to be beaten with rods. And when they had inflicted many blows upon them, they threw them into prison, commanding the jailer to guard them securely; and he, having received such a command, threw them into the inner prison, and fastened their feet in the stocks. But about midnight Paul and Silas were praying and singing hymns of praise to God, and the prisoners were listening to them; and suddenly there came a great earthquake, so that the foundations of the prison house were shaken; and immediately all the doors were opened, and everyone's chains were unfastened. And when the jailer had been roused out of sleep and had seen the prison doors opened, he drew his sword and was about to kill himself, supposing that the prisoners had escaped. But Paul cried out with a loud voice, saying, "Do yourself no harm, for we are all here!" And he called for lights and rushed in and, trembling with fear, he fell down before Paul and Silas, and after he brought them out, he said, "Sirs, what must I do to be saved?" And they said, "Believe in the Lord Jesus, and you shall be saved, you and your household." And they spoke the word of the Lord to him together with all who were in his house. And he took them that very hour of the night and washed their wounds, and immediately he was baptized, he and all his household. And he brought them into his house and set food before them, and rejoiced greatly, having believed in God with his whole household. Now when day came, the chief magistrates sent their policemen, saying, "Release those men." And the jailer reported these words to Paul, saying, "The chief magistrates have sent to release you. Now therefore, come out and go in peace." But Paul said to them, "They have beaten us in public without trial, men who are Romans, and have thrown us into prison; and now are they sending us away secretly? No indeed! But let them come themselves and bring us out." And the policemen reported these words to the chief magistrates. And they were afraid when they heard that they were Romans, and they came and appealed to them, and when they had brought them out, they kept begging them to leave the city. And they went out of the prison and entered the house of Lydia, and when they saw the brethren, they encouraged them and departed. (16:19–40)

A very reassuring aspect of God's sovereign rule over the universe is His ability to bring good results out of bad circumstances. That is especially true when His people undergo persecution. God "causes all things to work together for good to those who love God, to those who are called according to His purpose" (Rom. 8:28), often by making "the wrath of man ... praise [Him]" (Ps. 76:10).

Sold into slavery in Egypt by his jealous brothers, Joseph rose to prominence in Pharaoh's court. In that exalted position he was able to provide for his father and brothers during the ensuing famine:

> And now do not be grieved or angry with yourselves, because you sold me here; for God sent me before you to preserve life. For the famine has been in the land these two years, and there are still five years in which there will be neither plowing nor harvesting. And God sent me before you to preserve for you a remnant in the earth, and to keep you alive by a great deliverance. Now, therefore, it was not you who sent me here, but God; and He has made me a father to Pharaoh and lord of all his household and ruler over all the land of Egypt. ... And as for you, you

meant evil against me, but God meant it for good in order to bring about this present result, to preserve many people alive. (Gen. 45:5–8; 50:20)

God used Joseph to preserve the ancestors of the nation of Israel.

Israel's apostasy led to her captivity at the hands of cruel foreign nations. But from the trauma and tragedy of that period emerged such shining lights as Daniel, Jeremiah, Ezekiel, Ezra, Nehemiah, and Esther.

The most heinous crime ever committed was the murder of God's Son, yet out of that evil act God brought salvation. In his sermon on the Day of Pentecost Peter declared:

Men of Israel, listen to these words: Jesus the Nazarene, a man attested to you by God with miracles and wonders and signs which God performed through Him in your midst, just as you yourselves know—this Man, delivered up by the predetermined plan and foreknowledge of God, you nailed to a cross by the hands of godless men and put Him to death. And God raised Him up again, putting an end to the agony of death, since it was impossible for Him to be held in its power. (Acts 2:22–24; cf. Heb. 2:10)

Acts chapters 4, 5, 7, 8, and 12 record the persecution of the early church. Yet all those instances only resulted in the strengthening of the church and an increase in its numbers (4:4). Verse 1 of chapter 8 notes that "on that day [of Stephen's martyrdom] a great persecution arose against the church in Jerusalem; and they were all scattered throughout the regions of Judea and Samaria, except the apostles." Acts 11:19–21 describes the results of that persecution:

So then those who were scattered because of the persecution that arose in connection with Stephen made their way to Phoenicia and Cyprus and Antioch, speaking the word to no one except to Jews alone. But there were some of them, men of Cyprus and Cyrene, who came to Antioch and began speaking to the Greeks also, preaching the Lord Jesus. And the hand of the Lord was with them, and a large number who believed turned to the Lord.

The sixteenth chapter of Acts records yet another illustration of God's turning bad circumstances into spiritual victory. Falsely accused, savagely beaten, and unjustly imprisoned, Paul and Silas saw God use those circumstances to bring salvation to an entire household.

This section moves to the results of Paul's miraculous deliverance of the demon-possessed girl (vv. 16–18). Paul's ministry had made its first beachhead in Europe at the important city of Philippi. Along with his fellow missionaries (Silas, Timothy, and Luke) he evangelized a group of women, both Jews and proselytes. One of the proselytes, Lydia, was converted along with her household (vv. 14–15), and the Philippian church was born.

Satan was quick to react, first attempting to infiltrate the young fellowship with a demon-possessed medium. When Paul's miraculous power thwarted that attempt, Satan tried to destroy the church through persecution. Those are always his two avenues of attack: infiltration—attacking the church from within; and persecution, attacking it from without. Verses 19–40 record the failure of Satan's attack through persecution, as God used that persecution to expand the Philippian church. God's marvelous turning of persecution into triumph unfolds in five sequential stages: persecution, praise, preaching, provision, and protection.

PERSECUTION

But when her masters saw that their hope of profit was gone, they seized Paul and Silas and dragged them into the market place before the authorities, and when they had brought them to the chief magistrates, they said, "These men are throwing our city into confusion, being Jews, and are proclaiming customs which it is not lawful for us to accept or to observe, being Romans." And the crowd rose up together against them, and the chief magistrates tore their robes off them, and proceeded to order them to be beaten with rods. And when they had inflicted many blows upon them, they threw them into prison, commanding the jailer to guard them securely; and he, having received such a command, threw them into the inner prison, and fastened their feet in the stocks. (16:19–24)

The reaction of the demon-possessed girl's **masters** reveals the inhumane cruelty of the institution of slavery. Instead of rejoicing in her deliverance, they became enraged when they **saw that their hope of profit was gone.** Their attitude is reminiscent of the Gerasenes in Mark 5. Instead of rejoicing over Jesus' deliverance of the demon-possessed maniac, they were angered over the loss of a herd of swine (v. 16). So upset were they that they "began to entreat [Jesus] to depart from their region" (v. 17). Later, in Ephesus, the craftsmen who made shrines of the goddess Artemis became violently hostile to Christianity. They feared the spread of the gospel would put them out of business, and the uproar was immense (Acts 19:23ff.).

Such reactions illustrate a sad spiritual reality: love of money blurs spiritual perception. "Those who want to get rich," Paul wrote to Timothy, "fall into temptation and a snare and many foolish and harmful desires which plunge men into ruin and destruction" (1 Tim. 6:9). That is true because "the love of money is a root of all sorts of evil, and some by longing for it have wandered away from the faith, and pierced themselves with many a pang" (v. 10).

Enraged at the loss of the income she provided, the girl's masters **seized Paul and Silas and dragged them into the market place before the authorities.** That was an interesting turn of events for Paul, who before his conversion had made a career of "dragging off men and women" to "put them in prison" (Acts 8:3). The *agora* (**market place**) was the central public square. It functioned not only as a marketplace, but also

> as the social center of the city. Here the unemployed waited for suitable work, the sick were healed, and the magistrates judged court cases. In those days, a plaintiff could drag a defendant into court and ask the judge to pass a verdict (James 2:6). The owners of the slave girl were acting according to Roman law when they laid their hands on Paul and Silas and put their grievance before the city authorities. (Simon J. Kistemaker, *New Testament Commentary: Acts* [Grand Rapids: Baker, 1990], 595)

Luke further describes the **authorities** as **the chief magistrates** (*stratēgos*; *praetor* in Latin). Every Roman colony was governed by two of these men, as was the case at Philippi.

Having dragged Paul and Silas before these authorities, their accusers opened the proceedings by declaring, **"These men are throwing our city into confusion, being Jews."** Anti-Semitism is not a modern phenomenon but has its origins in antiquity. At about this time, Emperor Claudius issued an order expelling the Jews from Rome (Acts 18:2). This anti-Semitism may explain why only Paul and Silas were apprehended, since Luke was a Gentile and Timothy a half-Gentile.

The charge that Paul and Silas were **proclaiming customs which it is not lawful for us to accept or to observe, being Romans** was technically true. There was a law forbidding Roman citizens to practice any foreign religion that had not been sanctioned by the state, although this law was rarely enforced. But the charge that the missionaries were creating mass confusion in the city was false. It had its basis not in fact but in anger over lost profits.

The charges against Paul and Silas, although false, were enough to manipulate a reaction and stir up the **crowd** in the marketplace. Mob mentality took over, and the crowd mindlessly **rose up together**

against the two missionaries. Caught up in the mob's anti-Semitic frenzy, the **chief magistrates** failed miserably to uphold the highly prized standards of Roman justice. They did not bother to investigate the charges, conduct a proper hearing, or give Paul and Silas a chance to defend themselves (which would have revealed, first of all, that they were Roman citizens). Instead, **the chief magistrates tore their robes off them, and proceeded to order them to be beaten** (illegally, cf. v. 37) **with rods.** Any semblance of just legal procedure was nonexistent. The beating was administered by the lictors (the "policemen" of vv. 35, 38), who were under the command of the magistrates (v. 35). Each lictor carried a bundle of rods tied together—ironically, as a symbol of Roman law and justice. With those rods they brutally beat the men, a punishment Paul endured three times (2 Cor. 11:25).

After Paul and Silas had received **many blows** from the lictors' rods, the magistrates ordered them to be thrown **into prison.** To the illegal beating they added an unjust imprisonment. They ordered Paul and Silas to be placed in maximum security, **commanding the jailer to guard them securely. He, having received such a command, threw them into the inner prison, and fastened their feet in the stocks.** Taking no chances with such important prisoners, the jailer threw the two battered and bleeding men into the **inner**, most secure, part of the prison. He then took the further precaution of fastening **their feet in the stocks.** All those safeguards were to prove futile, however. Like Herod (Acts 12:6–11) and the Sanhedrin (Acts 5:19–25) before them, the authorities at Philippi were to learn that no prison can hold those whom God wants released.

Nor did this satanically inspired persecution intimidate Paul and Silas; it encouraged them to even further boldness. Writing of this incident to the Thessalonians, Paul said, "After we had already suffered and been mistreated in Philippi, as you know, we had the boldness in our God to speak to you the gospel of God amid much opposition" (1 Thess. 2:2). Paul's indomitable spirit, and joyous anticipation of being with Christ in heaven, gave him an almost reckless boldness in proclaiming the gospel. No amount of opposition could keep him from fulfilling his calling. Writing to the Philippians from prison in Rome, Paul rejoiced that his "circumstances [had] turned out for the greater progress of the gospel" (Phil. 1:12). Far from ending his ministry, that imprisonment saw it spread even to "those of Caesar's household" (Phil. 4:22). Paul could accept whatever suffering resulted from his ministry because he viewed himself as expendable. To the Philippians he wrote, "But even if I am being poured out as a drink offering upon the sacrifice and service of your faith, I rejoice and share my joy with you all" (Phil. 2:17). Paul and Silas manifested that same attitude of joy amid suffering while in prison at Philippi, turning persecution into praise.

PRAISE

But about midnight Paul and Silas were praying and singing hymns of praise to God, and the prisoners were listening to them; and suddenly there came a great earthquake, so that the foundations of the prison house were shaken; and immediately all the doors were opened, and everyone's chains were unfastened. And when the jailer had been roused out of sleep and had seen the prison doors opened, he drew his sword and was about to kill himself, supposing that the prisoners had escaped. But Paul cried out with a loud voice, saying, "Do yourself no harm, for we are all here!" And he called for lights and rushed in and, trembling with fear, he fell down before Paul and Silas, (16:25–29)

Paul and Barnabas were understandably unable to sleep due to their appalling circumstances. After having been severely beaten, they found themselves in a filthy dungeon. Their feet were fastened in stocks designed to induce painful cramping by spreading their legs as wide as possible. In spite of it all, they maintained a joyful attitude. As **midnight** arrived, **Paul and Silas were praying and singing hymns of praise to God.** Their attitude astounded **the** other **prisoners, who were listening to them,** and provided a powerful testimony of God's transforming grace.

How could the two missionaries praise God under such conditions? They understood what many Christians seem to forget—praising God does not depend on circumstances. "Rejoice in the Lord *always*," wrote Paul to the Philippian church (Phil. 4:4; cf. 1 Thess. 5:16, 18). Christians do not rejoice in their *circumstances;* not even Paul did that. He knew what it was to experience affliction so severe that he was "burdened excessively" and "despaired even of life" (2 Cor. 1:8). Christians rejoice in the glorious truth that the sovereign God controls every circumstance of life. They "know that God causes all things to work together for good to those who love God, to those who are called according to His purpose" (Rom. 8:28). When trials come, believers can take comfort in the truth expressed by Peter in 1 Peter 5:10: "After you have suffered for a little while, the God of all grace, who called you to His eternal glory in Christ, will Himself perfect, confirm, strengthen and establish you." Like Paul in 2 Corinthians 4:16–17 they can say:

> Therefore we do not lose heart, but though our outer man is decaying, yet our inner man is being renewed day by day. For momentary, light affliction is producing for us an eternal weight of glory far beyond all comparison.

He adds in 2 Corinthians 12:9–10:

> He has said to me, "My grace is sufficient for you, for power is perfected in weakness." Most gladly, therefore, I will rather boast about my weaknesses, that the power of Christ may dwell in me. Therefore I am well content with weaknesses, with insults, with distresses, with persecutions, with difficulties, for Christ's sake; for when I am weak, then I am strong.

The key to having joy in every circumstance of life is to be filled with the Spirit. Joy is a part of the fruit of the Spirit (Gal. 5:22), and yielding to His control produces songs of joy (Eph. 5:18–19). The problem with sad, miserable Christians is not their circumstances but the lack of living a Spirit-controlled life.

Paul and Silas's reaction underscores another vitally important truth in living the Christian life: How Christians live is directly related to their concept of God. No one expressed that truth more clearly than A. W. Tozer:

> What comes into our minds when we think about God is the most important thing about us.
>
> The history of mankind will probably show that no people has ever risen above its religion, and man's spiritual history will positively demonstrate that no religion has ever been greater than its idea of God....
>
> Were we able to extract from any man a complete answer to the question, "What comes into your mind when you think about God?" we might predict with certainty the spiritual future of that man....
>
> A right conception of God is basic not only to systematic theology but to practical Christian living as well. It is to worship what the foundation is to the temple; where it is inadequate or out of plumb the whole structure must sooner or later collapse. I believe there is scarcely an error in doctrine or a failure in applying Christian ethics that cannot be traced finally to imperfect and ignoble thoughts about God. (*The Knowledge of the Holy* [New York: Harper & Row, 1975], 9, 10)

Paul and Silas did not base their theology on their circumstances. Instead, they evaluated those circumstances in light of what they knew to be true about God. Their songs expressed confident trust that God would use their circumstances for their good and His glory. They did not have long to wait until He did.

Suddenly the chorus of praises was interrupted by **a great earthquake,** as God intervened on behalf of his saints. So powerful was the earthquake **that the foundations of the prison house were shaken; and immediately all the doors were opened, and everyone's chains were unfastened** from the walls. God had sent an angel to release Peter from prison (Acts 12:7ff.); here He used the natural means of an earthquake. Both the supernatural and the natural realms are under His sovereign control.

The earthquake also rocked the jailer's house, probably located next to the prison. Having been **roused out of** his **sleep, and** seeing that **the prison doors** had been **opened, he drew his sword and was about to kill himself,** naturally **supposing that the prisoners had escaped.** He knew all too well that a Roman soldier who allowed a prisoner to escape, no matter what the cause, paid with his own life (cf. Acts 12:19; 27:42). Rather than anticipate facing the humiliating and painful execution that would surely follow, the jailer chose **to kill himself** immediately.

Before he could do that, a voice out of the darkness stopped him. From inside the prison, **Paul cried out with a loud voice, saying, "Do yourself no harm, for we are all here!"** Not only Paul and Silas, but all the rest of the prisoners also had remained (they were probably all in the same dungeon). Why the other prisoners did not attempt to escape is not noted. Perhaps they were still stunned by the earthquake and fearful of aftershocks. Possibly they feared the consequences if they tried to escape and were recaptured. Or it may have been that their respect for Paul and Silas allowed the two missionaries to restrain them. In any case, they remained inside the prison.

Astonished at this unbelievable turn of events, the jailer **called for lights and rushed in and, trembling with fear, he fell down before Paul and Silas.** The tables were turned, and the jailer fell to his knees before his prisoners. He was no doubt aware of the message Paul and Silas had preached, and he regarded the earthquake as supernatural confirmation that they spoke the truth. That supernatural confirmation of the preachers and their message led the jailer to view them as speaking divine truth and to seek the salvation they offered. As in the case of Paul (cf. Acts 9:1ff.), it took a striking manifestation of God's power to bring the jailer to his knees. His defenses had been stripped away, and his heart was now opened to respond to the preaching of the gospel.

PREACHING

and after he brought them out, he said, "Sirs, what must I do to be saved?" And they said, "Believe in the Lord Jesus, and you

shall be saved, you and your household." And they spoke the word of the Lord to him together with all who were in his house. (16:30–32)

No doubt having first made sure the other prisoners were secure, the jailer **brought** Paul and Silas **out** into the courtyard. There he asked the question that was burning in his heart, **"Sirs, what must I do to be saved?"** Some have interpreted his question in terms of being saved from punishment, but that is not the case. Since no prisoners had escaped, he faced no punishment from his superiors. And why ask two prisoners such a question? The jailer's question expressed the deep longing of his heart to be right with God. Having undoubtedly heard the testimony of the demon-possessed girl (v. 17), either in person or from others, he believed Paul and Silas had the answer.

To the jailer's simple and direct question the missionaries gave an equally simple and direct answer: **"Believe in the Lord Jesus, and you shall be saved."** Unlike the rich young ruler (Luke 18:18–23), his heart was ready; nothing stood in his way.

The truth that salvation is wholly by faith in the Lord Jesus Christ permeates the Scriptures. "There is salvation in no one else," according to Acts 4:12, "for there is no other name under heaven that has been given among men, by which we must be saved." That glorious truth was at the heart of apostolic preaching (see also Acts 2:38–39; 5:14; 8:12; 10:43; 11:17, 21; 13:12, 38–39, 48; 14:1; 15:11; 17:12; 18:8). Jesus Himself declared, "I am the way, and the truth, and the life; no one comes to the Father, but through Me" (John 14:6). It is also the constant theme of the epistles (cf. Rom. 3:20–25; 5:1; 1 Cor. 6:11; Gal. 2:16; 3:24; Eph. 2:8–9; 2 Tim. 3:15; Titus 3:7).

To **believe in the Lord Jesus** means first to believe He is who He claimed to be. The apostle John wrote, "These have been written that you may believe that Jesus is the Christ, the Son of God; and that believing you may have life in His name" (John 20:31). Second, it means to believe in what He did. Paul succinctly summarized the work of Christ in 1 Corinthians 15:3–4:

> For I delivered to you as of first importance what I also received, that Christ died for our sins according to the Scriptures, and that He was buried, and that He was raised on the third day according to the Scriptures.

To the Romans he wrote:

> If you confess with your mouth Jesus as Lord, and believe in your heart that God raised Him from the dead, you shall be saved; for with the heart man believes, resulting in righteousness, and with the mouth he confesses, resulting in salvation. (Rom. 10:9–10)

The message of salvation was preached not to the jailer alone but also to the rest of his **household.** Accordingly, the two missionaries **spoke the word of the Lord to him together with all who were in his house.** His family, servants, and perhaps relatives or guests who were staying with him all heard the gospel (cf. v. 15; Acts 11:14; 18:8). That the others in the jailer's household individually believed the gospel becomes clear in v. 34 (cf. Acts 10:44).

PROVISION

And he took them that very hour of the night and washed their wounds, and immediately he was baptized, he and all his household. And he brought them into his house and set food before them, and rejoiced greatly, having believed in God with his whole household. (16:33–34)

When the gospel is preached to hearts prepared by God, results are inevitable. The jailer and each member of his household were saved. That his salvation was genuine is evident from four considerations. First, he expressed genuine love for Paul and Silas when **he took them that very hour of the night and washed their wounds.** Jesus said in John 13:35, "By this all men will know that you are My disciples, if you have love for one another." Second, **immediately he was baptized, he and all his household.** By that act they publicly identified themselves with Jesus Christ. Though the hour was late, other people were no doubt still outdoors because of the earthquake. Even if there were no others to witness the baptisms, word of them would surely get around. Third, he showed hospitality, as had Lydia before him (v. 15), by bringing Paul and Silas into the **house** and setting **food before them.** James 2:14-17 shows the importance of hospitality in relation to faith. Finally, he **rejoiced greatly, having believed in God with his whole household.** A short time earlier he was ready to commit suicide. Now he radiated the joy that comes from knowing one's sins are forgiven (cf. Ps. 32:1; Rom. 4:7). Only the grace of God could effect such an instantaneous transformation.

PROTECTION

Now when day came, the chief magistrates sent their policemen, saying, "Release those men." And the jailer reported these words to Paul, saying, "The chief magistrates have sent to release you. Now therefore, come out and go in peace." But Paul said to them, "They have beaten us in public without trial, men who are Romans, and have thrown us into prison; and now are they sending us away secretly? No indeed! But let them come themselves and bring us out." And the policemen reported these words to the chief magistrates. And they were afraid when they heard that they were Romans, and they came and appealed to them, and when they had brought them out, they kept begging them to leave the city. And they went out of the prison and entered the house of Lydia, and when they saw the brethren, they encouraged them and departed. (16:35–40)

Ever the faithful shepherd concerned for his flock, Paul knew he had to take steps to protect the newborn Philippian church from official government harassment. The opportunity presented itself **when day came,** and **the chief magistrates sent their policemen** (the same individuals who had beaten Paul and Silas)**, saying, "Release those men."** They no doubt hoped that the chastened missionaries would quietly limp out of town. Paul, however, had other ideas.

No doubt pleased at the good news he brought, **the jailer reported these words to Paul, saying, "The chief magistrates have sent to release you. Now therefore, come out and go in peace."** But Paul refused to be disposed of so flippantly. He did not seek revenge, but He did not want his and Silas's ill-treatment to become a precedent for the mistreatment of other Christians. For Paul and Silas to have departed quietly could have set a dangerous precedent for the future treatment of missionaries and exposed the believers to arbitrary and abusive action from the magistrates.

The magistrates had made a serious error, as Paul pointed out: **"They have beaten us in public without trial, men who are Romans, and have thrown us into prison."** To inflict corporal punishment on a citizen was a grave violation of Roman law, all the more so since it had been done **without trial.** The consequences, both for the magistrates and for the city, were potentially very serious. The magistrates could have been removed from office, and the emperor could have rescinded Philippi's privileges as a Roman colony.

Paul refused to allow the magistrates to compound their injustice by **sending** him and Silas **away secretly. "No indeed!"** he responded, **"but let them come themselves and bring us out."** If the magistrates want us to leave, Paul declares, let them show us the respect due to Roman citizens.

When **the policemen reported** Paul's **words to the chief magistrates** the latter **were afraid when they heard that** the two men **were Romans.** They knew the consequences of their actions could be devastating for them and their city. Trying to defuse the situation and placate Paul and Silas, the magistrates **came** in person to the prison in a conciliatory manner **and appealed to them, and when they had brought them out,** as Paul had demanded, **they kept begging them to leave the city.** The magistrates were in an awkward position. On the one hand, they had no legal grounds for expelling two Roman citizens who were guilty of no crime. On the other hand, Paul and Silas's continued presence in Philippi could have provoked further violence. Their self-exaltation of the day before suitably deflated, the humbled magistrates could only resort to **begging** Paul and Silas to **leave the city.** This they did, but on their own terms. First **they went out of the prison and entered the house of Lydia,** where they **saw the brethren** and **encouraged them and** only then **departed.**

Once again Satan's plans were frustrated and overruled by God's sovereign control of events. The persecution Satan unleashed to destroy the Philippian church merely added another household to it and gained it protection from the city's rulers. For those who boldly preach the gospel and praise Him no matter what the circumstances, God stands ready to turn persecution into production.

Men Who Turned the World Upside Down (Acts 17:1–15)

9

Now when they had traveled through Amphipolis and Apollonia, they came to Thessalonica, where there was a synagogue of the Jews. And according to Paul's custom, he went to them, and for three Sabbaths reasoned with them from the Scriptures, explaining and giving evidence that the Christ had to suffer and rise again from the dead, and saying, "This Jesus whom I am proclaiming to you is the Christ." And some of them were persuaded and joined Paul and Silas, along with a great multitude of the God-fearing Greeks and a number of the leading women. But the Jews, becoming jealous and taking along some wicked men from the market place, formed a mob and set the city in an uproar; and coming upon the house of Jason, they were seeking to bring them out to the people. And when they did not find them, they began dragging Jason and some brethren before the city authorities, shouting, "These men who have upset the world have come here also; and Jason has welcomed them, and they all act contrary to the decrees of Caesar, saying that there is another king, Jesus." And they stirred up the crowd and the city authorities who heard these things. And when they had received a pledge from Jason and the others, they released them. And the brethren immediately sent Paul and Silas away by night to Berea; and

when they arrived, they went into the synagogue of the Jews. Now these were more noble-minded than those in Thessalonica, for they received the word with great eagerness, examining the Scriptures daily, to see whether these things were so. Many of them therefore believed, along with a number of prominent Greek women and men. But when the Jews of Thessalonica found out that the word of God had been proclaimed by Paul in Berea also, they came there likewise, agitating and stirring up the crowds. And then immediately the brethren sent Paul out to go as far as the sea; and Silas and Timothy remained there. Now those who conducted Paul brought him as far as Athens; and receiving a command for Silas and Timothy to come to him as soon as possible, they departed. (17:1–15)

The world is not now as it was when God created it. The Fall of man, and God's resultant curse on the earth and its environment, toppled it from its spiritual axis. Fallen man is now trapped in an evil world system that is hostile to God. Ours is truly a world turned upside down.

The universe, however, will not remain that way forever. Ultimately, the Lord of glory will return (Rev. 19:11–21), take back the earth (Rev. 5), and establish His sovereign rule over all of it (Ps. 2:6–8). The curse will be lifted, and the earth will be restored to something of its original character. Finally, after the kingdom of Jesus Christ on earth, the whole universe will be uncreated (2 Pet. 3:10–13; Rev. 21:1–4).

That does not mean God is standing idly by until then. Throughout redemptive history He has sent His messengers to proclaim the light of His truth to the lost, sin-darkened world. Such people upset the system and disturb the comfort of sinners, thus incurring their wrath. They turn things right side up from God's perspective, but upside down from the world's.

Elijah ministered during the dark days of Ahab's reign. Ahab was an evil man, more so than any of his predecessors on Israel's throne (1 Kings 16:30). Even worse, he was married to Jezebel, the wicked daughter of the pagan king of Sidon. With her inciting him (1 Kings 21:25), he led the nation down the ruinous path to idolatry. Sent to confront Ahab's wickedness, Elijah prophesied that a devastating drought would strike Israel (1 Kings 17:1). He so upset Ahab's world that when the two finally met face-to-face the exasperated Ahab exclaimed, "Is this you, you troubler of Israel?" (1 Kings 18:17).

Another troublesome man was brought before the last king of Judah, Zedekiah. The powerful Babylonian army that had been besieging Jerusalem had temporarily withdrawn to deal with the threat of Pharaoh's forces (Jer. 37:11). Yet despite that encouraging sign, Jeremiah kept insisting that the city would fall. Even worse for morale, he had solemnly declared:

> Thus says the Lord, "He who stays in this city will die by the sword and by famine and by pestilence, but he who goes out to the Chaldeans will live and have his own life as booty and stay alive." Thus says the Lord, "This city will certainly be given into the hand of the army of the king of Babylon, and he will capture it." (Jer. 38:2–3)

A group of infuriated court officials dragged Jeremiah before King Zedekiah, demanding

> let this man be put to death, inasmuch as he is discouraging the men of war who are left in this city and all the people, by speaking such words to them; for this man is not seeking the well-being of this people, but rather their harm. (Jer. 38:4)

Jeremiah was proclaiming God's message to His doomed, rebellious people. Yet, from their upside-down perspective, he was guilty of treason.

The prophet Amos lived during the troubled times of the divided kingdom. Although a native of the southern kingdom of Judah, God sent him with a message of doom to the northern kingdom of Israel. Instead of heeding Amos's divinely inspired warning,

> Amaziah, the priest of Bethel, sent word to Jeroboam, king of Israel, saying, "Amos has conspired against you in the midst of the house of Israel; the land is unable to endure all his words. For thus Amos says, 'Jeroboam will die by the sword and Israel will certainly go from its land into exile.'" (Amos 7:10–11)

Amaziah then contemptuously "said to Amos, 'Go, you seer, flee away to the land of Judah, and there eat bread and there do your prophesying!'" (Amos 7:12). Amos was turning Amaziah's world upside down, and he didn't like it.

Like Elijah, Jeremiah, and Amos, the apostle Paul also shook up complacent sinners. In virtually every city he visited he caused a disturbance. In fact, as chapter 17 opens, he has just left Philippi, where his ministry had upset the pagan Greeks. To his enemies, Paul was "a real pest and a fellow who stirs up dissension among all the Jews throughout the world" (Acts 24:5).

What characterizes a person who shakes up the world for the gospel? From the narrative of Acts 17 emerge four key words that provide the answer: courage, content, converts, and conflict. The accounts of Paul's ministry at Thessalonica and Berea are closely parallel and need to be considered together.

COURAGE

Now when they had traveled through Amphipolis and Apollonia, they came to Thessalonica, where there was a synagogue of the Jews. And according to Paul's custom, he went to them, . . . And the brethren immediately sent Paul and Silas away by night to Berea; and when they arrived, they went into the synagogue of the Jews. (17:1–2a, 10)

No one will ever influence the world for Christ who lacks courage; it is courageous people who make a difference. Paul reminded Timothy of that in 2 Timothy 1:7. Courage and boldness were essential to the impact of the early church, and there is no more consistent illustration of that than Paul himself. The prospect of trials and persecution did not deter him from carrying out his ministry. Addressing the elders of the church at Ephesus, he summed up his attitude:

> Behold, bound in spirit, I am on my way to Jerusalem, not knowing what will happen to me there, except that the Holy Spirit solemnly testifies to me in every city, saying that bonds and afflictions await me. But I do not consider my life of any account as dear to myself, in order that I may finish my course, and the ministry which I received from the Lord Jesus, to testify solemnly of the gospel of the grace of God. (Acts 20:22–24)

The incidents at Thessalonica and Berea display Paul's remarkable courage.

Paul, Silas, and Timothy had left Philippi in the wake of the riot provoked by Paul's healing of a demon-possessed slave girl (16:16–40). Luke apparently did not accompany them, since the Acts narrative now shifts to the third person (cf. 16:19). Perhaps he remained behind in Philippi to minister to the young church there. As a Gentile, he may have been immune to the anti-Jewish sentiment that had arisen against Paul and Silas.

Leaving Philippi, the missionaries traveled southwest along the important Roman highway known as the Egnatian Way, **through Amphipolis and Apollonia,** and finally **to Thessalonica. Amphipolis** was about thirty miles from Philippi, **Apollonia** about thirty miles from **Amphipolis,** and **Thessalonica** just under forty miles from **Apollonia.** The narrative implies that they made the journey from Philippi to Thessalonica in three days, stopping for the night at **Amphipolis** and again at **Apollonia.** If so, they covered about thirty miles a day, leading some commentators to speculate that they traveled on horses (perhaps supplied through the generosity of the Philippian church). It is difficult to imagine that Paul and Silas, weakened by their beating at Philippi, could have walked nearly one hundred miles in three days.

There is no indication that Paul and his companions preached the gospel in either **Amphipolis** or **Apollonia,** although **Amphipolis** was a larger and more important city than Philippi. The reason seems to be that neither city had a synagogue. Luke's note that **there was a synagogue of the Jews** at Thessalonica implies an absence of one in the other cities—no evidence of a synagogue has been identified in either Amphipolis or Apollonia.

Thessalonica was the capital and most important city of Macedonia, having an estimated population of 200,000. It had been founded either by Philip of Macedon (the father of Alexander the Great) or, more likely, by one of his generals, Cassander, and named after Alexander the Great's stepsister. In Paul's day, Thessalonica was a major port and an important commercial center. Known today as Thessaloniki, it is still a significant city in Greece.

Paul was driven by a burning desire to see his fellow Jews saved (Rom. 9:1–3; 10:1). Not surprisingly, then, **according to** his **custom, he went to** the Jews when he arrived in Thessalonica. Despite his frequent mistreatment at their hands, Paul never lost his passion for the souls of his people.

Paul had faced much Jewish opposition on his first missionary journey. On the island of Cyprus, he was opposed by the Jewish false prophet Bar-Jesus (Acts 13:6ff.). Leaving there, he went to Pisidian Antioch, where "when the Jews saw the crowds [listening to Paul preach], they were filled with jealousy, and began contradicting the things spoken by Paul, and were blaspheming" (Acts 13:45). Later, "the Jews aroused the devout women of prominence and the leading men of the city, and instigated a persecution against Paul and Barnabas, and drove them out of their district" (Acts 13:50). They went to Iconium, where "the Jews who disbelieved stirred up the minds of the Gentiles, and embittered them against the brethren" (Acts 14:2). Forced to flee Iconium (Acts 14:5–6), Paul and Barnabas went to Lystra, where Paul very nearly lost his life (Acts 14:19). In spite of all that, and his recent persecution in Philippi at the hands of Gentiles, Paul did not hesitate to courageously enter the synagogue at Thessalonica.

Sadly, Jewish opposition was to force Paul to flee Thessalonica too. Verse 10 notes that **the brethren** at Thessalonica **immediately sent Paul and Silas away by night to Berea.** Located some fifty miles from Thessalonica, **Berea** was a much less important town; the Roman writer Cicero described it as "off the beaten track." Undaunted by the constant opposition from his Jewish brethren, Paul immediately entered **the synagogue of the Jews** when he arrived in Berea. His love for his people and his God left him no option. As he wrote in 1 Corinthians 9:16, "If I preach the gospel, I have nothing to boast of, for I am under compulsion; for woe is me if I do not preach the gospel." Such courage is the result of several spiritual virtues.

First, courage is built on faith—trusting God. David also knew the importance of that truth. Often troubled and pursued by his enemies, he nevertheless repeatedly proclaimed his absolute trust in God. In Psalm 27 he said:

> The Lord is my light and my salvation; whom shall I fear? The Lord is the defense of my life; whom shall I dread? When evildoers came upon me to devour my flesh, my adversaries and my enemies, they stumbled and fell. Though a host encamp against me, my heart will not fear; though war arise against me, in spite of this I shall be confident. (vv. 1–3)

Paul echoed that thought in Ephesians 6:10 when he wrote, "Be strong in the Lord, and in the strength of His might" (cf. 2 Tim. 2:1). The key to courage is trust in the sovereign power and care of God and dependence on His strength. In any circumstance of life, Christians can be confident that "the Lord preserves the faithful" (Ps. 31:23). Lack of courage stems ultimately from an inadequate understanding of God.

Second, courage results from purity—confessing sin. In Psalm 7, David wrote:

> O Lord my God, in Thee I have taken refuge; save me from all those who pursue me, and deliver me, lest he tear my soul like a lion, dragging me away, while there is none to deliver. O Lord my God, if I have done this, if there is injustice in my hands, if I have rewarded evil to my friend, or have plundered him who without cause was my adversary, let the enemy pursue my soul and overtake it; and let him trample my life down to the ground, and lay my glory in the dust. . . . My shield is with God, who saves the upright in heart. (vv. 1– 5, 10)

Faced with a difficult trial, David declared there was no unconfessed sin in his life. On that basis, he asked God to deliver him. He knew that attempting to fight a spiritual battle with gaping holes in his breastplate of righteousness was foolish.

Third, courage comes from hope—thanking God in advance for the victory. In 2 Chronicles 20, Judah faced an invasion by a combined force of Moabites and Ammonites. King Jehoshaphat, knowing Judah was powerless against her enemies, prayed to the Lord for help (v. 12). He then led his people out to meet the attackers. Verse 21 records that before the battle began, Jehoshaphat "appointed those who sang to the Lord and those who praised Him in holy attire." They "went out before the army and said, 'Give thanks to the Lord, for His lovingkindness is everlasting.'" In response to their thankful trust, "the Lord set ambushes against the sons of Ammon, Moab, and Mount Seir, who had come against Judah; so they were routed" (v. 22). Thanking God in advance gave the people courage to anticipate the victory.

CONTENT

and for three Sabbaths reasoned with them from the Scriptures, explaining and giving evidence that the Christ had to suffer and rise again from the dead, and saying, "This Jesus whom I am proclaiming to you is the Christ." . . . Now these were more noble-minded than those in Thessalonica, for they received the word with great eagerness, examining the Scriptures daily, to see whether these things were so. (17:2b–3, 11)

Courage must be coupled with the proper content if a believer is to shake the world. To have the right message, but not the boldness to proclaim it, renders it useless. On the other hand, to boldly proclaim error, as the cults do, causes even greater harm. Proclaiming the truth with great boldness, as Paul did, cannot help but change the world.

Some Christians believe it is all-important not to offend nonbelievers. Accordingly, they focus their gospel presentations only on what Christ has to offer the sinner to improve his life in time and eternity. To declare to the non-Christian that his sinful life is an offense to a holy God and call him to mourn and repent is considered poor marketing technique.

Such an imbalanced approach to evangelism finds no support in Scripture. The true gospel *must* offend the nonbeliever by confronting him with his sin and judgment. Romans 9:33 says, "Behold, I lay in Zion a stone of stumbling and a rock of offense, and he who believes in Him will not be disappointed." Peter quoted that same Old Testament passage (Isa. 28:16), as well as Psalm 118:22 and Isaiah 8:14:

For this is contained in Scripture: "Behold I lay in Zion a choice stone, a precious corner stone, and he who believes in Him shall not be disappointed." This precious value, then, is for you who believe. But for those who disbelieve, "The stone which the builders rejected, this became the very corner stone," and, "A stone of stumbling and a rock of offense"; for they stumble because they are disobedient to the word, and to this doom they were also appointed. (1 Pet. 2:6–8)

Sinners are a constant offense to God (cf. Ps. 7:11); they need to know that.

Paul boldly confronted the Jews of Thessalonica, **and for three Sabbaths reasoned with them from the Scriptures, explaining and giving evidence that the Christ had to suffer and rise again from the dead, and saying, "This Jesus whom I am proclaiming to you is the Christ."**

The common Jewish view of the Messiah pictured Him as a conquering political ruler who would restore their fortunes, defeat their enemies, and usher in the kingdom. That the Messiah would come to die at the hands of His own people was beyond their comprehension. Even the apostles had taken a long time to understand that truth (cf. Matt. 16:21–22; Luke 24:25–26). Paul wrote of the difficulty Jewish people had in accepting the death of Messiah in 1 Corinthians 1:23, when he said that "Christ crucified" was "to Jews a stumbling block," and even to the Gentiles it was "foolishness."

Reasoned is from *dialegomai*, from which the English word *dialogue* derives. It describes not a formal sermon but a discussion, during which Paul repeatedly fielded questions from his hearers. That was the way he commonly ministered in the synagogues (cf. Acts 18:4, 19; 19:8–9). Effective Christian witness includes being able to answer questions about the faith. Peter commanded believers to "sanctify Christ as Lord in your hearts, always being ready to make a defense to everyone who asks you to give an account for the hope that is in you, yet with gentleness and reverence" (1 Pet. 3:15).

Scripture provides the truth for such a defense. The foundation of Paul's apologetic method was not the emptiness of human wisdom, or the extrabiblical traditions so revered by the Jews. Instead, Paul **reasoned with them from the** Old Testament **Scriptures.** He proved his case from the very source the Jews revered, **explaining and giving evidence that the Christ had to suffer and rise again from the dead.** Luke does not record the details of Paul's arguments (for a summary of one of his messages, see Acts 13:16ff.). He may have referred to the types in the sacrificial system of Moses' law, and undoubtedly he appealed to such passages as Psalm 22 and Isaiah 53 to prove the Messiah had to die, and to Psalm 16 to show that the Messiah would rise from the dead.

Having thus shown that the Old Testament prophesied the death and resurrection of the Messiah, Paul's powerful conclusion was that **this Jesus whom I am proclaiming to you is the Christ.** He alone fulfilled those prophecies, having "died for our sins according to the Scriptures," been "buried, and ... raised on the third day according to the Scriptures" (1 Cor. 15:3–4). Those who would turn the world upside down must use the Word of God as the lever.

Paul used the same approach in evangelizing the Berean Jews. **Now these** Luke notes, **were more noble-minded than those in Thessalonica, for they received the word with great eagerness, examining the Scriptures daily, to see whether these things were so.** Evidently, they did not have the prejudices to overcome that the Thessalonian Jews did. Significantly, when persecution arose in Berea it was led by Jews from Thessalonica (v. 13). Unlike the Thessalonians, whom Paul had to reason with and persuade (v. 4), the Bereans **received the word with great eagerness, examining the Scriptures daily, to see whether** the **things** preached by Paul **were so.** They were open to the truth and searched their scrolls for themselves. No wonder Luke describes them as **more noble-minded than those in Thessalonica**.

Examining is from *anakrinō*, a word sometimes used of a judicial investigation. The noble Bereans carefully sifted the evidence and concluded that the gospel Paul proclaimed was the truth that fulfilled Old Testament promise. Those who honestly examine the Scriptures will always come to that conclusion. In John 5:39, Jesus said to the Jewish leaders, "You search the Scriptures, because you think that in them you have eternal life; and it is these that bear witness of Me." In verse 46 He added, "For if you believed Moses, you would believe Me; for he wrote of Me." In John 7:17 Jesus called for a willing heart when He said, "If any man is willing to do His will, he shall know of the teaching, whether it is of God, or whether I speak from Myself." In Luke 24:25–27 Jesus Himself used the Old Testament Scripture to convince the disciples:

> And He said to them, "O foolish men and slow of heart to believe in all that the prophets have spoken! Was it not necessary for the Christ to suffer these things and to enter into His glory?" And beginning with Moses and with all the prophets, He explained to them the things concerning Himself in all the Scriptures.

Of course now we have both testaments to prove that Jesus is the Christ.

Most people who reject the gospel have little knowledge of the Scriptures. Some of the Bible's harshest critics over the centuries have displayed a shocking ignorance of its teachings. The primary duty in evangelism, then, must be to demonstrate the truth of Christianity from the Scriptures.

How can a Christian know God's Word well enough to use it effectively?

First, the prerequisite for Bible study is confession of sin. First Peter 2:1–2 states that truth succinctly: "Therefore, putting aside all malice and all guile and hypocrisy and envy and all slander, like newborn babes, long for the pure milk of the word, that by it you may grow in respect to salvation." It is impossible to study the Scriptures profitably with an impure mind.

Second, Bible study must be diligent. Paul commanded his beloved son in the faith, Timothy, to "be diligent to present yourself approved to God as a workman who does not need to be ashamed, handling accurately the word of truth" (2 Tim. 2:15). Lazy, haphazard, careless Bible study will not produce a Christian who is "mighty in the Scriptures" (Acts 18:24).

Third, believers must be committed to practicing the truths they learn. James charged Christians to "prove yourselves doers of the word, and not merely hearers who delude themselves" (James 1:22). The ultimate goal of all Bible study is not increased knowledge but increased holiness and Christlikeness.

Finally, an excellent way to learn the truth is to teach it to others (2 Tim. 2:2). We retain far more of what we study to teach others than of what we learn for our own benefit.

The Old Testament believer Ezra is an example for Christians to follow. According to Ezra 7:10, he "set his heart to study the law of the Lord, and to practice it, and to teach His statutes and ordinances in Israel."

CONVERTS

And some of them were persuaded and joined Paul and Silas, along with a great multitude of the God-fearing Greeks and a number of the leading women. . . . Many of them therefore believed, along with a number of prominent Greek women and men. (17:4, 12)

Those who would influence the world for Christ must recognize that they cannot do it alone. Discipling others, who in turn disciple still others (cf. 2 Tim. 2:2), causes exponential growth and magnifies Christianity's impact on the world. Such spiritual reproductivity was a key element in Paul's ministry.

Paul's presentation of the gospel was so compelling that **some of** the Thessalonian Jews, though resistant, **were persuaded and**

joined Paul and Silas. The Thessalonians were not as open to the truth as the Bereans, yet Paul's convincing exposition of the Old Testament, coupled with the work of the Holy Spirit (1 Thess. 1:5), led to their response. Not only some of the Jews, but also **a great multitude of the God-fearing Greeks and a number of the leading women** came to a saving knowledge of the gospel.

The Thessalonian church was a spiritually reproducing church. Two of its members, Aristarchus and Secundus, joined Paul in his evangelistic work (Acts 20:4). Paul commended all the church members in 1 Thessalonians 1:8, because "the word of the Lord [had] sounded forth from [them], not only in Macedonia and Achaia, but also in every place [their] faith toward God [had] gone forth." The Thessalonians used their strategic location on the Egnatian Way to spread the gospel far beyond their own city.

A similar rich harvest was reaped in Berea, where **many of** the Jews, eager to understand, **believed, along with a number of prominent Greek women and men.** The Thessalonians had to be persuaded; the Bereans were ready and **believed.** Their hearts were more open to the truth, as evidenced by their eager searching of the Scriptures. The Thessalonians and Bereans typify two kinds of people encountered in evangelism. The Word of God can persuade the closed and the open; the obstinate and the pliant; because of those who seek the truth, and those who do not.

CONFLICT

But the Jews, becoming jealous and taking along some wicked men from the market place, formed a mob and set the city in an uproar; and coming upon the house of Jason, they were seeking to bring them out to the people. And when they did not find them, they began dragging Jason and some brethren before the city authorities, shouting, "These men who have upset the world have come here also; and Jason has welcomed them, and they all act contrary to the decrees of Caesar, saying that there is another king, Jesus." And they stirred up the crowd and the city authorities who heard these things. And when they had received a pledge from Jason and the others, they released them. . . . But when the Jews of Thessalonica found out that the word of God had been proclaimed by Paul in Berea also, they came there likewise, agitating and stirring up the crowds. And then immediately the brethren sent Paul out to go as far as the sea; and Silas and Timothy remained there. Now those who conducted Paul brought him as far as Athens; and receiving a command for Silas

and Timothy to come to him as soon as possible, they departed. (17:5–9, 13–15)

This last point is the result of the first three. Those who courageously proclaim the right message and win converts will face conflict. Success will be accompanied by opposition. Paul and his companions were no exception. The unbelieving **Jews** at Thessalonica were enraged by the success of the gospel. They "loved the darkness rather than the light; for their deeds were evil" (John 3:19). **Becoming jealous and taking along some wicked men from the market place,** they **formed a mob and set the city in an uproar**—ironically, the very thing they accused the missionaries of doing (v. 6). **Coming upon the house of Jason,** where the crowd assumed the missionaries were staying, **they were seeking to bring them out to the people.**

Paul, Silas, and Timothy were not there, and the mob had to content itself with **dragging Jason and some brethren before the city authorities.** Luke's description is accurate; he uses the term *politarchs* for the officials—the exact term that occurs for the local magistrates in inscriptions uncovered in Macedonia. Nothing is known of **Jason,** except that he was probably Jewish, since Jason was a name often taken by Diaspora Jews.

The Jewish leaders brought two charges against the believers. The first was that **these men who have upset the world have come here also; and Jason has welcomed them.** This vague charge that the missionaries were troublemakers was not substantiated. In fact, it was the mob that had created the disturbance (v. 5). By declaring that **Jason has welcomed them,** they accused him of harboring criminals. The second charge against the missionaries was far more serious: **they all act contrary to the decrees of Caesar, saying that there is another king, Jesus.** To acknowledge any other king but Caesar was one of the most serious crimes in the Roman Empire. It was for allegedly claiming to be a rival earthly ruler to Caesar that the Romans crucified Jesus (cf. John 19:12). Failure to worship Caesar surely led to Paul's execution.

These charges **stirred up the crowd and the city authorities who heard these things.** The latter, like their counterparts at Philippi, decided the simplest solution was to expel the "troublemakers." Accordingly, having demanded and **received a pledge from Jason and the others, they released them.** Since that bond would be forfeited if there was any more trouble, Paul and his companions had no choice but to leave. The anguish that expulsion caused Paul is reflected in his comments in 1 Thessalonians 2:17–18:

But we, brethren, having been bereft of you for a short while—in person, not in spirit—were all the more eager with great desire to see your face. For we wanted to come to you—I, Paul, more than once—and yet Satan thwarted us.

When the missionaries were expelled from Thessalonica and moved on to Berea (v. 10), unfortunately the satanically inspired opposition to the gospel followed them (cf. 1 Thess. 2:14–16). **When the Jews of Thessalonica found out that the word of God had been proclaimed by Paul in Berea also, they came there likewise, agitating and stirring up the crowds.** Luke does not give the details of what happened, but Paul, at least, was forced to leave. Accordingly, **the brethren sent Paul out to go as far as the sea,** from where he could take ship to Athens. (Exactly how Paul got from Berea to Athens is unclear. Due to variant readings in the Greek manuscripts, commentators disagree about whether he traveled by ship or by land.) Unlike the situation in Thessalonica, **Silas and Timothy** were able to remain behind to carry on the work in Berea. Meanwhile **those who conducted Paul brought him as far as Athens; and receiving a command for Silas and Timothy to come to him as soon as possible, they departed.** Apparently the Berean Christians decided that there was no safe place anywhere in Macedonia for Paul, hence the decision to send him to Athens.

Christians who would shake the world as did Paul and his companions must be courageous. They must proclaim the right message and recognize the importance of enlisting the aid of others. They must also be prepared to weather the storm of persecution that will surely follow. In the words of G. Campbell Morgan,

> the measure of our triumph in work for God is always the measure of our travail. No propagative work is done save at cost; and every genuine triumph of the Cross brings after it the travail of some new affliction, and some new sorrow. So we share the travail that makes the Kingdom come. (*The Acts of the Apostles* [New York: Revell, 1924], 405–6)

Getting to Know the Unknown God (Acts 17:16–34)

10

Now while Paul was waiting for them at Athens, his spirit was being provoked within him as he was beholding the city full of idols. So he was reasoning in the synagogue with the Jews and the God-fearing Gentiles, and in the market place every day with those who happened to be present. And also some of the Epicurean and Stoic philosophers were conversing with him. And some were saying, "What would this idle babbler wish to say?" Others, "He seems to be a proclaimer of strange deities,"—because he was preaching Jesus and the resurrection. And they took him and brought him to the Areopagus, saying, "May we know what this new teaching is which you are proclaiming? For you are bringing some strange things to our ears; we want to know therefore what these things mean." (Now all the Athenians and the strangers visiting there used to spend their time in nothing other than telling or hearing something new.) And Paul stood in the midst of the Areopagus and said, "Men of Athens, I observe that you are very religious in all respects. For while I was passing through and examining the objects of your worship, I also found an altar with this inscription, 'TO AN UNKNOWN GOD.' What therefore you worship in ignorance, this I proclaim to you. The God who made the world and all things in it, since

He is Lord of heaven and earth, does not dwell in temples made
with hands; neither is He served by human hands, as though He
needed anything, since He Himself gives to all life and breath
and all things; and He made from one, every nation of mankind
to live on all the face of the earth, having determined their
appointed times, and the boundaries of their habitation, that
they should seek God, if perhaps they might grope for Him and
find Him, though He is not far from each one of us; for in Him we
live and move and exist, as even some of your own poets have
said, 'For we also are His offspring.' Being then the offspring of
God, we ought not to think that the Divine Nature is like gold or
silver or stone, an image formed by the art and thought of man.
Therefore having overlooked the times of ignorance, God is now
declaring to men that all everywhere should repent, because He
has fixed a day in which He will judge the world in righteousness
through a Man whom He has appointed, having furnished proof
to all men by raising Him from the dead." Now when they heard
of the resurrection of the dead, some began to sneer, but others
said, "We shall hear you again concerning this." So Paul went out
of their midst. But some men joined him and believed, among
whom also were Dionysius the Areopagite and a woman named
Damaris and others with them. (17:16–34)

In his Sunday morning message of January 7, 1855, a young
Charles Haddon Spurgeon addressed the following words to his congregation:

> It has been said by someone that "the proper study of mankind is man."
> I will not oppose the idea, but I believe it is equally true that the prop-
> er study of God's elect is God; the proper study of a Christian is the
> Godhead. The highest science, the loftiest speculation, the mightiest
> philosophy, which can ever engage the attention of a child of God, is
> the name, the nature, the person, the work, the doings, and the exis-
> tence of the great God whom he calls his Father....
>
> Would you lose your sorrows? Would you drown your cares? Then go,
> plunge yourself in the Godhead's deepest sea; be lost in his immensity;
> and you shall come forth as from a couch of rest, refreshed and invig-
> orated. I know nothing which can so comfort the soul; so calm the
> swelling billows of grief and sorrow; so speak peace to the winds of
> trial, as a devout musing upon the subject of the Godhead. ("The
> Immutability of God," in *The New Park Street Pulpit* [Pasadena, Tex.:
> Pilgrim, 1981], 1)

Although spoken well over a century ago, Spurgeon's words speak forcefully to today's church. In this age of liberalism, neoorthodoxy, pragmatism, psychology, emotionalism, experientialism, and man-centered theology, the church desperately needs a proper perspective of God.

To the unbelieving world, rife with skepticism, antisupernaturalism, rationalism, mysticism, and the hopeless despair each produces, the Christian offers the only message of hope. Man is not a cosmic accident, a personal being trapped in an impersonal universe. There is a God, who is both the creator of the universe and its sovereign ruler. Not only does He exist, but He is also knowable and has revealed Himself to man. God created men to know Him (John 17:3) and through that knowledge to glorify Him (Matt. 5:16; Rom. 15:6; 1 Cor. 6:20). Man's intimate knowledge of God was lost in the Fall but is restored through the atoning sacrifice of Jesus Christ. Sin is forgiven, and alienated people are reconciled to God for time and eternity.

For the believer, the highest level of spiritual maturity belongs to those who "know Him who has been from the beginning" (1 John 2:13). Knowing God is the key to contentment (Phil. 4:11), happiness (Pss. 33:12; 144:15), and peace (Isa. 26:3; Rom. 8:6). Faced with a crisis, it is "the people who know their God" who "will display strength and take action" (Dan. 11:32).

In Acts 17:16–34, Paul proclaims the good news that the one and only true and living God is knowable to the pagan city of Athens. The apostle had arrived there alone after having been forced to flee Thessalonica and Berea (17:1–15). He sent word back with his escort for Silas and Timothy to meet him there (17:15). It was not in his nature, however, to remain idle while he waited. The result was a classic confrontation between God's man and Satan's city.

As a Hellenized Jew, Paul had been exposed to Greek culture with its outstanding traditions in art and philosophy. Athens was the center of that culture. In its heyday, several centuries before Christ, it had been the greatest city in the world. Socrates, his brilliant student Plato, and Plato's student Aristotle, perhaps the greatest and most influential philosopher of all time, taught there. So also did Epicurus, founder of Epicureanism, and Zeno, founder of Stoicism, two dominant philosophies.

By Paul's day, Corinth had replaced Athens as the most important political and commercial center in Greece. Yet Athens had lost none of its cultural significance, was still the philosophical center of the ancient world, and was the home of the world's most famous university. Athens was also a religious center, where almost every god in existence was worshiped. The pagan writer Petronius sarcastically quipped that it was easier to find a god in Athens than a man (R. C. H. Lenski, *The*

Interpretation of the Acts of the Apostles [Minneapolis: Augsburg, 1961],
708). Every public building was dedicated to a god, and statues of gods
filled the city (17:16, 23).

It was that gross manifestation of pagan idolatry that stirred Paul
to action. Luke notes that **while Paul was waiting for** Silas and
Timothy **at Athens, his spirit was being provoked within him as he
was beholding the city full of idols.** Rather than viewing it from the
perspective of a tourist, he saw Athens as a city full of lost men and
women, doomed to a Christless eternity.

Jerusalem moved the Lord both to tears and to anger, and
Athens likewise stirred Paul to holy anger. **Provoked** does not bring out
the full force of *paroxunō*, which means "to become angry, or infuriated."
Luke used the corresponding noun to describe the "sharp disagreement" between Paul and Barnabas (Acts 15:39). Paul hated idolatry
because it robbed God of His glory (cf. Rom. 1:23). Nineteenth-century
missionary Henry Martyn expressed what Paul must have felt. He wrote
concerning a discussion he had with a Muslim:

> Mirza Seid Ali told me of a distich (couplet) made by his friend in hon-
> our of a victory over the Russians. The sentiment was that Prince Abbas
> Mirza had killed so many Christians that Christ from the fourth heaven
> took hold of Mahomet's [Muhammad's] skirt to entreat him to desist. I
> was cut to the soul at this blasphemy. Mirza Seid Ali perceived that I was
> considerably disordered and asked what it was that was so offensive? I
> told him that "I could not endure existence if Jesus was not glorified; it
> would be hell to me, if He were to be always thus dishonoured." He was
> astonished and again asked "Why?" "If any one pluck out your eyes," I
> replied, "there is no saying *why* you feel pain;—it is feeling. It is because
> I am one with Christ that I am thus dreadfully wounded." (Constance E.
> Padwick, *Henry Martyn* [Chicago: Moody, 1980], 225–26. Italics in the
> original.)

Paul channeled his emotion into action. **So**, because of his outrage over the Athenians' blasphemy of the Lord God by their idolatry, he
**was reasoning in the synagogue with the Jews and the God-fear-
ing Gentiles, and in the market place every day with those who
happened to be present.** Following his normal pattern of ministry, Paul
went on the Sabbath to his countrymen, **reasoning in the synagogue
with the Jews and the God-fearing Gentiles.** The rest of the week,
he took on all comers **in the market place** (Athens's famed *agora*), dia-
loguing **every day with those who happened to be present.**

Not only did Athens affect Paul, but he also made an impact on
the city. Among those he engaged in debate were **some of the Epi-**

curean and Stoic philosophers. They, along with the Cynics, represented the three most popular contemporary schools of philosophy.

Central to **Epicurean** philosophy was the teaching that pleasure and the avoidance of pain are the chief end of man. They were materialists, who, while not denying the existence of the gods, believed they did not intervene in the affairs of men. They taught that, at death, the body and soul (both composed of atoms) disintegrate; there is no afterlife.

The **Stoic philosophers,** on the other hand, saw self-mastery as the greatest virtue. They believed self-mastery comes from being indifferent to both pleasure and pain, reaching the place where one feels nothing. In contrast to the practical atheism of the Epicureans, the Stoics were pantheists.

The extremes of Stoicism and Epicureanism sum up the futility of man's existence apart from God. F. F. Bruce writes:

> Stoicism and Epicureanism represent alternative attempts in pre-Christian paganism to come to terms with life, especially in times of uncertainty and hardship, and post-Christian paganism down to our own day has not been able to devise anything appreciably better. (*The Book of the Acts*, The New International Commentary on the New Testament [Grand Rapids: Eerdmans, 1971], 351)

Although they differed radically in their philosophic beliefs, both Stoics and Epicureans were united in their contempt for Paul's teaching. **Some** of them **were saying** derisively, **"What would this idle babbler wish to say?"** *Spermologos* (**idle babbler**) literally means "seed picker." The word

> evoked images of a bird pecking indiscriminately at seeds in a barnyard. It referred to a dilettante, someone who picked up scraps of ideas here and there and passed them off as profundity with no depth of understanding at all. (John B. Polhill, *The New American Commentary: Acts* [Nashville: Broadman, 1992], 367)

Others, misunderstanding completely Paul's message, thought him **to be a proclaimer of strange deities—because he was preaching Jesus and the resurrection.** They may have thought Paul used the term *anastasis* (**resurrection**) as the proper name of a goddess.

Paul created enough of a stir that finally **they took him and brought him to the Areopagus.** The **Areopagus** was a court, so named for the hill on which it had once met. The power of that tribunal had fluctuated over the centuries but in Roman times was considerable. (Athens was a free city in the Roman Empire, with the right of self-government.) Paul was not formally tried before this court (which several centuries earlier had condemned Socrates), but he was informally required to give an account of his teaching.

The proceedings opened with the question, **"May we know what this new teaching is which you are proclaiming? For you are bringing some strange things to our ears; we want to know therefore what these things mean."** They had no genuine interest in the gospel, however, as Luke's parenthetical comment shows: **(Now all the Athenians and the strangers visiting there used to spend their time in nothing other than telling or hearing something new.)** Luke's opinion of the Athenians' love of novelty finds an echo in other ancient writers.

The theme of Paul's message to the assembly was how to know the unknown God. That involves three steps: recognizing that God is, recognizing who He is, and recognizing what He has said.

RECOGNIZING THAT GOD IS

And Paul stood in the midst of the Areopagus and said, "Men of Athens, I observe that you are very religious in all respects. For while I was passing through and examining the objects of your worship, I also found an altar with this inscription, 'TO AN UNKNOWN GOD.' What therefore you worship in ignorance, this I proclaim to you. (17:22–23)

Standing **in the midst of the Areopagus,** Paul began his address by conceding to them their religious devotion: **"Men of Athens, I observe that you are very religious in all respects.** He took as a point of contact something he observed **while passing through and examining the objects of** their **worship: an altar with this inscription, 'TO AN UNKNOWN GOD.'**

The Athenians had taken the first step toward knowing God in that they were supernaturalists. It is obviously impossible for those who deny God's existence to know Him, since "he who comes to God must believe that He is" (Heb. 11:6). No one will search for a path to a destination they believe does not exist. And they must have believed there was a god (among all their deities) whom they did not know.

The Bible does not offer formal arguments for God's existence. His existence is ultimately a matter of revelation and faith (Heb. 11:6; cf. John 1:18; 20:29). Such faith, however, is not a blind leap in the dark but is founded on fact. It is true that while God's existence is not provable in the sense of a scientific experiment or a mathematical equation, it is rational and logical in a cause-and-effect world.

The Bible reveals powerful and convincing evidence for God's existence. Externally, "The heavens are telling of the glory of God; and their expanse is declaring the work of His hands" (Ps. 19:1). Internally, "that which is known about God is evident within [people]; for God made it evident to them" (Rom. 1:19).

The law of cause and effect argues for God's existence. Common sense dictates that every effect must have a cause. Yet there cannot be an endless chain of such causes. Therefore, there must be an uncaused first cause. Theologians refer to that line of reasoning as the cosmological argument. (For an exposition of this form of the cosmological argument, see Norman L. Geisler and Winfried Corduan, *Philosophy of Religion* [Grand Rapids: Baker, 1988], 175ff.) An alternate form of the cosmological argument runs as follows: Everything that begins to exist has a cause. The universe began to exist. Therefore the universe must have a cause. (For a defense of this form of the cosmological argument, see William Lane Craig, *Apologetics* [Chicago: Moody, 1984], 73ff.; Francis J. Beckwith, "Philosophy and Belief in God: The Resurgence of Theism in Philosophical Circles," *The Master's Seminary Journal* 2 [Spring 1991]: 72ff.)

The Bible acknowledges the principle of cause and effect in Hebrews 3:4, where the writer of Hebrews asserts that "every house is built by someone, but the builder of all things is God." A house requires an efficient cause; it would be absurd to put a pile of building material in the path of a hurricane and expect the storm to assemble a house. How much more absurd is it to imagine that the immensely complex universe in which we live had no efficient cause?

Nature also displays remarkable evidence of design. Biologist Michael Pitman writes, "Through any but blinkered eyes the biological world shows clear signs of planning and order" (*Adam and Evolution* [London: Rider, 1984], 27). From the baffling complexity of the cell, to the miraculous transformation of caterpillars into butterflies, to the precise engineering of the earth to support life, examples of design are everywhere. Botanist Alan Radcliffe Smith cites one:

> The Lady's Slipper Orchid is an example of a 2-stamen orchid. As the common name implies, the lip is very distinctive, being shaped like a shoe or slipper. The inside of the lip is very smooth and this, together with the inrolled edges, prevents the easy departure of an insect visitor by the same way in which it came. Instead, it is forced by the shape of the lip and the nature of the surface to move towards the back, or point of attachment, where there are two small exits. In order to gain these exits, the insect must first pass beneath a stigma and then brush past

one or other of the two stamens, which deposits pollen onto it, after which it is free to fly off. If it then goes to another slipper, it will pollinate it with the pollen gained from the previous one; the second slipper will not be on the same plant as only one flower is open on a given plant at any one time, and thus cross-fertilization is very efficiently effected. . . . The complexity of interaction between plant and insect is truly staggering and, for those who will see, it clearly bears the hallmark of the all-wise creator. (Cited by Pitman, *Adam and Evolution*, 82)

A plan requires a planner, a program requires a programmer, and design requires a designer. Since the world so clearly exhibits evidence of design, it must have had a Designer. That is the essence of the teleological argument for God's existence: the order and complexity of the universe could not have arisen by random chance. The Bible also presents that truth. In Psalm 94:9 the psalmist wrote, "He who planted the ear, does He not hear? He who formed the eye, does He not see?" Intelligence comes from intelligence, moral judgment from a moral being. To argue that they came from dead matter is the height of folly.

Since the evidence for God's existence is so overwhelming, the question arises as to why there are atheists. The Bible teaches that the reason is not intellectual and rational but moral and spiritual. David wrote in Psalm 14:1, "The fool has said in his heart, 'There is no God.'" That the foolishness in view is moral, not intellectual, is clear from the rest of the verse: "They are corrupt, they have committed abominable deeds; there is no one who does good." Atheism's rejection of God appeals to people who wish to avoid judgment for their sinful lifestyle.

Romans 1:18–23 makes clear that the matter of rejecting God is willful and due to the love of sin:

For the wrath of God is revealed from heaven against all ungodliness and unrighteousness of men, who suppress the truth in unrighteousness, because that which is known about God is evident within them; for God made it evident to them. For since the creation of the world His invisible attributes, His eternal power and divine nature, have been clearly seen, being understood through what has been made, so that they are without excuse. For even though they knew God, they did not honor Him as God, or give thanks; but they became futile in their speculations, and their foolish heart was darkened. Professing to be wise, they became fools, and exchanged the glory of the incorruptible God for an image in the form of corruptible man and of birds and four-footed animals and crawling creatures.

Into the confusion caused by conflicting philosophies and idolatry, Paul spoke forcefully the truth that the one true God not only exists but can also be known: **What therefore you worship in ignorance, this I proclaim to you.** That God can be known is the clear teaching of the Bible (Deut. 4:35; 1 Kings 8:43; 1 Chron. 28:9; Ps. 9:10; Jer. 9:24; 24:7; 31:34; John 17:3). This God who can be known is the believer's message of hope to the lost world.

RECOGNIZING WHO GOD IS

The God who made the world and all things in it, since He is Lord of heaven and earth, does not dwell in temples made with hands; neither is He served by human hands, as though He needed anything, since He Himself gives to all life and breath and all things; and He made from one, every nation of mankind to live on all the face of the earth, having determined their appointed times, and the boundaries of their habitation, that they should seek God, if perhaps they might grope for Him and find Him, though He is not far from each one of us; for in Him we live and move and exist, as even some of your own poets have said, 'For we also are His offspring.' Being then the offspring of God, we ought not to think that the Divine Nature is like gold or silver or stone, an image formed by the art and thought of man. (17:24–29)

Having established that God exists and can be known by men, Paul introduces his hearers to Him. He presents God as creator, ruler, giver, controller, and revealer.

CREATOR

The God who made the world and all things in it (17:24*a*)

Paul's bold assertion that **God made the world and all things in it** was a powerful and upsetting truth for some of the Athenians to hear. It ran contrary to the Epicureans, who believed matter was eternal and therefore had no creator, and to the Stoics, who as pantheists believed everything was part of God—who certainly couldn't have created Himself. But it was still the basic approach required. Whenever the logic of a creator has been eliminated, people are cut off completely from God.

The truth that God is the creator of the universe and all it contains is just as unpopular in our day. The prevailing explanation by the ungodly for the origin of all things is evolution. It is taught dogmatically by its zealous adherents (including, sadly, many Christians) as a scientific fact as firmly established as the law of gravity. Yet evolution is not even a scientific theory (since it is not observable, repeatable, or testable), let alone an established fact.

The impressive scientific evidence against evolution can be briefly summarized as follows. First, the second law of thermodynamics shows that evolution is theoretically impossible. Second, the evidence of the fossil record shows evolution in fact did not take place. (Among the many helpful books presenting the scientific case against evolution are Michael Denton, *Evolution: A Theory in Crisis* [Bethesda, Md.: Adler and Adler, 1985]; Duane T. Gish, *Evolution: The Fossils Still Say NO!* [El Cajon, Calif.: Institute for Creation Research, 1995]; Henry M. Morris, *The Biblical Basis for Modern Science* [Grand Rapids: Baker, 1985]; Henry M. Morris and Gary E. Parker, *What Is Creation Science?* [San Diego: Master Book Publishers, 1984].)

The second law of thermodynamics, one of the most well-established principles in all of science, states that the natural tendency is for things to go from a more ordered to a less ordered state. Noted atheist Isaac Asimov acknowledged that "as far as we know, all changes are in the direction of increasing entropy, of increasing disorder, of increasing randomness, of running down" (cited in Henry M. Morris, ed., *Scientific Creationism* [San Diego: Creation-Life, 1976], 39). Yet, incredibly, evolutionists argue that precisely the opposite has happened. According to them, things have gone from a less ordered state to a more ordered one. Attempts to harmonize evolution with the second law of thermodynamics have not been successful, and it remains a powerful witness against evolution (cf. Emmett L. Williams, ed., *Thermodynamics and the Development of Order* [Norcross, Ga.: Creation Research Society Books, 1987]).

The only way to determine if evolution has happened is to examine the fossil record, which contains the history of life on earth. Although presented in popular literature and textbooks as proof for evolution, the fossil record is actually a major source of embarrassment for evolutionists. The innumerable transitional forms between phylogenetic groups demanded by evolution are simply not found. Although an evolutionist, David B. Kitts of the University of Oklahoma admits,

> Despite the bright promise that paleontology provides a means of "seeing" evolution, it has presented some nasty difficulties for evolutionists the most notorious of which is the presence of "gaps" in the fossil record. Evolution requires intermediate forms between species and paleontology does not provide them. ("Paleontology and Evolutionary Theory," *Evolution* 28 [September 1974]: 467)

Even Stephen Jay Gould of Harvard University, perhaps the most well-known contemporary defender of evolution, candidly admits,

> The extreme rarity of transitional forms in the fossil record persists as the trade secret of paleontology. The evolutionary trees that adorn our textbooks have data only at the tips and nodes of their branches; the rest is inference, however reasonable, not the evidence of fossils. ("Evolution's Erratic Pace," *Natural History* LXXXVI [May 1977]: 14)

Paul's affirmation that **God made the world and all things in it** finds its support in Scripture. The Bible opens with the simple declaration "In the beginning God created the heavens and the earth" (Gen. 1:1). In Psalm 146:5–6 the psalmist writes, "How blessed is he whose help is the God of Jacob, whose hope is in the Lord his God; Who made heaven and earth, the sea and all that is in them." Isaiah asks rhetorically, "Do you not know? Have you not heard? The Everlasting God, the Lord, the Creator of the ends of the earth does not become weary or tired. His understanding is inscrutable" (Isa. 40:28). In Isaiah 45:18, Isaiah describes God as "the God who formed the earth and made it." Jeremiah 10:12 says of God, "It is He who made the earth by His power, who established the world by His wisdom; and by His understanding He has stretched out the heavens." Taking comfort in God's power, Jeremiah exclaims, "Ah Lord God! Behold, Thou hast made the heavens and the earth by Thy great power and by Thine outstretched arm! Nothing is too difficult for Thee" (Jer. 32:17). Zechariah 12:1 refers to God as He "who stretches out the heavens, lays the foundation of the earth, and forms the spirit of man within him."

The New Testament also teaches that God is the creator. Ephesians 3:9 declares that God "created all things." Colossians 1:16 says of Jesus Christ, "By Him all things were created, both in the heavens and on earth, visible and invisible, whether thrones or dominions or rulers or authorities—all things have been created by Him and for Him." The great hymn of praise to God in Revelation 4:11 reads, "Worthy art Thou, our Lord and our God, to receive glory and honor and power; for Thou didst create all things, and because of Thy will they existed, and were created." In Revelation 10:6 an angel "swore by Him who lives forever and ever, who created heaven and the things in it, and the earth and the things in it, and the sea and the things in it."

Still, the truth that God is the creator of all things is widely rejected—even by some who profess to believe in His existence. They see Him as a remote first cause, who merely set in motion the evolutionary process and can make no claim on anyone's life. But the creator God can and does. Sinful men are uncomfortable with the thought that they are accountable to One who created them and hence owns them.

When preaching to Jews, Paul began with the Old Testament Scripture; but with Gentiles, he began with the need to explain the first cause (see the discussion of 14:15 in chapter 7 of this volume).

RULER

since He is Lord of heaven and earth, does not dwell in temples made with hands (17:24b)

Because God created them, **He is Lord of heaven and earth**, and their rightful ruler. Genesis 14:19 describes God as "possessor of heaven and earth," while David says in Psalm 24:1, "The earth is the Lord's, and all it contains, the world, and those who dwell in it." The psalmist wrote: "The Lord has established His throne in the heavens; and His sovereignty rules over all" (Ps. 103:19). Humbled by God's devastating judgment on him, the pagan king of Babylon, Nebuchadnezzar, was forced to admit:

> [God's] dominion is an everlasting dominion, and His kingdom endures from generation to generation. And all the inhabitants of the earth are accounted as nothing, but He does according to His will in the host of heaven and among the inhabitants of earth; and no one can ward off His hand or say to Him, "What hast Thou done?" (Dan. 4:34–35)

The God who created the universe obviously **does not dwell in temples made with hands.** In 1 Kings 8:27 Solomon said, "But will God indeed dwell on the earth? Behold, heaven and the highest heaven cannot contain Thee, how much less this house which I have built!" (cf. 2 Chron. 2:6; 6:18). David expressed that same truth in Psalm 139:1–12:

> O Lord, Thou hast searched me and known me. Thou dost know when I sit down and when I rise up; Thou dost understand my thought from afar. Thou dost scrutinize my path and my lying down, and art intimately acquainted with all my ways. Even before there is a word on my tongue, behold, O Lord, Thou dost know it all. Thou hast enclosed me behind and before, and laid Thy hand upon me. Such knowledge is too wonderful for me; it is too high, I cannot attain to it. Where can I go from Thy Spirit? Or where can I flee from Thy presence? If I ascend to heaven, Thou art there; if I make my bed in Sheol, behold, Thou art there. If I take the wings of the dawn, if I dwell in the remotest part of

the sea, even there Thy hand will lead me, and Thy right hand will lay hold of me. If I say, "Surely the darkness will overwhelm me, and the light around me will be night," even the darkness is not dark to Thee, and the night is as bright as the day. Darkness and light are alike to Thee.

The folly of idolatry is most clearly seen in its denial of God's infinity.

GIVER

neither is He served by human hands, as though He needed anything, since He Himself gives to all life and breath and all things; (17:25)

Paul points out the absurdity of imagining that God, the creator and ruler of the universe, should need to be **served by human hands, as though He needed anything**. Job 22:2–3 asks, "Can a vigorous man be of use to God. . . . Is there any pleasure to the Almighty if you are righteous, or profit if you make your ways perfect?" God declares to Israel:

I shall take no young bull out of your house, nor male goats out of your folds. For every beast of the forest is Mine, the cattle on a thousand hills. I know every bird of the mountains, and everything that moves in the field is Mine. If I were hungry, I would not tell you; for the world is Mine, and all it contains. (Ps. 50:9–12)

Far from needing anything from men, God **gives to all life and breath and all things**. Psalm 104:14–15 reads:

[God] causes the grass to grow for the cattle, and vegetation for the labor of man, so that he may bring forth food from the earth, and wine which makes man's heart glad, so that he may make his face glisten with oil, and food which sustains man's heart.

To the Romans Paul wrote, "For from Him and through Him and to Him are all things. To Him be the glory forever. Amen" (Rom. 11:36). He commanded Timothy to "instruct those who are rich in this present world not to be conceited or to fix their hope on the uncertainty of riches, but on God, who richly supplies us with all things to enjoy" (1 Tim. 6:17). "Every good thing bestowed and every perfect gift is from above," notes James, "coming down from the Father of lights, with whom there is no variation, or shifting shadow" (James 1:17).

Nor does God give only to His children. Jesus said in Matthew 5:45 that God "causes His sun to rise on the evil and the good, and sends rain on the righteous and the unrighteous." God blesses all men, even the most hardened sinners, with the benefits of common grace.

CONTROLLER

and He made from one, every nation of mankind to live on all the face of the earth, having determined their appointed times, and the boundaries of their habitation, (17:26)

God is not only the sovereign ruler of the universe but also the controller of the affairs and destinies of men and nations. Paul declares that He made **from one** (Adam) **every nation of mankind to live on all the face of the earth.** That statement was a blow to the national pride of the Greeks, who scornfully referred to non-Greeks as "barbarians." All men are equal, because all were created by God. He **determined their appointed times;** the rise and fall of nations and empires are in His hands (cf. Dan. 2:36ff.; Luke 21:24). God also set **the boundaries of their habitation,** placing certain nations in specific geographical locations (Deut. 32:8) and determining the extent of their conquests (cf. Isa. 10:12–15).

REVEALER

that they should seek God, if perhaps they might grope for Him and find Him, though He is not far from each one of us; for in Him we live and move and exist, as even some of your own poets have said, 'For we also are His offspring.' Being then the offspring of God, we ought not to think that the Divine Nature is like gold or silver or stone, an image formed by the art and thought of man. (17:27–29)

God's providential activity as creator, ruler, giver, and controller should move men to **seek** Him. Reason should send them from the greatest effect (the universe) back to the first cause—God. In all that He has done in creating and sustaining the universe, God has revealed Himself to mankind. Such self–disclosure should encourage men to **grope for Him and find Him.** The natural revelation of God in the human conscience (Rom. 2:14–15) and the physical world leaves all men without excuse (Rom. 1:18ff.), since **He is not far from each one**

of us. Even those who never heard the gospel are still accountable to God for failing to live up to natural revelation. Had they done so, God would have brought them the special revelation they needed to be saved.

The Greeks certainly could not plead ignorance. Even their **poets** acknowledged the revelation of God in nature, though they wrongly saw it as a revelation of their false gods. The Cretan poet Epimenides noted that **in Him we live and move and exist,** while Aratus, from Paul's home region of Cilicia, added, **For we also are His offspring.** Those quotes illustrate the universal revelation of God as creator, ruler, and sustainer. While Paul could easily have documented those truths from the Old Testament, he chose instead illustrations familiar to his pagan audience, who were unfamiliar with Scripture.

Since man is **the offspring of God,** as even the pagan poets acknowledged, it is foolish **to think that the Divine Nature is like gold or silver or stone, an image formed by the art and thought of man.** If God created man, He must be more than a mere man-made idol. Paul used quotes from their own poets to highlight to his audience the absurdity of idolatry.

The best starting point for evangelizing pagans with no knowledge of the Scripture is to explain the power and Person behind the creation. Satan's invention of evolution cuts off that path of reason that leads to God.

RECOGNIZING WHAT GOD HAS SAID

Therefore having overlooked the times of ignorance, God is now declaring to men that all everywhere should repent, because He has fixed a day in which He will judge the world in righteousness through a Man whom He has appointed, having furnished proof to all men by raising Him from the dead. (17:30–31)

To recognize that God exists, and even understand who He is, will not lead to a saving knowledge of Him. That comes only from an understanding of special revelation. Accordingly, Paul concludes his message by presenting to his hearers God's special revelation in the Person of Jesus Christ.

The coming of Christ brought about a change in God's dealing with humanity. In the past, God **overlooked the times of ignorance,** that is, He didn't always intervene with special judgment (though sin always caused consequences) against the nations who did not know Him. But **God is now declaring to men that all everywhere should repent.** Natural revelation is insufficient to save, and merely serves to draw men to God. There is no salvation apart from Jesus Christ, "for there is no other name under heaven that has been given among men, by which we must be saved" (Acts 4:12).

There is coming **a day in which** God **will judge the world in righteousness through a Man whom He has appointed**—Jesus Christ. In John 5:22–27 Jesus said:

> For not even the Father judges anyone, but He has given all judgment to the Son, in order that all may honor the Son, even as they honor the Father. He who does not honor the Son does not honor the Father who sent Him. Truly, truly, I say to you, he who hears My word, and believes Him who sent Me, has eternal life, and does not come into judgment, but has passed out of death into life. Truly, truly, I say to you, an hour is coming and now is, when the dead shall hear the voice of the Son of God; and those who hear shall live. For just as the Father has life in Himself, even so He gave to the Son also to have life in Himself; and He gave Him authority to execute judgment, because He is the Son of Man.

God **furnished proof** of that **to all men by raising Him from the dead.** The resurrection of Jesus Christ showed God's approval of Him, and qualified Him as judge. There are no excuses now—the proof of the Word of the Lord is all in. Sinners will be judged by what they do with that truth.

The response to Paul's message was predictable, considering the contempt his hearers had previously expressed toward him (cf. v. 18). **When they heard** Paul speak **of the resurrection of the dead, some began to sneer,** since there was no place in Greek thought for a bodily resurrection. **Others**, a little more charitably, **said, "We shall hear you again concerning this."** They never would however, since **Paul went out of their midst** and soon left Athens, never to return.

Paul's apologetic for Christianity was not entirely ignored, however. Luke notes that **some men joined** him **and believed.** They included **Dionysius the Areopagite,** a member of the Areopagus court, **a woman named Damaris, and others with them.** They not only recognized God's existence and who He is but also took the final step and listened to what He said to them through His messenger. Because of that, they alone came to know the "unknown God."

Encouraging the Servant of God (Acts 18:1–17)

11

After these things he left Athens and went to Corinth. And he found a certain Jew named Aquila, a native of Pontus, having recently come from Italy with his wife Priscilla, because Claudius had commanded all the Jews to leave Rome. He came to them, and because he was of the same trade, he stayed with them and they were working; for by trade they were tent-makers. And he was reasoning in the synagogue every Sabbath and trying to persuade Jews and Greeks. But when Silas and Timothy came down from Macedonia, Paul began devoting himself completely to the word, solemnly testifying to the Jews that Jesus was the Christ. And when they resisted and blasphemed, he shook out his garments and said to them, "Your blood be upon your own heads! I am clean. From now on I shall go to the Gentiles." And he departed from there and went to the house of a certain man named Titius Justus, a worshiper of God, whose house was next to the synagogue. And Crispus, the leader of the synagogue, believed in the Lord with all his household, and many of the Corinthians when they heard were believing and being baptized. And the Lord said to Paul in the night by a vision, "Do not be afraid any longer, but go on speaking and do not be silent; for I am with you, and no man will attack you in order to harm you, for I have

many people in this city." And he settled there a year and six months, teaching the word of God among them. But while Gallio was proconsul of Achaia, the Jews with one accord rose up against Paul and brought him before the judgment seat, saying, "This man persuades men to worship God contrary to the law." But when Paul was about to open his mouth, Gallio said to the Jews, "If it were a matter of wrong or of vicious crime, O Jews, it would be reasonable for me to put up with you; but if there are questions about words and names and your own law, look after it yourselves; I am unwilling to be a judge of these matters." And he drove them away from the judgment seat. And they all took hold of Sosthenes, the leader of the synagogue, and began beating him in front of the judgment seat. And Gallio was not concerned about any of these things. (18:1–17)

A little-appreciated truth about the ministry is that pastors and missionaries, perhaps more than other believers, are subject to discouragement. Charles Spurgeon explains that

> good men are promised tribulation in this world, and ministers may expect a larger share than others, that they may learn sympathy with the Lord's suffering people, and so may be fitting shepherds of an ailing flock. ("The Minister's Fainting Fits," in *Lectures to My Students: First Series* [reprint; Grand Rapids: Baker, 1980], 168)

Some of God's choicest servants have undergone times of severe despondency and despair. Burdened with the weight of a rebellious, grumbling people, Moses cried out to the Lord:

> Why hast Thou been so hard on Thy servant? And why have I not found favor in Thy sight, that Thou hast laid the burden of all this people on me? Was it I who conceived all this people? Was it I who brought them forth, that Thou shouldest say to me, "Carry them in your bosom as a nurse carries a nursing infant, to the land which Thou didst swear to their fathers"? Where am I to get meat to give to all this people? For they weep before me, saying, "Give us meat that we may eat!" I alone am not able to carry all this people, because it is too burdensome for me. So if Thou art going to deal thus with me, please kill me at once, if I have found favor in Thy sight, and do not let me see my wretchedness. (Num. 11:11–15)

Following Israel's defeat at Ai, Joshua said, "Alas, O Lord God, why didst Thou ever bring this people over the Jordan, only to deliver us into the hand of the Amorites, to destroy us? If only we had been willing to dwell beyond the Jordan!" (Josh. 7:7) Elijah knew what it was to plunge from the height of success to the pit of despair. Following his dramatic victory over the prophets of Baal on Mount Carmel (1 Kings 18:20ff.), he fled into the wilderness in fear of Jezebel. There he despaired of life and said, "It is enough; now, O Lord, take my life, for I am not better than my fathers" (1 Kings 19:4). Faced with the prospect of imminent death, godly king Hezekiah wept and pleaded with the Lord (Isa. 38:1–20). After his world collapsed and his God seemingly abandoned him, Job cursed the day of his birth (Job 3:1ff.) and complained bitterly about God's treatment of him (Job 9:16ff.). Jeremiah was known as the weeping prophet, and even our Lord was described as "a man of sorrows, and acquainted with grief" (Isa. 53:3).

Nor did the apostle Paul escape the throes of discouragement. The opening of Acts 18 finds him at a low point in his grueling ministry. His second missionary journey had been arduous. After traveling through Asia Minor "strengthening the churches" (Acts 15:41), he crossed the Aegean Sea to the Greek mainland. His healing of a demon-possessed girl in Philippi sparked a riot, and he and Silas had been beaten and thrown into prison. After being released following a devastating earthquake, he was forced to leave the city (16:39–40). From there he went to Thessalonica, where his ministry enjoyed great success (17:4). Persecution forced him to flee to Berea (17:10), where many also responded to his preaching and teaching (17:12). When persecution followed him there from Thessalonica, Paul was again forced to escape danger (17:14). He arrived alone in the great city of Athens, where his brilliant speech in defense of Christianity had largely been ignored (17:19–32). He then **left Athens and went to Corinth,** a fifty-three mile walk.

By Paul's day Corinth had replaced Athens as the leading political and commercial center in Greece. Corinth enjoyed a strategic location on the isthmus of Corinth, which connected the Peloponnesian peninsula with the rest of Greece. Nearly all traffic between northern and southern Greece passed through the city. Because it was a 200-mile sail around the peninsula, some ships were put on rollers and pulled across the 4-mile bridge of land. In A.D. 67 Nero began work on a canal, but one was not completed until 1893.

As a trade center, Corinth was cosmopolitan, with a largely unsettled population. Pfeiffer and Vos note that "much of the population was mobile (sailors, businessmen, government officials, *et al.*) and was therefore cut off from the inhibitions of a settled society" (*The Wycliffe Historical Geography of Bible Lands* [Chicago: Moody, 1967], 481). As a result, Corinth was one of the most debauched cities of antiquity. R. C. H. Lenski writes:

Corinth was a wicked city even as larger cities of the empire went at this period. The very term "Corinthian" came to mean a profligate. *Korinthiazomai,* "to Corinthianize," meant to practice whoredom; *Korinthiastēs* = a whoremonger; *Korinthia korē* (girl) = a courtesan. (*The Interpretation of the Acts of the Apostles* [Minneapolis: Augsburg, 1961], 744)

Towering some 1,500 feet above Corinth was the Acropolis, on top of which was the temple of Aphrodite, the goddess of love. Each evening the temple's one thousand priestesses, who were ritual prostitutes, would descend into the city to ply their trade. In sharp contrast to the sedate (by comparison) intellectual and cultural center of Athens, Corinth was "undeniably a rip-roaring town where 'none but the tough could survive' (Horace, *Epistles* 1.17.36)" (David J. Williams, *New International Biblical Commentary: Acts* [Peabody, Mass.: Hendrickson, 1990], 313).

As he arrived in Corinth, Paul felt greater discouragement. "The combination of only limited success at Athens, loneliness, and the prospect of facing this city, with its commerce and vice, accounts for the weakness and fear that gripped the apostle as he arrived to begin his work" (Everett F. Harrison, *Interpreting Acts: The Expanding Church* [Grand Rapids: Zondervan, 1986], 292). Reflecting on his state of mind when he first arrived in their city, Paul later wrote to the Corinthians, "I was with you in weakness and in fear and in much trembling" (1 Cor. 2:3). He also spoke of his trial in his first letter to the Thessalonians, written from Corinth. In 1 Thessalonians 3:7, Paul wrote, "For this reason, brethren, in all our distress and affliction we were comforted about you through your faith." Their faith was a beacon of hope in his darkness. Besides his discouragement, he may have been physically ill, perhaps from the lingering effects of the ill-treatment he had received in Philippi (16:22–24). Physical weakness often makes discouragement even worse.

But the "God of all comfort" (2 Cor. 1:3), who "comforts the depressed" (2 Cor. 7:6), did not leave Paul in his downtrodden condition. He encouraged his struggling servant through four means: the companionship of friends, the blessing of converts, the fellowship of God, and the frustration of his enemies. These are the very blessings any depressed servant of the Lord can cling to for encouragement.

THE COMPANIONSHIP OF FRIENDS

And he found a certain Jew named Aquila, a native of Pontus, having recently come from Italy with his wife Priscilla, because Claudius had commanded all the Jews to leave Rome. He came

to them, and because he was of the same trade, he stayed with them and they were working; for by trade they were tent-makers. And he was reasoning in the synagogue every Sabbath and trying to persuade Jews and Greeks. But when Silas and Timothy came down from Macedonia, (18:2–5a)

Paul's struggle was made more intense because he had to bear it alone. With Silas and Timothy still in Macedonia (v. 5), God knew Paul needed someone else to help him shoulder the formidable burdens he carried. Paul **found** that desperately needed companionship in **a certain Jew named Aquila, a native of Pontus,** who had **recently come from Italy with his wife Priscilla, because Claudius had commanded all the Jews to leave Rome.** In Corinth Paul first met this husband and wife team who were to become two of his closest friends, even eventually risking their lives for him (Rom. 16:3–4). **Pontus,** Aquila's home region, was located in Asia Minor, on the south shore of the Black Sea. Because **his wife Priscilla** is named first four out of the six times the couple is mentioned, some have speculated that she was a Roman woman of higher social rank than Aquila. More likely, she is mentioned first because she was the more prominent of the two in service to the church. Paul always refers to her by her formal name, Prisca (Rom. 16:3; 1 Cor. 16:19; 2 Tim. 4:19), while Luke always uses the diminutive form **Priscilla** (cf. vv. 18, 26).

The Bible does not record the conversions of Aquila and Priscilla, but they were probably already Christians when Paul met them. They had come from Rome, where a church already existed (Rom. 1:7–8), and they are not listed among the Corinthian converts, either in this chapter or anywhere else in the New Testament. Had two such prominent individuals been saved under Paul's ministry, their conversions would no doubt have been recorded.

In accounting for their relocation to Corinth, Luke explains that the two had **recently come from Italy because** Emperor **Claudius had commanded all the Jews to leave Rome.** That decree is mentioned by Roman historian Suetonius, who wrote, "As the Jews were indulging in constant riots at the instigation of Chrestus, [Claudius] banished them from Rome" (*Life of Claudius* 25.4, cited in F. F. Bruce, *The Book of the Acts*, The New International Commentary on the New Testament [Grand Rapids: Eerdmans, 1971], 368). Since Chrestus differs in only one letter from Christus (Latin for "Christ"), it is commonly assumed that Suetonius refers to disturbances in the Jewish community sparked by the preaching of Christ. Writing seventy years after the fact, he wrongly assumed Chrestus (Christ) to have been in Rome instigating the riots.

Having been forced to leave Rome, Aquila and Priscilla moved their business to Corinth. Paul, no doubt looking for work to support himself, met them there, **and because he was of the same trade, he stayed with them and they were working; for by trade they were tent-makers.** *Skēnopoios* (**tent-makers**) could also refer to leather workers, a trade that included the making of tents, which were often made out of leather. It was customary for all Jewish boys, even rabbis' sons, to learn their father's trade. Paul had no doubt learned from his father to work with this skill.

Paul, of course, did not neglect his ministry. While working along-side Aquila and Priscilla during the week, **he was reasoning in the synagogue every Sabbath and trying to persuade Jews and Greeks.** As noted in the discussion of 17:2 in chapter 9 of this volume, **reasoning** denotes a dialogue. Though the gospel was his single subject (cf. 1 Cor. 2:1–4), Paul did not only preach; there was the give-and-take of questions and answers. His goal was **to persuade** the **Jews** and God-fearing **Greeks** (prosyletes to Judaism) that Jesus Christ was Israel's Lord and Messiah and the Savior from sin and hell.

The God of all comfort met the need of his discouraged servant for companionship not only by providing two new friends but also by bringing back two familiar ones. The arrival of **Silas and Timothy** from **Macedonia** no doubt greatly encouraged him. Although Acts does not record it, Silas and Timothy had apparently rejoined Paul at Athens as he intended (17:15). From there he sent Timothy back to Thessalonica (1 Thess. 3:1–6). Silas was also sent somewhere in Macedonia, since he, too, came to Corinth from that province. He may have gone to Philippi (cf. Phil. 4:15; 2 Cor. 11:9), since Paul kept frequent communication at this time with his first European church.

THE BLESSING OF CONVERTS

Paul began devoting himself completely to the word, solemnly testifying to the Jews that Jesus was the Christ. And when they resisted and blasphemed, he shook out his garments and said to them, "Your blood be upon your own heads! I am clean. From now on I shall go to the Gentiles." And he departed from there and went to the house of a certain man named Titius Justus, a worshiper of God, whose house was next to the synagogue. And Crispus, the leader of the synagogue, believed in the Lord with all his household, and many of the Corinthians when they heard were believing and being baptized. (18:5b–8)

The generous gifts from the Macedonians (2 Cor. 11:9; Phil. 4:15) brought by Silas and Timothy allowed Paul to cease leather working and begin **devoting himself completely to the word** (cf. Luke 24:27; John 5:39, 46; Acts 6:4; 1 Cor. 9:6ff.). Using the Old Testament, he was **solemnly testifying to the Jews that Jesus was the Christ** (cf. Acts 13:16–41).

As so often happened when Paul presented the gospel to his countrymen, many in Corinth's Jewish community rejected it. **Resisted** is from *antitassō*, and literally means "to arrange in battle array" (Lenski, *Acts*, 748). They organized themselves to fight Paul's teaching and even **blasphemed** the name of Christ—the most serious sin (cf. Matt. 12:31–32; Luke 22:64–65).

At length Paul, realizing the futility of continuing to throw pearls before swine (Matt. 7:6), **shook out his garments** in the traditional, dramatic Jewish gesture of rejection. Jews returning from Gentile lands customarily shook the Gentile dust off their sandals, an act which became a symbol of their hatred of non-Jews (cf. Luke 9:5; Acts 13:51). Paul's act symbolized his rejection of the Jews—an infuriating act to them by one of their own. It also showed his abhorrence of their blasphemy; he did not want any of the dust from the synagogue where that blasphemy had taken place to cling to his clothes. His shocking statement, **your blood be upon your own heads! I am clean** (cf. Josh. 2:19; 2 Sam. 1:16; 1 Kings 2:37; Ezek. 18:13; 33:4; Matt. 27:25) indicated that his opponents were fully responsible for what they were doing. Like the faithful watchman of Ezekiel 33:2–5, Paul absolved himself from any guilt connected with their rejection.

His ministry of the gospel was then to **go to the Gentiles,** so Paul **departed** from the synagogue **and went to the house of a certain man named Titius Justus, a worshiper of God.** As **a worshiper of God, Titius Justus,** though a Gentile, had shown an interest in the God of Israel and had attached himself to the synagogue. His name indicates that he was a Roman, and, since Romans often had three names, some have speculated that his full name was Gaius Titius Justus, thus identifying him with the Gaius of Romans 16:23 and 1 Corinthians 1:14.

Paul's passion to reach his fellow Jews with the gospel (cf. Rom. 9:1; 10:1) did not allow him to go far from the synagogue. In fact, the house of Titius Justus **was next to the synagogue,** which no doubt further infuriated the unbelieving Jews. Still worse (from their perspective) was the startling news that **Crispus, the leader of the synagogue, believed in the Lord with all his household.** That astonishing conversion must have sent shock waves through Corinth's Jewish community, which watched in mounting alarm as **many of the Corinthians when they heard were believing and being baptized.** Desperate to halt the rising tide of belief in Jesus as Messiah, they soon hauled Paul before the Roman authorities. Before that ordeal, however, the Lord provided the apostle with the most encouraging comfort—He came Himself to Paul.

THE FELLOWSHIP OF GOD

And the Lord said to Paul in the night by a vision, "Do not be afraid any longer, but go on speaking and do not be silent; for I am with you, and no man will attack you in order to harm you, for I have many people in this city." And he settled there a year and six months, teaching the word of God among them. (18:9–11)

Paul's friends, both his newfound ones and his old ones, gave much encouragement to him, as did the many Corinthian converts. Yet those very converts brought intensifying opposition from Corinth's Jewish community—to the extent that Paul was struggling with whether he should continue to preach at Corinth. To encourage His servant at the highest and most strengthening level, **the Lord** Himself **said to Paul in the night by a vision, "Do not be afraid any longer, but go on speaking and do not be silent."** This is one of six visions Paul received in Acts (9:12; 16:9–10; 22:17–18; 23:11; 27:23–24), all coming at crucial points in his ministry.

The Lord's encouraging message, **"Do not be afraid any longer, but go on speaking and do not be silent"** answered the struggle in Paul's mind. The supernatural vision provided four reasons for him not to give up proclaiming the gospel in that city. First, God commanded it specifically when He said **"go on speaking."** Second, God reminded him, **"I am with you."** He gave a similar revelation to Joshua when he assumed the leadership of Israel after Moses' death:

> No man will be able to stand before you all the days of your life. Just as I have been with Moses, I will be with you; I will not fail you or forsake you.... Have I not commanded you? Be strong and courageous! Do not tremble or be dismayed, for the Lord your God is with you wherever you go. (Josh. 1:5, 9)

With the Lord's powerful presence aiding his ministry, Paul could accomplish whatever God intended him to. The Lord stood by him until the very end of his ministry (2 Tim. 4:16–18) and promises His presence to all believers (Matt. 28:20; cf. Isa. 41:10; Jer. 1:17–19).

Third, God promised Paul that **"no man will attack you in order to harm you."** Those under God's protection are invulnerable (cf. Isa. 54:17; Rev. 11:5).

The final reason God gave Paul to keep preaching was that He had **many people in this city.** All those in Corinth who "had been appointed to eternal life" had not yet "believed" (Acts 13:48). The truth of election expressed in verse 10 balances the truth of human responsibility in verse 6. As always, Scripture presents those two inscrutable truths without attempting to harmonize them. Both are true, and there is no real contradiction between them. (For further discussion of this issue, see the exposition of Acts 13:46, 48 in chapter 3 of this volume.) Here it is clear that some people belong to the Lord who are not yet saved, and they will not be saved without the preaching of the gospel (cf. Rom. 10:13–15). Paul defined his preaching as having the purpose of bringing the elect to faith (cf. Titus 1:1).

His strength fully renewed by God's promise to him, Paul **settled** in Corinth for another **year and six months, teaching the word of God among them.** He continued to minister in that strategic location, and the elect continued to be saved and grow in their faith. During that period a certain incident provided the final source of God's encouragement to Paul.

THE FRUSTRATION OF HIS ENEMIES

But while Gallio was proconsul of Achaia, the Jews with one accord rose up against Paul and brought him before the judgment seat, saying, "This man persuades men to worship God contrary to the law." But when Paul was about to open his mouth, Gallio said to the Jews, "If it were a matter of wrong or of vicious crime, O Jews, it would be reasonable for me to put up with you; but if there are questions about words and names and your own law, look after it yourselves; I am unwilling to be a judge of these matters." And he drove them away from the judgment seat. And they all took hold of Sosthenes, the leader of the synagogue, and began beating him in front of the judgment seat. And Gallio was not concerned about any of these things. (18:12–17)

Paul's Jewish opponents had watched in frustrated rage as more and more people came to faith in Christ. Finally, in desperation, they tried to get the Roman authorities to put a halt to Paul's preaching.

That authority was vested in **Gallio**, the **proconsul of Achaia**. **Gallio** was the brother of Seneca, the famed Roman philosopher and tutor of Nero. Seneca described his brother as "an intelligent person who hated flattery, and was blessed with an 'unaffectedly pleasant personality'" (Simon J. Kistemaker, *New Testament Commentary: Acts* [Grand Rapids: Baker, 1990], 659). He was **proconsul of Achaia** from July, A.D. 51

to June A.D. 52. Luke's use of the title **proconsul** is another important testimony to his painstaking accuracy as an historian, as Richard N. Longenecker explains:

> That Luke distinguishes correctly between senatorial and imperial provinces and has the former governed by a proconsul on behalf of the senate and the latter governed by a propraetor representing the emperor says much for his accuracy, for the status of provinces changed with the times. Achaia was a senatorial province from 27 B.C. to A.D. 15 and then again from A.D. 44 onwards ... It was therefore governed by a proconsul. . . . Macedonia, however, was an imperial province, and therefore Luke rightly called the magistrates at Philippi praetors. ("The Acts of the Apostles," in Frank E. Gaebelein, ed., *The Expositor's Bible Commentary* [Grand Rapids: Zondervan, 1981], 9:485)

Hoping to capitalize on Gallio's inexperienced authority, **the Jews with one accord rose up against Paul and brought him before the judgment seat.** The **judgment seat** was a large, raised stone platform that stood in the *agora* (marketplace) in front of the residence of the proconsul and served as the public court where he tried cases. The Jews hoped for a favorable verdict from Gallio, which could then be cited as a precedent in other places where the gospel was preached. They began the proceedings by **saying, "This man persuades men to worship God contrary to the law."** Judaism was officially tolerated by the Romans, who at this early date viewed Christianity as nothing more than a sect of Judaism. Their charge challenged that conventional wisdom by saying that since Paul's Christian teaching was outside the bounds of Judaism, Christianity should not receive the toleration from the Romans that Judaism did.

This was a charge with far-reaching implications. Had Gallio ruled in the Jews' favor, Christianity could have been banned not only in Corinth but also throughout the Empire. Gallio, however, was not to be so easily duped. As **Paul was about to open his mouth** to defend himself, Gallio cut him off. The proconsul refused to meddle in what he viewed as an internal dispute within Judaism. Accordingly he **said to the Jews, "If it were a matter of wrong or of vicious crime, O Jews, it would be reasonable for me to put up with you; but if there are questions about words and names and your own law, look after it yourselves; I am unwilling to be a judge of these matters."** Gallio rendered what in today's courts would be called a summary judgment and threw the case out. He officially ruled that there was no crime involved but that the issue was merely one of semantics. When the Jews persisted in arguing their case against Paul, Gallio **drove them away from the judgment seat.**

Though the specific antecedent of **they all** is not clear, the most reasonable interpretation is that it refers to the angry Jews who vented their frustration by taking **hold of Sosthenes, the leader of the synagogue, and beating him in front of the judgment seat.** That seems most consistent with Gallio's refusal to stop the beating (see the discussion below). Whether **Sosthenes** was a Christian at this time is not known, but he later is identified as one (1 Cor. 1:1). If he had already become a Christian, the Jews' motive for roughing him up is obvious. If he had not, his fellow Jews were probably upset with his bungling their case before Gallio. As a **leader of the synagogue** (as was Crispus, v. 8) he no doubt had presented the case against Paul to the judge. But consistent with his refusal to meddle in the internal affairs of the Jews, and in recognition that it was a religious issue for them, **Gallio was not concerned about any of these things.**

God strengthened Paul through friends, converts, His own presence, and through the discomfiture of Paul's enemies. He was faithful to His promise recorded in Isaiah 40:29–31:

> He gives strength to the weary, and to him who lacks might He increases power. Though youths grow weary and tired, and vigorous young men stumble badly, yet those who wait for the Lord will gain new strength; they will mount up with wings like eagles, they will run and not get tired, they will walk and not become weary.

That same comfort and encouragement is available to all who faithfully serve our Lord.

Breaking with the Past (Acts 18:18–19:7)

12

And Paul, having remained many days longer, took leave of the brethren and put out to sea for Syria, and with him were Priscilla and Aquila. In Cenchrea he had his hair cut, for he was keeping a vow. And they came to Ephesus, and he left them there. Now he himself entered the synagogue and reasoned with the Jews. And when they asked him to stay for a longer time, he did not consent, but taking leave of them and saying, "I will return to you again if God wills," he set sail from Ephesus. And when he had landed at Caesarea, he went up and greeted the church, and went down to Antioch. And having spent some time there, he departed and passed successively through the Galatian region and Phrygia, strengthening all the disciples. Now a certain Jew named Apollos, an Alexandrian by birth, an eloquent man, came to Ephesus; and he was mighty in the Scriptures. This man had been instructed in the way of the Lord; and being fervent in spirit, he was speaking and teaching accurately the things concerning Jesus, being acquainted only with the baptism of John; and he began to speak out boldly in the synagogue. But when Priscilla and Aquila heard him, they took him aside and explained to him the way of God more accurately. And when he wanted to go across to Achaia, the brethren encouraged him and

wrote to the disciples to welcome him; and when he had arrived, he helped greatly those who had believed through grace; for he powerfully refuted the Jews in public, demonstrating by the Scriptures that Jesus was the Christ. And it came about that while Apollos was at Corinth, Paul having passed through the upper country came to Ephesus, and found some disciples, and he said to them, "Did you receive the Holy Spirit when you believed?" And they said to him, "No, we have not even heard whether there is a Holy Spirit." And he said, "Into what then were you baptized?" And they said, "Into John's baptism." And Paul said, "John baptized with the baptism of repentance, telling the people to believe in Him who was coming after him, that is, in Jesus." And when they heard this, they were baptized in the name of the Lord Jesus. And when Paul had laid his hands upon them, the Holy Spirit came on them, and they began speaking with tongues and prophesying. And there were in all about twelve men. (18:18–19:7)

Although the atoning work of Jesus Christ inaugurated the New Covenant, it took time for the early Jewish believers to fully abandon the ceremonial practices of the revered and dutifully followed Old Covenant. The book of Hebrews contains the theology of that transition, showing Christ's superiority to everyone and everything connected with the Old Covenant. The book of Acts records the transition's historical outworking, as a new entity entered the stage of redemptive history. Clearly, God had temporarily set aside Israel (cf. Matt. 21:33–43; 22:1–9; 23:37–38; Rom. 10:19–21; 11:20–24), whose long history of apostasy reached an appalling climax in the killing of its Messiah. God began working out His kingdom purposes through the church. Yet it took time for the new church to separate itself completely from its old religious habits (cf. Acts 10, 11, 15).

First-century Judaism was far more than a religion; it was a combination of divinely ordained laws covering many features of daily life, along with which developed a man-made national and cultural tradition. To be Jewish was not merely to embrace a biblical creed or affirm an Old Testament theology. Being Jewish also meant embracing a traditional interpretation of Scripture and an expansion of legal prescriptions into nearly every area of life. To be Jewish meant not only to *believe* differently from one's Gentile neighbors but also to *behave* differently. In fact, the purpose of many Old Covenant ceremonies and observances was to keep Israel separate from her Gentile neighbors.

The Jews were uniquely God's people, and He wanted them to stand apart from the corrupting influence of the rest of the world, that they might be a witness to the nations of the power and grace of the true

God. This divine design was compounded and even adulterated by the "traditions of men," which Jesus said substituted for the "commandment of God" (cf. Matt. 15:3, 9).

Not surprisingly, even the apostles had difficulty shedding the old demands and patterns and making the transition. Acts 2:46 finds the church they led still meeting in the temple, and 3:1 shows that Peter and John were still observing the prescribed times of prayer. Peter strenuously and repeatedly resisted abandoning the dietary regulations (10:9–16). The Jewish believers, including the other apostles, were shocked that Peter violated Jewish custom by eating with Gentiles (11:2–3). Even Paul, the apostle to the Gentiles, twice took a Jewish vow (18:18; 21:26). It should be noted that the Lord was patient with this transition. He likewise urged believers to understand that those who still observed the Old Testament laws should not be hurried into some freedom that would violate their consciences or cause them to engage in self-condemnation. This is the subject of Paul's instruction in Romans 14:1–15:6.

The church, even in the Gentile world, was usually associated with the synagogues. Paul's custom, when entering a city, was to preach the gospel first to the Jews gathered on the Sabbath. Jewish believers would often continue to operate within the framework of the synagogue for as long as possible (cf. 19:8–9). So common was that association that the Romans initially viewed Christianity as nothing more than a sect within Judaism. For that reason, the proconsul Gallio refused to rule in the Corinthian Jews' case against Paul, declaring it to be an internal dispute within Judaism (18:12–15).

The text of Acts 18:18–19:7 is linked together by three examples of those caught up in this transition from the Old to the New Covenant: Paul, Apollos, and twelve Old Testament saints.

PAUL IN TRANSITION

And Paul, having remained many days longer, took leave of the brethren and put out to sea for Syria, and with him were Priscilla and Aquila. In Cenchrea he had his hair cut, for he was keeping a vow. And they came to Ephesus, and he left them there. Now he himself entered the synagogue and reasoned with the Jews. And when they asked him to stay for a longer time, he did not consent, but taking leave of them and saying, "I will return to you again if God wills," he set sail from Ephesus. And when he had landed at Caesarea, he went up and greeted the church, and went down to Antioch. And having spent some time there, he

departed and passed successively through the Galatian region and Phrygia, strengthening all the disciples. (18:18–23)

Gallio's favorable ruling (18:14–15) allowed **Paul** to remain **many days longer** at Corinth. At last, however, he felt the need to return to Palestine. He **took leave of the brethren** at Corinth **and put out to sea for Syria,** taking **with him Priscilla and Aquila,** who had become two of Paul's closest friends. That he felt the freedom to invite them to accompany him shows that other leaders had already emerged within the Corinthian church, such as Gaius, Sosthenes, Stephanus, and Crispus. And the fact that Priscilla and Aquila would leave their business to go with Paul indicates their loyalty and devotion to him.

Arriving at **Cenchrea,** the eastern port of Corinth, where he could find a ship going east, Paul **had his hair cut, for he was keeping a vow.** His action seems puzzling at first glance, since he was well aware that the Old Covenant and all its rituals had passed away. Yet he had been reared according to the strictest standards of the Jewish faith. In Galatians 1:13–14 Paul wrote:

> For you have heard of my former manner of life in Judaism, how I used to persecute the church of God beyond measure, and tried to destroy it; and I was advancing in Judaism beyond many of my contemporaries among my countrymen, being more extremely zealous for my ancestral traditions.

To the Philippians he described himself as

> circumcised the eighth day, of the nation of Israel, of the tribe of Benjamin, a Hebrew of Hebrews; as to the Law, a Pharisee; as to zeal, a persecutor of the church; as to the righteousness which is in the Law, found blameless. (Phil. 3:5–6)

After he became a Christian, Paul realized the worthlessness of all the efforts at self-salvation by ritual, tradition, legalism, sincerity, and external goodness compared to the true righteousness and knowledge of God that came through knowing Christ (Phil. 3:7–9). But he had a genuine love for God's law in Scripture (cf. Rom. 7:12, 14) and was still influenced by his Jewish heritage. And when he wanted to show his deep thanks for God's marvelous encouragement during the difficult times in Corinth (cf. chapter 11 of this volume), he naturally thought of a typically Jewish way of doing so.

The vow Paul made was a Nazirite vow—a special pledge of separation and devotion to God (cf. 2 Cor. 6:17). It was usually made in gratitude to the Almighty for gracious blessing or deliverance. In Numbers 6, God Himself inaugurated the Nazirite vow, saying to Moses,

> Speak to the sons of Israel, and say to them, "When a man or woman makes a special vow, the vow of a Nazirite, to dedicate himself to the Lord, he shall abstain from wine and strong drink; he shall drink no vinegar, whether made from wine or strong drink, neither shall he drink any grape juice, nor eat fresh or dried grapes. All the days of his separation he shall not eat anything that is produced by the grape vine, from the seeds even to the skin. All the days of his vow of separation no razor shall pass over his head. He shall be holy until the days are fulfilled for which he separated himself to the Lord; he shall let the locks of hair on his head grow long." (Num. 6:2–5)

The vow was for a specific period (usually a month, although Samson [Judg. 16:17], Samuel [1 Sam. 1:11], and John the Baptist [Luke 1:15] were Nazirites for life). At the end of that time there was an elaborate ceremony:

> Now this is the law of the Nazirite when the days of his separation are fulfilled, he shall bring the offering to the doorway of the tent of meeting. And he shall present his offering to the Lord: one male lamb a year old without defect for a burnt offering and one ewe-lamb a year old without defect for a sin offering and one ram without defect for a peace offering, and a basket of unleavened cakes of fine flour mixed with oil and unleavened wafers spread with oil, along with their grain offering and their libations. Then the priest shall present them before the Lord and shall offer his sin offering and his burnt offering. He shall also offer the ram for a sacrifice of peace offerings to the Lord, together with the basket of unleavened cakes; the priest shall likewise offer its grain offering and its libation. The Nazirite shall then shave his dedicated head of hair at the doorway of the tent of meeting, and take the dedicated hair of his head and put it on the fire which is under the sacrifice of peace offerings. And the priest shall take the ram's shoulder when it has been boiled, and one unleavened cake out of the basket, and one unleavened wafer, and shall put them on the hands of the Nazirite after he has shaved his dedicated hair. Then the priest shall wave them for a wave offering before the Lord. It is holy for the priest, together with the breast offered by waving and the thigh offered by lifting up; and afterward the Nazirite may drink wine. This is the law of the Nazirite who vows his offering to the Lord according to his separation, in addition to what else he can afford; according to his vow which he takes, so he shall do according to the law of his separation. (Num. 6:13–21)

In Paul's day, provision was made for those away from Jerusalem at the termination of their vow to shave their heads, as Paul did, then within thirty days present the hair at the Temple (cf. Josephus *Wars*, 2.15.1). The phrase **he was keeping a vow** indicates a process not yet completed. That required his arrival in Jerusalem.

Having crossed the Aegean Sea as they sailed eastward, Paul and his party **came to Ephesus,** the most important city in Asia Minor. Paul **left** Priscilla and Aquila **there** to become settled and establish their business. They apparently remained in Ephesus for a few years, had a church meet in their home (1 Cor. 16:19), and eventually returned to Rome (Rom. 16:3–5). Paul **himself,** as was his common strategy, **entered the synagogue and reasoned with the Jews.** As in Berea, he was well received, so much so that the Jews **asked him to stay for a longer time.** His response to this great opportunity gives a clear testimony to the seriousness of his vow. He refused to stay! In a hurry to reach Jerusalem because of his vow, and (as some Greek manuscripts add) to reach the city before the Feast (probably Passover), **he did not consent**. Regretfully **taking leave of them and saying, "I will return to you again if God wills," he set sail from Ephesus.** He did not leave the city without a Christian witness, however, since Priscilla and Aquila remained there. And, as will be seen shortly, they were soon to have help.

Arriving in Palestine, Paul **landed at Caesarea,** the Roman city and port of call for travelers bound for Jerusalem. From there he went on to fulfill his vow, and then **greeted the church.** That Paul did visit Jerusalem, although the city is not mentioned, is clear from the requirement of the vow, as well as from Luke's use of the terms **went up** and **went down.** One naturally **went up** from Caesarea, located on the coast, to Jerusalem, located on Mount Zion, then **went down** from Jerusalem to anywhere else. Paul, then, completed his second missionary journey in **Antioch,** from where it had begun (15:35–36).

With those few short verses, focusing on the apostle in transition from the old ways, Luke sums up a long and arduous journey. William Barclay observes:

> We may see very clearly here how much we do not know about Paul. Acts 18:23–19:1 describe a journey of no less than 1,500 miles and it is dismissed with barely a reference. There are untold tales of heroism of Paul which we will never know. (*The Acts of the Apostles* [Philadelphia: Westminster, 1955], 150)

Paul's burning desire to reach the lost world for Christ did not let him remain for long in his home church at Antioch. After **having spent some time there, he departed and passed successively through**

the Galatian region and Phrygia, strengthening all the disciples.
With those words Luke begins the account of Paul's third missionary
journey. But before continuing with the record of that mission, he returns
to recount what took place at Ephesus after Paul's departure. He tells the
story of a second individual in transition: Apollos.

APOLLOS IN TRANSITION

**Now a certain Jew named Apollos, an Alexandrian by birth, an
eloquent man, came to Ephesus; and he was mighty in the
Scriptures. This man had been instructed in the way of the Lord;
and being fervent in spirit, he was speaking and teaching accurately the things concerning Jesus, being acquainted only with
the baptism of John; and he began to speak out boldly in the synagogue. But when Priscilla and Aquila heard him, they took him
aside and explained to him the way of God more accurately. And
when he wanted to go across to Achaia, the brethren encouraged
him and wrote to the disciples to welcome him; and when he had
arrived, he helped greatly those who had believed through
grace; for he powerfully refuted the Jews in public, demonstrating by the Scriptures that Jesus was the Christ.** (18:24–28)

As the scene shifts to Ephesus, the inspired physician introduces
a certain Jew named Apollos, an Alexandrian by birth. At the
time, Alexandria, located in Egypt near the mouth of the Nile, had a large
Jewish population. So although reared outside Israel, Apollos grew up in
a Jewish cultural setting. *Logios* (**eloquent**) appears only here in the
New Testament. The word "can mean either a man of words ... or a man
of ideas" (A. T. Robertson, *Word Pictures in the New Testament* [reprint,
1930; Grand Rapids: Baker, n.d.], 3:306). Apollos may well have been
both a learned and eloquent man.

More important, **he was mighty in the Scriptures.** *Dunatos*
(**mighty**) is related to *dunamis*, from which the English word "dynamite"
derives. *Graphais* (**Scriptures**), as always in the New Testament, identifies the Old Testament. His learning and eloquence, coupled with his
powerful treatment of the Old Testament, made Apollos a devastating
debater (cf. v. 28). The rarity of such preachers is indicated by the fact
that no one else is so designated as powerful in dealing with the
Scriptures. The church today is in desperate need of men like Apollos.

That Apollos **had been instructed in the way of the Lord**
does not mean he was already a Christian (cf. v. 26). The phrase **the way
of the Lord** is an Old Testament term for instruction in the things of
God. God said of Abraham in Genesis 18:19:

I have chosen him, in order that he may command his children and his household after him to keep the way of the Lord by doing righteousness and justice; in order that the Lord may bring upon Abraham what He has spoken about him.

Judges 2:22 describes God's intent "to test Israel" to see "whether they will keep the way of the Lord to walk in it as their fathers did, or not." In Psalm 25:8–9 the psalmist declares, "Good and upright is the Lord; therefore He instructs sinners in the way. He leads the humble in justice, and He teaches the humble His way." The way of the Lord, then, was the path of spiritual and moral standards God expected His people to follow (cf. 1 Sam. 12:23; 2 Kings 21:22; Prov. 10:29; Jer. 5:4–5).

Apollos combined his deep knowledge and eloquence with a passionate heart. Luke describes him as **fervent in spirit,** having a soul fired with enthusiasm for the things of God. His zeal translated into action, as **he was speaking and teaching accurately the things concerning Jesus, being acquainted only with the baptism of John; and he began to speak out boldly in the synagogue.** Based on his limited knowledge, Apollos **was speaking and teaching accurately the things concerning Jesus.** He did not have a full understanding of the gospel, however, being **acquainted only with the baptism of John.** John's baptism was one of preparation for Messiah's coming (Luke 1:16–17). Apollos accepted John the Baptist's message that Messiah was coming. He even believed that Jesus was that Lamb of God (John 1:29) and Messiah. He surely expounded with force and persuasion the Scriptures that pointed to Jesus. But he did not understand the significance of Christ's death and resurrection. Nor was he acquainted with the coming of the Spirit and the birth of the church on the Day of Pentecost. In short, he was a redeemed Old Testament saint; he was saved but was not able to be called a Christian yet.

Although his teaching was accurate, as far as it went, Apollos needed the rest of the story concerning Jesus. Accordingly, **when Priscilla and Aquila heard him, they took him aside and explained to him the way of God more accurately.** Instead of publicly instructing Apollos, they tactfully **took him aside,** possibly into their home, to speak to him. Having done so, they explained to him the rich fullness of the truth concerning the Messiah's atoning death and resurrection. That the mighty preacher and scholar would consent to be taught by a lowly tentmaker and his wife attests to his godly humility.

After this wonderful instruction and completion of his faith, Apollos, armed with his newfound knowledge of God's gospel, **wanted to go across** the Aegean Sea **to Achaia**—specifically to its capital, Corinth (19:1). The **brethren** in Ephesus **encouraged him** to do so

and even **wrote to the disciples** in Corinth **to welcome him** as a fellow Christian. Fulfilling his plan and arriving at Corinth, the eloquent preacher soon made his presence felt in both the Christian and Jewish communities. Luke notes that **he helped greatly those who had believed through grace.** The designation of Christians here as **those who had believed through grace** is the Spirit's way of reminding all that faith is a gift of grace (cf. Eph. 2:8). Apollos assisted the believers in their spiritual growth through his powerful preaching.

This fervent, brilliant Old Testament scholar also exploded like a bombshell on Corinth's unconverted Jewish community. Like Stephen (6:8–10) and Paul (9:22) before him, Apollos **powerfully refuted the Jews in public, demonstrating by the Scriptures that Jesus was the Christ. Refuted** is from *diakatelegchomai,* an intense double compound word. Apollos was so effective in his discourse that he crushed his opponents, totally disproving them at every point.

His devastating performance in the public debates made a profound impression on the Corinthian church. They soon held him in the same high esteem in which they held Peter and Paul (1 Cor. 1:12; 3:4,6). It must have pained him (as it did Paul and Peter), to have one of the developing Corinthian church's factions identify with him. His successful transition from Old Covenant believer to New Testament saint was an immense blessing for the church.

OLD TESTAMENT SAINTS IN TRANSITION

And it came about that while Apollos was at Corinth, Paul having passed through the upper country came to Ephesus, and found some disciples, and he said to them, "Did you receive the Holy Spirit when you believed?" And they said to him, "No, we have not even heard whether there is a Holy Spirit." And he said, "Into what then were you baptized?" And they said, "Into John's baptism." And Paul said, "John baptized with the baptism of repentance, telling the people to believe in Him who was coming after him, that is, in Jesus." And when they heard this, they were baptized in the name of the Lord Jesus. And when Paul had laid his hands upon them, the Holy Spirit came on them, and they began speaking with tongues and prophesying. And there were in all about twelve men. (19:1–7)

After the interlude describing Apollos's conversion and ministry, Luke returns to the story of Paul for his final example of transition. He notes **that while Apollos was at Corinth, Paul** (on his third missionary journey) **having passed through the upper country came to**

Ephesus. The beloved apostle was making good on his promise to return to Ephesus (18:21), with the hope that the Jews would still be eager to hear. He arrived there by way of the **upper country.** By doing so, Paul took the more direct route, not the regular trade route on the lower level through the Lycus and Maender valleys. He thus approached Ephesus from the north, where he had been ministering (18:23).

Once in Ephesus, Paul **found some disciples.** Much controversy surrounds the spiritual status of these men. Those who insist they were already Christians use this passage as a proof text for their view that receiving the Holy Spirit is a subsequent, postsalvation, or "second blessing," experience. Such an interpretation, however, is untenable. First, it commits the methodological error of failing to consider the transitional nature of Acts, which means that the experiences and phenomena described in Acts are not normative for today. Second, this is a faulty interpretation because it commits the comparative scriptural error. Other texts make obvious that this passage cannot be used to teach that some Christians today may not have the Holy Spirit. That would contradict the explicit teaching of the New Testament epistles, which declare unequivocally that every Christian receives the Spirit at salvation (1 Cor. 6:19; 12:13; 2 Cor. 6:16; Eph. 1:13), and define those without the Spirit as unsaved (Rom. 8:9; Jude 19). (For a further discussion of the error of making the experiences recorded in Acts normative for today, see my book *Charismatic Chaos* [Grand Rapids: Zondervan, 1992], 171ff.)

Nor does Luke's description of them as **disciples** prove that these men were Christians. *Mathētēs* ("disciple") simply means "learner" or "follower" and does not always in the New Testament refer to Christians (although every Christian is a disciple of Jesus Christ). The Bible speaks of the disciples of the Pharisees (Mark 2:18; Luke 5:33) and of John the Baptist (Matt. 9:14; 11:2; Luke 5:33; 7:18–19; 11:1; John 1:35; 3:25). Even all those called disciples of Jesus Christ were not saved. John 6:66 says, "As a result of this many of His disciples withdrew, and were not walking with Him anymore."

Paul certainly did not assume these twelve disciples were Christians. His question, **"Did you receive the Holy Spirit when you believed?"** sought to determine their status. Commentator David Williams explains the significance of Paul's question:

> His [Paul's] criterion for what distinguished the Christian is significant. So, too, is the way in which his question is framed. It implies that the Holy Spirit is received at a definite point in time and that that time is the moment of initial belief (the aorist participle, *pisteusantes*, being construed here as coincidental with the verb, *elabete*). The same thought is expressed, for example, in Ephesians 1:13: "Having believed, you were marked in him with a seal, the promised Holy Spirit" (cf. Acts

11:17). No space of time is envisaged between the two events; nor is the possibility entertained of believing without also receiving the "seal of the Spirit." (*New International Biblical Commentary: Acts* [Peabody, Mass.: Hendrickson, 1990], 329)

Their answer **"No, we have not even heard whether there is a Holy Spirit"** confirmed to the apostle that they were not yet Christians. That they were unacquainted with the coming of the Spirit at Pentecost showed that they were in fact Old Testament saints. Their response to Paul's next question, **"Into what then were you baptized?"** further clarified their status. They responded, **"Into John's baptism,"** showing that they were disciples of John the Baptist. That Paul would encounter followers of John the Baptist nearly a quarter of a century after his death is not unusual. J. B. Lightfoot notes that such groups still existed in the second century (*Saint Paul's Epistles to the Colossians and to Philemon* [reprint of the 1879 edition; Grand Rapids: Zondervan], 402ff.). And had these twelve already believed in Jesus Christ, they would have been baptized into His name.

Having learned that they were Old Testament saints, Paul explained that **"John baptized with the baptism of repentance, telling the people to believe in Him who was coming after him, that is, in Jesus."** The apostle's statement offers further proof that these disciples were not Christians; they apparently did not know that Jesus was the promised Messiah whom John proclaimed. Significantly, Paul did not instruct them about how to receive the Spirit, but about Jesus.

The light of truth dawned in their hearts **when they heard** Paul's teaching, and **they were baptized** in water **in the name of the Lord Jesus,** signifying their spiritual union with Him by faith. Immediately, in a gesture of apostolic affirmation, **Paul laid his hands upon them.** Some of the apostles had been present at each new phase of the church (Acts 2, 8, 10) so that they would be authoritative witnesses to the reality that all who believed in Jesus Christ were one in Him. I. Howard Marshall notes that

> laying on of hands should be understood as a special act of fellowship, incorporating the people concerned into the fellowship of the church. This was necessary in the case of the Samaritan converts in chapter 8 to make it quite clear that they were accepted fully into the Jewish church centred on Jerusalem; and it was necessary in the present instance to make it clear to these members of a semi-Christian group that they were now becoming part of the universal church. (*The Acts of the Apostles* [Grand Rapids: Eerdmans, 1992], 308)

As Paul made this gesture, **the Holy Spirit came upon them** and, as had others before them (cf. 2:1–4; 8:14–17), **they began speaking with tongues and prophesying.** That was a further indication that they were now a part of the one true church (cf. 11:15, 17). And since they had not even heard that the Spirit had come, they needed tangible proof that He had indeed come into their lives.

These **twelve men,** like Paul and Apollos before them, illustrate the transitional nature of Acts. The church, which had embraced Jews, Gentiles, and Samaritans, now gathered in the last group: Old Testament saints. And the same miraculous gifts were present, so that all would know what was said of the Gentiles in Acts 11:17–18:

> If God therefore gave to them the same gift as He gave to us also after believing in the Lord Jesus Christ, who was I that I could stand in God's way? And when they heard this, they quieted down, and glorified God, saying, "Well then, God has granted to the Gentiles also the repentance that leads to life."

So all the groups were gathered in. And in each case apostles were present to verify that all received the same Holy Spirit in the same way. That having been completed, Paul could write to the Ephesians, "There is one body and one Spirit, just as also you were called in one hope of your calling; one Lord, one faith, one baptism" (Eph. 4:4–5). From then on, the Holy Spirit would come to every heart at salvation, as the epistles teach.

The Powerful Word
(Acts 19:8–20)

13

And he entered the synagogue and continued speaking out boldly for three months, reasoning and persuading them about the
kingdom of God. But when some were becoming hardened and
disobedient, speaking evil of the Way before the multitude, he
withdrew from them and took away the disciples, reasoning
daily in the school of Tyrannus. And this took place for two
years, so that all who lived in Asia heard the word of the Lord,
both Jews and Greeks. And God was performing extraordinary
miracles by the hands of Paul, so that handkerchiefs or aprons
were even carried from his body to the sick, and the diseases left
them and the evil spirits went out. But also some of the Jewish
exorcists, who went from place to place, attempted to name over
those who had the evil spirits the name of the Lord Jesus, saying,
"I adjure you by Jesus whom Paul preaches." And seven sons of
one Sceva, a Jewish chief priest, were doing this. And the evil
spirit answered and said to them, "I recognize Jesus, and I know
about Paul, but who are you?" And the man, in whom was the
evil spirit, leaped on them and subdued all of them and overpowered them, so that they fled out of that house naked and
wounded. And this became known to all, both Jews and Greeks,
who lived in Ephesus; and fear fell upon them all and the name

of the Lord Jesus was being magnified. Many also of those who had believed kept coming, confessing and disclosing their practices. And many of those who practiced magic brought their books together and began burning them in the sight of all; and they counted up the price of them and found it fifty thousand pieces of silver. So the word of the Lord was growing mightily and prevailing. (19:8–20)

Ever since the Fall, members of the human race have been in rebellion against God. Having (so they think) torn God's "fetters apart, and cast away [His] cords from [themselves]" (Ps. 2:3), they imagine themselves to be free. In reality, they have become enslaved to sin (John 8:34; Rom. 6:17) and Satan (1 John 5:19). The apostle Paul reminded the Ephesians:

> You were dead in your trespasses and sins, in which you formerly walked according to the course of this world, according to the prince of the power of the air, of the spirit that is now working in the sons of disobedience. (Eph. 2:1–2)

Satan manipulates fallen men by two means. First, he influences their minds. "A natural man," wrote Paul to the Corinthians, "does not accept the things of the Spirit of God; for they are foolishness to him, and he cannot understand them, because they are spiritually appraised" (1 Cor. 2:14). Lacking the Holy Spirit's illumination, unregenerate men and women fall prey to Satan, who seeks to blind "the minds of the unbelieving, that they might not see the light of the gospel of the glory of Christ, who is the image of God" (2 Cor. 4:4).

This is confirmed by the spiritual strategy for war with Satan's kingdom given in 2 Corinthians 10:3–5, where Paul writes:

> For though we walk in the flesh, we do not war according to the flesh, for the weapons of our warfare are not of the flesh, but divinely powerful for the destruction of fortresses. We are destroying speculations and every lofty thing raised up against the knowledge of God, and we are taking every thought captive to the obedience of Christ.

We are waging war against ideas, proud philosophies and thoughts in an effort to tear down human idealogies and bring every thought captive to Christ. That can be done only with the truth of Scripture.

Second, Satan exerts a sinister influence over the fallen human will, though he cannot force it to act. He does so by temptation, both externally, through the evil world system and internally through sinful human nature. Jesus expressed the fearful effect of that influence to the Pharisees when He said, "You are of your father the devil, and you want to do the desires of your father" (John 8:44).

Satan does not have things all his own way, however. Into this fallen, rebellious, evil world "the Son of God appeared for this purpose, that He might destroy the works of the devil" (1 John 3:8). His death on the cross assured Satan's ultimate defeat:

> Since then the children share in flesh and blood, He Himself likewise also partook of the same, that through death He might render powerless him who had the power of death, that is, the devil. (Heb. 2:14; cf. Col. 2:15; 1 Pet. 3:18–22)

When the glorious earthly kingdom of the Lord Jesus Christ comes, Satan will not be permitted to tarnish it with his presence (Rev. 20:1–3). Released for one last burst of evil activity at the end of that Millennium, he and all his wicked, rebelling forces, both angelic and human, will then be cast into the lake of fire forever (Rev. 20:10–15).

The earthly ministry of Jesus Christ foreshadowed Satan's ultimate defeat. From the very outset, He exercised absolute power and authority over Satan and his demons. Tempted three times by Satan himself, Jesus emerged from the struggle victorious. The gospels are replete with examples of His power over the demonic realm. Matthew 17:14–18 relates one such incident:

> And when they came to the multitude, a man came up to Him, falling on his knees before Him, and saying, "Lord, have mercy on my son, for he is a lunatic, and is very ill; for he often falls into the fire, and often into the water. And I brought him to Your disciples, and they could not cure him." And Jesus answered and said, "O unbelieving and perverted generation, how long shall I be with you? How long shall I put up with you? Bring him here to Me." And Jesus rebuked him, and the demon came out of him, and the boy was cured at once.

Mark 1:32–34 yields another insight into Jesus' amazing power over demons:

> And when evening had come, after the sun had set, they began bringing to Him all who were ill and those who were demon-possessed. And the whole city had gathered at the door. And He healed many who were ill with various diseases, and cast out many demons; and He was not permitting the demons to speak, because they knew who He was.

Not only did Jesus have the authority to cast out demons, but He also had such absolute control over them that He could forbid them to speak. Mark 5:1–13 describes one of the most terrifying examples of demon possession in all of Scripture:

> And they came to the other side of the sea, into the country of the Gerasenes. And when He had come out of the boat, immediately a man from the tombs with an unclean spirit met Him, and he had his dwelling among the tombs. And no one was able to bind him anymore, even with a chain; because he had often been bound with shackles and chains, and the chains had been torn apart by him, and the shackles broken in pieces, and no one was strong enough to subdue him. And constantly night and day, among the tombs and in the mountains, he was crying out and gashing himself with stones. And seeing Jesus from a distance, he ran up and bowed down before Him; and crying out with a loud voice, he said, "What do I have to do with You, Jesus, Son of the Most High God? I implore You by God, do not torment me!" For He had been saying to him, "Come out of the man, you unclean spirit!" And He was asking him, "What is your name?" And he said to Him, "My name is Legion; for we are many." And he began to entreat Him earnestly not to send them out of the country. Now there was a big herd of swine feeding there on the mountain. And the demons entreated Him, saying, "Send us into the swine so that we may enter them." And He gave them permission. And coming out, the unclean spirits entered the swine; and the herd rushed down the steep bank into the sea, about two thousand of them; and they were drowned in the sea.

The cure of even this individual, infested with numerous demons, posed no difficulty for Jesus. He commanded them to enter the pigs, so that all watching would have no doubt that they obeyed Him. It was a dramatic display of His power over the spiritual forces of evil.

The demons exhibited a terror that stems from their knowledge of their ultimate fate. Luke 4:33–35 relates that

> there was a man in the synagogue possessed by the spirit of an unclean demon, and he cried out with a loud voice, "Ha! What do we have to do with You, Jesus of Nazareth? Have You come to destroy us? I know who You are—the Holy One of God!" And Jesus rebuked him, saying, "Be quiet and come out of him!" And when the demon had thrown him down in their midst, he came out of him without doing him any harm.

Aware of the fate that awaited him—eternal destruction in hell—the demon fearfully asked if this was the time and if Jesus was going to destroy him on the spot (cf. Matt. 8:29). Interestingly, while men through the centuries have debated Jesus' identity, the demons have no such doubts. This fallen angel knew that he was in the presence of "the Holy One of God," and such awareness terrified him (cf. James 2:19). It should be noted that in this instance, as in all the instances recorded in the gospels, there was no struggle. Jesus spoke, and the demons instantly acquiesced.

Jesus also extended His power over demons by delegating it to some of His followers. During His earthly ministry, He sent out seventy of His disciples to proclaim the gospel of the kingdom. When they returned they exclaimed, "Lord, even the demons are subject to us in Your name" (Luke 10:17). The twelve were given power over demons (cf. Matt. 10:8). Acts 5:16 records that "the people from the cities in the vicinity of Jerusalem were coming together, bringing people who were sick or afflicted with unclean spirits; and they were all being healed" by the apostles. Through the ministry of Philip the evangelist, "in the case of many who had unclean spirits, they were coming out of them shouting with a loud voice" (Acts 8:7). Encountering a demon-possessed girl in Philippi, "Paul was greatly annoyed, and turned and said to the spirit, 'I command you in the name of Jesus Christ to come out of her!' And it came out at that very moment" (Acts 16:18).

Such miraculous power over demons was unique to a few individuals during the apostolic age, being basically one of the "signs and wonders and miracles" that constituted "the signs of a true apostle" (2 Cor. 12:12). By the time Hebrews was written, its author spoke of such miraculous signs in the past tense:

> How shall we escape if we neglect so great a salvation? After it was at the first spoken through the Lord, it was confirmed to us by those who heard, God also bearing witness with them, both by signs and wonders and by various miracles and by gifts of the Holy Spirit according to His own will. (Heb. 2:3–4)

The fascination, seen today in some Christian circles, with exorcising demons is without biblical support and dangerous. The assumption that a believer has authority to command demons and Satan, or to bind them, is fiction. Even Michael the archangel would not be so bold (cf. Jude 9). And reducing the Christian life to a demon hunt obviates believers' biblically mandated responsibility to pursue true sanctification by holiness and godly living.

Nowhere in the epistles is there any promise to Christians that they can deliver the unsaved from demons. Nor is there any command for believers to exorcise demons out of each other. Nowhere in Scripture are demons ever cast out of believers. Since there is no evidence in

Scripture that demons reside in Christians, it is not surprising that there is no record of demons ever being cast out of believers. Indeed, the definitive New Testament passage on spiritual warfare (Eph. 6:10–17) emphasizes the believer's victory through the means of a righteous, holy life armed with the Word. (For further discussion of these issues, see my books *Charismatic Chaos* [Grand Rapids: Zondervan, 1992] and, particularly, *How to Meet the Enemy* [Wheaton, Ill: Victor, 1992].)

The weapon Christians are to wield in their personal battle with the forces of darkness is "the sword of the Spirit, which is the word of God" (Eph. 6:17). As it is through the power of the Word alone that the intellectual fortresses of Satan fall, so Christians by that truth can successfully battle Satan and his demon hosts. Even the book of Acts, which records the apostles' evangelistic ministry, emphasizes the preaching of the Word over signs, wonders, miracles, and exorcisms. And in Acts 6:4 the apostles defined the priorities of their ministry in the church: "We will devote ourselves to prayer, and to the ministry of the word."

This rich text shows how powerfully the Word of God dominated the city of Ephesus. Verse 20 summarizes the passage: "So the word of the Lord was growing mightily and prevailing." The power of God's Word is evident through its proclamation, confirmation, competition, conviction, and domination.

PROCLAMATION

And he entered the synagogue and continued speaking out boldly for three months, reasoning and persuading them about the kingdom of God. But when some were becoming hardened and disobedient, speaking evil of the Way before the multitude, he withdrew from them and took away the disciples, reasoning daily in the school of Tyrannus. And this took place for two years, so that all who lived in Asia heard the word of the Lord, both Jews and Greeks. (19:8–10)

The first step in unleashing the power of the Word is to proclaim it, and Paul did just that. He had established cordial relationships with the Ephesian Jews on his previous, brief visit (18:19–21). Returning to Ephesus, he found the door still open, so **he entered the synagogue and continued speaking out boldly for three months, reasoning and persuading them about the kingdom of God.** The imperfect tense of *parrēsiazomai* (**speaking out boldly**) emphasizes the continual nature of Paul's proclamation. Boldness was a hallmark of apostolic preaching (Acts 4:29) and of Paul's desire for ministry (Eph. 6:19). The content of his preaching was uncompromisingly confrontational; he held back nothing out of fear of rejection or hostility. Paul spent **three months** boldly proclaiming the gospel in the **synagogue,** his longest stretch in any synagogue, except possibly at Corinth. During that time, Paul was **reasoning** with the Jews **and persuading them about the kingdom of God. Reasoning** is from *dialegomai,* from which the English word *dialogue* derives. Paul did not merely lecture, but again was responding to their questions and challenges. **Persuading** is the present participle of *peithō,* and means "to convince by argument" (cf. Acts 28:23). He was obviously in the midst of a whole congregation of unbelieving Jews. Yet he unflinchingly and directly challenged their whole religious system, calling them to repent and believe in Jesus as their Messiah and God.

Preaching the **kingdom of God** encompasses more than the eschatological thousand-year reign of Christ on the earth. To teach the kingdom of God is to teach the things concerning Christ and salvation (cf. Acts 28:31) and righteousness (Rom. 14:17). It is to teach how to enter the sphere of salvation and live there in communion with God.

Although Paul was able to minister in the synagogue for an unusually long time, the inevitable finally happened. **Some** of the Jews became **hardened and disobedient, speaking evil of the Way before the multitude. Hardened** is from *sklērunō,* a word always used in the New Testament to speak of a heart hardened against God (Rom. 9:18; Heb. 3:8, 13, 15; 4:7). The imperfect tense of the verb shows that the hardening was a process. Over the course of Paul's three-month ministry in the Ephesian synagogue, some hearts gradually hardened against the gospel. When the truth is rejected repeatedly, it hardens the heart, and the message of salvation becomes an "aroma from death to death" (2 Cor. 2:16). Their refusing to repent and believe the gospel is classified as being **disobedient,** since belief is a divine command (Acts 17:30; cf. Mark 1:15).

The outward manifestation of their hardened inward disobedience manifested itself not only in a refusal to repent and believe but also in **speaking evil of the Way.** As the capitalization in the *New American Standard Bible* text suggests, **the Way** was an early title for Christianity (cf. Acts 9:2; 19:23; 24:14, 22). Paul's opponents began an aggressive public campaign of slander **before the multitude** in an attempt to destroy the apostle's influence with them.

Realizing nothing was to be gained by remaining in the synagogue any longer, Paul **withdrew from** there **and took away the disciples** (those who had repented and confessed Jesus as Lord), and began **reasoning daily in the school of Tyrannus. Tyrannus** may have been the owner of the lecture hall or a philosopher who taught there. If he was a teacher, his name, which means "our tyrant," may be a nickname given him by his students. Some New Testament manuscripts add that Paul taught in that school from the fifth to the tenth hours (11:00 A.M. to 4:00 P.M.), perhaps the time when Tyrannus would have dismissed his students for the midday rest. F. F. Bruce, for example, wrote:

> Tyrannus no doubt held his classes in the early morning hours. Public activity ceased in the cities of Ionia for several hours at 11 A.M., and ... more people would be asleep at 1 P.M. than at 1 A.M. But Paul, after spending the early hours of the day at his tent-making (cf. Ch. 20:34), devoted the hours of burden and heat to his more important and more exhausting business, and must have infected his hearers with his own energy and zeal, so that they were willing to sacrifice their siesta for the sake of listening to Paul. (*The Book of the Acts*, The New International Commentary on the New Testament [Grand Rapids: Eerdmans, 1971], 388–89)

Paul did not go off duty at 4:00 P.M. but continued ministering well into the evening hours (Acts 20:31), no doubt instructing from house to house.

Paul maintained this grueling schedule **for two years**, with the result **that all who lived in Asia heard the word of the Lord, both Jews and Greeks**. Without (as far as is known) ever leaving Ephesus, Paul, through his converts, evangelized the entire province of **Asia** (cf. v. 26). During this time, the churches at Colossae and Hierapolis, and probably also the seven churches of Revelation 2–3, were founded. Paul's very effective strategy for evangelism was to teach the Word, make disciples, and let them spread the gospel. Spiritually reproducing Christians are the heart of any successful method of evangelism.

So the kingdom of darkness was effectively assaulted by the proclamation of the gospel.

CONFIRMATION

And God was performing extraordinary miracles by the hands of Paul, so that handkerchiefs or aprons were even carried from his body to the sick, and the diseases left them and the evil spirits went out. (19:11–12)

To provide incontrovertible evidence that the message was true, God **was performing extraordinary miracles by the hands of Paul.** Such miraculous confirmation was a standard feature of apostolic preaching. In the absence of a written New Testament by which to measure someone's teaching, God used signs and wonders to authenticate His message (2 Cor. 12:12; Heb. 2:3–4; cf. Acts 2:22).

Steeped in superstition and failing to understand that Paul was merely the human channel for God's power, the Ephesians did some amazing things. The **handkerchiefs,** or sweatbands, and **aprons** Paul wore during his tentmaking labor **were even carried from his body to the sick.** The idea that healing power could be so magically transmitted was prevalent in the ancient world (cf. Matt. 9:21; Acts 5:15). That **the diseases left them and the evil spirits went out** through those means does not commend that method (as some would-be healers would have people believe). It must instead be viewed as nothing more than God's accommodation to the mentality of those people. And it further proved that Paul was from God and thus spoke for God. As a doctor, Luke carefully distinguishes between **diseases** and afflictions caused by **evil spirits** to make clear that not all illness stems from demonic causes.

The miracles God performed through Paul were essential to convince the Ephesians that he was from God. Impressed with him as the messenger of God, their hearts were prepared to hear his message of salvation.

COMPETITION

But also some of the Jewish exorcists, who went from place to place, attempted to name over those who had the evil spirits the name of the Lord Jesus, saying, "I adjure you by Jesus whom Paul preaches." And seven sons of one Sceva, a Jewish chief priest, were doing this. And the evil spirit answered and said to them, "I recognize Jesus, and I know about Paul, but who are you?" And the man, in whom was the evil spirit, leaped on them and subdued all of them and overpowered them, so that they fled out of that house naked and wounded. (19:13–16)

Seeing the potency of the name of Jesus, **some of the** itinerant **Jewish exorcists** decided to add it to their repertoire of incantations. As John Polhill explains,

> Ancient magicians were syncretists and would borrow terms from any religion that sounded sufficiently strange to be deemed effective. These Jewish exorcists of Ephesus were only plying their trade. Paul's "spell" in Jesus' name seemed effective for him, so they gave it a try. (*The New American Commentary: Acts* [Nashville: Broadman, 1992], 403)

Like Simon Magus (Acts 8), the **exorcists** thought the power of the Spirit operative in the apostles was no more than their own fakery or demonic activity, and could be manipulated for their own ends. Accordingly, they **attempted to name over those who had the evil spirits the name of the Lord Jesus, saying, "I adjure you by Jesus whom Paul preaches."** These, of course, were not Christian Jews, since they only knew Jesus as the one **whom Paul preaches.** *Exorkistōn* (**exorcists**) appears only here in the New Testament. It derives from a root word meaning "to bind with an oath"; ancient exorcists attempted to expel demons by invoking the name of a more powerful spirit being. Exorcists were common in the ancient world, even among the Jews (Matt. 12:27; Acts 13:6). Their fanciful spells and ritual formulas were very different from the absolute authority delegated by Christ and exercised by the apostles.

The name of Jesus is no magical charm to be used by whoever wants to use it, as these **exorcists** soon learned the hard way. They addressed the demon with the incantation **"I adjure you by Jesus whom Paul preaches."** Unlike Paul, however, they did not know the Person they named nor have His power delegated to them. Luke adds the parenthetical note that **seven sons of one Sceva, a Jewish chief priest, were doing this.** Nothing further is known of **Sceva,** and there was never a **Jewish** high **priest** by that name. Either he was a member of one of the high priestly families, or, more likely, he appropriated the title to impress his clients. That is not unlike those charlatans in our own day who falsely claim to be doctors or professors.

Though they may have fooled the gullible Ephesians, these would-be exorcists could not fool the demon. He knew that they did not have any power over him. Speaking through the voice of his human victim, **the evil spirit** scornfully **said to them, "I recognize Jesus, and I know about Paul, but who are you?"** He knew very well who Jesus was, and was aware that Paul had received supernatural power over the demonic realm from Him. By demanding of the exorcists **"who are you?"** the demon challenged their authority over him.

The exorcists, of course, had neither the right to use the name of Jesus nor the power to command demons, so the demon attacked them viciously. With the supernatural strength that sometimes accompanied demon possession (cf. Mark 5:3–4), **the man, in whom was the evil spirit, leaped on them and subdued all** seven **of them and overpowered them, so that they fled out of that house naked and wounded.** Battered, defrocked, and humiliated, they beat a hasty and ignominious retreat. They were no doubt shocked that their attempted exorcism had so utterly failed. Presumably, Satan had allowed them in the past to appear to succeed. It can be helpful to remember that Satan's kingdom is inconsistent and random. Even his demons do not act consistently, and they form a house divided against itself, which cannot stand (Matt. 12:25–26). Here, however, God overruled the confused efforts of these fools for his own purposes.

This story vividly illustrates the danger for any who assume messianic or apostolic power over demons and Satan and thus carelessly meddle in the supernatural realm.

Satan would have wished these sons of Sceva to succeed, so that the domain of darkness could compete with God, as Pharaoh's magicians did with Moses (Ex. 7:22). But the attempt to provide competition for the Word was thwarted. In fact, it completely backfired and only brought greater conviction among the Ephesians of the power of Jesus' name and the truth of Paul's preaching.

CONVICTION

And this became known to all, both Jews and Greeks, who lived in Ephesus; and fear fell upon them all and the name of the Lord Jesus was being magnified. Many also of those who had believed kept coming, confessing and disclosing their practices. And many of those who practiced magic brought their books together and began burning them in the sight of all; and they counted up the price of them and found it fifty thousand pieces of silver. (19:17–19)

The would-be exorcists' fate soon **became known to all, both Jews and Greeks, who lived in Ephesus.** As a result, **fear fell upon them all and the name of the Lord Jesus was being magnified.** The tremendous reality of the name (encompassing all that is true about Him) of Jesus was evident to everyone. They recognized that He was no one to trifle with but someone before whom to bow in faith. Shaken by what had happened, and recognizing the futility of pagan magic, **many also of those who had believed kept coming, confessing and disclosing their practices.** Thus they displayed the turning from sin that marks genuine repentance. *Praxeis* (**practices**) here refers to their secret magic spells, which were generally believed to be rendered useless if they were divulged. They turned from their magic as the Thessalonians turned from their idols (1 Thess. 1:9).

Not content with merely ruining their spells by revealing them, **many of those who practiced magic brought their books together and began burning them in the sight of all; and they counted up the price of them and found it fifty thousand pieces of silver.** They destroyed all their magic paraphernalia publicly, **in the sight of all.** The staggering value of it, noted as **fifty thousand pieces of silver** (equivalent to 50,000 days' wages for an average laborer), was given to indicate Ephesus's widespread involvement in the magic arts.

DOMINATION

So the word of the Lord was growing mightily and prevailing.
(19:20)

Luke's brief summary statement (cf. Acts 6:7; 12:24) pulls the passage together and emphasizes the dominant position the Word of God achieved in Ephesus. All the satanic forces of the occult and magic arrayed against the Word could not overpower it. The bold preaching of the gospel, the confirming miracles, the defeat of the exorcists, the resultant awe and respect for the name of Jesus, and the public repudiation of the magical arts demonstrated the invincible might of God's Word.

The Riot at Ephesus (Acts 19:21–41)

14

Now after these things were finished, Paul purposed in the spirit to go to Jerusalem after he had passed through Macedonia and Achaia, saying, "After I have been there, I must also see Rome." And having sent into Macedonia two of those who ministered to him, Timothy and Erastus, he himself stayed in Asia for a while. And about that time there arose no small disturbance concerning the Way. For a certain man named Demetrius, a silversmith, who made silver shrines of Artemis, was bringing no little business to the craftsmen; these he gathered together with the workmen of similar trades, and said, "Men, you know that our prosperity depends upon this business. And you see and hear that not only in Ephesus, but in almost all of Asia, this Paul has persuaded and turned away a considerable number of people, saying that gods made with hands are no gods at all. And not only is there danger that this trade of ours fall into disrepute, but also that the temple of the great goddess Artemis be regarded as worthless and that she whom all of Asia and the world worship should even be dethroned from her magnificence." And when they heard this and were filled with rage, they began crying out, saying, "Great is Artemis of the Ephesians!" And the city was filled with the confusion, and they rushed with one accord into the theater, dragging along Gaius and Aristarchus, Paul's traveling companions from Macedonia. And when Paul wanted to go into the assembly, the disciples would not let him. And also some of the Asiarchs who were friends of his sent to him and repeatedly urged him not to venture into the theater. So then, some were shouting one thing and some another, for the assembly was in confusion, and the majority did not know for what cause they had come together. And some of the crowd concluded it was Alexander, since the Jews had put him forward; and having motioned with his hand, Alexander was intending to make a defense to the assembly. But when they recognized that he was a Jew, a single outcry arose from them all as they shouted for about two hours, "Great is Artemis of the Ephesians!" And after quieting the multitude, the town clerk said, "Men of Ephesus, what man is there after all who does not know that the city of the Ephesians is guardian of the temple of the great Artemis, and of the image which fell down from heaven? Since then these are undeniable facts, you ought to keep calm and to do nothing rash. For you have brought these men here who are neither robbers of temples nor blasphemers of our goddess. So then, if Demetrius and the craftsmen who are with him have a complaint against any man, the courts are in session and proconsuls are available; let them bring charges against one another. But if you want anything beyond this, it shall be settled in the lawful assembly. For indeed we are in danger of being accused of a riot in connection with today's affair, since there is no real cause for it; and in this connection we shall be unable to account for this disorderly gathering." And after saying this he dismissed the assembly. (19:21–41)

One lesson that history teaches is the paradoxical truth that the church thrives under persecution. Effectiveness and persecution usually go hand in hand, since an effective church is a bold church, and a bold church is often a church made strong through suffering. The Lord Jesus Christ called His church to be salt and light in the world (Matt. 5:13–14); salt stings when rubbed in wounds, and light reveals the evil deeds done in darkness. Both can provoke a hostile reaction.

The early church faced persecution from its inception. In Jerusalem, that persecution came from organized religion (Acts 4:1–31; 5:17–42; 6:9–15; 8:1–4). In Antioch, it stemmed from prejudice and envy (Acts 13:44–52). In Lystra, it was the result of ignorant paganism (Acts 14:8–19). In Philippi, it was the reaction to a victory over the demonic realm (Acts 16:16–40). In Thessalonica, it came from an unruly mob, urged on by jealous religious leaders (Acts 17:1–9). In Athens, the gospel faced the opposition of worldly philosophy (Acts 17:16–34). In Corinth, as in Jerusalem, it came from Judaism, this time in a Roman court (Acts 18:5–17). Wherever the church boldly and faithfully proclaims the gospel it faces Satanic opposition. It comes as no surprise, then, that persecution also arose in Ephesus, stemming from a pseudo-religious materialism. Hardened hearts, hypocrisy, and hatred energized the opposition to the gospel.

Before describing the chaos of the riot, Luke gives a brief note on Paul's plans. As his three-year ministry in Ephesus drew to a close, the apostle made plans **to go to Jerusalem** by way of **Macedonia** and **Achaia.** His itinerary seems puzzling, since Macedonia and Achaia were in the opposite direction from Jerusalem. Further, he had just ministered in those regions before coming to Ephesus (18:23). But Paul had a definite plan in mind, one that reveals his deep concern for the unity of the church.

Many in the church at Jerusalem were poor and in need of sustained financial assistance. To meet that need, Paul wanted to take to Jerusalem with him a love offering from the largely Gentile churches he had founded. Before returning to Jerusalem, he revisited Macedonia and Achaia to collect that offering (Rom. 15:25–27; 1 Cor. 16:1–4; 2 Cor. 8–9). By contributing to the financial needs of the Jewish believers at Jerusalem, those Gentiles would emphasize the church's unity (cf. 1 Cor. 12:26), while confirming in a very practical way their love for their Jewish brethren. James 2:15–16 describes the importance of such care:

> If a brother or sister is without clothing and in need of daily food, and one of you says to them, "Go in peace, be warmed and be filled," and yet you do not give them what is necessary for their body, what use is that?

Jerusalem was not Paul's ultimate goal, however. **"After I have been there,"** he declared, **"I must also see Rome."** In keeping with his desire "to preach the gospel, not where Christ was already named, that I might not build upon another man's foundation" (Rom. 15:20), he had not yet visited the imperial capital. Yet, so strategic was the church there that he could not stay away indefinitely. As he explained to the members there, "I long to see you in order that I may impart some spiritual gift to you, that you may be established" (Rom. 1:11).

But even mighty Rome was merely a stop on the way to somewhere else for Paul. In Romans 15:22–24 he wrote:

> I have often been hindered from coming to you; but now, with no further place for me in these regions, and since I have had for many years

a longing to come to you whenever I go to Spain—for I hope to see you in passing, and to be helped on my way there by you, when I have first enjoyed your company for a while.

Since setting out from Antioch on his first missionary journey, Paul had been extending his ministry farther and farther west. Spain was yet westward from Rome. It was also home to some of the most influential people in the Roman Empire, such as the noted philosopher Seneca. Paul, the master strategist, was planning to reach Spain with the gospel.

Paul's brief expression of his desire to visit Rome marks a turning point in Acts. From this point until the end of the book, the target in the apostle's mind is Rome. He would eventually get there, although not by the means he envisioned.

In the meantime, Paul **sent into Macedonia two of those who ministered to him, Timothy and Erastus**, to pave the way for his own return and for the collection. **Timothy**, Paul's friend, disciple, co-worker, and beloved spiritual son, had been ministering in Corinth (18:5) before joining Paul in Ephesus at some unspecified time. Nothing further is known of **Erastus** or whether he is the same individual mentioned in Romans 16:23 or 2 Timothy 4:20. Paul **himself,** however, **stayed in Asia for a while.** He delayed all his travel plans temporarily because, as he wrote at this time to the Corinthians, "I shall remain in Ephesus until Pentecost; for a wide door for effective service has opened to me, and there are many adversaries" (1 Cor. 16:8–9). Those adversaries soon made themselves known, as a riot erupted in Ephesus over the success of Paul's ministry. Luke's account of that riot relates its causes, characteristics, and calming.

THE CAUSES OF THE RIOT

And about that time there arose no small disturbance concerning the Way. For a certain man named Demetrius, a silversmith, who made silver shrines of Artemis, was bringing no little business to the craftsmen; these he gathered together with the workmen of similar trades, and said, "Men, you know that our prosperity depends upon this business. And you see and hear that not only in Ephesus, but in almost all of Asia, this Paul has persuaded and turned away a considerable number of people, saying that gods made with hands are no gods at all. And not only is there danger that this trade of ours fall into disrepute, but also that the temple of the great goddess Artemis be regarded as worthless and that she whom all of Asia and the world worship should even be dethroned from her magnificence." (19:23–27)

Luke informs us that **about that time**—before Paul left Ephesus as he planned (cf. vv. 21–22)—**there arose no small disturbance concerning the Way.** As noted in chapter 13 of this volume, **the Way** was an early title for the Christian faith (cf. Acts 9:2; 19:9; 22:4; 24:14, 22), probably deriving from Jesus' description of Himself as "the way, and the truth, and the life" (John 14:6).

The unseen cause of the riot was the satanic realm's antagonism to the prevailing of the Word (19:20). Demons stirred up human agents to oppose the gospel, which was spreading rapidly throughout the province of Asia (v. 26; cf. v. 10). The instigator of the riot was **a certain man named Demetrius, a silversmith.** Demetrius was a common name, and there is no reason to assume that he is the individual mentioned in 3 John 12. His business was making **silver shrines of** the goddess **Artemis** (probably depicting her seated in the temple). The shrines served as household idols and were presented at the temple as votive offerings. Archaeologists have unearthed numerous terra cotta shrines, but no silver ones. The latter were most likely melted down for their silver content, probably even by the temple priests.

Demetrius was a prominent businessman, **bringing no little business to the craftsmen** to whom he contracted out work. He may even have been the head of the silversmith's guild. The trade they were involved in was an important and lucrative one. The worship of the goddess Artemis was widespread throughout the Roman Empire. There appears to have been at least thirty-three shrines to Artemis throughout the Roman Empire, making it perhaps the most popular cult of all. Ephesus, site of the impressive Temple of Artemis (one of the Seven Wonders of the Ancient World), was the center of Artemis worship. Pilgrims flocked to the city, especially during the annual festival to Artemis held each spring. The trade generated by this influx of pilgrims was an essential part of the Ephesian economy. It is likely that the riot described in this passage took place during that festival, at the peak season for the sale of the paraphernalia of Artemis.

Alarmed at the spread of the Christian gospel and its rejection of idol worship, Demetrius **gathered together** his fellow silversmiths **with the workmen of similar trades.** Although he would later mention more noble issues, Demetrius began his speech by bluntly stating his real concern: **"Men, you know that our prosperity depends upon this business."** The gospel was threatening their business, and they were compelled to take action. Demetrius then reminded them of the extent of the threat posed by the Christian faith and its leading spokesman: **You see and hear that not only in Ephesus, but in almost all of Asia, this Paul has persuaded and turned away a considerable number of people, saying that gods made with hands are no gods at all.** The Christian preachers were denying the reality of **gods made with hands** (cf. 1 Cor. 8:4–6), and they had already persuaded **a considerable number of people** of that truth. Like the Thessalonians, the Ephesians were turning from idols to serve the "living and true God" (1 Thess. 1:9).

Demetrius, a bitter opponent of the Christian faith, was forced to confess that the preaching of the gospel was successful. Significantly, he could come up with no legitimate charge of wrongdoing by the Christians (cf. v. 37). His concern was purely financial; as more people became Christians, the market for the shrines would shrink. The crafts-men's thriving business was thus in jeopardy.

What caused the success of the gospel in Ephesus? First, the powerful presence and diligent, relentless labor of one man totally com-mitted to Jesus Christ. Paul was an example of the influence one man can have on a city, province, state, or nation. The key to his influence was not a charismatic personality, a clever marketing strategy, or political influence. In his farewell speech to the elders of the Ephesian church, Paul reminded them, "I did not shrink from declaring to you the whole purpose of God. . . . night and day for a period of three years I did not cease to admonish each one with tears" (Acts 20:27, 31). Paul's influence flowed from his devotion to his Lord and to the Word of truth.

A second factor in the gospel's success was a purged church. Acts 19:18–19 records that

> many also of those who had believed [at Ephesus] kept coming, con-fessing and disclosing their practices. And many of those who prac-ticed magic brought their books together and began burning them in the sight of all; and they counted up the price of them and found it fifty thousand pieces of silver.

Because of the purging, the church was clean and "the word of the Lord was growing mightily and prevailing" (19:20).

A third reason for the success of the gospel was the church's use of proper spiritual means. The Ephesian believers did not lobby the city authorities, picket the silversmiths' shops, or organize demonstrations against Artemis worship. They did not try to be popular. They preached and lived out the message and let the power of their changed lives con-front and push out the old ways.

Demetrius, then, began his speech by playing on his hearers' fears of financial ruin, warning of the **danger that** their **trade fall into disrepute.** How typical of a depraved mind to focus on crass material-ism when eternal souls are at stake! The Lord Jesus Christ exposed the folly of that type of thinking when He asked, "What does it profit a man to gain the whole world, and forfeit his soul? For what shall a man give in exchange for his soul" (Mark 8:36–37)? Hell will be filled with people who, like Judas, loved money more than God.

Moving up a level from personal financial considerations, Demetrius next appealed to their religious devotion. He raised the disturbing possibility that **the temple of the great goddess Artemis** might come to **be regarded as worthless.** The Christians, he warned, were challenging the majesty of Artemis.

Finally, Demetrius appealed directly to the issue of income. If **she whom all of Asia and the world** worshiped were to be **dethroned from her magnificence,** Ephesus would suffer. The temple of Artemis was famous throughout the Roman world, and it had been built with gifts from many rulers. Anything that tarnished Artemis's reputation would lower Ephesus's status, hinder civic pride, and disastrously cripple the city's economy. Loyalty to Ephesus demanded that the craftsmen oppose the new religion that threatened to undermine the city's claim to fame and source of revenue.

THE CHARACTERISTICS OF THE RIOT

And when they heard this and were filled with rage, they began crying out, saying, "Great is Artemis of the Ephesians!" And the city was filled with the confusion, and they rushed with one accord into the theater, dragging along Gaius and Aristarchus, Paul's traveling companions from Macedonia. And when Paul wanted to go into the assembly, the disciples would not let him. And also some of the Asiarchs who were friends of his sent to him and repeatedly urged him not to venture into the theater. So then, some were shouting one thing and some another, for the assembly was in confusion, and the majority did not know for what cause they had come together. And some of the crowd concluded it was Alexander, since the Jews had put him forward; and having motioned with his hand, Alexander was intending to make a defense to the assembly. But when they recognized that he was a Jew, a single outcry arose from them all as they shouted for about two hours, "Great is Artemis of the Ephesians!" (19:28–34)

The specter of financial disaster, the challenge to their fervently held religious beliefs, and the threat to their civic pride were too much for the crowd to bear. **When they heard** Demetrius's speech, they **were filled with rage,** and **began crying out, saying, "Great is Artemis of the Ephesians!"** Demetrius had accomplished his goal and whipped the crowd into a frenzy. Inflamed by his incendiary speech, the people surged into the streets, invoking the name of their goddess. Like the Chaldeans of Jeremiah's day, they were "mad over fearsome idols" (Jer. 50:38).

The infuriated crowd manifested the first characteristic of the riot: anger. Such mindless fury typifies riots, when anger runs rampant and violence is indiscriminate. It is also typical of the way the world reacts to Christianity. When the Jewish leaders heard Stephen's masterful speech in defense of Christianity, "they were cut to the quick, and they began gnashing their teeth at him" (Acts 7:54). Similarly, the enraged mob at Philippi "rose up together against [Paul and Silas] and the chief magistrates tore their robes off them, and proceeded to order them to be beaten with rods. And when they had inflicted many blows upon them, they threw them into prison" (Acts 16:22–23). In Jerusalem,

> the Jews from Asia, upon seeing [Paul] in the temple, began to stir up all the multitude and laid hands on him, crying out, "Men of Israel, come to our aid! This is the man who preaches to all men everywhere against our people, and the Law, and this place; and besides he has even brought Greeks into the temple and has defiled this holy place." For they had previously seen Trophimus the Ephesian in the city with him, and they supposed that Paul had brought him into the temple. And all the city was aroused, and the people rushed together; and taking hold of Paul, they dragged him out of the temple; and immediately the doors were shut. And while they were seeking to kill him, a report came up to the commander of the Roman cohort that all Jerusalem was in confusion. (Acts 21:27b–31)

The gospel makes people angry because it confronts them with their false religion and their sin and forces them to recognize the inadequacy of their world view, exposing the emptiness of their lifestyle.

A second characteristic of the riot was confusion. As the frenzied rioters swarmed through Ephesus, **the city was filled with the confusion**, chaos, and disorder they caused. Surging through the main streets, they came down the hill where **they rushed with one accord into the theater,** and seized **Gaius and Aristarchus, Paul's traveling companions from Macedonia.** According to Acts 20:4, Aristarchus was from Thessalonica, a city in Macedonia. That same verse, however, lists **Gaius**'s hometown as Derbe, a city of Galatia. It may be, as some commentators argue, that the plural genitive *Makedonas* ("from Macedonia") was originally a singular. In that case, it would describe only Aristarchus. However Gaius was a common name (cf. 1 Cor. 1:14; 3 John 1), and the one mentioned in 20:4 may be a different individual. **Aristarchus** was a beloved companion of Paul, who would accompany him on his ill-fated voyage to Rome (Acts 27:2) and share his imprisonment in that city (Col. 4:10). He was a Jewish believer, since Paul describes him, along with "Barnabas' cousin Mark" and "Jesus who is called Justus," as "fellow workers for the kingdom of God who are from the circumcision" (Col. 4:10–11). The **theater,** the ruins of which are remarkably preserved today, was the normal place for town meetings to be held. As the largest public building in the city (holding approximately 25,000 people), it was the only place such a large crowd could gather.

When he heard what was happening, **Paul wanted to go into the assembly.** The courageous apostle wanted to charge into the theater to rescue his friends and defend the cause of Christ against Demetrius's charges. Realizing that for Paul to appear before the unruly mob would only endanger his life (and those of his companions), **the disciples would not let him**. Although the apostle did not "consider [his] life of any account as dear to [himself]" (Acts 20:24), the other believers would not allow him to risk his life needlessly (cf. Acts 9:25, 30; 17:10, 14).

Not only did Paul's fellow Christians restrain him, but **also some of the Asiarchs who were friends of his sent to him and repeatedly urged him not to venture into the theater.** The **Asiarchs**

> were members of the noblest and wealthiest families of the province of Asia and were bound together in a league for promoting the cult of the emperor and Rome. . . . Every year an Asiarch was elected for the entire province, and additional Asiarchs were elected for each city that had a temple honoring the emperor. The title was probably borne for life by officers in the league; so in Paul's day there could have been a number of Asiarchs at Ephesus. (Richard N. Longenecker, "The Acts of the Apostles," in Frank E. Gaebelein, ed., *The Expositor's Bible Commentary* [Grand Rapids: Zondervan, 1981], 9:503–4)

Fearing for Paul's safety, the Asiarchs **repeatedly urged him not to venture into the theater.** That such prominent individuals were friendly to Paul is significant. Everett F. Harrison writes:

> The very fact that such men of prominence and wealth were Paul's friends reveals with utmost clearness that they did not regard him as dangerous or as carrying on an unlawful activity. Here is positive proof that the imperial cult (the worship of the Roman emperor) had not yet come to the point of opposing the Christian cause. The action of Gallio (18:14–15) may have been influential in making the officials of the province [the Asiarchs] favorable to Paul. (*Interpreting Acts: The Expanding Church* [Grand Rapids: Zondervan, 1986], 319)

Meanwhile, the situation in the theater was one of complete

chaos: **some were shouting one thing and some another, for the assembly was in confusion.** Then Luke adds with a touch of satire, **the majority did not know for what cause they had come together.** Swept up in mob hysteria, most people in the crowd didn't even understand the issue.

A final characteristic of the riot was the closed-mindedness it produced. According to the NASB translation, **some of the crowd concluded** the cause of the commotion **was Alexander, since the Jews had put him forward.** *Sunbibazō* (**concluded**) can, as the NASB marginal note indicates, be translated "instructed." In that case, the text would be saying that some in the crowd (the Jews) instructed Alexander to speak for them. Climbing onto the stage and **having motioned with his hand, Alexander was intending to make a defense to the assembly.** He may have been a Christian Jew or, more likely, a spokesman for the unbelieving Jews. (Any identification of him with the Alexanders of the pastoral epistles [1 Tim. 1:20; 2 Tim. 4:14] is doubtful, due to the commonness of the name.) In either case, the Jews' purpose for putting **him forward** was the same. Fearing that the riot might turn into a pogrom, they wanted to disassociate themselves from the Christians.

Their attempt, however, backfired. When the mob **recognized that** Alexander **was a Jew, a single outcry arose from them all as they shouted for about two hours, "Great is Artemis of the Ephesians!"** To the pagan crowd, there would have been little difference between Christians and Jews. Both worshiped an invisible God, and both rejected idolatry. The minds of the pagans were closed to what Alexander might have to say. Instead, they drowned him out with their shouts of **"Great is Artemis of the Ephesians!"** Completely out of control, they kept up their screaming **for about two hours.**

THE CALMING OF THE RIOT

And after quieting the multitude, the town clerk said, "Men of Ephesus, what man is there after all who does not know that the city of the Ephesians is guardian of the temple of the great Artemis, and of the image which fell down from heaven? Since then these are undeniable facts, you ought to keep calm and to do nothing rash. For you have brought these men here who are neither robbers of temples nor blasphemers of our goddess. So then, if Demetrius and the craftsmen who are with him have a complaint against any man, the courts are in session and proconsuls are available; let them bring charges against one another. But if you want anything beyond this, it shall be settled in the

lawful assembly. For indeed we are in danger of being accused of a riot in connection with today's affair, since there is no real cause for it; and in this connection we shall be unable to account for this disorderly gathering." And after saying this he dismissed the assembly. (19:35–41)

Finally, after two hours of riotous confusion, order was restored by **the town clerk.** As the city's chief administrative officer (the equivalent of the mayor of a modern city) and liaison between the city council and the Roman authorities, he was Ephesus's leading citizen. As such, he knew the Romans would hold him responsible for what happened. **After quieting the multitude,** he began to address its members: **"Men of Ephesus, what man is there after all who does not know that the city of the Ephesians is guardian of the temple of the great Artemis, and of the image which fell down from heaven?"** He reminded them that it was common knowledge throughout the Roman world that **the city of the Ephesians is guardian of the temple of the great Artemis. The image which fell down from heaven** probably refers to a meteorite. John Polhill notes:

> Meteorites were often associated with the worship of the Mother Goddess [Artemis]. The most famous of these was the sacred stone taken from Pessinus to Rome in 204 B.C. A meteorite also seems to have been associated with the cult of the Taurian Artemis. Although there is no evidence beyond this text for such a sacred stone being connected with the Ephesian cult, it is altogether likely that one existed, given this common association of the mother goddess with a "stone from heaven." (_Acts,_ 413)

The town clerk went on to point out that **since then these are undeniable facts, you ought to keep calm and to do nothing rash.** Nothing the Christian preachers could do, he insisted, could possibly affect their great goddess; Artemis's power was undeniable, and her reputation secure. Although the man was sincere, he was tragically mistaken. Today, no one worships Artemis, yet millions worship the Lord Jesus Christ.

The **town clerk** then turned to a more serious issue and rebuked them. **You have brought these men here who are neither robbers of temples nor blasphemers of our goddess.** Even this pagan official testified to the Christians' character; they were not thieves, nor did they use insulting language. Despite Demetrius's claims, the Christians had not acted improperly.

Having reassured the crowd, he next criticized **Demetrius and**

the craftsmen for sparking the riot. Rather than resorting to mob action, they should have followed the due process of the law. After all, he reminded them, **the courts are in session and proconsuls are available; let them bring charges against one another.** Anything that could not be settled in the courts should **be settled in the lawful assembly.**

The town clerk then concluded his speech with a sobering warning: **For indeed we are in danger of being accused of a riot in connection with today's affair, since there is no real cause for it; and in this connection we shall be unable to account for this disorderly gathering.** Again, he exonerated the Christians, admitting that **there is no real cause** for the **riot.** Consequently, they were **in danger of being accused of a riot** by the Roman government, and they would **be unable to account for this disorderly gathering.** If the Romans investigated the disturbance, the Ephesians would be unable to defend their actions. That could result in the loss of the privileges the Romans had granted them. His arguments were persuasive, and when **he dismissed the assembly** they went quietly. As far as is known, Demetrius and his fellow craftsmen did not pursue the matter any further.

The Ephesian believers weathered the storm of persecution unleashed by Demetrius's speech and the resulting riot. Indeed, the church at Ephesus would play a prominent role in church history for several centuries. So again in Acts, God caused the wrath of men to praise Him (Ps. 76:10).

For the Love of the Church
(Acts 20:1–17)

15

And after the uproar had ceased, Paul sent for the disciples and when he had exhorted them and taken his leave of them, he departed to go to Macedonia. And when he had gone through those districts and had given them much exhortation, he came to Greece. And there he spent three months, and when a plot was formed against him by the Jews as he was about to set sail for Syria, he determined to return through Macedonia. And he was accompanied by Sopater of Berea, the son of Pyrrhus; and by Aristarchus and Secundus of the Thessalonians; and Gaius of Derbe, and Timothy; and Tychicus and Trophimus of Asia. But these had gone on ahead and were waiting for us at Troas. And we sailed from Philippi after the days of Unleavened Bread, and came to them at Troas within five days; and there we stayed seven days. And on the first day of the week, when we were gathered together to break bread, Paul began talking to them, intending to depart the next day, and he prolonged his message until midnight. And there were many lamps in the upper room where we were gathered together. And there was a certain young man named Eutychus sitting on the window sill, sinking into a deep sleep; and as Paul kept on talking, he was overcome by sleep and fell down from the third floor, and was picked up dead. But Paul went down and fell upon him and after embracing him, he said, "Do not be troubled, for his life is in him." And when he had gone back up, and had broken the bread and eaten, he talked with them a long while, until daybreak, and so departed. And they took away the boy alive, and were greatly comforted. But we, going ahead to the ship, set sail for Assos, intending from there to take Paul on board; for thus he had arranged it, intending himself to go by land. And when he met us at Assos, we took him on board and came to Mitylene. And sailing from there, we arrived the following day opposite Chios; and the next day we crossed over to Samos; and the day following we came to Miletus. For Paul had decided to sail past Ephesus in order that he might not have to spend time in Asia; for he was hurrying to be in Jerusalem, if possible, on the day of Pentecost. And from Miletus he sent to Ephesus and called to him the elders of the church. (20:1–17)

If one were to ask the question, "What are the most important qualities of a minister of Jesus Christ?" he would expect to receive a list of several. Skill in preaching and teaching, boldness, and godliness are among the foundational qualities that must be enumerated. Shepherding ability, wise oversight, and the ability to work with people are also crucial.

Behind all those qualities must be love; love for the Lord, love for the truth, and love for the church—not the organization but the people. Such love, flowing from devotion to the Lord Jesus Christ and the Word of God, marks all those who exercise noble leadership in the church.

There have always been dedicated pastors who sacrificed in life and death for the church. It was love for the church that drove the busy Reformers Luther and Calvin to preach constantly to their flocks—not merely on Sundays, but throughout the week. Many Puritan pastors continued to preach the Word after being forbidden to do so by the authorities. They knew they risked being imprisoned (as was John Bunyan), but love for the church compelled them to take that risk. Love for the church consumed the godly nineteenth-century Scottish pastor Robert Murray McCheyne. Ill health could not deter him from his loving service, and, consequently, he died at a young age. It was his love for the church that motivated Charles Spurgeon to speak out against the modernism that was creeping into the evangelical church of his day. During the resulting "Down-Grade Controversy," Spurgeon was sharply criticized for his stand. Some of those close to him deserted him. Yet he refused to back down, although the stress the controversy generated hastened his death.

Church history is replete with examples of those who sacrificially loved the church. Yet no man has ever loved the church more than the apostle Paul. He expressed that love frequently in his letters. To the Philippians he wrote:

> I thank my God in all my remembrance of you, always offering prayer with joy in my every prayer for you all, in view of your participation in the gospel from the first day until now. For I am confident of this very thing, that He who began a good work in you will perfect it until the day of Christ Jesus. For it is only right for me to feel this way about you all, because I have you in my heart. (Phil. 1:3–7)

"You are our letter," he told the Corinthians, "written in our hearts" (2 Cor. 3:2). He also wrote to them, "You are in our hearts to die together and to live together" (2 Cor. 7:3). In 1 Thessalonians 2:7–8, Paul expressed his intimate love for the Thessalonian church:

> We proved to be gentle among you, as a nursing mother tenderly cares for her own children. Having thus a fond affection for you, we were well–pleased to impart to you not only the gospel of God but also our own lives, because you had become very dear to us.

Paul, however, did not merely "love with word or with tongue, but in deed and truth" (1 John 3:18). Jesus said in John 15:13, "Greater love has no one than this, that one lay down his life for his friends." Paul made that ultimate sacrifice, giving his life to serve the church Jesus gave His life to redeem.

Not only did the apostle give his life for the church, but he also endured much suffering for it. He chronicles some of that suffering in 2 Corinthians 11:23–28:

> Are they servants of Christ? (I speak as if insane) I more so; in far more labors, in far more imprisonments, beaten times without number, often in danger of death. Five times I received from the Jews thirty-nine lashes. Three times I was beaten with rods, once I was stoned, three times I was shipwrecked, a night and a day I have spent in the deep. I have been on frequent journeys, in dangers from rivers, dangers from robbers, dangers from my countrymen, dangers from the Gentiles, dangers in the city, dangers in the wilderness, dangers on the sea, dangers among false brethren; I have been in labor and hardship, through many sleepless nights, in hunger and thirst, often without food, in cold and exposure. Apart from such external things, there is the daily pressure upon me of concern for all the churches.

The worst suffering Paul endured was not the physical suffering resulting from being beaten, stoned, or shipwrecked. Far more relentlessly painful was his loving "concern for all the churches" (v. 28). "Who is weak," he exclaims in verse 29, "without my being weak? Who is led into sin without my intense concern?"

When false doctrine threatened the Galatian churches, it caused Paul much anguish. His turbulent emotions are reflected in the disjointed Greek constructions in the book of Galatians. The defections of those he loved and trusted, such as John Mark (Acts 13:13) and Demas (2 Tim. 4:10), wounded him deeply. The chronic sin and mutiny at Corinth depressed him (2 Cor. 7:5–6).

So great was Paul's love for the church that he willingly, even joyfully, suffered for it. "But even if I am being poured out as a drink offering upon the sacrifice and service of your faith," he wrote to the Philippians, "I rejoice and share my joy with you all" (Phil. 2:17). He echoed that same theme in his letter to the Colossians: "Now I rejoice in my sufferings for your sake, and in my flesh I do my share on behalf of His body (which is the church) in filling up that which is lacking in Christ's afflictions" (Col. 1:24).

Acts 20:1–17 does not describe love in the soaring terms of 1 Corinthians 13. In fact, it contains no doctrine or practical exhortation at all. But this simple, straightforward narrative illustrates Paul's love for the church in action (where love is best seen). That love is made visible in his exhortation, giving, persistence, availability, and concern.

EXHORTATION

And after the uproar had ceased, Paul sent for the disciples and when he had exhorted them and taken his leave of them . . . and had given them much exhortation (20:1a, 2b)

Calm returned to Ephesus **after the uproar** (the riot described in 19:23–41) **had ceased.** The word *thorubos* (**uproar**) is a fitting descriptive for those tumultuous events sparked by Demetrius the silversmith. Matthew used it to describe the disturbance that took place during Pilate's trial of Jesus (Matt. 27:24). Luke used it later in Acts to describe the riot that broke out when Paul visited the temple in Jerusalem (21:34). In all three instances the word describes an uncontrollable, hysterical mob.

After such a traumatic event, most men would have been content to escape with their lives. Paul's concern for the church's spiritual security, however, overrode any concern for his personal safety. He could not leave Ephesus until he had **sent for the disciples and exhorted**

them one last time. Paul was well aware, as he would shortly warn the leaders of the Ephesian church (20:29–31), of the serious danger posed by false teachers. He no doubt also was concerned that the Ephesian believers might be intimidated by the threat of further rioting. The cure for both problems was instruction from and exhortation to follow God's Word. Only after charging the Ephesian believers did Paul take **his leave of them** to begin his planned trip to Jerusalem via Macedonia and Achaia (cf. 19:21).

Leaving Ephesus, Paul crossed the Aegean Sea to Macedonia, probably by way of Troas. The main purpose of his journey through Macedonia was to collect an offering for the poor believers at Jerusalem (see the next section). Still, he could not pass up the opportunity to instruct the Macedonian believers. While he was with them he gave them, as he had the Ephesians, **much exhortation.** This biblical counsel and warning formed the content of his preaching to them.

As Paul set out for Jerusalem, he must have had a sense of finality. His third missionary journey had seen opposition reach fever pitch. Almost everywhere he went he had faced violent persecution. He believed that he would not be coming back, that he would never again see the churches of Asia, Macedonia, and Achaia that had become so dear to him (cf. 20:25). (Paul may have visited some of them again after his release from his first Roman imprisonment. However he could not have foreseen that possibility at this time.) It is the measure of his love that Paul remained at Ephesus, exposing himself to further risk. He spent those final hours giving them **much exhortation** with the Word—the source of their life and strength.

Unfortunately, Paul's commitment to proclaim the truth of God is not in vogue today. Preaching that exhorts from the Word no longer holds the central place it held in the early church (Acts 10:42; 13:5, 32; 14:7, 15, 21; 15:35; 16:10; 17:3, 13; 20:25; 28:31). Paul's charge to Timothy to "give attention to the public reading of Scripture, to exhortation and teaching" (1 Tim. 4:13) is too often ignored. (For a discussion of the importance of preaching, see *Acts 1–12*, MacArthur New Testament Commentary [Chicago: Moody, 1994], 48–50.)

The results of downplaying strong, biblical preaching are tragic. When pastors neglect their responsibility for "the equipping of the saints" (Eph. 4:12*a*), then the saints cannot do their "work of service" (Eph. 4:12*b*). As a result, the "building up of the body of Christ" (Eph. 4:12*c*) does not take place. The disastrous consequences include lack of true unity (4:13*a*), imperfect knowledge of Jesus Christ (4:13*b*), and lack of spiritual maturity (4:13*c*), resulting in immature "children" who are "tossed here and there by waves, and carried about by every wind of doctrine, by the trickery of men, by craftiness in deceitful scheming" (4:14).

Why is preaching being minimized? First, because of the widespread assault on the authority of Scripture. Never in the history of the church has the Bible been subjected to the savage attacks it has endured in the last century and a half. Skeptical unbelievers deny the inspiration of the Scriptures, deriding them as the prescientific myths of the Hebrew tribes. They assert that the Bible is rife with gross scientific blunders, historical errors, even moral blemishes.

More subtle attacks have come from those within the church. Some agree with the skeptics that the Bible contains errors, yet claim that it is still authoritative. The absurdity of such a view is obvious,

> for while it is no doubt a mystery that eternal truth is revealed in temporal events and presented in human words, it is sheer unreason to say that this truth is revealed in and through that which is erroneous. (Geoffrey W. Bromiley, "The Authority of Scripture," in Donald Guthrie, J. A. Motyer, Alan M. Stibbs, and Donald J. Wiseman, eds., *The New Bible Commentary: Revised* [Grand Rapids: Eerdmans, 1970], 10)

Others affirm the Bible's inspiration and inerrancy but deny in practice its uniqueness as a source of divine revelation. The claim that God speaks today through prophecies, visions, and dreams denies that the Bible alone contains "the faith which was once for all delivered to the saints" (Jude 3) and "everything pertaining to life and godliness" (2 Pet. 1:3). (For a further discussion of this point, see my books *Charismatic Chaos* [Grand Rapids: Zondervan, 1992], and *Reckless Faith* [Wheaton, Ill.: Crossway, 1994].)

Paul's exhortation was firmly based on the authoritative Scriptures (as were his writings—cf. Rom. 4:3; 9:17; 10:11; 11:2; Gal. 3:8, 22; 4:30; 1 Tim. 5:18). Acts 17:2 notes that "according to Paul's custom, he went to them, and for three Sabbaths reasoned with them from the Scriptures." To the Corinthians he wrote:

> For I delivered to you as of first importance what I also received, that Christ died for our sins according to the Scriptures, and that He was buried, and that He was raised on the third day according to the Scriptures. (1 Cor. 15:3–4)

He instructed the young pastor Timothy to "give attention to the public reading of Scripture, to exhortation and teaching" (1 Tim. 4:13), since "all Scripture is inspired by God and profitable for teaching, for reproof, for correction, for training in righteousness; that the man of God may be adequate, equipped for every good work" (2 Tim. 3:16–17).

The loss of belief in an authoritative Scripture seriously undermines preaching. In fact, there can be no truly biblical preaching if the Bible's authority and singular preeminence are rejected, since that would leave no divine revelation to proclaim. What is left is humanistic rationalism on the one hand or subjective mysticism on the other, both of which are antithetical to biblical preaching. (Biblical preaching is defined in John MacArthur et al., *Rediscovering Expository Preaching* [Dallas, Word, 1992].)

A second contribution to the demise of biblical preaching comes from some who claim to uphold the authority of Scripture. A sad legacy of the fundamentalist and evangelical movements has been those narrow-minded and legalistic pastors who are overbearing, compassionless, and harsh. They abuse the authority of the pulpit. Ignoring Peter's warning against "lording it over those allotted to [their] charge" (1 Pet. 5:3), they have in effect set themselves up as little gods in their churches. They not only exercise abusive authority in the church but often also in their people's private lives, with tragic results. God expects the shepherds of His flock to feed the sheep, not beat them.

The preaching of such men is often bombastic denunciation of those with whom they disagree, or dogmatic declarations of their particular legalistic concerns. They play on their people's emotions, intimidating them into abject fear. Such ungracious pulpitism may have contributed as much to the demise of biblical preaching as the undermining of Scripture's authority.

How pastors and congregations view the ministry hinders sound doctrinal preaching. The apostolic focus of the ministry on "prayer" and "the ministry of the word" (Acts 6:4) can be lost amid the demands placed on pastors. A man who is expected to be visitor, evangelist, counselor, social worker, and administrator of the church schedule will obviously have little time left for long hours of rich study in preparation for preaching. (For a biblical view of pastoral ministry, see John MacArthur, ed., *Rediscovering Pastoral Ministry* [Dallas: Word, 1995].) Personal sin factors, such as laziness and apathy toward study by some pastors, have also contributed to preaching's demise.

But nothing currently contributes more to the decline of biblical preaching than the rise of a market-driven philosophy of ministry. Attempting to be "user-friendly," churches have jettisoned preaching in favor of movies, drama, concerts, the testimonies of Christian superstars, and other forms of entertainment. And no wonder, since preaching the biblical truths of sin, judgment, and God's sovereignty in salvation is decidedly not user-friendly. In a philosophy of ministry where pragmatism reigns supreme, the large crowds drawn by such alternative "worship" services serve to validate them. Such shortsighted thinking, however, misses the point. The problem with churches is not poor attendance but poor spiritual health. And what people need most is not to be entertained, but to be taught the truths of God's Word (2 Tim. 4:1–4). (I critique the market-driven philosophy of ministry that pervades today's church in my book *Ashamed of the Gospel* [Wheaton, Ill.: Crossway, 1993].)

A sure mark of genuine love for the church is selfless, tireless exhortation from the Word of God. Though weary, busy, and persecuted, Paul devoted himself to teaching everywhere he went. His consuming passion, even at the risk of his life, was to see believers brought to spiritual maturity. As he expressed it in Colossians 1:28, "We proclaim Him, admonishing every man and teaching every man with all wisdom, that we may present every man complete in Christ."

GIVING

he departed to go to Macedonia. And when he had gone through those districts (20:1b–2a)

Paul planned to travel from Ephesus to Jerusalem through the Greek **districts** of **Macedonia** (the northern section) and Achaia (the southern section). That itinerary took him in the opposite direction from his ultimate goal of Jerusalem. Paul, however, had a definite purpose in mind—to take up a collection for the poor believers at Jerusalem. He mentions his plans in three of his epistles written at this time—1 Corinthians, 2 Corinthians, and Romans. In 1 Corinthians, written shortly before he left Ephesus (1 Cor. 16:5–8), Paul wrote:

> Now concerning the collection for the saints, as I directed the churches of Galatia, so do you also. On the first day of every week let each one of you put aside and save, as he may prosper, that no collections be made when I come. And when I arrive, whomever you may approve, I shall send them with letters to carry your gift to Jerusalem; and if it is fitting for me to go also, they will go with me. (16:1–4)

In 2 Corinthians, written from Macedonia (2 Cor. 2:12–13; 7:5–6), Paul devotes two entire chapters to the collection (2 Cor. 8–9). In Romans, written from the Achaian city of Corinth (Rom. 16:23; 1 Cor. 1:14), he penned the following:

> But now, I am going to Jerusalem serving the saints. For Macedonia and Achaia have been pleased to make a contribution for the poor among the saints in Jerusalem. Yes, they were pleased to do so, and they are indebted to them. For if the Gentiles have shared in their spiritual

things, they are indebted to minister to them also in material things. Therefore, when I have finished this, and have put my seal on this fruit of theirs, I will go on by way of you to Spain. (15:25–28)

Why was the collection so important to Paul? First, because he had a love for the saints in Jerusalem who were impoverished by persecution. Those believers also carried the burden of the believers who had been pilgrims in Jerusalem when they were saved at Pentecost and then remained and needed provision. Furthermore, the other apostles at Jerusalem had asked him to remember the poor (Gal. 2:10).

To compound the difficulty of the Jerusalem church, the land of Israel had suffered a severe famine (cf. Acts 11:28). Had it not been for the relief efforts organized by the Jewish proselyte Queen Helena of Adiabene (a region in northern Mesopotamia east of Syria), many would have perished. Wealthy believers were selling their property from the start to provide money for the many who were poor (Acts 4:32–37). Such resources were not limitless, but the problem of poverty continued. Help was needed from outside the exhausted resources of the Jerusalem church.

When Paul finally reached Jerusalem with the collection, the Jews, incensed at his presence, tried to kill him. The Romans rescued him, but he was to remain their prisoner for more than two years (Acts 24:27), endure a hazardous sea voyage to Rome, and stand trial before the emperor. The sacrifices Paul willingly endured reveal his great love for the church.

An equally important reason for taking up the collection was Paul's deep concern for the unity of the church. Paul knew that the cultural tensions between Jews and Gentiles posed an ever-present danger to that unity. By generously meeting the needs of the poor Jewish believers at Jerusalem, the Gentiles would affirm their love for them (1 John 3:17; cf. James 2:15–16). That in turn would cement the bond of unity so important to Paul (Rom. 10:12; Gal. 3:28; Col. 3:11).

Clearly, Paul's love for the church was expressed by sacrificial giving. The apostle John expressed the inseparable link between giving and loving in 1 John 3:16–18:

We know love by this, that He laid down His life for us; and we ought to lay down our lives for the brethren. But whoever has the world's goods, and beholds his brother in need and closes his heart against him, how does the love of God abide in him? Little children, let us not love with word or with tongue, but in deed and truth.

PERSISTENCE

And there he spent three months, and when a plot was formed against him by the Jews as he was about to set sail for Syria, he determined to return through Macedonia. And he was accompanied by Sopater of Berea, the son of Pyrrhus; and by Aristarchus and Secundus of the Thessalonians; and Gaius of Derbe, and Timothy; and Tychicus and Trophimus of Asia. But these had gone on ahead and were waiting for us at Troas. And we sailed from Philippi after the days of Unleavened Bread, and came to them at Troas within five days; and there we stayed seven days. (20:3–6)

After **three months** in Achaia (most or all of it spent in Corinth), it was time for Paul to continue his journey. He had intended to catch a ship at Cenchrea (Corinth's port) carrying Jewish pilgrims to Palestine for Passover. However, as he had so often in the past, Paul faced danger from his countrymen (2 Cor. 11:26). When he **was about to set sail for Syria,** he became aware of **a plot** that had been **formed against him by the Jews** of Corinth. They had not forgotten the shocking conversions of the synagogue leaders Crispus (18:8) and Sosthenes (18:17; 1 Cor. 1:1) or their humiliating defeat before the proconsul Gallio (18:12–17). Luke does not record the details of this plot, but Paul would have been an easy target for murder on a small ship—especially one crowded with Jewish pilgrims.

The plot delayed Paul by depriving him of the direct sea route to Syria. Therefore, he **determined to return** to Palestine **through Macedonia.** He would retrace his steps through Achaia north into Macedonia. From there he would cross the Aegean Sea to find another ship in Asia Minor headed toward Israel. That delay and detour cost Paul his opportunity to be in Jerusalem for Passover; all he could hope for now was to arrive in time for Pentecost, fifty days after Passover (20:16).

Paul did not travel alone. **He was accompanied by Sopater of Berea, the son of Pyrrhus; and by Aristarchus and Secundus of the Thessalonians; and Gaius of Derbe, and Timothy; and Tychicus and Trophimus of Asia.** The party apparently separated in Philippi, since Luke notes that those mentioned in verse 4 **had gone on ahead and were waiting for us at Troas.** The use of the pronouns "us" (v. 5) and "we" (v. 6) reveals that Luke was again Paul's traveling companion, rejoining him at Philippi. Luke had apparently remained in that city after Paul and Silas had been forced to leave (as the use of "they" in 17:1 suggests).

Paul's companions came from the Roman provinces in which he

had ministered. They were likely the official representatives of their churches and had taken collections for the church at Jerusalem. **Sopater (Berea)**, and **Aristarchus and Secundus** (Thessalonica) were from Macedonia; **Gaius (Derbe)** and **Timothy** (Lystra, Acts 16:1) from Galatia; and **Tychicus and Trophimus** (both probably from Ephesus, cf. Acts 21:29) from Asia. Luke probably represented Philippi, and Titus Achaia (Corinth, cf. 2 Cor. 8:16–19). The remainder of the party (Paul, Luke, and possibly Titus) **sailed from Philippi after the days of Unleavened Bread** (Passover), **and came to them at Troas within five days.** After celebrating Passover at Philippi, they sailed from Neapolis (Acts 16:11–12) to rejoin their companions **at Troas.** Paul's trip across the Aegean Sea from Troas to Neapolis on the second missionary journey had taken only two days (16:11). This voyage, however, took **five days,** possibly because the winds were against them. Reunited in Troas, the party **stayed** there for **seven days.**

Paul's persistence is another mark of his love for the church. In this passage, he modeled the persistence of love he wrote about in 1 Corinthians 13, where he described it as patient (v. 4), enduring all things (v. 7), and never failing (v. 8). Love relentlessly, persistently pursues the good of others.

AVAILABILITY

And on the first day of the week, when we were gathered together to break bread, Paul began talking to them, intending to depart the next day, and he prolonged his message until midnight. And there were many lamps in the upper room where we were gathered together. And there was a certain young man named Eutychus sitting on the window sill, sinking into a deep sleep; and as Paul kept on talking, he was overcome by sleep and fell down from the third floor, and was picked up dead. But Paul went down and fell upon him and after embracing him, he said, "Do not be troubled, for his life is in him." And when he had gone back up, and had broken the bread and eaten, he talked with them a long while, until daybreak, and so departed. And they took away the boy alive, and were greatly comforted. But we, going ahead to the ship, set sail for Assos, intending from there to take Paul on board; for thus he had arranged it, intending himself to go by land. And when he met us at Assos, we took him on board and came to Mitylene. And sailing from there, we arrived the following day opposite Chios; and the next day we crossed over to Samos; and the day following we came to Miletus. For Paul had decided to sail past Ephesus in order that he might

not have to spend time in Asia; for he was hurrying to be in Jerusalem, if possible, on the day of Pentecost. And from Miletus he sent to Ephesus and called to him the elders of the church. (20:7–17)

This passage is the earliest recorded description of a Christian worship service, and several features are noteworthy. First, the believers **gathered together** for worship not on the Sabbath (Saturday) but on **the first day of the week** (Sunday). Despite the claims of some, Christians are not required to observe the Sabbath, as the following considerations reveal.

First, although a day of rest and worship is demonstrated by God in the creation, the Saturday Sabbath was given to Israel as the sign of the Mosaic Covenant (Ex. 31:16–17; Ezek. 20:12; Neh. 9:14). Since Christians are under the New Covenant (2 Cor. 3:6ff.; Heb. 8), they are not required to observe the sign associated with the Mosaic Covenant.

Second, there is no command in the New Testament for Christians to observe the Sabbath.

Third, even during the Mosaic economy, the Old Testament neither commanded the Gentile nations to observe the Sabbath nor condemned them for failing to do so. That offers further proof that the Sabbath was given to Israel only.

Fourth, there is no record in the Bible of anyone's observing the Sabbath before the time of Moses. Similarly, the first command to keep the Sabbath appears in the law given to Moses at Sinai (Ex. 20:8).

Fifth, the Jerusalem Council (Acts 15) did not impose Sabbath-keeping on the Gentile believers.

Sixth, the apostle Paul warned the Gentiles about many different sins in his epistles but never about breaking the Sabbath.

Seventh, Colossians 2:16–17 describes the Sabbath as a shadow of Christ; the shadow is no longer binding on us since the substance (Christ) has come.

Eighth, in Galatians 4:10–11, Paul rebukes the Galatians for thinking that God expected them to observe special days, such as the Sabbath.

Ninth, Romans 14:5 declares observing the Sabbath to be a matter of personal preference among converted Jews. It was to be tolerated until they became more mature in the understanding of their Christian liberty. Therefore it could not be something God requires believers to do.

Tenth, the book of Acts and the subsequent writings of the early church Fathers make clear that the church from earliest times met for worship on Sunday. For example, the *Epistle of Barnabas*, written at the close of the first century, says:

Your present Sabbaths are not acceptable to Me, but that is which I have made, [namely this,] when, giving rest to all things, I shall make a beginning of the eighth day, that is, a beginning of another world. Wherefore, also, we keep the eighth day with joyfulness, the day also on which Jesus rose again from the dead. (XV; *The Ante-Nicene Fathers* [reprint; Grand Rapids: Eerdmans, 1973], 1:147)

Early in the second century, Ignatius wrote, "Let every friend of Christ keep the Lord's Day as a festival, the resurrection-day, the queen and chief of all the days" (*Epistle to the Magnesians*, IX; *The Ante-Nicene Fathers* [reprint; Grand Rapids: Eerdmans, 1973], 1:63). Later in the second century, Justin Martyr described how Christians of his day worshiped:

On the day called Sunday, all who live in cities or in the country gather together to one place, and the memoirs of the apostles or the writings of the prophets are read, as long as time permits. . . . Sunday is the day on which we all hold our common assembly, because . . . Jesus Christ our Saviour on the same day rose from the dead. (*First Apology*, LXVII; [reprint; Grand Rapids: Eerdmans, 1973], 1:186)

Tertullian, who lived in the late second and early third centuries, referred to Christians as those "to whom Sabbaths are strange" (*On Idolatry*, XIV [reprint; Grand Rapids: Eerdmans, 1973], 3:70).

Luke gives a second feature of early Christian worship by recording the location of the meeting as **the upper room** of a house. New Testament churches met in homes (Rom. 16:5; 1 Cor. 16:19; Col. 4:15; Philem. 2); the earliest known church building dates from the first half of the third century (E. M. Blaiklock, "Dura Europos," in E. M. Blaiklock and R. K. Harrison, eds., *The New International Dictionary of Biblical Archaeology* [Grand Rapids: Zondervan, 1983], 165).

Luke adds that the purpose of the meeting was **to break bread**—to celebrate the Agape (love feast, or common meal—cf. 1 Cor. 11:20–22) and communion. In preparation for that, **Paul began talking to them. Talking** is from *dialegomai*, from which the English word "dialogue" derives. Paul did not stop with preaching; there was discussion, and he answered their questions. Sometimes those questions demanded lengthy explanations, as in this case. Although he was **intending to depart the next day, he prolonged his message until midnight.** Paul was about to leave on a long, difficult journey, yet his love for the church made him available as long as the members needed him. Giving no thought to his own need for rest, he used every available minute to teach the believers at Troas. As verse 11 indicates, Paul kept at it until it was time for him to leave.

Luke was also at the meeting and provides the eyewitness detail in verse 8 that **there were many lamps in the upper room where we were gathered together.** He may have mentioned the lamps to show that the church had nothing to hide from its pagan neighbors. More likely, however, Luke mentions the lamps to help explain why Eutychus fell asleep. The many oil-burning lamps would have added fumes and smoke to the stuffy atmosphere in the room.

Eutychus had found his way to the most advantageous location and was **sitting on the sill** of the open **window,** where the air would be freshest and coolest. Even there, however, he began gradually (as the present tense of the participle *katapheromenos* [**sinking**] indicates) **sinking into a deep sleep.** The fumes, the stuffiness of the crowded room, his youth (the word *pais* ["boy"] in v. 11 suggests he was between seven and fourteen years old), and the lateness of the hour finally took their toll. **As Paul kept on talking, he was overcome by sleep and fell down from the third floor, and was picked up dead.** Luke declares that Eutychus was dead. As a physician (Col. 4:14), he was obviously able to determine that.

The shocking event broke up the meeting, and the stunned believers gathered around Eutychus's body. The tragedy, however, was shortly to be turned to triumph. **Paul went down** with the rest **and fell upon him and after embracing him, he said, "Do not be troubled, for his life is in him."** That Paul **fell upon him**, **embracing him** is reminiscent of Elijah (1 Kings 17:21) and Elisha (2 Kings 4:34). The apostle's statement that **his life is in him** does not mean that Eutychus had not died (cf. v. 9) but that his life had been restored. Accordingly, Paul commanded them to stop being **troubled;** that is, to stop the shock, sorrow, and wailing that must have begun. **Troubled** is from *thorubeō*, the verb form of the word "uproar" in verse 1. It is used to describe such lamenting in Matthew 9:23 and Mark 5:38.

Having taken **away the boy alive,** the believers naturally **were greatly comforted.** The teaching was not over, however, so they all went **back up** to the upper chamber. When they **had broken the bread and eaten,** Paul **talked with them a long while, until daybreak.** After the break for a love feast and Communion service, the apostle continued teaching them through the night. Given the dramatic confirmation of his apostolic authority they had just witnessed, Paul no doubt had their undivided attention.

At daybreak, Paul had to leave. Luke and the others went **ahead to the ship** and **set sail for Assos,** twenty miles from Troas. **There** they planned **to take Paul on board; for thus he had arranged it, intending himself to go by land.** Why Paul chose to walk to Assos is not stated. It is most likely that it gave him more time to instruct the disciples from Troas who accompanied him.

Paul's selfless love for the church is notably clear. He was available to minister for an entire night and through a twenty-mile walk the next morning. No sacrifice was too great for the apostle to make for the building up of the saints. He was tirelessly available to his beloved people.

Luke further demonstrates Paul's availability in the next segment of this narrative:

> **And when he met us at Assos, we took him on board and came to Mitylene. And sailing from there, we arrived the following day opposite Chios; and the next day we crossed over to Samos; and the day following we came to Miletus. For Paul had decided to sail past Ephesus in order that he might not have to spend time in Asia; for he was hurrying to be in Jerusalem, if possible, on the day of Pentecost. And from Miletus he sent to Ephesus and called to him the elders of the church.** (20:14–17)

After his long walk from Troas, Paul **met** the rest of his party **at Assos.** Having taken **him on board,** the ship sailed **to Mitylene,** the leading city of the island of Lesbos. Paul and his companions continued their voyage through the coastal islands of Asia Minor, stopping successively at **Chios** (the birthplace of Homer) and **Samos** (the birthplace of the mathematician Pythagoras) before landing on the mainland at **Miletus,** a city thirty miles south of Ephesus. Luke notes parenthetically that **Paul had decided to sail past Ephesus in order that he might not have to spend time in Asia; for he was hurrying to be in Jerusalem, if possible, on the day of Pentecost.** The delay caused by the plot against his life at Corinth (20:3) had forced Paul to miss celebrating Passover in Jerusalem. He was still determined to **be in Jerusalem on the day of Pentecost,** fifty days after Passover. Accordingly, he did not want to **have to spend time in Asia,** especially at Ephesus. Paul no doubt felt that a personal visit to the church there would be too time-consuming, so he decided instead to send to **Ephesus and** instruct **the elders of the church** to come down to meet him at Miletus. That explains his decision to take a ship at Troas that would make port at Miletus instead of Ephesus.

The ship in which Paul was sailing evidently was to remain at Miletus for several days. Instead of resting, Paul used that time to further instruct and exhort the leaders of the key church at Ephesus. So great was his concern that he could not pass up the opportunity to give them a final word of exhortation. They were crucial to the work of Christ and the gospel, and they were to face very difficult times. He had a special love for that church, which he had spent three years building.

Paul's love for the church sets the standard for all Christians to follow (cf. Rom. 12:10ff.). May God give all believers, not just church leaders, such a teaching, giving, persistent, available love for the church Christ "purchased with His own blood" (Acts 20:28).

Paul's View of the Ministry (Acts 20:17–24)

16

And from Miletus he sent to Ephesus and called to him the elders of the church. And when they had come to him, he said to them, "You yourselves know, from the first day that I set foot in Asia, how I was with you the whole time, serving the Lord with all humility and with tears and with trials which came upon me through the plots of the Jews; how I did not shrink from declaring to you anything that was profitable, and teaching you publicly and from house to house, solemnly testifying to both Jews and Greeks of repentance toward God and faith in our Lord Jesus Christ. And now, behold, bound in spirit, I am on my way to Jerusalem, not knowing what will happen to me there, except that the Holy Spirit solemnly testifies to me in every city, saying that bonds and afflictions await me. But I do not consider my life of any account as dear to myself, in order that I may finish my course, and the ministry which I received from the Lord Jesus, to testify solemnly of the gospel of the grace of God." (20:17–24)

Expertise is a highly sought after commodity in this complex world. Seminars given by experts in everything from technology to time management to investments to relationships are packed with people, and books on such topics are often best-sellers. Almost anyone who has succeeded at something will find an audience eager to learn how they, too, can succeed.

The advice of experts is also sought in the church, particularly in the area of church growth, where the advice of specialists in cultural analysis and marketing techniques is greatly valued. Some seminaries even have departments of church growth, attempting to impart to prospective pastors those techniques the schools believe will ensure growth.

If the apostle Paul were alive, he would be the most sought after and mimicked church growth expert of them all. After all, it was largely through his ministry that Christianity grew from a small Palestinian sect to an empire-wide phenomenon.

Trying to copy the apostle's style would be wrongheaded, however, for Paul's success was not based on his ministry methodology. The apostle's successful ministry flowed from his devotion to truth, spiritual character, commitment to serving God, and the resultant powerful example his life set for others. There was no credibility gap between the truth he proclaimed and the way he lived.

The New Testament teaches that the heart of leadership is example. Jesus reminded His disciples in John 13:15, "I gave you an example that you also should do as I did to you." Luke described his gospel as the record of "all that Jesus began to *do* and teach" (Acts 1:1). The writer of Hebrews commanded his readers to "remember those who led you, who spoke the word of God to you; and considering the result of their conduct, imitate their faith" (Heb. 13:7). Peter exhorted his fellow elders to "be examples to the flock" (1 Pet. 5:3). To the Corinthians Paul wrote, "I exhort you therefore, be imitators of me" (1 Cor. 4:16; cf. 11:1). He instructed the Philippians, "Join in following my example, and observe those who walk according to the pattern you have in us" (Phil. 3:17; cf. 4:9). He commended the Thessalonians because they "became imitators of us and of the Lord" (1 Thess. 1:6). His advice to Timothy on how to be a leader was to "in speech, conduct, love, faith and purity, show yourself an example of those who believe" (1 Tim. 4:12).

This passage in Acts 20 gives insights into Paul's view of the ministry. It does not focus on technique but on the godly attitudes he modeled. Paul saw his ministry related to four dimensions: toward God, the church, the lost, and himself. Having the proper perspective in those four areas is foundational to a successful ministry.

The setting in which Paul revealed these principles was his farewell speech to the elders of the Ephesian church. He was on his way to Jerusalem, bringing an offering from the Gentile churches for the needy in the Jerusalem church. By so doing he hoped to ease their physical burden, as well as to cement the spiritual bond between Jews and Gentiles in the church. The ship on which he and his companions were traveling had made a stopover at **Miletus,** on the coast of Asia Minor thirty miles south of Ephesus. From there, Paul **sent to Ephesus and called to him the elders of the church.** He had decided (for reasons of time) not to visit the church at Ephesus (20:16). However his love and concern for that church compelled him to give this final exhortation to its leaders.

These men were especially dear to Paul's heart. He was their spiritual father and the founder of the local church they served. For three years he had nurtured and taught them, enduring persecution from the Jews and a riot caused by the Gentiles. They had grown to spiritual maturity under Paul's ministry, and he had released to them the oversight of the Ephesian congregation. The term **elders** identifies them as pastors, with emphasis on their spiritual maturity, while **overseers** (v. 28) describes their function. They were spiritually mature individuals who ruled the church. The two terms describe the same man, along with the word "shepherd" (or "pastor," v. 28), which emphasizes the task of feeding or teaching. All three are used to refer to those in the highest place of spiritual leadership in the church

After **they had come to him,** Paul began to share what was on his heart. His speech, the only one of his addressed to Christians that Luke records, is filled with Pauline phraseology. He began by saying **to them, "You yourselves know, from the first day that I set foot in Asia, how I was with you the whole time."** The Ephesian elders had observed his ministry during his three years in their city. Paul's appeal to their personal knowledge of him is reminiscent of his words to the Thessalonians:

> For you yourselves know, brethren, that our coming to you was not in vain ... For we never came with flattering speech, as you know, nor with a pretext for greed—God is witness ... You are witnesses, and so is God, how devoutly and uprightly and blamelessly we behaved toward you believers; just as you know how we were exhorting and encouraging and imploring each one of you as a father would his own children. (1 Thess. 2:1, 5, 10–11)

By reminding the Ephesian elders of their firsthand knowledge of his ministry, Paul was not only establishing himself as an example for them to emulate but also may have been defending himself. False teachers constantly attempted to tear down what he had built up, often by attacking his credibility (cf. 2 Cor. 10:10–12; 11:1ff.; Gal. 1:6–9; 3:1; 5:12; Phil. 3:2). That such enemies of the gospel threatened Ephesus is clear from Paul's warning in verses 29–31. On the other hand, he may simply have been setting forth his own ministry as an example for the elders to follow.

Toward God—Service

serving the Lord with all humility and with tears and with trials which came upon me through the plots of the Jews; (20:19)

Paul viewed the ministry primarily as **serving the Lord** and commonly referred to himself as a "bond-servant of Jesus Christ" (Rom. 1:1; cf. Gal. 1:10; Col. 1:7; 4:7; Titus 1:1). He was the one Paul sought to please, not men. In the midst of a raging storm at sea, he testified of that devotion to serve his Lord by telling the others on board, "This very night an angel of the God to whom I belong and whom I serve stood before me" (Acts 27:23). To the Galatians he wrote, "For am I now seeking the favor of men, or of God? Or am I striving to please men? If I were still trying to please men, I would not be a bond-servant of Christ" (Gal. 1:10). In 1 Thessalonians 2:4 he declared, "Just as we have been approved by God to be entrusted with the gospel, so we speak, not as pleasing men but God, who examines our hearts." Paul knew well the truth that "the fear of man brings a snare, but he who trusts in the Lord will be exalted" (Prov. 29:25).

Everyone in the ministry is called to serve God rather than men. That applies to all Christians, for everything believers do, first of all, is service to Him (1 Cor. 10:31; Matt. 25:34–40). Serving God defines the motive for doing what is right in His sight above every other consideration. It means a preacher does not serve the will and desires of the congregation or even the leaders of the church, but God. It means an employee does not merely serve an employer, but God (Eph. 6:5–7). As Paul expressed it to the Colossians, "It is the Lord Christ whom you serve" (Col. 3:24).

Serving is from *douleuō*, the verb form of *doulos* ("bond-servant; slave"). Paul uses the verb form seventeen times in his epistles, primarily to refer to obedience to the Lord. He considered it a great honor and privilege to serve the King of kings and Lord of lords.

Two attitudes mark a bond-servant of the Lord. First, such service must be rendered in **all humility,** since a servant is not greater than his master (Matt. 10:24). Despite his position and accomplishments, Paul was a humble man. "What then is Apollos?" he asked the factious Corinthians. "And what is Paul? Servants through whom you believed, even as the Lord gave opportunity to each one" (1 Cor. 3:5). In 1 Corinthians 15:9 he described himself as "the least of the apostles ... not fit to be called an apostle, because I persecuted the church of God." In 2 Corinthians 3:5 he wrote, "Not that we are adequate in ourselves to consider anything as coming from ourselves, but our adequacy is from God." Though he considered himself "not in the least inferior to the most eminent apostles" (2 Cor. 11:5), in Ephesians 3:8 he referred to himself as "the very least of all saints" and in 1 Timothy 1:15 as the "foremost of all [sinners]."

Ambrose, the fourth-century bishop of Milan, was one of the most noted leaders of the early church. It was under his ministry that Augustine was converted. Ambrose had been the governor of the Roman province that included the city of Milan. When that city's bishop died, the people met in the cathedral to elect a new bishop. As governor, Ambrose got up to speak a few words to the crowd. Suddenly someone cried out, "Ambrose for bishop!" Others in the crowd echoed his shout. To his surprise and dismay (though he had been a Christian for a long time, he was not ordained and hadn't even been baptized yet), Ambrose was elected bishop. He fled and tried unsuccessfully to hide but was finally persuaded that his appointment was God's will. His first act as bishop was to give away his wealth to the poor.

Called to become a preacher of the gospel, Scottish Reformer John Knox

> burst forth in most abundant tears, and withdrew himself to his chamber. His countenance and behaviour, from that day till the day that he was compelled to present himself to the public place of preaching, did sufficiently declare the grief and trouble of his heart; for no man saw any sign of mirth in him, neither yet had he pleasure to accompany any man, many days together. (William Barclay, *The Letters to Timothy, Titus, and Philemon* [Philadelphia: Westminster, 1975], 50)

Second, serving the Lord involves a willingness to endure suffering, since suffering is the lot of any servant. The Lord Jesus Christ was the foremost example of a suffering servant. Such passages as Psalm 22 and Isaiah 53 depict His suffering in graphic detail. Peter wrote in 1 Peter 2:21, "Christ also suffered for you, leaving you an example for you to follow in His steps." Just as Christ suffered, so also "all who desire to live godly in Christ Jesus will be persecuted" (2 Tim. 3:12), because "through many tribulations we must enter the kingdom of God" (Acts 14:22).

Paul lists two areas from which suffering comes. The apostle's reference to serving the Lord **with tears** speaks of internal suffering. Paul's zeal for the Lord caused him to be grieved and pained when God was dishonored by unbelievers and believers. Those who share Paul's passion will share his tears.

Three things in particular moved Paul to tears. First, he grieved over the state of the lost. In Romans 9:2–3 he writes, "I have great sorrow and unceasing grief in my heart. For I could wish that I myself were accursed, separated from Christ for the sake of my brethren, my kinsmen according to the flesh."

Second, he cried over weak, struggling, sinning Christians. To such believers at Corinth he wrote, "Out of much affliction and anguish of heart I wrote to you with many tears" (2 Cor. 2:4).

Finally, the sinister threat posed by false teachers caused Paul to say to the Ephesian elders, "Therefore [because of the false teachers mentioned in vv. 29–30] be on the alert, remembering that night and day for a period of three years I did not cease to admonish each one with tears" (v. 31). To the Philippians he wrote, "For many walk, of whom I often told you, and now tell you even weeping, that they are enemies of the cross of Christ" (Phil. 3:18).

But the tears of a servant of God are not in vain. The psalmist wrote in Psalm 126:6, "He who goes to and fro weeping, carrying his bag of seed, shall indeed come again with a shout of joy, bringing his sheaves with him." To those with caring, compassionate hearts, who faithfully spread the precious seed of the Word, God promises a rich spiritual harvest.

Not all suffering is internal. Paul also faced the external **trials which came upon** him **through the plots of the Jews.** He faced the hostility and opposition of his countrymen throughout his ministry (2 Cor. 11:24, 26). Acts 9:20 notes that "immediately [following his conversion] he began to proclaim Jesus in the synagogues, saying, 'He is the Son of God.'" It did not take long for opposition to develop; verse 23 of that same chapter notes that "the Jews plotted together to do away with him." On Cyprus, Paul faced opposition from "a Jewish false prophet whose name was Bar-Jesus" (Acts 13:6). At Pisidian Antioch, "when the Jews saw the crowds [assembled to hear Paul speak], they were filled with jealousy, and began contradicting the things spoken by Paul, and were blaspheming" (Acts 13:45). At Iconium (14:2), Lystra (14:19), Thessalonica (17:5ff.), Berea (17:13), Corinth (18:6, 12–13), and Ephesus (19:9) the sad story of Jewish hostility was repeated. The beginning of Paul's present journey to Jerusalem had witnessed a Jewish plot to take his life (20:3), and when he arrived there he would face still more Jewish opposition (21:27ff., 23:12ff.). Truly did the Lord's words to Ananias about Paul come true: "I will show him how much he must suffer for My name's sake" (Acts 9:16).

Some judge the success of a servant of God by how large or widespread his ministry is, how many degrees he has, or how much publicity he receives. But the true measure of a servant of God is whether he focuses solely on pleasing God, which gives him the willingness to serve with humility and suffer opposition from those hostile to the truth.

TOWARD THE CHURCH—TEACHING

how I did not shrink from declaring to you anything that was

profitable, and teaching you publicly and from house to house, (20:20)

Paul saw clearly that his obligation toward the church was to teach. As he wrote in Ephesians 4:12, the primary task of leaders in the church is "the equipping of the saints for the work of service, to the building up of the body of Christ"—a goal that can only be accomplished through the consistent, thorough teaching of God's Word. Therefore Paul reminds the Ephesian leaders that he **did not shrink from declaring to** them **anything that was profitable. Shrink from** is from *hupostellō*, which also appears in verse 27 and means "to draw back" or "to withhold." Paul held back nothing of the wise counsel and holy, sovereign purpose of God; he withheld no doctrine, exhortation, or admonition that was profitable.

Well does Proverbs 29:25 warn, "The fear of man brings a snare." But Paul had no such fears—even when confronting another apostle. In Galatians 2:11–21 he recounted the story of his dramatic public rebuke of Peter:

> When Cephas [Peter] came to Antioch, I opposed him to his face, because he stood condemned. For prior to the coming of certain men from James, he used to eat with the Gentiles; but when they came, he began to withdraw and hold himself aloof, fearing the party of the circumcision. And the rest of the Jews joined him in hypocrisy, with the result that even Barnabas was carried away by their hypocrisy. But when I saw that they were not straightforward about the truth of the gospel, I said to Cephas in the presence of all, "If you, being a Jew, live like the Gentiles and not like the Jews, how is it that you compel the Gentiles to live like Jews? We are Jews by nature, and not sinners from among the Gentiles; nevertheless knowing that a man is not justified by the works of the Law but through faith in Christ Jesus, even we have believed in Christ Jesus, that we may be justified by faith in Christ, and not by the works of the Law; since by the works of the Law shall no flesh be justified. But if, while seeking to be justified in Christ, we ourselves have also been found sinners, is Christ then a minister of sin? May it never be! For if I rebuild what I have once destroyed, I prove myself to be a transgressor. For through the Law I died to the Law, that I might live to God. I have been crucified with Christ; and it is no longer I who live, but Christ lives in me; and the life which I now live in the flesh I live by faith in the Son of God, who loved me, and delivered Himself up for me. I do not nullify the grace of God; for if righteousness comes through the Law, then Christ died needlessly."

Paul's zeal for the purity of the gospel allowed him to play no favorites. He would boldly confront anyone—even the respected leader of the twelve, or his close friend Barnabas—who compromised biblical truth. Unlike many today, Paul could declare, "Am I now seeking the favor of men, or of God? Or am I striving to please men? If I were still trying to please men, I would not be a bond-servant of Christ" (Gal. 1:10). When he commanded Timothy to "preach the word; be ready in season and out of season; reprove, rebuke, exhort, with great patience and instruction" (2 Tim. 4:2), the apostle was himself an example of one who had done just that. He had to speak his convictions regarding the truth, as he said in 2 Corinthians 4:13, "I believed, therefore I spoke."

That a man of God must boldly proclaim the truth is not just a New Testament idea. David wrote:

> I have proclaimed glad tidings of righteousness in the great congregation; behold, I will not restrain my lips, O Lord, Thou knowest. I have not hidden Thy righteousness within my heart; I have spoken of Thy faithfulness and Thy salvation; I have not concealed Thy lovingkindness and Thy truth from the great congregation. (Ps. 40:9–10)

Ezekiel 33:7–9 contains a sobering warning of the consequences of failing to declare God's truth:

> Now as for you, son of man, I have appointed you a watchman for the house of Israel; so you will hear a message from My mouth, and give them warning from Me. When I say to the wicked, "O wicked man, you shall surely die," and you do not speak to warn the wicked from his way, that wicked man shall die in his iniquity, but his blood I will require from your hand. But if you on your part warn a wicked man to turn from his way, and he does not turn from his way, he will die in his iniquity; but you have delivered your life.

Those who shrink from proclaiming God's truth are subject to God's chastening.

Second Timothy 3:16 defines what is **profitable:** "All Scripture is inspired by God and profitable for teaching, for reproof, for correction, for training in righteousness." "Teaching" involves communicating the principles of God's Word; "reproof" refers to applying Scripture to produce conviction of sin; "correction" gives repentant sinners the biblical direction to turn from sin and follow Christ; and "training in righteousness" moves believers along the path toward Christlikeness. Thus armed with the Scriptures, "the man of God [will] be adequate, equipped for every good work" (2 Tim. 3:17).

There were two outlets for Paul's **teaching.** He taught **publicly.**

Acts 19:8 records that when he came to Ephesus, he taught in the synagogue for three months. After being forced to leave there, he taught in a rented hall for two more years (19:10). But not only did he publicly proclaim the Word, he also taught privately **from house to house.** He took the truths he publicly proclaimed and applied them to individuals' and families' daily concerns.

Whether in public or in private, the servant of Jesus Christ does not fail to declare the profitable truths of God's Word. And in the preparation and the proclamation, he handles the Scripture as a "workman who does not need to be ashamed, handling accurately the word of truth" (2 Tim. 2:15).

TOWARD THE LOST—EVANGELISM

solemnly testifying to both Jews and Greeks of repentance toward God and faith in our Lord Jesus Christ. (20:21)

No view of the ministry is complete that fails to have a proper perspective on reaching the lost. Paul saw himself as an evangelist, having a mandate to reach sinners with the truth of the gospel. To the Romans he wrote:

> I am under obligation both to Greeks and to barbarians, both to the wise and to the foolish. . . . For I am not ashamed of the gospel, for it is the power of God for salvation to everyone who believes, to the Jew first and also to the Greek. (1:14, 16)

First Corinthians 9:19–23 reveals Paul's passionate desire to fulfill that mandate:

> For though I am free from all men, I have made myself a slave to all, that I might win the more. And to the Jews I became as a Jew, that I might win Jews; to those who are under the Law, as under the Law, though not being myself under the Law, that I might win those who are under the Law; to those who are without law, as without law, though not being without the law of God but under the law of Christ, that I might win those who are without law. To the weak I became weak, that I might win the weak; I have become all things to all men, that I may by all means save some. And I do all things for the sake of the gospel, that I may become a fellow partaker of it.

So intense was Paul's concern for the lost that he cried out, "Woe is me if I do not preach the gospel" (1 Cor. 9:16). He even made the shocking statement that, if possible, he would be willing to give up his own salvation to see unredeemed Jews saved (Rom. 9:3).

Paul's intense zeal for proclaiming the gospel compelled him to make his presentation of it thorough and complete. **Testifying** is from *diamarturomai*, a compound word made up of a verb intensified by the addition of a preposition. Paul's gospel presentations were never shallow or partial but detailed and comprehensive (cf. vv. 20, 27). As the apostle to the Gentiles (Rom. 11:13; cf. 1 Tim. 2:7), he evangelized **both Jews and Greeks.**

A biblically sound gospel presentation must contain two components. First, it must include **repentance toward God.** *Metanoia* (**repentance**) is a rich and important New Testament word, meaning "to change one's mind or purpose." It describes a change of mind that results in a change of behavior; it is the conscious act of a sinner turning from his sins to God. Nineteenth-century theologian Heinrich Heppe defined repentance as "a gracious power, bestowed only on the elect, by which they lay aside the life of sin and busy themselves with righteousness" (*Reformed Dogmatics* [reprint; Grand Rapids: Baker, 1978], 571). Remorse, such as that expressed by Judas (Matt. 27:3) or Saul (1 Sam. 15:24–25), must not be confused with repentance. Repentance involves sorrow for the act of sin, remorse sorrow for its consequences. A repentant person is sorry he sinned, whereas a remorseful person is sorry he got caught.

Repentance involves the entire person, intellect, emotion, and will. In Acts 2:36, Peter concluded his sermon on the Day of Pentecost by boldly declaring, "Therefore let all the house of Israel know for certain that God has made Him both Lord and Christ—this Jesus whom you crucified." He had clearly and powerfully presented his hearers with the facts of the gospel. Verse 37 describes the emotional aspect of repentance: "When they heard this, they were pierced to the heart, and said to Peter and the rest of the apostles, 'Brethren, what shall we do?'" But true repentance also involves an act of the will: "So then, those who had received his word were baptized" (v. 41). By publicly identifying themselves with Jesus Christ through baptism, these new believers made a decisive break with their past.

The New Testament knows nothing of a gospel that lacks a call to repentance. John the Baptist insisted that his hearers "bring forth fruits in keeping with repentance" (Luke 3:8). The Lord Jesus Christ also called people to repent (Matt. 4:17); in fact, He described His ministry as one of calling sinners to repentance (Luke 5:32). Paul's message to both Jews and Gentiles was "that they should repent and turn to God, performing deeds appropriate to repentance" (Acts 26:20). The words of the Lord Jesus Christ that "repentance for forgiveness of sins should be proclaimed in His name to all the nations, beginning from Jerusalem" (Luke 24:47; cf. Acts 17:30), mark repentance as central to the gospel message. (For a detailed discussion of repentance see my books *The Gospel According to Jesus* (rev. ed.) [Grand Rapids: Zondervan, 1994], and *Faith Works* [Dallas: Word, 1993].)

The gospel message also includes **faith in our Lord Jesus Christ.** Sinners must not only turn away from sin but turn toward God (cf. 1 Thess. 1:9). Saving faith, like repentance, has an intellectual, emotional, and volitional aspect. Theologians use three Latin words, *notitia*, *assensus*, and *fiducia*, to describe those aspects. *Notitia* (knowledge) is the intellectual aspect, *assensus* (assent) the emotional, and *fiducia* (trust) the volitional aspect of saving faith. Saving faith thus involves the total person trusting wholly in the **Lord Jesus Christ** alone for salvation. (For further instruction on saving faith, see my book *Faith Works* [Dallas: Word, 1993], 37–54.)

Paul saw himself not only as a servant, feeding the household of God, but as a herald, announcing to lost sinners the good news of salvation. Those two essential aspects of ministry must be the concern of all believers.

TOWARD HIMSELF—SACRIFICE

And now, behold, bound in spirit, I am on my way to Jerusalem, not knowing what will happen to me there, except that the Holy Spirit solemnly testifies to me in every city, saying that bonds and afflictions await me. But I do not consider my life of any account as dear to myself, in order that I may finish my course, and the ministry which I received from the Lord Jesus, to testify solemnly of the gospel of the grace of God. (20:22–24)

As an excellent servant of Jesus Christ, Paul had a single-minded devotion to his one life's purpose. He described himself as **bound in spirit** by his strong compulsion to fulfill his ministry. *Deō* (**bound**) is commonly used to refer to physical binding with chains or ropes (cf. Matt. 14:3; 21:2; 27:2; Acts 9:2; 12:6; 21:11). It is used figuratively to speak of the powerful tie of the marriage bond (Rom. 7:2; 1 Cor. 7:27, 39). Paul's sense of duty and responsibility to his Master drove him on his **way to Jerusalem**, **not knowing** specifically **what** would **happen to** him once he arrived **there.** He did know, however, that the **Holy Spirit solemnly** testified **to** him **in every city** he visited **that bonds and afflictions** awaited him (cf. Rom. 15:31). It was revealed to Paul that he faced persecution in Jerusalem, though what that specifically would entail had not yet been disclosed. That would later be made clear to him by the prophet Agabus when he arrived in Palestine (21:10–11).

Paul's response to the situation reveals his sacrificial spirit: **I do not consider my life of any account as dear to myself,** he told them, **in order that I may finish my course, and the ministry which I received from the Lord Jesus, to testify solemnly of the gospel of the grace of God.** Only one thing mattered to Paul: to finish the work God had given him to do. What happened to him was of no consequence (cf. 21:13) when compared to the unique nature of his calling from Christ Himself—on which all the accusations against him hinged.

It must be noted that the message the apostle preached and all preachers echo is called **the gospel of the grace of God.** The clear emphasis is on grace, the unmerited favor of God by which He forgives undeserving sinners the totality of their sins and freely, mercifully gives them the complete righteousness of Jesus Christ.

Paul successfully fulfilled his ministry to the very end of his life. As his death drew near, he wrote triumphantly to Timothy, "I have fought the good fight, I have finished the course, I have kept the faith" (2 Tim. 4:7). And after he paid the ultimate price for his devoted, loyal service to Jesus Christ, he no doubt heard from his beloved Master the words "Well done, good and faithful slave ... enter into the joy of your master" (Matt. 25:21).

It should be the goal of all Christians to complete successfully the ministry God has given them. To do so requires that they maintain a proper perspective of their ministry as it relates to God, believers, unbelievers, and themselves. To do less is unworthy of the Lord who graciously called them into His service.

A Charge to New Testament Church Leaders (Acts 20:25–38)

17

"And now, behold, I know that all of you, among whom I went about preaching the kingdom, will see my face no more. Therefore I testify to you this day, that I am innocent of the blood of all men. For I did not shrink from declaring to you the whole purpose of God. Be on guard for yourselves and for all the flock, among which the Holy Spirit has made you overseers, to shepherd the church of God which He purchased with His own blood. I know that after my departure savage wolves will come in among you, not sparing the flock; and from among your own selves men will arise, speaking perverse things, to draw away the disciples after them. Therefore be on the alert, remembering that night and day for a period of three years I did not cease to admonish each one with tears. And now I commend you to God and to the word of His grace, which is able to build you up and to give you the inheritance among all those who are sanctified. I have coveted no one's silver or gold or clothes. You yourselves know that these hands ministered to my own needs and to the men who were with me. In everything I showed you that by working hard in this manner you must help the weak and remember the words of the Lord Jesus, that He Himself said, 'It is more blessed to give than to receive.' And when he had said

these things, he knelt down and prayed with them all. And they began to weep aloud and embraced Paul, and repeatedly kissed him, grieving especially over the word which he had spoken, that they should see his face no more. And they were accompanying him to the ship. (20:25–38)

The crucial component in any organization, institution, or business is its leadership. Good leadership can lift an organization to the heights of success, whereas poor leadership can plunge it into the depths of ruin. Not surprisingly, a vast amount of material is available for those wishing to sharpen their leadership skills. Leadership is treated as an essential element because it is.

God is even more concerned about leadership in His kingdom. The Bible, both in its teaching and the examples it presents, speaks about leadership. The Old Testament presents good leaders, such as Moses, Samuel, and David. It also reveals the disastrous consequences that come because of poor leaders, such as Saul, Ahab, and Manasseh. The Old Testament contains wise counsel on how to be a good leader (Prov. 8:15; 14:28; 16:10, 12; 20:8, 26, 28; 29:4, 14; 31:4), and it has denunciations of poor leadership practices (Isa. 9:14–16; Jer. 5:31; Ezek. 22:26–28; Hosea 4:9).

The New Testament presents poor leaders such as the Pharisees, whom Jesus described as "blind guides of the blind," serving only to lead themselves and their followers into a pit (Matt. 15:14). The results of their inept and deadly leadership greatly distressed our Lord. When He saw "the multitudes, He felt compassion for them, because they were distressed and downcast like sheep without a shepherd" (Matt. 9:36). Bereft of competent spiritual leadership, the Jews drifted aimlessly. The wise, selfless, sacrificial leadership of the apostles stands in sharp contrast to the incompetent leadership of Israel's leaders.

The pastoral epistles set forth the high standards for leaders in the church (1 Tim. 3:1–13; Titus 1:5–9). All of those guidelines are summarized in the requirement that a leader be "above reproach" (1 Tim. 3:2; Titus 1:6). The standards are high because the responsibility is great. James cautioned, "Let not many of you become teachers, my brethren, knowing that as such we shall incur a stricter judgment" (James 3:1). Paul instructed Timothy that leaders who continue in sin are to be publicly rebuked (1 Tim. 5:20). On the other hand, those "who rule well [are to] be considered worthy of double honor, especially those who work hard at preaching and teaching" (1 Tim. 5:17). There is in spiritual leadership the potential for great blessing or serious condemnation.

A primary task of the apostles and evangelists was the appointing of pastors in the early congregations. Paul directed Titus, ministering on the island of Crete, to "appoint elders in every city" (Titus 1:5), as he and Barnabas had done on their first missionary journey (Acts 14:23). In the present passage, Paul addresses the elders he had appointed in Ephesus. His ship had stopped on its voyage to Palestine at Miletus (20:15), not far from Ephesus. He summoned the Ephesian elders to meet him there (20:17) so that he could give them one final exhortation. In verses 17–24 Paul describes four essential attitudinal perspectives on ministry: toward God, the church, the lost, and himself. Having given that general overview of the dimensions of ministry, he now narrows his focus to instruction regarding ministry in the church.

Before giving them the priorities for leading the church, Paul laid a foundation by summarizing his own ministry at Ephesus. He opened on a sad note, informing them, **I know that all of you, among whom I went about preaching the kingdom, will see my face no more.** He had served with them for three years, and his work with them was done. Having been taught and discipled by the apostle, they were ready to minister on their own. The term **kingdom** encompasses God's rule in the sphere of salvation, not just the future millennial reign of Jesus Christ (cf. Acts 28:31). **Preaching the kingdom** meant proclaiming the gospel, the good news that sinners in the realm of Satan, death, and destruction ("the kingdom of darkness") could enter the realm of salvation, life, and glory ("the kingdom of God's Son"). Paul preached this gospel thoroughly and clearly, as he indicated in verses 20 and 27.

Because he thoroughly fulfilled his obligation to teach, Paul could **testify** to them that he was **innocent of the blood of all men—** both Jews and Gentiles. He had not only taught the church but also evangelized the lost. He had not been unfaithful in any aspect of ministry.

Paul's declaration that he was **innocent of the blood of all men** is reminiscent of God's words to Ezekiel:

> Now as for you, son of man, I have appointed you a watchman for the house of Israel; so you will hear a message from My mouth, and give them warning from Me. When I say to the wicked, "O wicked man, you shall surely die," and you do not speak to warn the wicked from his way, that wicked man shall die in his iniquity, but his blood I will require from your hand. But if you on your part warn a wicked man to turn from his way, and he does not turn from his way, he will die in his iniquity; but you have delivered your life. (Ezek. 33:7–9)

That is a sobering reminder of the serious responsibility that all believers, but especially leaders, have to speak God's truth (cf. James 3:1). Paul declared himself innocent because he **did not shrink from declaring to** them **the whole purpose of God.** The implication is that those elders must follow Paul's example of preaching a complete gospel of God's redemption of sinners or face God's chastisement. That is still true for all pastors.

After that personal note, Paul charged the church leaders to maintain five priorities: be right with God, shepherd the flock, guard the flock, study and pray, and be free from self-interest.

BE RIGHT WITH GOD

Be on guard for yourselves (20:28a)

The first priority for anyone involved in spiritual leadership is his own relationship with God. Effective ministry is not mere outward activity; it is the overflow of a rich, deep relationship with God. As John Owen wisely observed,

> A minister may fill his pews, his communion roll, the mouths of the public, but what that minister is on his knees in secret before God Almighty, that he is and no more. (Cited in I. D. E. Thomas, *A Puritan Golden Treasury* [Edinburgh: Banner of Truth, 1977], 192)

No one is ready to face the pressures and responsibilities of ministry who is not right with God. Those pressures, as well as the demand to set the example, require that leaders constantly be on guard (Mark 13:9; Luke 21:34).

The first step in being on guard is self-examination. After a whole chapter of exhortation to the young preacher (1 Tim. 4:1–15), Paul summed up what he had said by calling Timothy to examine himself (verse 16): "Pay close attention to yourself and to your teaching; persevere in these things; for as you do this you will insure salvation both for yourself and for those who hear you." He charged Timothy to scrutinize his life and doctrine to make sure both honored God. Such was crucial to his own perseverance and to the salvation and perseverance of others. Paul expressed that same truth in his second letter to Timothy:

> Now in a large house there are not only gold and silver vessels, but also vessels of wood and of earthenware, and some to honor and some to dishonor. Therefore, if a man cleanses himself from these things, he will be a vessel for honor, sanctified, useful to the Master, prepared for every good work. (2 Tim. 2:20–21)

In a house there were vessels for dishonorable uses, such as garbage and other waste. There were also vessels for honorable uses, such as food and drink. Only clean ones of high quality were fit for honor. Since God uses clean and holy instruments, vessels of honor, self-examination and forsaking sin are essential for leaders. Although God does bless His truth in spite of the preacher, He does not bless the unholy leader, no matter what title, position, or office he might hold.

In a powerful passage from his classic work *The Reformed Pastor*, Richard Baxter gives a stirring call for pastors to examine themselves:

> Take heed to yourselves, lest you live in those sins which you preach against in others, and lest you be guilty of that which daily you condemn. Will you make it your work to magnify God, and, when you have done, dishonour him as much as others? Will you proclaim Christ's governing power, and yet contemn it, and rebel yourselves? Will you preach his laws, and wilfully break them? If sin be evil, why do you live in it? if it be not, why do you dissuade men from it? If it be dangerous, how dare you venture on it? if it be not, why do you tell men so? If God's threatenings be true, why do you not fear them? if they be false, why do you needlessly trouble men with them, and put them into such frights without a cause? Do you "know the judgment of God, that they who commit such things are worthy of death"; and yet will you do them? "Thou that teachest another, teachest thou not thyself?" Thou that sayest a man should not commit adultery, or be drunk, or covetous, art thou such thyself? "Thou that makest thy boast of the law, through breaking the law dishonourest thou God?" What! shall the same tongue speak evil that speakest against evil? Shall those lips censure, and slander, and backbite your neighbour, that cry down these and the like things in others? Take heed to yourselves, lest you cry down sin, and yet do not overcome it; lest, while you seek to bring it down in others, you bow to it, and become its slaves yourselves: "For of whom a man is overcome, of the same is he brought into bondage." "To whom ye yield yourselves servants to obey, his servants ye are to whom ye obey, whether of sin unto death, or of obedience unto righteousness." O brethren! it is easier to chide at sin, than to overcome it. (*The Reformed Pastor* [Edinburgh: Banner of Truth, 1979], 67–68)

Personal holiness is the requirement of true and powerful spiritual leadership. God calls for holiness that is not just outward, in the eyes of men. Paul had that outward virtue even before his salvation, when he described himself as blameless as to the law (Phil. 3:6). But he called it "rubbish" (v. 8) compared to true righteousness. True holiness is inward, so that one can say with Paul, "For our proud confidence is this, the testimony of our conscience, that in holiness and godly sincerity, not in fleshly wisdom but in the grace of God, we have conducted ourselves in the world, and especially toward you" (2 Cor. 1:12).

SHEPHERD THE FLOCK

and for all the flock, among which the Holy Spirit has made you overseers, to shepherd the church of God which He purchased with His own blood. (20:28b)

After making sure that his own life (and consequently that of his family, 1 Tim. 3:4–5) is in order, a leader's second priority is the spiritual care of his flock. Positively, that care involves the feeding and leading of **all the flock.** The metaphor of a flock and a shepherd is often used to describe God's relationship to His people. It is an apt one, since sheep are helpless, timid, dirty, and in need of constant protection and care. The Old Testament frequently describes Israel as God's flock (Pss. 77:20; 78:52; 80:1; Isa. 40:11; 63:11; Jer. 13:17; 23:2–3; 31:10; Ezek. 34:2ff.; Mic. 2:12; 5:4; 7:14; Zech. 10:3), and the New Testament pictures the church as a flock with the Lord Jesus Christ as its Shepherd (John 10:1ff.; Heb. 13:20; 1 Pet. 2:25; 5:2–4).

Jesus Christ, the Chief Shepherd (1 Pet. 5:4), has taken His flock and divided it into many smaller flocks (cf. 1 Pet. 5:2, "the flock of God among [or apportioned to] you"; 1 Pet. 5:3, "those allotted to your charge"). The **Holy Spirit** sovereignly raises up **overseers,** or under-shepherds, who are responsible to **shepherd** their flocks. **Shepherd** is from *poimainō*, a comprehensive term encompassing the entire task of a shepherd. The most important part of that task, however, is to feed. In John 21:15–17, Jesus three times instructed Peter to care for His sheep. The second time He used *poimainō*, but the first and third times *boskō*, which has the more restricted meaning of "to feed." Obviously, then, the primary task of an undershepherd of the Lord's flock is to feed the sheep. Sadly, many undershepherds today fail to do that, seemingly content to lead their sheep from one barren wasteland to another. The tragic result is a spiritually weak flock, ready to eat the poisonous weeds of false doctrine, or to follow false shepherds who deceitfully promise them greener pastures, while leading them to barren desert.

Since sheep are followers, the shepherds' task also involves leading the flock. They must set the direction for the sheep to follow. The New Testament knows nothing of congregational rule; instead it commands believers to "obey your leaders, and submit to them" (Heb. 13:17). Paul reminded the Thessalonians that their pastors were given "charge over you in the Lord" and were to be appreciated, esteemed, loved, and followed without conflict (1 Thess. 5:12–13). God has committed the leadership of the church to the **overseers** (elders, pastors). Those who serve faithfully are to be doubly honored (1 Tim. 5:17); those who fall into sin are to be publicly rebuked (1 Tim. 5:20). It is a sobering realization that elders will someday give an account to God for how they lead those committed to their charge (Heb. 13:17).

The motive for such high standards of leadership lies in the fact that **the church** belongs not to men, but to **God** (cf. 1 Pet. 5:2). Church leaders have a stewardship over His property and must discharge that stewardship faithfully (cf. 1 Cor. 4:2). Further, the church is the most precious reality on earth, since the ultimate price was paid for it when the Lord Jesus Christ **purchased** it **with His own blood** (cf. 1 Pet. 1:18–19). That demands that every leader treat the church as the precious fellowship that it is. God is a spirit and has no body, hence no blood. Yet Paul can say that God as much as purchased the church with His own blood because he "believed so strongly in the deity of Jesus Christ and His essential unity with the Father that [he] hesitated not to speak of His sacrifice on Calvary as a shedding of the blood of God" (G. T. Stokes, "The Acts of the Apostles," in W. Robertson Nicoll, ed., *The Expositor's Bible* [New York: A. C. Armstrong and Son, 1903], 2:419).

The Lord Jesus Christ set the example of loving concern for the church that all leaders must follow. In Ephesians 5:25–27, Paul describes Christ's sacrificial love for the church:

> Christ ... loved the church and gave Himself up for her; that He might sanctify her, having cleansed her by the washing of water with the word, that He might present to Himself the church in all her glory, having no spot or wrinkle or any such thing; but that she should be holy and blameless.

The undershepherd must have the same concern for the purity of the church as did the Great Shepherd. Paul certainly did. To the Corinthians he wrote, "I am jealous for you with a godly jealousy; for I betrothed you to one husband, that to Christ I might present you as a pure virgin" (2 Cor. 11:2). Those undershepherds who truly value the church will shepherd their flocks by feeding them the Word of God and faithfully leading them.

GUARD THE FLOCK

I know that after my departure savage wolves will come in among you, not sparing the flock; and from among your own selves men will arise, speaking perverse things, to draw away the

disciples after them. Therefore be on the alert, remembering that night and day for a period of three years I did not cease to admonish each one with tears. (20:29–31)

It is not enough for a faithful shepherd to feed and lead his flock, he must also protect it from predators. Paul had no doubt that **after** his **departure** false teachers would threaten the Ephesian church, as they already had entered the church at Corinth (2 Cor. 11:4) and the churches of Galatia (Gal. 1:6). Whenever the truth is proclaimed, Satan can be expected to counter it with the lies of false doctrine. It has always been so. Paul's striking description of false teachers as **savage wolves** ...**not sparing the flock** echoes that of the Lord Jesus Christ (Matt. 7:15; 10:16). Because of the serious danger they pose to the church, the Scriptures condemn false teachers in the strongest language. Peter vividly describes them in 2 Peter 2 as "those who indulge the flesh in its corrupt desires and despise authority" (v. 10); "unreasoning animals" (v. 12); "stains and blemishes" (v. 13); "having eyes full of adultery . . . having a heart trained in greed . . . accursed children" (v. 14); "springs without water . . . mists driven by a storm, for whom the black darkness has been reserved" (v. 17); "slaves of corruption" (v. 19); dogs returning to their own vomit and pigs wallowing in the mud (v. 22).

True to Paul's prediction, false teachers did **come in among** the flock at Ephesus and attack it (cf. Rev. 2:2). Even more subtle than the attack of false teachers from outside the church, however, is the defection of those within. Accordingly, Paul warned them that **from among your own selves men will arise, speaking perverse things, to draw away the disciples after them. Perverse** is from *diastrephō*, which means "to distort," or "to twist." False teachers twist God's truth for their own perverted ends. **Draw away** is from *apospaō* and could be translated "to drag away" or "to tear away." If the undershepherds are not vigilant, Paul warns, the wolves will drag their sheep away to devour them.

Tragically, even the Ephesian church, where Paul himself ministered for three years, saw such defections among its leadership. In his letters to Timothy (who was then the pastor of the Ephesian church), Paul condemned the false teachers who had arisen from within the Ephesian congregation (1 Tim. 1:3–7; 2 Tim. 3:1–9), even naming some of them (1 Tim. 1:20; 2 Tim. 1:15; 2:17).

Jude also warned in his epistle of the insidious danger of false teachers who arise from within the church:

> Beloved, while I was making every effort to write you about our common salvation, I felt the necessity to write to you appealing that you

contend earnestly for the faith which was once for all delivered to the saints. For certain persons have crept in unnoticed, those who were long beforehand marked out for this condemnation, ungodly persons who turn the grace of our God into licentiousness and deny our only Master and Lord, Jesus Christ. (vv. 3–4)

But these men revile the things which they do not understand; and the things which they know by instinct, like unreasoning animals, by these things they are destroyed. Woe to them! For they have gone the way of Cain, and for pay they have rushed headlong into the error of Balaam, and perished in the rebellion of Korah. These men are those who are hidden reefs in your love feasts when they feast with you without fear, caring for themselves; clouds without water, carried along by winds; autumn trees without fruit, doubly dead, uprooted; wild waves of the sea, casting up their own shame like foam; wandering stars, for whom the black darkness has been reserved forever. (vv. 10–13)

These are grumblers, finding fault, following after their own lusts; they speak arrogantly, flattering people for the sake of gaining an advantage. (v. 16)

To guard their flocks from attacks from both outside and inside the church, the undershepherds must do two things. First, they must **be on the alert.** Knowing that the savage wolves are awaiting an opening to attack their flocks, they must be vigilant. Charles Jefferson describes the importance of the shepherd's vigilance:

The Eastern shepherd was, first of all, a watchman. He had a watchtower. It was his business to keep a wide-open eye, constantly searching the horizon for the possible approach of foes. He was bound to be circumspect and attentive. Vigilance was a cardinal virtue. An alert wakefulness was for him a necessity. He could not indulge in fits of drowsiness, for the foe was always near. Only by his alertness could the enemy be circumvented. There were many kinds of enemies, all of them terrible, each in a different way. At certain seasons of the year there were floods. Streams became quickly swollen and overflowed their banks. Swift action was necessary in order to escape destruction There were enemies of a more subtle kind—animals, rapacious and treacherous: lions, bears, hyenas, jackals, wolves. There were enemies in the air; huge birds of prey were always soaring aloft ready to swoop down upon a lamb or kid. And then, most dangerous of all, were the human birds and beasts of prey—robbers, bandits, men who made a business of robbing sheepfolds and murdering shepherds. That Eastern world was full of perils. It teemed with forces hostile to the shepherd and his flock.

When Ezekiel, Jeremiah, Isaiah, and Habakkuk talk about shepherds, they call them watchmen set to warn and save.

Many a minister fails as a pastor because he is not vigilant. He allows his church to be torn to pieces because he is half asleep. He took it for granted that there were no wolves, no birds of prey, no robbers, and while he was drowsing the enemy arrived. False ideas, destructive interpretations, demoralizing teachings came into his group, and he never knew it. He was interested, perhaps, in literary research; he was absorbed in the discussion contained in the last theological quarterly, and did not know what his young people were reading, or what strange ideas had been lodged in the heads of a group of his leading members. There are errors which are as fierce as wolves and pitiless as hyenas; they tear faith and hope and love to pieces and leave churches, once prosperous, mangled and half dead. (*The Minister as Shepherd* [Hong Kong: Living Books for All, 1980], 41–42, 43–44)

The faithful shepherd must also warn his flock. Paul had done so during his own ministry at Ephesus; he reminds the Ephesian elders of how **night and day for a period of three years** he **did not cease to admonish each one with tears. Admonish** is from *noutheteō*, which refers to giving counsel with a warning involved (cf. Col. 1:28). The pattern of Paul's ministry shows the importance of warning believers about false teachers. He admonished the Ephesians **for a period of three years,** caring for **each one** of the flock (cf. v. 20). So compelled was he to warn them that he hardly had time for sleep, ministering **night and day** (cf. 1 Thess. 2:9; 2 Thess. 3:8). Nor was it a mere academic exercise for Paul—he punctuated his warnings **with** his **tears.** He wept because he knew the terrible consequences when false teachers infiltrate. Only by following Paul's example can the faithful undershepherd protect Christ's flock from the savage wolves and diseased sheep who constantly threaten it.

STUDY AND PRAY

And now I commend you to God and to the word of His grace, which is able to build you up and to give you the inheritance among all those who are sanctified. (20:32)

If an undershepherd is to feed and protect his flock, he must be a student of the Scriptures and devoted to prayer. Only then will he have true knowledge and the wisdom to apply that knowledge. This dual priority of ministry goes back to the example of the apostles, who declared in Acts 6:4, "We will devote ourselves to prayer, and to the ministry of the word." Those exercises are the heart of a leader's effectiveness.

Here is another illustration of Paul's constant practice to **commend** believers **to God** in prayer (Rom. 1:9–10; Eph. 1:15–16; Phil. 1:4; 1 Thess. 1:2–3; 2 Thess. 1:11; 2 Tim. 1:3; Philem. 4). Though not specifically a call for pastors to pray, it is surely a reminder of the centrality of prayer in Paul's life. The church in Acts lived in a constant atmosphere of prayer (1:14; 2:42). It prayed when choosing Judas's successor (1:24), when facing persecution (4:23–31; 16:25); at the choosing of seven men to administer the church's relief efforts (6:6), for Peter's release from prison (12:5, 12), at the sending of Paul and Barnabas to the mission field (13:2), when appointing elders in local churches (14:23); in short, every aspect of the life of the early church was bathed in prayer.

There is no substitute for prayer, for prayer acknowledges dependence on God and lines us up with His purposes. Prayer also allows God to glorify Himself by answering (John 14:13). Without it the undershepherds' attempts to feed, lead, and guard the flock will be in vain. Good intentions, good ideas, or good programs cannot overcome the effects of prayerlessness.

Study of the Word is the other foundational pillar of ministry, since it is **the word of His grace** that **is able to build** believers **up and to give** them **the inheritance among all those who are sanctified.** In 1 Peter 2:2, Peter echoed Paul's thought: "Like newborn babes, long for the pure milk of the word, that by it you may grow in respect to salvation." Paul told Timothy that the church was "the pillar and support of the truth" (1 Tim. 3:15), thus requiring that its leaders know that truth.

The Word is the source of spiritual growth (1 Thess. 2:13; 2 Tim. 3:16–17; 2 Pet. 3:18). The Word is also the source of assurance, convincing believers that they have an **inheritance among all those who are sanctified.** Weak, struggling believers who lack assurance of salvation need to be fed the Word of God that they might "grow in the grace and knowledge of our Lord and Savior Jesus Christ" (2 Pet. 3:18).

Prayer and the ministry of the Word must be the main occupation of the shepherd. If the undershepherd ignores these elements, both he and his flock suffer greatly.

Be Free from Self-Interest

I have coveted no one's silver or gold or clothes. You yourselves know that these hands ministered to my own needs and to the men who were with me. In everything I showed you that by working hard in this manner you must help the weak and remember the words of the Lord Jesus, that He Himself said, 'It

is more blessed to give than to receive.' And when he had said these things, he knelt down and prayed with them all. And they began to weep aloud and embraced Paul, and repeatedly kissed him, grieving especially over the word which he had spoken, that they should see his face no more. And they were accompanying him to the ship. (20:33–38)

A truly God-honoring ministry must focus on giving, not getting. God will not bless the ministry of someone who is preoccupied with money. The Lord Jesus Christ put it simply and directly when He said, "You cannot serve God and mammon" (Matt. 6:24). All believers are commanded, "Let your character be free from the love of money, being content with what you have" (Heb. 13:5); that is doubly true of those in positions of spiritual leadership (1 Tim. 3:3; Titus 1:7). Those who care for the flock of God must not do so for material gain.

Love of money has always characterized false teachers. In the Old Testament, Isaiah (56:11), Jeremiah (6:13; 8:10), and Micah (3:11) denounced the greedy false leaders of Israel. In the New Testament, Paul described false teachers as those who teach "things they should not teach, for the sake of sordid gain" (Titus 1:11). Peter also warned against the greed of false teachers (2 Pet. 2:3).

Paul's ministry was not characterized by self-seeking materialism. The apostle emphatically declared **I have coveted no one's silver or gold or clothes.** He then appealed to their firsthand observation of his three years of ministry at Ephesus. **You yourselves know**, he reminded them, no doubt holding up his hands as he spoke, **that these hands ministered to my own needs and to the men who were with me.** Although Paul had every right to receive support for his ministry (1 Cor. 9:3ff.) and sometimes did (2 Cor. 11:8–9; Phil. 4:10–19), it was his custom to support himself (2 Cor. 11:7; 12:13; 1 Thess. 2:9; 2 Thess. 3:8). He did so that he might "offer the gospel without charge" (1 Cor. 9:18).

Paul then appealed to them to follow his example: **In everything I showed you that by working hard in this manner you must help the weak and remember the words of the Lord Jesus, that He Himself said, 'It is more blessed to give than to receive.'** The apostle not only supported himself but also worked to help others in need. This quotation of Jesus is not recorded in the gospels but was nonetheless known among the early Christians. It is of great consequence that this is the only quotation recorded outside the gospels of a statement spoken by Jesus while He was on earth. That gives significant weight to the truth it reveals. The gospels no more contain every word our Lord spoke during His earthly ministry than they do all His deeds (John 21:25). Only the divinely inspired Bible, however, contains those words and deeds that He wished us to remember. The fanciful deeds and sayings recorded in extrabiblical writings are to be rejected.

Having **said these things,** Paul **knelt down and prayed with them all.** His exhortation was finished, and he had to leave, no doubt because his ship was ready to sail. When the time of prayer was over, **they began to weep aloud and embraced Paul, and repeatedly kissed him, grieving especially over the word which he had spoken, that they should see his face no more.** The parting was an emotional one, reflecting the Ephesian elders' deep love for Paul and their immense sorrow that they would never see him again. Even when the beloved apostle finally tore himself away, they could not bear to part with him and **were accompanying him to the ship.**

Paul's ministry was successful because his life was right with God, he made it his priority to feed and guard the flock, he devoted himself to prayer and the ministry of the word, and he was totally free of self-interest. The result was the devoted love of his people and, more important, the approval of God.

The Courage of Conviction (Acts 21:1–16)

18

And when it came about that we had parted from them and had set sail, we ran a straight course to Cos and the next day to Rhodes and from there to Patara; and having found a ship crossing over to Phoenicia, we went aboard and set sail. And when we had come in sight of Cyprus, leaving it on the left, we kept sailing to Syria and landed at Tyre; for there the ship was to unload its cargo. And after looking up the disciples, we stayed there seven days; and they kept telling Paul through the Spirit not to set foot in Jerusalem. And when it came about that our days there were ended, we departed and started on our journey, while they all, with wives and children, escorted us until we were out of the city. And after kneeling down on the beach and praying, we said farewell to one another. Then we went on board the ship, and they returned home again. And when we had finished the voyage from Tyre, we arrived at Ptolemais; and after greeting the brethren, we stayed with them for a day. And on the next day we departed and came to Caesarea; and entering the house of Philip the evangelist, who was one of the seven, we stayed with him. Now this man had four virgin daughters who were prophetesses. And as we were staying there for some days, a certain prophet named Agabus came down from Judea. And

coming to us, he took Paul's belt and bound his own feet and hands, and said, "This is what the Holy Spirit says: 'In this way the Jews at Jerusalem will bind the man who owns this belt and deliver him into the hands of the Gentiles.'" And when we had heard this, we as well as the local residents began begging him not to go up to Jerusalem. Then Paul answered, "What are you doing, weeping and breaking my heart? For I am ready not only to be bound, but even to die at Jerusalem for the name of the Lord Jesus." And since he would not be persuaded, we fell silent, remarking, "The will of the Lord be done!" And after these days we got ready and started on our way up to Jerusalem. And some of the disciples from Caesarea also came with us, taking us to Mnason of Cyprus, a disciple of long standing with whom we were to lodge. (21:1–16)

Courageous commitment, stemming from strong convictions, is an essential quality found in all those whom God chooses to lead. Convinced that God had given Israel the land of Canaan, Joshua and Caleb argued forcefully for an immediate invasion (Num. 13:30; 14:7–9)—despite the fearful, cowardly recommendations of the other ten spies. Believing that God would grant His people victory over the Canaanite forces led by Sisera, Deborah urged Barak to lead the Israelites against him (Judg. 4:4–14). Such was David's conviction that God would defeat Goliath (one of the cursed Anakim) and deliver Israel from the Philistines that he willingly risked his life in battle with the giant (1 Sam. 17:32–37). Shadrach, Meshach, and Abed-nego were willing to forfeit their lives rather than give up their conviction that God alone is to be worshiped (Dan. 3:16–18). Daniel, too, was willing to die rather than cease worshiping the true God (Dan. 6:10).

The apostle Paul stood in the line of those saints who held such strong convictions. He was completing a critical mission to deliver relief funds from the Gentile churches in Asia Minor and Greece to the many poor in the Jerusalem church. Because of the many pilgrims in that church, and the alienation and persecution of the Jerusalem believers, there were many poor among the congregation who were in constant need. The church had surely depleted its resources in the generosity of the early years (cf. Acts 4:32–37) and now it needed generous help (cf. 2 Cor. 8:20; 9:5). Paul's goal was not only to meet the basic needs of the Jerusalem congregation (cf. Gal. 2:9–10) but also to solidify the loving unity between the Jewish and the Gentile churches (cf. Eph. 2:11–17). As the apostle traveled to Jerusalem to deliver the money, he was repeatedly warned of the trials and persecution he would face when he got there (Acts 20:23). Despite those warnings, he never wavered in his conviction that he was to fulfill God's will in the matter, which gave him the courage to see his ministry through no matter what the personal consequences.

From the narrative in verses 1–16 emerge four aspects of the courage of conviction displayed by the apostle Paul: such courage knows its purpose, cannot be diverted, pays any price, and motivates others.

THE COURAGE OF CONVICTION KNOWS ITS PURPOSE

And when it came about that we had parted from them and had set sail, we ran a straight course to Cos and the next day to Rhodes and from there to Patara; and having found a ship crossing over to Phoenicia, we went aboard and set sail. And when we had come in sight of Cyprus, leaving it on the left, we kept sailing to Syria and landed at Tyre; for there the ship was to unload its cargo. (21:1–3)

Conviction presupposes a clear purpose. Joshua and Caleb were convinced God had given Israel the land of Canaan. Deborah was convinced God would give victory to Israel. David was convinced God would judge Goliath and preserve Israel from the Philistines. Daniel, Shadrach, Meshach, and Abed-nego were convinced that the true God was to be worshiped instead of idols. Paul was convinced that he moved and ministered in the purpose and power of God. From that unshakable conviction came his indomitable courage.

The Acts 21 narrative begins with a reminder of Paul's emotional farewell to the Ephesian elders. Luke, one of Paul's main traveling companions and the author of Acts, notes that **when it came about that we had parted from them and had set sail, we ran a straight course to Cos and the next day to Rhodes and from there to Patara.** Luke's use of the term *apospaō* (**parted**), which means "to tear away" (cf. 20:30; Luke 22:41), shows the trauma of that parting. So great was the Ephesian elders' love for him that Paul literally had to tear himself away from his sorrowing friends.

Having with difficulty **parted from them,** Paul and his companions **set sail** to resume their sea journey to Palestine. Leaving Miletus, they **ran a straight course to Cos,** capital city of the island of the same name. From there they sailed to **Rhodes,** passing as they entered the harbor there the famed Colossus of Rhodes, one of the Seven Wonders of the Ancient World. From Rhodes they rounded the southwestern corner of Asia Minor, stopping at **Patara.** Each of those ports represents a day's voyage; the ship sailed during the day and anchored in each port for the night.

> The reason [the ship did not sail at night] lies in the wind, which in the Aegean during the summer generally blows from the north, beginning at a very early hour in the morning; in the late afternoon it dies away; at sunset there is a dead calm, and thereafter a gentle south wind arises and blows during the night. (Sir William M. Ramsay, *St. Paul the Traveller and the Roman Citizen* [reprint; Grand Rapids: Baker, 1975], 293)

It was that north wind that allowed the ship to run **a straight course** from Miletus to Cos.

Patara, located on the mainland of Asia Minor near the mouth of the Xanthus River, was a large and busy port. In his haste to reach Jerusalem before the Day of Pentecost (20:16), Paul decided to risk crossing the Mediterranean Sea, rather than continuing to hug the coast. The prevailing west winds made such a crossing of the open sea possible. Accordingly, **having found a ship crossing over** the Mediterranean from Patara **to Phoenicia,** Paul and his friends **went aboard and set sail.** This ship was undoubtedly much larger than the smaller coastal vessel they had been sailing on. The ship that would bear Paul across the Mediterranean on his eventful voyage to Rome carried 276 people (Acts 27:37), and this one may have been similar in size.

Crossing the Mediterranean, they passed to the south of **Cyprus, leaving it on the left.** The ship did not anchor at Cyprus but **kept sailing to Syria and landed at Tyre.** The crossing from Patara to Tyre, on the east coast of the Mediterranean, normally took five days. Paul and his party then had seven days (v. 4) to wait before the ship was ready to continue its voyage.

This simple recounting of Paul's travels portrays a man driven to fulfill the priority of meeting the needs of the poor and unifying the church. It shows that the strength of his courage stemmed from devotion to obey what he knew were divine priorities.

THE COURAGE OF CONVICTION CANNOT BE DIVERTED

And after looking up the disciples, we stayed there seven days; and they kept telling Paul through the Spirit not to set foot in Jerusalem. And when it came about that our days there were ended, we departed and started on our journey, while they all, with wives and children, escorted us until we were out of the city. And after kneeling down on the beach and praying, we said farewell to one another. Then we went on board the ship, and they returned home again. (21:4–6)

Traveling on the ship that sailed directly across the Mediterranean to Palestine allowed Paul and his party to spend time in Tyre and still arrive in Jerusalem on schedule for Pentecost. Paul had not founded the church at Tyre and may not have known the Christians in that city, since the church there had been founded by believers fleeing the persecution that broke out in Jerusalem after Stephen's martyrdom (Acts 11:19)—a persecution led, ironically, by Paul himself. That Paul was unfamiliar with the church in Tyre required his **looking up the disciples.** Having found them, Paul and his companions **stayed** with them during the **seven days** they remained in Tyre.

The Christians there quickly attached their love to the apostle and, fearing for his safety, **they kept telling Paul through the Spirit not to set foot in Jerusalem.** The question arises as to whether Paul received here a direct command from the Holy Spirit that he obstinately disobeyed. Some argue that Paul, driven by his passionate concern for the poor and the unity of the church, was disobedient in going to Jerusalem. The Bible quite candidly reveals the shortcomings of even the greatest men of God. Scripture presents the failings, as well as the triumphs, of men such as Noah, Abraham, Jacob, David, Peter, John, and the rest of the apostles. Paul was no more immune to failure than they were; in fact, Luke has already recorded Paul's quarrel with Barnabas over John Mark (15:37–39). That Paul was not disobedient on this occasion, however, is evident from several considerations.

First, the phrase **through the Spirit** is inconclusive; it merely means that someone spoke as from a spiritual gift of prophecy. As Paul notes in 1 Corinthians 14:29, however, not every manifestation of the gift of prophecy is legitimate. Whether it was legitimate in this instance must be determined by other factors.

Second, Paul lived a life sensitive to the Spirit's leading. When forbidden by the Spirit to preach in certain regions, Paul did not disobey (Acts 16:6–7). When led by the Spirit to minister in Macedonia, Paul immediately obeyed (Acts 16:9–10). That long-term pattern of obedience makes it unlikely that he was disobedient in this matter.

Third, the Holy Spirit had never before prohibited Paul from going to Jerusalem. According to Acts 20:22–23, He warned Paul repeatedly of what would happen to him when he got there but did not tell him not to go.

Fourth, Paul described his mission to Jerusalem as "the ministry which I received from the Lord Jesus" (Acts 20:24). How could the Holy Spirit forbid Paul from doing what the Lord Jesus Christ had commanded him to? Further, Acts 19:21 records that "Paul purposed in the spirit to go to Jerusalem," while in Acts 20:22 the apostle describes himself as "bound in spirit . . . on my way to Jerusalem." He was compelled in his innermost being by the Holy Spirit to undertake this mission.

Finally, the Scriptures nowhere suggest that Paul sinned by going to Jerusalem. After he got there he declared, "I have lived my life with a perfectly good conscience before God up to this day" (Acts 23:1; cf. 24:16). It is difficult to see how he could have said that if he had just flagrantly sinned against God.

In Tyre, as in so many other places, the Holy Spirit warned Paul of the persecution he faced in Jerusalem. The believers in Tyre, through the Spirit, foresaw the suffering he would endure when he reached his goal. It was only natural that they would try to dissuade him from going to Jerusalem—just as some of his older friends would soon do (21:12). The Spirit's message to Paul in Tyre, as elsewhere, was a warning, not a prohibition.

After a week of fellowship and ministry at Tyre, it was time for Paul and his group to leave. Luke writes, **when it came about that our days there were ended**—the ship had finished unloading its cargo and was ready to sail—**we departed and started on our journey.** So devoted had the Christians at Tyre become to them that **they all, with wives and children, escorted** Paul and his companions **until** they **were out of the city** (cf. 20:38). At the shore they held an impromptu prayer meeting. Luke records that **after kneeling down on the beach and praying, we said farewell to one another.** Then Paul and his companions **went on board the ship, and** the believers from Tyre **returned home again.**

Neither the threat of persecution nor the pleadings of well-meaning fellow believers could divert Paul from fulfilling his calling. He retained the courage of his conviction despite the repeated warnings of severe persecution once he reached Jerusalem (Acts 20:23). Nothing could dissuade him from carrying out the task the Lord had assigned him.

THE COURAGE OF CONVICTION PAYS ANY PRICE

And when we had finished the voyage from Tyre, we arrived at Ptolemais; and after greeting the brethren, we stayed with them for a day. And on the next day we departed and came to Caesarea; and entering the house of Philip the evangelist, who was one of the seven, we stayed with him. Now this man had four virgin daughters who were prophetesses. And as we were staying there for some days, a certain prophet named Agabus came down from Judea. And coming to us, he took Paul's belt and bound his own feet and hands, and said, "This is what the Holy Spirit says: 'In this way the Jews at Jerusalem will bind the man who owns this belt and deliver him into the hands of the Gentiles.'" And when we had heard this, we as well as the local

residents began begging him not to go up to Jerusalem. Then Paul answered, "What are you doing, weeping and breaking my heart? For I am ready not only to be bound, but even to die at Jerusalem for the name of the Lord Jesus." And since he would not be persuaded, we fell silent, remarking, "The will of the Lord be done!" (21:7–14)

Having completed **the voyage from Tyre,** Paul and the others **arrived at Ptolemais.** Known in Old Testament times as Acco (Judg. 1:31), Ptolemais was about twenty-five miles south of Tyre. Never one to waste ministry opportunities (cf. Eph. 5:16), Paul immediately sought out the Christians in that city. **After greeting the brethren,** Paul and his companions **stayed with them for a day.** The church at Ptolemais, like that of Tyre, had likely been founded by those who fled Jerusalem following Stephen's martyrdom (Acts 11:19). Paul's care for them was no less because he had not founded their church; his was a "concern for all the churches" (2 Cor. 11:28).

After a day's delay, the ship resumed its journey south along the coast. **On the next day** it covered the forty miles to **Caesarea,** Jerusalem's port, located about sixty miles northwest of the holy city. It was the seat of the Roman government in Judea and the official residence of its governors (most notably Pilate). Caesarea had a mixed population of Jews and Gentiles. It was also home to **Philip the evangelist, who was one of the seven** faithful men chosen by the early church some twenty years earlier to oversee the distribution of food to widows (Acts 6:5–6). God honored his service and called Philip to be an evangelist. It was he who preached the gospel in Samaria (Acts 8:5) and many other nearby cities (8:40). Philip also was the pioneer in preaching the gospel to non-Jews, first to the half-breed Samaritans, then to the Gentile Ethiopian eunuch (8:26ff.). He richly deserved the appellation **evangelist**—a title given to no one else in Acts (though Timothy was told to do the work of an evangelist [2 Tim. 4:5]).

Although many years earlier Paul had been a bitter enemy of Philip and the gospel he preached, they were now fellow preachers of salvation. The Christians' chief persecutor, once so feared (cf. Gal. 1:22–24), was welcomed into his **house,** and he and his friends **stayed with him.**

Philip's household included his **four virgin daughters who were prophetesses.** That Luke describes them as virgins suggests that they may have been set aside by God for special ministry (cf. 1 Cor. 7:34). Prophets, like apostles, were specially appointed by God in the church. They must be distinguished from individual believers with the gift of prophecy (1 Cor. 12:10). They complemented the ministry of the apostles (Eph. 4:11), functioning exclusively within a particular local congregation, while the apostles had a broader ministry. In contrast to the apostles, whose doctrinal revelation was foundational to the church (Acts 2:42; Eph. 2:20), the message of the prophets was more personal and practical. They sometimes received new revelation from God concerning matters that would later be covered in Scripture. The main thrust of their ministry, however, was the reiteration or exposition of existing divine revelation (1 Cor. 14:3), much like today's preachers and teachers of the Word.

The revelatory aspect of the gift of prophecy ceased at the close of the apostolic era with the completing of Scripture. The nonrevelatory, reiterative aspect of the prophets' ministry of doctrinal and practical exhortation has been taken over by the evangelists, pastors, and teachers. In fact, in the last letters he wrote, the pastoral epistles, Paul does not refer to prophets at all; instead, teaching is to be done by the elders (1 Tim. 3:2; Titus 1:9). This lack of references to prophets is especially significant in epistles devoted largely to church structure, officers, and service (cf. 1 Tim. 3:15). (For a further discussion of prophets and the gift of prophecy, see *1 Corinthians*, MacArthur New Testament Commentary [Chicago: Moody, 1984], 323–24; *Charismatic Chaos* [Grand Rapids: Zondervan, 1992], 69–70; and *Reckless Faith* [Wheaton, Ill.: Crossway, 1994], 177–99.)

Luke records no details regarding Philip's daughters' prophetic ministry. It is therefore impossible to know how often they prophesied or even if they did so more than once. However the New Testament does not permit women to assume the role of preachers or teachers in the church (1 Cor. 14:34–36; 1 Tim. 2:11–12). It is likely, therefore, that they prophesied by receiving divine revelation, rather than preaching sermons. It is also possible that they spoke instructively to individuals rather than to congregations.

It has been recorded that early believers regarded these women as valuable sources of information on the early history of the church. The historian Eusebius notes that the church Father Papias received information from them (*Ecclesiastical History*, III.XXXIX; [Grand Rapids: Baker, 1973], 126). Perhaps Luke used them as a source of information in writing his gospel and Acts. He would have had many opportunities to talk with them, not only during this visit, but also during Paul's two-year imprisonment at Caesarea (Acts 24:27).

Whatever the nature of their prophetic ministry, the four women did not prophesy on this occasion regarding Paul. It was left to another prophet to do that. After the apostolic party had stayed **for some days** in Philip's house, **a certain prophet named Agabus came down from Judea.** Although located in Judea, Caesarea was considered a foreign city by the Jews, since it was the seat of the hated Roman occupation forces. Scripture mentions an earlier prophecy by Agabus (Acts

11:28) and prophecies by Judas and Silas (Acts 15:32), but only here is a verbatim prophecy recorded. That prophecy graphically depicts Paul's impending arrest at Jerusalem. In a dramatic enactment reminiscent of the Old Testament prophets (cf. 1 Kings 11:29–39; Isa. 20:2–6; Jer. 13:1–11; Ezek. 4–5), Agabus **took Paul's belt and bound his own feet and hands.** He then explained the significance of his actions: **"This is what the Holy Spirit says: 'In this way the Jews at Jerusalem will bind the man who owns this belt and deliver him into the hands of the Gentiles.'"** Agabus's dramatic actions and words were a warning to Paul of what awaited him in Jerusalem, and a test of his courage.

Like the believers in Tyre, the Caesarean Christians were appalled when they learned of Paul's fate. Along with Luke and the rest of the apostle's companions, **the local residents began begging him not to go up to Jerusalem.** Their love and concern for the beloved apostle caused them, in view of his inevitable capture, to try to dissuade him from risking his life.

Paul's response reflected his willingness to pay any price required to complete the task the Lord had assigned him. To their appeals **Paul answered, "What are you doing, weeping and breaking my heart? For I am ready not only to be bound, but even to die at Jerusalem for the name of the Lord Jesus."** Paul would not be turned aside from his goal, even by the concerns of well-meaning friends. His determination mirrored that of Ezekiel:

> For you are not being sent to a people of unintelligible speech or difficult language, but to the house of Israel, nor to many peoples of unintelligible speech or difficult language, whose words you cannot understand. But I have sent you to them who should listen to you; yet the house of Israel will not be willing to listen to you, since they are not willing to listen to Me. Surely the whole house of Israel is stubborn and obstinate. Behold, I have made your face as hard as their faces, and your forehead as hard as their foreheads. Like emery harder than flint I have made your forehead. Do not be afraid of them or be dismayed before them, though they are a rebellious house. (Ezek. 3:5–9)

Because of Israel's stubborn and obstinate refusal to heed his message, Ezekiel would have to be even more stubborn and obstinate in his determination to deliver it.

At last, realizing Paul **would not be persuaded** to cancel his plans to go to Jerusalem, the rest of the believers **fell silent, remarking, "The will of the Lord be done!"** That was not fatalistic resignation but confident trust in God's sovereign and perfect will (cf. 1 Sam. 3:18; Matt. 6:10; Luke 22:42). They committed Paul into His care.

THE COURAGE OF CONVICTION MOTIVATES OTHERS

And after these days we got ready and started on our way up to Jerusalem. And some of the disciples from Caesarea also came with us, taking us to Mnason of Cyprus, a disciple of long standing with whom we were to lodge. (21:15–16)

Unable to dissuade Paul, his companions **got ready and started on** their **way up to Jerusalem**. Despite their forebodings, **some of the disciples from Caesarea also came with** Paul and his party, **taking** them **to Mnason of Cyprus, a disciple of long standing with whom** Paul and his party **were to lodge**. Instead of their fears affecting him, his courage motivated them. They knew he would be a marked man in Jerusalem, facing hatred, imprisonment, even death. They also knew that by identifying with him they put themselves at risk. Yet they were willing to accept that risk because the apostle was. His courage was contagious.

The Civil War battle of Antietam was one of the bloodiest days in American military history. On that September day in 1862 nearly 6,000 Union and Confederate soldiers were killed and 17,000 others wounded. To put that in perspective:

> The casualties at Antietam numbered four times the total suffered by American soldiers at the Normandy beaches on June 6, 1944. More than twice as many Americans lost their lives in one day at Sharpsburg [Antietam] as fell in combat in the War of 1812, the Mexican War, and the Spanish-American war *combined*. (James M. McPherson, *Battle Cry of Freedom* [New York: Oxford, 1988], 544. Italics in original.)

Some of the fiercest fighting on that awful day took place in a part of the battlefield known as the Cornfield. Some Union soldiers, their ranks decimated by heavy Confederate fire, fled toward the rear in wild panic—only to be stopped by the contagious courage of one man. Historian Bruce Catton describes the scene:

> The Pennsylvanians broke and ran again—to be stopped, incomprehensibly, a few yards in the rear by a boyish private who stood on a little hillock and kept swinging his hat, shouting: "Rally, boys, rally! Die like men, don't run like dogs!"

> Strangely, on that desperate field where men were madly heroic and full of abject panic by turns, this lone private stopped the retreat. (*Mr. Lincoln's Army* [New York: The Fairfax Press, 1984], 162)

Like that nameless soldier, Paul had the courage not only to face the enemy himself but also to inspire others to do likewise.

Paul's Arrival at Jerusalem (Acts 21:17–26)

19

And when we had come to Jerusalem, the brethren received us gladly. And now the following day Paul went in with us to James, and all the elders were present. And after he had greeted them, he began to relate one by one the things which God had done among the Gentiles through his ministry. And when they heard it they began glorifying God; and they said to him, "You see, brother, how many thousands there are among the Jews of those who have believed, and they are all zealous for the Law; and they have been told about you, that you are teaching all the Jews who are among the Gentiles to forsake Moses, telling them not to circumcise their children nor to walk according to the customs. What, then, is to be done? They will certainly hear that you have come. Therefore do this that we tell you. We have four men who are under a vow; take them and purify yourself along with them, and pay their expenses in order that they may shave their heads; and all will know that there is nothing to the things which they have been told about you, but that you yourself also walk orderly, keeping the Law. But concerning the Gentiles who have believed, we wrote, having decided that they should abstain from meat sacrificed to idols and from blood and from what is strangled and from fornication." Then Paul took the men, and

the next day, purifying himself along with them, went into the temple, giving notice of the completion of the days of purification, until the sacrifice was offered for each one of them. (21:17–26)

The book of Acts reveals many aspects of the apostle Paul's character. He was a powerful, clear preacher and a man of great learning and wisdom. He was bold and fearless in the face of the fiercest opposition. Possessing remarkable self-discipline and holding strong, unwavering commitments, Paul was persistent in carrying out the tasks the Lord assigned him. The apostle was also a leader who inspired others to imitate his godly life (1 Cor. 11:1). His love for the lost drove him across the Roman world, restlessly seeking new regions to evangelize (cf. Rom. 15:20). And he himself testified that his loving concern for the churches was the greatest burden he bore (2 Cor. 11:28).

Yet that description of Paul is incomplete; it lacks one essential element of his character: humility.

Paul certainly had much to boast of. He had impeccable Jewish credentials as a member of the elite Pharisees and a student of the greatest rabbi of the day, Gamaliel. Further, he was "advancing in Judaism beyond many of [his] contemporaries among [his] countrymen, being more extremely zealous for [his] ancestral traditions" (Gal. 1:14; cf. Phil. 3:5–6). No wonder that Paul characterized himself to the Philippians as a "Hebrew of Hebrews" (Phil. 3:5). His credentials following his dramatic conversion are no less impressive. As the "apostle to the Gentiles" (Rom. 11:13; 1 Tim. 2:7), Paul spearheaded the spread of the gospel and the establishment of churches throughout the Roman world. Besides his vision on the Damascus road, he was personally visited by the resurrected, glorified Christ several other times. Paul also had the unique privilege of being "caught up to the third heaven" (2 Cor. 12:2). And his sufferings for the cause of Christ were unmatched by anyone else (2 Cor. 11:22ff.; Gal. 6:17). He had performed all the signs of an apostle (2 Cor. 12:12) and was in no sense "inferior to the most eminent apostles" (2 Cor. 11:5).

All of the revelations he received, along with his knowledge and accomplishments, could have made Paul proud, boastful, egotistical, and arrogant. Instead, like the Lord Jesus Christ (Matt. 11:29), he was a gentle, gracious, humble man (2 Cor. 10:1; 1 Tim. 1:12–17). His humility can be seen clearly in this section.

The collection of the offering, which had consumed Paul for many months and endless miles of travel, was about to culminate in his long-anticipated arrival at Jerusalem. There he would present to the Jerusalem church that offering, which he had painstakingly received from the Gentile congregations of Asia Minor and Greece. Their substantial gift of love and gesture of unity would help meet the needs of the poor believers at Jerusalem and conciliate the Jewish and Gentile churches.

Paul's last stop before Jerusalem was the port city of Caesarea. From there he and his companions "started on [their] way up to Jerusalem" (Acts 21:15), about sixty-five miles to the southeast. Travelers always went "up" to Jerusalem, since it is located on a plateau. As was customary (cf. Acts 20:38; 21:5), some of the Caesarean Christians accompanied Paul's party to Jerusalem (21:16). Luke notes that their destination was the house of "Mnason of Cyprus, a disciple of long standing with whom [they] were to lodge" (21:16). Mnason's Greek name suggests that he was a Hellenistic Jew. His familiarity with Gentiles and with Greek culture was no doubt why Paul and his Gentile companions stayed with him. Mnason would have been more comfortable housing them than the more strict Palestinian Jews. Luke's description of him as a "disciple of long standing" may mean that he was one of those converted on the Day of Pentecost. If so, he may have been one of Luke's sources on the early days of the church.

Paul's arrival in Jerusalem marked the end of his missionary journeys. He would soon be arrested and remain an "ambassador in chains" (Eph. 6:20) for the remainder of the period covered by Acts. This transitional passage depicts the apostle's fellowship with the Jerusalem church and the events leading to his arrest. To capture the features of this monumental meeting, we may divide the text into three sections: communion, concern, and compromise.

COMMUNION

And when we had come to Jerusalem, the brethren received us gladly. And now the following day Paul went in with us to James, and all the elders were present. And after he had greeted them, he began to relate one by one the things which God had done among the Gentiles through his ministry. And when they heard it they began glorifying God; (21:17–20a)

Paul no doubt arrived in **Jerusalem** by the Day of Pentecost as he had planned (20:16). The **brethren** there **received** the apostle and his party **gladly**. Certainly they were pleased at the generous (2 Cor. 8:20) expression of love from the Gentile churches in the much-needed offering Paul and the others brought. But more significantly, they were overjoyed at the Gentile converts who accompanied Paul. They provided firsthand evidence of God's gracious saving work throughout the Roman world. There was no doubt a time of warm communion.

After the initial, unofficial reception (possibly at Mnason's house), on **the following day Paul** and the others **went in to James, and all the elders were present.** This was the official reception by the leaders of the church. The mention of **James and all the elders** marks a significant change in that leadership. When the church at Jerusalem began, it was ruled by the apostles (2:42; 4:35–37; 5:2). As the church grew, the apostles recognized the need for assistance with the administrative details, and seven men were chosen to serve under them (6:2–6). Elders are first mentioned in 11:30, and by the time of the Jerusalem Council they had assumed a prominent role (15:2, 4, 6, 22, 23; 16:4). Now Paul and the others found the church led by the **elders** alone; the apostles are not mentioned. At least one was already dead—James the brother of John (Acts 12:2). The others had turned over the leadership responsibilities to the elders and left the city to engage in missionary work. Elder rule was thus being established as the New Testament pattern of church government (cf. Acts 14:23; 20:17; 1 Tim. 5:17; Titus 1:5; James 5:14; 1 Pet. 5:1, 5).

The number of those elders is not given. Some have speculated that there were seventy, paralleling the Jewish Sanhedrin. Given the enormous size of the Jerusalem church (cf. v. 20), there may have been at least that many and probably more. Just as Peter often functioned as spokesman for the apostles, **James** filled that role for the elders. Paul described him as having been, with Peter and John, one of the pillars of the Jerusalem church (Gal. 2:9). Significantly, following his own miraculous release from Herod's prison, Peter had commanded the believers to "report these things to James and the brethren" (Acts 12:17). James held a recognized position of leadership even at that early date.

Strangely, Luke does not mention the presentation of the collection. In fact, except for an allusion to it in 24:17, he does not refer to it at all in Acts. We can assume, however, that it was presented and gratefully accepted.

After he had greeted the assembled elders, Paul **began to relate one by one the things which God had done among the Gentiles through his ministry.** He did not couch his report in vague generalities or tedious statistics. Instead, he told them **one by one** (cf. Acts 11:4) of specific incidents in his missionary journeys. Nor did the apostle boast of what he had accomplished; instead, he recounted **the things which God had done among the Gentiles through his ministry.** As in his previous reports (14:27; 15:4, 12), Paul humbly gave all the credit and glory to God. He saw himself only as an instrument God graciously called to preach the gospel to the Gentiles (cf. Rom. 15:18; Eph. 3:8; 1 Thess. 2:4).

Paul expressed his humility in his rebuke of the hero-worshiping Corinthians. Writing to them in 1 Corinthians 3:5–7 he declared:

What then is Apollos? And what is Paul? Servants through whom you believed, even as the Lord gave opportunity to each one. I planted, Apollos watered, but God was causing the growth. So then neither the one who plants nor the one who waters is anything, but God who causes the growth.

Later in that same letter he added, "By the grace of God I am what I am, and His grace toward me did not prove vain; but I labored even more than all of them, yet not I, but the grace of God with me" (1 Cor. 15:10). To the Romans he wrote, "I will not presume to speak of anything except what Christ has accomplished through me, resulting in the obedience of the Gentiles by word and deed" (Rom. 15:18). It is the mark of a godly man that he exalts the Lord and not himself. "He who boasts," wrote Paul in 2 Corinthians 10:17, "let him boast in the Lord."

Paul's God-centered report produced a corresponding response by the assembled elders. Instead of praising him, **when they heard it, they began glorifying God.** As when Peter reported the salvation of Cornelius's household (11:18), Paul's report produced rejoicing. (The salvation of sinners has the same effect in heaven, as Luke 15:7, 10, 32 indicate.) By glorifying God, the elders acknowledged that salvation is His work, not man's.

CONCERN

and they said to him, "You see, brother, how many thousands there are among the Jews of those who have believed, and they are all zealous for the Law; and they have been told about you, that you are teaching all the Jews who are among the Gentiles to forsake Moses, telling them not to circumcise their children nor to walk according to the customs. What, then, is to be done? They will certainly hear that you have come." (21:20b–22)

The joy of the Jerusalem leaders was mixed with concern. A potentially serious problem had developed, one they needed Paul's help to resolve. They reminded their beloved **brother** of something he himself had observed (**you see** is from *theoreō*, which means "to perceive, discern, or reflect on"): There were **many thousands** (*muriades*, literally "myriads," "tens of thousands") ... **among the Jews ... who** had **believed** who were **all zealous for the Law.** The Greek text uses a noun and actually reads "zealots for the law." These were Jewish Christians who remained devoted to the ceremonial aspects of the law. While not viewing it as a means of salvation, they still observed its required feasts, Sabbath regulations, ritual vows (v. 23), and dietary restrictions.

Why were they still clinging to the customs and rituals of the Old Covenant? First, because those customs and rituals had been established by God. Coming to faith in Jesus Christ enhanced these Jewish believers' love for God and desire to obey Him and thus may have motivated a greater zeal for the old ceremonies.

Second, the apostles and other leaders in the Jerusalem church did not oppose the continuation of these practices. Nowhere in the New Testament are Jewish believers condemned for observing them. In fact, Paul commands tolerance for such "weaker brothers" (Rom. 14:1ff.; 1 Cor. 8–10) until they grow to understand their freedom and can use it with clear consciences. The Jerusalem Council (Acts 15), while forbidding the imposition of Old Covenant rituals on Gentiles, did not prohibit Jewish believers from continuing to observe them.

God Himself was tolerant during this period of transition, knowing how difficult it was for the Jewish Christians to break with their past (see the discussion of this point in chapter 12 of this volume). He also knew that in a few years this would no longer be a dominant issue in the church. After the Jewish revolt against Rome (A.D. 66–70), which culminated in the destruction of Jerusalem, the influence of the Jerusalem church waned. Christianity gradually became a predominantly Gentile faith, and other churches (such as Antioch and Alexandria) ascended to the forefront.

James and the elders then set forth the specific problem that was troubling them. They warned Paul, "The zealots for the law **have been told about you that you are teaching all the Jews who are among the Gentiles to forsake Moses, telling them not to circumcise their children nor to walk according to the customs."** This large group of zealous Jewish believers provided fertile soil for false teachers—Paul's old nemeses the Judaizers. These bitter enemies of the gospel of grace had dogged Paul's footsteps throughout his missionary journeys. In fact, he wrote Galatians largely to counter their dangerous false teachings. They denied that salvation is by grace through faith alone, insisting that keeping the Mosaic law was required for salvation (cf. Acts 15:1). The Jerusalem Council explicitly rejected their heretical teachings.

The phrase **they have been told** indicates that these troubling reports were far more than mere rumors from the Diaspora Jews (those living outside Palestine). The underlying Greek verb is *katēcheō*, from which the English word "catechism," implying learning by repetition, derives. The Judaizers had literally drilled their lies about Paul into the heads of the Jewish Christians. By claiming that Paul was **teaching all the Jews who are among the Gentiles to forsake Moses, telling them not to circumcise their children nor to walk according to**

the customs, the Judaizers sought to destroy his credibility with the Hebrew Christian community, which still revered the Mosaic law.

The charges against Paul were unsettling for the Jerusalem church, since they dealt with issues that went to the heart of what set the Jews apart as God's people. Further, this was

> a time of intense Jewish nationalism and political unrest. One insurrection after another rose to challenge the Roman overlords, and Felix brutally suppressed them all. This only increased the Jewish hatred for Rome and inflamed anti-Gentile sentiments. It was a time when pro-Jewish sentiment was at its height, and friendliness with outsiders was viewed askance. (John B. Polhill, *The New American Commentary: Acts* [Nashville: Broadman, 1992], 447)

Thus, the allegations against Paul posed a serious threat to the Jerusalem church's efforts to evangelize unbelieving Jews.

The Judaizer's accusations were, of course, completely false. Paul nowhere taught Jewish Christians to abandon their Jewish heritage. In keeping with the decision of the Jerusalem Council he did, however, insist that Gentiles not be pressured to observe the ceremonies of the law. All this discussion brings up the question: If Paul really opposed circumcision, why did he circumcise Timothy (Acts 16:1–3)? And if he taught others not to observe the Jewish customs, why did he take a Nazirite vow (Acts 18:18)? Further, the Judaizers' lies about Paul were contradictory. In Galatia, they falsely accused him of advocating circumcision (Gal. 5:11); here in Jerusalem they falsely accused him of abrogating it. Like all inveterate liars, they said whatever was expedient at the moment.

It is hardly surprising that the children of the father of lies resort to lies (John 8:44). Lies are one of the main ways Satan attacks the work of God. Believers should be slow to accept accusations against other Christians (particularly leaders, 1 Tim. 5:19), especially when such charges originate with opponents of the Christian faith.

False or not, the accusations posed a serious threat that had to be dealt with. As a way of introducing their proposed solution, the elders asked Paul **"What, then, is to be done? They will certainly hear that you have come."** Something had to be decided, for the news of Paul's presence in Jerusalem could hardly be kept secret.

COMPROMISE

"Therefore do this that we tell you. We have four men who are under a vow; take them and purify yourself along with them, and

pay their expenses in order that they may shave their heads; and all will know that there is nothing to the things which they have been told about you, but that you yourself also walk orderly, keeping the Law. But concerning the Gentiles who have believed, we wrote, having decided that they should abstain from meat sacrificed to idols and from blood and from what is strangled and from fornication." Then Paul took the men, and the next day, purifying himself along with them, went into the temple, giving notice of the completion of the days of purification, until the sacrifice was offered for each one of them. (21:23-26)

The elders feared a confrontation between the apostle to the Gentiles and the misinformed zealots for the law. To head that off, they suggested a compromise—not a sacrifice of truth for expediency but an act of self-sacrificial humility to promote unity and understanding. **"Therefore,"** they urged Paul, **"do this that we tell you."** They informed him of **four men** of their number **who** were **under a vow** (a Nazirite vow, as the reference to shaving their heads makes clear [cf. Num. 6:18]). The Nazirite vow, expounded at length in Numbers 6, symbolized total separation to God. It involved abstaining from alcoholic beverages and all other products derived from grapes, letting the hair of the head grow long, and avoiding contact with dead bodies. The usual length of the vow was thirty days (cf. Josephus *Wars* 2.15.1), although Samson (Judg. 16:17), Samuel (1 Sam. 1:11), and John the Baptist (Luke 1:15) were Nazirites for life. It manifested the highest level of spiritual devotion.

What it meant for Paul to **purify** himself **along with** the four is not clear. He could not have taken a Nazirite vow himself, since the four men's vows would expire in seven days (v. 27). Some have suggested that the four had incurred a ritual defilement during their vows. Numbers 6:9-12 describes the purification ritual, lasting seven days, that applied in those circumstances. That does not appear to be the case here, however, since those defiled and purified had to begin the period of their vows all over again (Num. 6:12). It would also not explain the preliminary visit to the temple, recorded in verse 26.

A more likely explanation is that Paul, having returned to Israel from Gentile lands, was considered ceremonially unclean. As their sponsor, Paul would participate in the ceremony marking the culmination of the four men's vows. But before he could do that, he would have to undergo ritual purification himself. His willingness to do that would show that he had no disdain for Jewish customs and tradition.

A second way the apostle could show his continuing devotion to his Jewish heritage was to **pay** the four men's **expenses in order**

that they might **shave their heads.** The expenses connected with the Nazirite vow (including paying for the hair-cutting ceremony in the temple and several expensive sacrifices [Num. 6:14ff.]) were considerable, and undertaking them for another was considered an act of piety. That would be further proof that the Judaizers' charges against Paul were false. **"All** those concerned about the Judaizers' allegations **will** then **know,"** James informed Paul, **"that there is nothing to the things which they have been told about you, but that you yourself also walk orderly, keeping the Law."**

James then added an important clarifying statement: **"But concerning the Gentiles who have believed, we wrote, having decided that they should abstain from meat sacrificed to idols and from blood and from what is strangled and from fornication."** By urging this course of action on Paul's part, the elders were by no means abrogating the decree of the Jerusalem Council regarding Gentiles. Gentiles were not to be required to observe the ceremonies and rituals of the Mosaic law. To make that absolutely clear, James summarized the decision of the council that Gentiles were only required to **abstain from meat sacrificed to idols and from blood and from what is strangled and from fornication.** Since Paul was Jewish, his participation in the ceremony would not violate that decision.

Displaying humility and a desire for unity, Paul agreed to the elders' proposal. Doing so would not compromise biblical truth since, as Paul himself had written in Romans 14 and 15, such matters were issues of Christian liberty. In fact, Paul's participation in the ceremony was an illustration of the principle he laid down in 1 Corinthians 9:19–23:

> For though I am free from all men, I have made myself a slave to all, that I might win the more. And to the Jews I became as a Jew, that I might win Jews; to those who are under the Law, as under the Law, though not being myself under the Law, that I might win those who are under the Law; to those who are without law, as without law, though not being without the law of God but under the law of Christ, that I might win those who are without law. To the weak I became weak, that I might win the weak; I have become all things to all men, that I may by all means save some. And I do all things for the sake of the gospel, that I may become a fellow partaker of it.

(For further discussion regarding Christian liberty, see *1 Corinthians*, MacArthur New Testament Commentary [Chicago: Moody, 1984], 243ff.) Accordingly, **Paul took the men, and the next day, purifying himself along with them, went into the temple, giving notice of the completion of the days of purification, until the sacrifice was**

offered for each one of them. Thus was set in motion the chain of events that would culminate in the apostle's arrest.

Some have argued that by heeding the elders' request, Paul made a tragic mistake. They accuse him of compromising his convictions and violating his conscience, although for the best of motives. Such a view is unlikely, however, for several reasons.

First, Paul had taken a Nazirite vow himself on his second missionary journey (18:18). Why, then, would it be wrong for him to participate in this ceremony?

Second, as noted, Paul's participation did not compromise any biblical truth. Instead, it was simply a matter of Christian liberty.

Third, if Paul made such a serious error, would not the Holy Spirit have made that clear in the text? Luke, under the Spirit's inspiration, recorded Paul's failures (cf. 15:37–39) as well as his strengths.

Fourth, Paul's motives were pure. That, coupled with the his vast knowledge of biblical truth, makes such a serious mistake unlikely.

Finally, the negative results do not prove he made a mistake. Such a pragmatic approach ignores the fact that Paul's arrest had been prophesied before he arrived in Jerusalem (21:4, 11; cf. 20:22-23).

Paul's humility permeates this straightforward historical narrative. He was humble before God, giving Him the glory for all that had been accomplished through his ministry. He showed his humility before other believers by agreeing to do what the elders asked of him. Finally, Paul humbly accepted the persecution he would shortly face.

Paul's Arrest
(Acts 21:27–22:29)

20

And when the seven days were almost over, the Jews from Asia, upon seeing him in the temple, began to stir up all the multitude and laid hands on him, crying out, "Men of Israel, come to our aid! This is the man who preaches to all men everywhere against our people, and the Law, and this place; and besides he has even brought Greeks into the temple and has defiled this holy place." For they had previously seen Trophimus the Ephesian in the city with him, and they supposed that Paul had brought him into the temple. And all the city was aroused, and the people rushed together; and taking hold of Paul, they dragged him out of the temple; and immediately the doors were shut. And while they were seeking to kill him, a report came up to the commander of the Roman cohort that all Jerusalem was in confusion. And at once he took along some soldiers and centurions, and ran down to them; and when they saw the commander and the soldiers, they stopped beating Paul. Then the commander came up and took hold of him, and ordered him to be bound with two chains; and he began asking who he was and what he had done. But among the crowd some were shouting one thing and some another; and when he could not find out the facts on account of the uproar, he ordered him to be brought into the barracks. And when he got to the stairs, it so happened that he was carried by the soldiers because of the violence of the mob; for the multitude of the people kept following behind, crying out, "Away with him!" And as Paul was about to be brought into the barracks, he said to the commander, "May I say something to you?" And he said, "Do you know Greek? Then you are not the Egyptian who some time ago stirred up a revolt and led the four thousand men of the Assassins out into the wilderness?" But Paul said, "I am a Jew of Tarsus in Cilicia, a citizen of no insignificant city; and I beg you, allow me to speak to the people." And when he had given him permission, Paul, standing on the stairs, motioned to the people with his hand; and when there was a great hush, he spoke to them in the Hebrew dialect, saying, "Brethren and fathers, hear my defense which I now offer to you." And when they heard that he was addressing them in the Hebrew dialect, they became even more quiet; and he said, "I am a Jew, born in Tarsus of Cilicia, but brought up in this city, educated under Gamaliel, strictly according to the law of our fathers, being zealous for God, just as you all are today. And I persecuted this Way to the death, binding and putting both men and women into prisons, as also the high priest and all the Council of the elders can testify. From them I also received letters to the brethren, and started off for Damascus in order to bring even those who were there to Jerusalem as prisoners to be punished. And it came about that as I was on my way, approaching Damascus about noontime, a very bright light suddenly flashed from heaven all around me, and I fell to the ground and heard a voice saying to me, 'Saul, Saul, why are you persecuting Me?' And I answered, 'Who art Thou, Lord?' And He said to me, 'I am Jesus the Nazarene, whom you are persecuting.' And those who were with me beheld the light, to be sure, but did not understand the voice of the One who was speaking to me. And I said, 'What shall I do, Lord?' And the Lord said to me, 'Arise and go on into Damascus; and there you will be told of all that has been appointed for you to do.' But since I could not see because of the brightness of that light, I was led by the hand by those who were with me, and came into Damascus. And a certain Ananias, a man who was devout by the standard of the Law, and well spoken of by all the Jews who lived there, came to me, and standing near said to me, 'Brother Saul, receive your sight!' And at that very time I looked up at him. And he said, 'The God of our fathers has appointed you to know His will, and to see the Righteous One, and to hear an utterance from His mouth. For you will be a witness for Him to all men of what you have seen and heard. And now why do you delay? Arise, and be baptized, and wash away your sins, call-ing on His name.' And it came about when I returned to Jerusalem and was praying in the temple, that I fell into a trance, and I saw Him saying to me, 'Make haste, and get out of Jerusalem quickly, because they will not accept your testimony about Me.' And I said, 'Lord, they themselves understand that in one synagogue after another I used to imprison and beat those who believed in Thee. And when the blood of Thy witness Stephen was being shed, I also was standing by approving, and watching out for the cloaks of those who were slaying him.' And He said to me, 'Go! For I will send you far away to the Gentiles.'" And they listened to him up to this statement, and then they raised their voices and said, "Away with such a fellow from the earth, for he should not be allowed to live!" And as they were crying out and throwing off their cloaks and tossing dust into the air, the commander ordered him to be brought into the barracks, stating that he should be examined by scourging so that he might find out the reason why they were shouting against him that way. And when they stretched him out with thongs, Paul said to the centurion who was standing by, "Is it lawful for you to scourge a man who is a Roman and uncondemned?" And when the centu-rion heard this, he went to the commander and told him, saying, "What are you about to do? For this man is a Roman." And the commander came and said to him, "Tell me, are you a Roman?" And he said, "Yes." And the commander answered, "I acquired this citizenship with a large sum of money." And Paul said, "But I was actually born a citizen." Therefore those who were about to examine him immediately let go of him; and the commander also was afraid when he found out that he was a Roman, and because he had put him in chains. (21:27–22:29)

This passage marks a major transition in the life and ministry of the apostle Paul. Since his conversion on the road to Damascus (Acts 9:1ff.), he had ministered freely (except for brief imprisonments such as in Philippi [Acts 16:23ff.; cf. 2 Cor. 11:23]). But from this point on in Acts, Paul will be a prisoner.

This turn of events did not end the apostle's ministry, however (cf. Acts 28:30–31; Phil. 1:12–13). No longer free to travel, he became an "ambassador in chains" (Eph. 6:20) for Jesus Christ. As a free man, he preached the gospel throughout the Roman world. As a prisoner, he preached the gospel to Roman officials—possibly including the emperor himself. And like John Bunyan, who wrote *The Pilgrim's Progress* while in Bedford jail, Paul wrote four New Testament books (Ephesians, Philip-pians, Colossians, and Philemon) during his imprisonment at Rome.

During this incarceration, Paul gave six separate defenses of his actions: before the unruly mob at Jerusalem (21:27ff.), the Sanhedrin (22:30ff.), Felix (24:1ff.), Festus (25:1–12), Herod Agrippa (25:13ff.), and the Jews at Rome (28:17–28). Those masterful defenses ably answered the false charges leveled against him—a fact even the Roman authorities acknowledged (26:30–32). This passage, describing his first defense, unfolds in five scenes: the attack of the mob, the arrest by the Romans, the apology of Paul, the action by the people, and the attitude of Paul.

THE ATTACK OF THE MOB

And when the seven days were almost over, the Jews from Asia, upon seeing him in the temple, began to stir up all the multitude and laid hands on him, crying out, "Men of Israel, come to our aid! This is the man who preaches to all men everywhere against our people, and the Law, and this place; and besides he has even brought Greeks into the temple and has defiled this holy place." For they had previously seen Trophimus the Ephesian in the city with him, and they supposed that Paul had brought him into the temple. And all the city was aroused, and the people rushed together; and taking hold of Paul, they dragged him out of the temple; and immediately the doors were shut. (21:27–30)

Paul, at the urging of James and the elders, had agreed to underwrite the expenses of four men who had taken a Nazirite vow (see chapter 19 of this volume). They hoped that doing so would silence those who falsely claimed he taught Jewish Christians to abandon Jewish customs (21:21). But since Paul had recently returned to Israel from Gentile lands, he needed to undergo ritual purification. Only then would he be ceremonially clean to participate with the four in the ceremony marking the end of their Nazirite vows.

The process of purification required Paul to visit the temple on the third and seventh days. On the latter visit, **when the seven days were almost over,** the apostle encountered some old enemies: **Jews from** the Roman province of **Asia,** in Jerusalem to celebrate the Feast of Pentecost. They were likely from Ephesus, since they recognized Trophimus, who was a resident of that city (v. 29). Since Paul had ministered in Ephesus for three years (Acts 20:31), they had no trouble recognizing him.

Upon seeing Paul **in the temple,** these enemies of the gospel wasted no time in seizing their opportunity. They immediately **began to stir up all the** vast **multitude** of devout pilgrims who were in the city for the festival. Having **laid hands on** Paul, his assailants began **crying**

out, **"Men of Israel, come to our aid!"** Acting as though Paul had committed an act of blasphemy, they called for help in dealing with it. To **stir up** the crowd against Paul, they made three false accusations (cf. the similar false accusations made against Stephen in 6:11–14). They first accused him of being anti-Semitic, an enemy of the Jewish people and their religion, identifying him as **the man who preaches to all men everywhere against our people.** That was the same false accusation that the Judaizers had used to poison the minds of the Jewish Christians against the apostle. But Paul was no enemy of Jews, as Romans 9:1–5 and 10:1 make clear. Paul nowhere taught Jewish believers to forsake their customs—merely that Gentiles not be pressured to observe them.

A second charge was that Paul opposed the **Law.** That was a particularly serious accusation in this setting, since the Jewish people were especially zealous for the law at Pentecost. Originally a celebration of the first fruits of the harvest, in Paul's day Pentecost had come to be a celebration of the giving of the law to Moses on Mount Sinai. Charging Paul at this time with teaching against the law was sure to infuriate the crowds.

Finally, the Jews falsely accused Paul of speaking against **this place** (the temple). Because the Jewish people revered the temple (the focal point of their worship), an accusation of blaspheming or defiling it was also a very serious matter. Jesus (Mark 14:57–58) and Stephen (Acts 6:13) were also falsely accused of speaking against the temple— accusations that helped lead to their deaths. Paul's accusers undoubtedly hoped for a similar outcome in his case.

To substantiate these general accusations, Paul's accusers came up with a specific one, crying out to the crowd **"he has even brought Greeks into the temple and has defiled this holy place."** Their "proof," Luke notes, was that **they had previously seen Trophimus the Ephesian in the city with him, and they supposed that Paul had brought him into the temple.** That charge was absurd. While taking part in a purification rite, Paul would hardly defile the temple by bringing a Gentile into it. And to do so, Paul would have had to bring Trophimus past the court of the Gentiles, where Gentiles were permitted. But that would have cost Trophimus his life, since the Romans allowed the Jews to execute any Gentile who entered there—even Roman citizens (cf. Josephus *Wars* 6.2.4). An inscription, found in 1935, solemnly warns, "No Gentile shall enter within the partition and barrier surrounding the temple, and whoever is caught shall be responsible to himself for his subsequent death" (E. M. Blaiklock and R. K. Harrison, eds., *The New International Dictionary of Biblical Archaeology* [Grand Rapids: Zondervan, 1983], 389). Paul would never have so endangered his friend's life. And if the Asian Jews had really seen Trophimus there, why had they not seized him then and executed him?

False or not, the accusations spread like wildfire. Soon **all the**

city was aroused (cf. Matt. 21:10), **and the people rushed together** to the vicinity of the temple. Determined to appear as if they desired to protect that sacred place from further defilement, they seized **Paul,** and **dragged him out of the temple; and immediately the doors were shut.** The temple guards shoved the frenzied mob outside (so Paul's death would not defile the temple; cf. 2 Kings 11:15) and then closed the doors (between the Court of the Women and the Court of the Gentiles). Their religious zeal inflamed by the false accusations of the Asian Jews, the infuriated and irrational crowd began savagely beating Paul. Too impatient to drag him out of the city and stone him (as had been done with Stephen), they intended to beat the apostle to death on the spot. They would have succeeded, but God providentially intervened to protect His servant. Help arrived in the form of Roman soldiers.

THE ARREST BY THE ROMANS

And while they were seeking to kill him, a report came up to the commander of the Roman cohort that all Jerusalem was in confusion. And at once he took along some soldiers and centurions, and ran down to them; and when they saw the commander and the soldiers, they stopped beating Paul. Then the commander came up and took hold of him, and ordered him to be bound with two chains; and he began asking who he was and what he had done. But among the crowd some were shouting one thing and some another, and when he could not find out the facts on account of the uproar, he ordered him to be brought into the barracks. And when he got to the stairs, it so happened that he was carried by the soldiers because of the violence of the mob; for the multitude of the people kept following behind, crying out, "Away with him!" (21:31–36)

The headquarters of the Roman occupation forces was Fort Antonia, located on a precipice overlooking the temple grounds. From its towers sentries had a clear view of the temple area, where civil unrest in Jerusalem was most likely to break out. During major religious celebrations, such as Pentecost, the Romans were especially watchful. Thus, it did not take the alert sentries long to spot the riot breaking out below them. **While** the mob was **seeking to kill** Paul, **a report came** from the sentries **to the commander of the Roman cohort that all Jerusalem was in confusion.** The **commander** (*chiliarchos*, from the Greek word for "one thousand"), or tribune, commanded the entire **Roman cohort** of one thousand men stationed at Fort Antonia. In Acts 23:26, Luke gives his name as Claudius Lysias. He was the ranking

Roman official in Jerusalem when the governor (whose official residence was in Caesarea) was not in the city. Lysias was thus the Roman official most concerned with maintaining order in Jerusalem.

Having received the report **that all Jerusalem was in confusion,** Lysias acted quickly and decisively to quell the riot. **At once he took along some soldiers and centurions, and ran down** the steps leading from Fort Antonia to the Court of the Gentiles, where the enraged crowd was beating Paul. Luke's use of the plural **centurions** suggests Lysias took two hundred soldiers or more, since a centurion commanded one hundred men. This massive show of force broke up the riot (and saved Paul's life). **When** the crowd **saw the commander and the soldiers, they stopped beating Paul,** since they did not want to be arrested themselves.

Because Paul was evidently the cause of the disturbance and must have done something very serious to excite the Jews to such fury, Lysias **took hold of** (arrested) him. As verse 38 reveals, he assumed (incorrectly) that Paul was an Egyptian terrorist. Having arrested him, Lysias **ordered him to be bound** between two soldiers **with two chains** (cf. 12:6), thus fulfilling Agabus's prophecy (21:10–11). Attempting to sort out the chaotic situation, Lysias then **began asking who** Paul **was and what he had done.** But in the confusion, with some **among the crowd shouting one thing and some another** (cf. 19:32), he could get no clear answer. Realizing that **he could not find out the facts on account of the uproar, he ordered** Paul **to be brought into the barracks.** There he intended to question the apostle in private and, if necessary, use torture to extract a confession.

The soldiers began escorting Paul through the crowd, and **when he got to the stairs, it so happened that he was carried by the soldiers because of the violence of the mob.** The Romans had lifted Paul up and transported him above the mob to the stairs. Seeing their intended victim being carried to safety, **the multitude of the people kept following behind** Paul and the soldiers. In mindless, faceless fury, losing all sense of fear for Roman soldiers, the crowd pushed and shoved, trying desperately to get at him. All the while they kept **crying out, "Away with him!"**—that is, "kill him" (cf. Luke 23:18; John 19:15; Acts 22:22).

THE APOLOGY OF PAUL

And as Paul was about to be brought into the barracks, he said to the commander, "May I say something to you?" And he said, "Do you know Greek? Then you are not the Egyptian who some time ago stirred up a revolt and led the four thousand men of the Assassins out into the wilderness?" But Paul said, "I am a Jew of

Tarsus in Cilicia, a citizen of no insignificant city; and I beg you, allow me to speak to the people." And when he had given him permission, Paul, standing on the stairs, motioned to the people with his hand; and when there was a great hush, he spoke to them in the Hebrew dialect, saying, "Brethren and fathers, hear my defense which I now offer to you." And when they heard that he was addressing them in the Hebrew dialect, they became even more quiet; and he said, "I am a Jew, born in Tarsus of Cilicia, but brought up in this city, educated under Gamaliel, strictly according to the law of our fathers, being zealous for God, just as you all are today. And I persecuted this Way to the death, binding and putting both men and women into prisons, as also the high priest and all the Council of the elders can testify. From them I also received letters to the brethren, and started off for Damascus in order to bring even those who were there to Jerusalem as prisoners to be punished. And it came about that as I was on my way, approaching Damascus about noontime, a very bright light suddenly flashed from heaven all around me, and I fell to the ground and heard a voice saying to me, 'Saul, Saul, why are you persecuting Me?' And I answered, 'Who art Thou, Lord?' And He said to me, 'I am Jesus the Nazarene, whom you are persecuting.' And those who were with me beheld the light, to be sure, but did not understand the voice of the One who was speaking to me. And I said, 'What shall I do, Lord?' And the Lord said to me, 'Arise and go on into Damascus; and there you will be told of all that has been appointed for you to do.' But since I could not see because of the brightness of that light, I was led by the hand by those who were with me, and came into Damascus. And a certain Ananias, a man who was devout by the standard of the Law, and well spoken of by all the Jews who lived there, came to me, and standing near said to me, 'Brother Saul, receive your sight!' And at that very time I looked up at him. And he said, 'The God of our fathers has appointed you to know His will, and to see the Righteous One, and to hear an utterance from His mouth. For you will be a witness for Him to all men of what you have seen and heard. And now why do you delay? Arise, and be baptized, and wash away your sins, calling on His name.' And it came about when I returned to Jerusalem and was praying in the temple, that I fell into a trance, and I saw Him saying to me, 'Make haste, and get out of Jerusalem quickly, because they will not accept your testimony about Me.' And I said, 'Lord, they themselves understand that in one synagogue after another I used to imprison and beat those who believed in Thee. And when the blood of Thy witness Stephen was being shed, I also

was standing by approving, and watching out for the cloaks of those who were slaying him.' And He said to me, 'Go! For I will send you far away to the Gentiles.'" (21:37–22:21)

Up to this point in his ordeal, Paul had remained silent. But reaching the top of the stairs, **as** he **was about to be brought into the barracks, he said to the commander, "May I say something to you?"** Shocked by the language Paul spoke, Lysias asked him incredulously, **"Do you know Greek?"** Greek was the language of cultured, educated men, not common criminals such as he assumed Paul to be. Lysias's next question revealed his wrong assumption of who his prisoner was: **"Then you are not the Egyptian who some time ago stirred up a revolt and led the four thousand men of the Assassins out into the wilderness?"** The question assumes a positive answer. Since Paul spoke Greek, he was probably not a local troublemaker, as Palestinians generally spoke Aramaic. Greek, however, was commonly spoken in Egypt, hence Lysias's assumption. The **Egyptian** was a false prophet who some years earlier led a group of his followers to the Mount of Olives. He proclaimed that the walls of Jerusalem would fall at his command and that the Romans would be driven out. Before that prophecy could come to pass, however, Roman troops led by Governor Felix arrived on the scene. They attacked the Egyptian and his followers and routed them. Several hundred were killed or captured and the rest (including the Egyptian) vanished. Josephus, who also records this incident, gives the number of the Egyptian's followers as 30,000, instead of the **four thousand** Luke mentions. Josephus, however, tends to exaggerate numbers. Some commentators have argued that Josephus's figure reflects the total number of the Egyptian's followers, whereas Luke gives only the number of fighting men. Still others have suggested a scribal error in the manuscripts of Josephus's writings to account for the discrepancy. They note the similarity in the Greek capital letters (which are used to represent numbers D (four) and L (thirty). In any case, it must be remembered that Luke was divinely inspired; Josephus was not.

Lysias described the Egyptian's followers as **Assassins.** The Assassins were a terrorist group that emerged during Felix's term as governor. Their strong Jewish nationalism made them bitter enemies of both the Romans and Jewish collaborators. The latter were the Assassins' primary targets. (*Sikariōn* [**Assassins**] derives from the Latin word *sica* [dagger].) Mingling with the crowds, they stabbed their victims. They would then either melt away into the crowd or brazenly join the mourners to escape detection. The Assassins were especially active during the Jewish festivals, such as Pentecost. Lysias no doubt assumed the crowd had caught one of them (maybe even the Egyptian himself) in the act of murder.

But Paul, of course, was neither an Egyptian nor an Assassin. He identified himself to Lysias as **a Jew of Tarsus in Cilicia, a citizen of no insignificant city.** As a **Jew**, he had every right to have been where he was in the temple. Withholding for the moment the fact of his Roman citizenship, Paul declared himself to be a **citizen** of **Tarsus in Cilicia.** Tarsus, as Paul notes, was not an **insignificant city** but rather a cultural center with a university rivaling those of Athens and Alexandria. Being a citizen of Tarsus explained the apostle's knowledge of Greek.

Having identified himself to Lysias, Paul courageously requested permission to **speak to the people.** Although battered, bruised, and in chains, the apostle did not think of his own safety and comfort. Instead, his passionate desire to see his countrymen saved (Rom. 10:1) drove him to seize the opportunity to recount his conversion to the crowd.

Hoping to calm the explosive situation and discover what had triggered it, Lysias consented. **When he had given him permission, Paul, standing on the stairs, motioned to the people with his hand** to quiet down and let him speak (cf. Acts 12:17; 13:16; 19:33). A **great hush** came over the unruly crowd, and then Paul **spoke to them in the Hebrew dialect** (Aramaic).

Paul's apology, or speech in defense of himself, is biographical. He defended both his motives (he was not anti-Jewish) and his actions (he acted only in submission to God). It was a strange place for Paul to preach—standing on the steps, surrounded by Roman soldiers, before the mob who sought his death. He began to address the crowd with courteous, conciliatory words reminiscent of Stephen (Acts 7:2): **"Brethren and fathers, hear my defense which I now offer to you."** Recognizing that **he was addressing them in** their own **Hebrew dialect, they became even more quiet.** Paul then told them of his dramatic conversion, as he went from Christianity's most violent persecutor to its greatest missionary. As in the other four New Testament accounts of his conversion (Acts 9, 26; Phil. 3; 1 Tim. 1), the emphasis is on God's power and sovereign grace, not Paul's achievements.

Paul's testimony may be divided into three sections: his conduct before his conversion, the circumstances of his conversion, and his commission after his conversion.

PAUL'S CONDUCT BEFORE HIS CONVERSION

and he said, "I am a Jew, born in Tarsus of Cilicia, but brought up in this city, educated under Gamaliel, strictly according to the law of our fathers, being zealous for God, just as you all are today. And I persecuted this Way to the death, binding and putting both men and women into prisons, as also the high priest

and all the Council of the elders can testify. From them I also received letters to the brethren, and started off for Damascus in order to bring even those who were there to Jerusalem as prisoners to be punished. (22:2d–5)

Paul began by refuting the spurious charge that he opposed the Jewish people (cf. 21:28), declaring emphatically, **"I am a Jew!"** Far from being anti- Jewish, the apostle had unimpeachable Jewish credentials. Although **born** among the Hellenistic Jews of the Diaspora **in Tarsus of Cilicia,** Paul had been **brought up in this city** (Jerusalem). Further, he was **educated under Gamaliel**—the most revered rabbi of that time and one of the greatest of all antiquity (for further information on Gamaliel, see *Acts 1–12*, MacArthur New Testament Commentary [Chicago: Moody, 1994], 172). As a student of Gamaliel, Paul was educated **strictly according to the law of our fathers.** He had been carefully and thoroughly instructed in the Old Testament law and the rabbinic traditions, and he was once a Pharisee who was blameless under the law (cf. Phil. 3:5–6). Considering that, the charge that he opposed the law (21:28) was ridiculous. His personal conviction was that the law was "holy . . . and righteous and good" (Rom. 7:12).

Nor was Paul's training a mere academic exercise. He was, he declared to the crowd, **zealous for God, just as you all are today** (cf. Rom. 10:2). Generously crediting to them the best of motives for their violent attack on him, Paul attributed it to zeal for God. But his zeal had far surpassed theirs, for because of it Paul had **persecuted this Way** (Christianity, cf. Acts 9:2; 19:9, 23; 24:14, 22) **to the death, binding and putting both men and women into prisons.** He had been the Christians' most-feared persecutor from Stephen's martyrdom until his conversion. His reputation as a persecutor of Christians was well known, as Paul acknowledged when he reminded the Galatians, "You have heard of my former manner of life in Judaism, how I used to persecute the church of God beyond measure, and tried to destroy it" (Gal. 1:13).

If any still doubted his zeal for God, Paul could call on **the high priest and all the Council of the elders** (the Sanhedrin) to **testify** for him. It was **from them** that he had **received letters to the brethren** (non-Christian Jews), **and started off for Damascus in order to bring even those who were there to Jerusalem as prisoners to be punished.** Such was Paul's zeal that the highest Jewish authorities chose him for the mission of arresting and extraditing the Christians, even as far away as Damascus.

Paul's conduct before his conversion refuted the false allegations against him. Far from being an enemy of his people, he had been "advancing in Judaism beyond many of [his] contemporaries among [his] countrymen, being more extremely zealous for [his] ancestral tra-

ditions" (Gal. 1:14). No one could legitimately question his regard for
God and His law.

**And it came about that as I was on my way, approaching
Damascus about noontime, a very bright light suddenly flashed
from heaven all around me, and I fell to the ground and heard a
voice saying to me, 'Saul, Saul, why are you persecuting Me?'
And I answered, 'Who art Thou, Lord?' And He said to me, 'I am
Jesus the Nazarene, whom you are persecuting.' And those who
were with me beheld the light, to be sure, but did not understand
the voice of the One who was speaking to me. And I said, 'What
shall I do, Lord?' And the Lord said to me, 'Arise and go on into
Damascus; and there you will be told of all that has been appointed for you to do.' But since I could not see because of the brightness of that light, I was led by the hand by those who were with
me, and came into Damascus. And a certain Ananias, a man who
was devout by the standard of the Law, and well spoken of by all
the Jews who lived there, came to me, and standing near said to
me, 'Brother Saul, receive your sight!' And at that very time I
looked up at him. And he said, 'The God of our fathers has
appointed you to know His will, and to see the Righteous One,
and to hear an utterance from His mouth. For you will be a witness for Him to all men of what you have seen and heard. And
now why do you delay? Arise, and be baptized, and wash away
your sins, calling on His name.'** (22:6–16)

Having shown the absurdity of the charge that he was motivated
by enmity toward the Jewish people, Paul then defended his actions. The
God of Israel had sovereignly, powerfully intervened in his life and
turned him from being Christianity's foremost persecutor to being its
foremost proponent. Paul had acted in submission to Him.

The account of Paul's dramatic conversion appears three times
in Acts (cf. 9:1ff.; 26:4–18), thus stressing its significance. Indeed, the conversion of Saul of Tarsus was a major turning point in both church and
world history. As the crowd listened intently, Paul recounted the events
of that remarkable day on the road to Damascus.

On a mission to extradite Christians back to Jerusalem for punishment (v. 5), Paul was **approaching Damascus about noontime.**
The time of day, absent from the account in chapter 9, stresses how **very
bright** the **light** was that **suddenly flashed from heaven all around**
Paul and his companions. The blazing glory of the glorified, exalted

Jesus Christ far outshone even the brilliant midday sun (26:13). Speechless with terror, Paul **fell to the ground and heard a voice saying to** him, **"Saul, Saul, why are you persecuting Me?"** Lying prostrate, stunned and blinded, Paul could only stammer out, **"Who art Thou, Lord?"** The Lord's reply, **"I am Jesus the Nazarene, whom you are persecuting,"** shocked and horrified him. Instantly Paul knew how terribly wrong he had been. The One whom he had despised and rejected as a charlatan, a blasphemer, and a false Messiah was in fact the Lord of glory. That **Jesus the Nazarene** had spoken to Paul from heaven was also disturbing news for the crowd to hear, since they, too, had despised and rejected Him. Perhaps some of the ones who cried out concerning Paul, "Away with him!" (21:36) had many years earlier raised that same cry against Jesus (cf. Luke 23:18; John 19:15).

Knowing that some in the crowd would question whether the Lord had really appeared to him, Paul introduced corroborating witnesses. Those **who were with** him on the road, he noted, **beheld the light, to be sure.** Momentarily stunned by its brilliance, they fell to the ground in terror with Paul (26:14) but unlike him were then able to stand up (9:7). Unable to **understand the voice of the One who was speaking,** they stood by speechless with fear while Jesus addressed his message singularly to Paul. Although some have imagined a contradiction between verse 9 and 9:7, this is not true. Because Jesus' message was only for Paul, he alone understood the words; his companions merely heard the sound (cf. John 12:29). Similarly, although his co-persecutors saw the light (v. 9), only Paul discerned the Person of Jesus Christ (9:7; cf. 9:17, 27; 22:14; 26:16; 1 Cor. 9:1; 15:8). Nevertheless, Paul's traveling companions on that fateful day could testify to the objective reality of what had happened. They saw the blinding light and heard the sound of Jesus' voice speaking to Paul. Paul's experience, therefore, could not be dismissed as either a subjective delusion or a lie.

Overwhelmed by the glorious confrontation by the Lord Jesus, the proud Pharisee could only humbly ask, **"What shall I do, Lord?"** In reply **the Lord said to** him, **"Arise and go on into Damascus."** Paul was to continue his journey to Damascus, but now as the Lord's servant, not His adversary. Upon arriving **there** he would **be told of all that** God had **appointed for** him **to do.** He was, as the Lord informed Ananias, "a chosen instrument of Mine, to bear My name before the Gentiles and kings and the sons of Israel" (9:15).

And so, **since** he **could not see because of the brightness of that light,** he **was led by the hand by those who were with** him, **and came into Damascus.** Paul finally reached his destination but under circumstances he could hardly have imagined when he started his journey. In Damascus, he met **a certain Ananias,** whom the Lord had sent to him (9:11–12). Though Ananias was one of the leading

Christians in Damascus, Paul described him to his hostile Jewish audience as **a man who was devout by the standard of the Law, and well spoken of by all the Jews who lived there.** Identified as a Christian, Ananias's testimony would have been suspect to them; identified as a devout member of the Jewish community, it offered further corroboration of Paul's story.

Ananias **came** (reluctantly, cf. 9:13–14) **to Paul, and standing near said to** him, **"Brother Saul, receive your sight!"** He declared that God had miraculously given him back his sight, **and at that very time** Paul **looked up at him.** He told Paul what God had said to him in his vision (9:15): **"The God of our fathers has appointed you to know His will, and to see the Righteous One, and to hear an utterance from His mouth. For you will be a witness for Him to all men of what you have seen and heard."**

Ananias's declaration "**the God of our fathers has appointed you**" stresses the biblical truth that God is sovereign in salvation. "No one can come to Me," declared Jesus, "unless the Father who sent Me draws him" (John 6:44; cf. Mark 13:20; Eph. 1:4; Col. 3:12; 2 Thess. 2:13; 2 Tim. 2:10; Titus 1:1; 1 Pet. 1:1–2). The Lord also sovereignly chooses those who serve Him (Luke 6:13; John 13:18; 15:16, 19; Acts 1:2). He chose Paul **to know His will, to see the Righteous One** (a messianic title, Isa. 53:11; Acts 3:14; 7:52), **to hear an utterance from His mouth** (leading to Paul's salvation), and to **be a witness for Him to all men of what** he had **seen and heard.** The dramatic conversion of Saul of Tarsus is compelling testimony to the sovereign purposes of God.

But the sovereign purpose of God in choosing individuals does not relieve them of their responsibility to respond properly. Therefore Ananias exhorted Paul: **"And now why do you delay? Arise, and be baptized, and wash away your sins, calling on His name."** Some have mistakenly sought support for baptismal regeneration (the false teaching that baptism is required for salvation) in this verse. Although baptism is an act of obedience required of all Christians, it does not save. Paul understood that clearly. To the Romans he wrote:

> [This is] the word of faith which we are preaching, that if you confess with your mouth Jesus as Lord, and believe in your heart that God raised Him from the dead, you shall be saved; for with the heart man believes, resulting in righteousness, and with the mouth he confesses, resulting in salvation. (Rom. 10:8–10)

Paul preached that salvation came from belief in the heart (cf. Acts 16:31; Rom. 3:28) and public confession of that faith (cf. Matt. 10:32;

Rom. 10:13). Obviously, he did not understand Ananias's words to mean that baptism saves.

Acts 10:44–48 clearly reveals the relationship of baptism to salvation. It was only *after* Cornelius and his friends had received the Holy Spirit (giving evidence that they were saved) that Peter ordered them baptized (10:47). Baptism thus follows salvation and does not cause it. (For further discussion of baptismal regeneration, see MacArthur, *Acts 1–12*, 73–75).

Ananias's words in verse 16, when properly understood, are in full agreement with the New Testament teaching that salvation is by faith alone. The phrase **wash away your sins** must be connected with **calling on His name,** since connecting it with **be baptized** leaves the participle *epikalesamenos* (**calling**) without an antecedent. Paul's sins were washed away not by baptism but by calling on the name of the Lord (cf. Rom. 10:13). A literal translation of the verse says, "Arise, get yourself baptized and your sins washed away, having called on His name." Both imperatives reflect the reality that Paul had already called on the Lord's name, which is the act that saves. Baptism and the washing away of sins follow.

By relating the circumstances of his conversion, Paul turned the tables on his adversaries. He had acted only in submission to God; therefore indicting him was tantamount to indicting God. His continued testimony reinforced that point.

PAUL'S COMMISSION AFTER HIS CONVERSION

And it came about when I returned to Jerusalem and was praying in the temple, that I fell into a trance, and I saw Him saying to me, "Make haste, and get out of Jerusalem quickly, because they will not accept your testimony about Me." And I said, "Lord, they themselves understand that in one synagogue after another I used to imprison and beat those who believed in Thee. And when the blood of Thy witness Stephen was being shed, I also was standing by approving, and watching out for the cloaks of those who were slaying him." And He said to me, "Go! For I will send you far away to the Gentiles." (22:17–21)

After his conversion and a brief period of ministry at Damascus (9:20–25), Paul spent three years in Nabataean Arabia (Gal. 1:17–18). Having **returned to Jerusalem**, Paul **was praying in the temple.** Here was further evidence that he had not rejected his Jewish heritage, as his accusers falsely insisted. While in the temple, Paul **fell into a trance.** *Ekstasis* (**trance**) describes the unique apostolic experience of being transported beyond the normal senses to the supernatural realm to receive divine revelation. The word is twice used to describe Peter's vision at Joppa (Acts 10:10; 11:5).

In his trance, Paul **saw** the Lord and heard **Him saying, "Make haste, and get out of Jerusalem quickly, because they will not accept your testimony about Me."** Since his arrival in the city, Paul had fearlessly proclaimed the faith he had once tried to destroy (9:28–29). His shocking turnabout, from Christian persecutor to Christian preacher, outraged the unbelieving Jews, who deemed him an apostate and blasphemer. Learning of a plot to kill him, the Christians hustled Paul out of Jerusalem and sent him home to Tarsus (9:30). Evidently it took this word from the risen, glorified Christ to persuade Paul to leave. Even then, he did not go willingly, protesting, **"Lord, they themselves understand that in one synagogue after another I used to imprison and beat those who believed in Thee. And when the blood of Thy witness Stephen was being shed, I also was standing by approving, and watching out for the cloaks of those who were slaying him."** Paul wrongly believed that seeing the radical transformation the Lord had wrought in his life would convince the unbelieving Jews of the truth of the gospel. The Lord knew better, however, and repeated His command for Paul to leave, saying to him, **"Go! For I will send you far away to the Gentiles."** The Lord now makes clear what was hinted at in the words of Ananias—that Paul would be a "witness for Him to all men" (22:15; cf. 9:15)—commissioning him as the apostle to the Gentiles.

Paul's conversion and commission were both unmistakably sovereign acts of God. By making those acts the focus of his defense to the crowd, the apostle put the crowd on the defensive. Since he had merely acted in obedience to divine confrontation and communication from God, how could they question, let alone condemn him?

THE ACTION BY THE PEOPLE

And they listened to him up to this statement, and then they raised their voices and said, "Away with such a fellow from the earth, for he should not be allowed to live!" And as they were crying out and throwing off their cloaks and tossing dust into the air, (22:22–23)

Members of the crowd had **listened to** Paul **up to** his **statement** that God had sent him to minister to the Gentiles. But that was the end of their interest, since they could not tolerate the suggestion that Gentiles could be saved without first becoming Jewish proselytes. That

would make them spiritually equal to the Jewish people before God—
the most blatant heresy imaginable to the crowd.

Their fury at Paul reignited: **they raised their voices and said,
"Away with such a fellow from the earth, for he should not be
allowed to live!"** Anyone who dared place Gentiles on an equal foot-
ing with Jews in God's saving purpose should not be allowed to pollute
the earth with his presence. Overcome with rage, **they were crying out
and throwing off their cloaks and tossing dust into the air.** The
Jews may have removed their cloaks in preparation to stone Paul, torn
them in an expression of horror at his "blasphemy," or thrown them and
the dust into the air as an expression of outrage. In any case, racial prejudice had pushed their passions further beyond the bounds of reason.
They stopped Paul before he could defend himself against the charge
that had sparked the riot in the first place—that he had brought a
Gentile into the inner court of the temple (21:28).

THE ATTITUDE OF PAUL

**the commander ordered him to be brought into the barracks,
stating that he should be examined by scourging so that he might
find out the reason why they were shouting against him that way.
And when they stretched him out with thongs, Paul said to the
centurion who was standing by, "Is it lawful for you to scourge a
man who is a Roman and uncondemned?" And when the centurion heard this, he went to the commander and told him, saying,
"What are you about to do? For this man is a Roman." And the
commander came and said to him, "Tell me, are you a Roman?"
And he said, "Yes." And the commander answered, "I acquired
this citizenship with a large sum of money." And Paul said, "But
I was actually born a citizen." Therefore those who were about
to examine him immediately let go of him; and the commander
also was afraid when he found out that he was a Roman, and
because he had put him in chains.** (22:24–29)

Since the riot was breaking out afresh and he was no nearer to
understanding its cause, **the commander** again **ordered** Paul **to be
brought into the barracks** (cf. 21:34). He made clear what his next
step in resolving the situation would be, **stating that** Paul **should be
examined by scourging so that he might find out the reason why
they were shouting against him that way. Scourging** by the Roman
flagellum (a wooden handle to which were attached leather thongs
tipped with bits of metal and bone) was a fearful ordeal from which
men frequently died (from loss of blood or infection). Jesus endured it

before His crucifixion (John 19:1). Such a beating would have surpassed anything Paul had previously experienced. In preparation, the guards **stretched him out with thongs** to make his body taut and magnify the effects of the flagellation.

Fortunately, Roman citizens were exempted from such brutal methods by the Valerian and Porcian laws (F. F. Bruce, *The Book of the Acts*, The New International Commentary on the New Testament [Grand Rapids: Eerdmans, 1971], 445 n. 34). Therefore **Paul said to the centurion who was standing by, "Is it lawful for you to scourge a man who is a Roman and uncondemned?"** As he had in the face of the crowd's hostility, Paul remained calm. He did not hurl invectives at the Romans but quietly informed them of the terrible injustice (and violation of his rights as a Roman citizen) they were about to do.

When the centurion supervising Paul's beating **heard** the apostle's claim to Roman citizenship, **he went to the commander and told him, saying, "What are you about to do? For this man is a Roman."** To subject a Roman citizen to the *flagellum* could have destroyed Lysias's military career or even cost him his life.

Gravely concerned, he **came and said to** Paul, **"Tell me, are you a Roman?" And he said, "Yes."** Claims to Roman citizenship were generally accepted at face value, since the penalty for making a false claim was death. Lysias's remark about his own citizenship and its value, **"I acquired this citizenship with a large sum of money,"** may indicate his relief at not having thrown it away by beating Paul. Or he may have been expressing sarcasm, lamenting that Roman citizenship had been greatly devalued if someone like Paul could obtain it. Roman citizenship was officially not for sale. However, particularly in the reign of Emperor Claudius (whose name Lysias may have taken when he acquired his citizenship), it could be obtained by bribing corrupt officials. Paul's devastating reply came with quiet dignity, **"But I was actually born a citizen."** Unlike Lysias, Paul had not obtained his citizenship by bribery but by birth. Lysias, again, had badly misjudged his prisoner.

The discovery that Paul was a Roman citizen brought an immediate halt to the proceedings. **Those who were about to examine him immediately let go of him; and the commander also was afraid when he found out that he was a Roman, and because he had put him in chains.** Alarmed at how close he had come to scourging a Roman citizen, Lysias immediately ordered his subordinates to release Paul. He **was** also **afraid** because he was guilty of putting a Roman citizen **in chains** without a preliminary hearing (which was also illegal). By now thoroughly perplexed, he decided to bring Paul before the Jewish judges, the Sanhedrin (v. 30).

Paul's conduct throughout his ordeal provides an example for all believers of how to give a positive testimony in negative circumstances. Several principles can be noted.

First, Paul accepted the situation as God ordained it. Facing persecution never caused him to be unfaithful to God's plan. He had known for some time that he faced arrest when he arrived at Jerusalem (20:22–23; 21:4, 10–13). He calmly accepted that as God's will, telling those trying to dissuade him from going to Jerusalem, "I am ready not only to be bound, but even to die at Jerusalem for the name of the Lord Jesus" (21:13).

Second, Paul used his circumstances as an opportunity. The crowd had not gathered to hear him preach but to beat and kill him. Paul, however, used that occasion to proclaim to them how God's saving power had transformed his life.

Third, Paul was conciliatory toward his persecutors. He did not threaten the hostile crowd or seek revenge. Instead, he courteously addressed them as "brethren and fathers" (22:1) and even assigned to their vicious beating of him the noble motive of zeal for God. Paul practiced the command he had earlier given to the Roman Christians: "Bless those who persecute you; bless and curse not" (Rom. 12:14). He was like his Lord Jesus, who "being reviled . . . did not revile in return; while suffering, He uttered no threats, but kept entrusting Himself to Him who judges righteously" (1 Pet. 2:23).

Fourth, Paul exalted the Lord. His defense to the crowd focused not on his impressive credentials and achievements but on what God had accomplished in his life. That was consistent with his words to the Corinthians: "Let him who boasts, boast in the Lord" (1 Cor. 1:31). Exalting the Lord also served to exonerate Paul and put the crowd in the position of opposing God.

Finally, and most important, Paul maintained the proper attitude—one of selfless love. It was his love for other believers that brought him to Jerusalem (to deliver the offering). It was his love for his weaker brethren and desire for unity in the church that brought him to the temple. It was his love for his unsaved countrymen (cf. Rom. 9:1-3) that led him to evangelize the hostile crowd. And it was his love for God that motivated his love for people and caused him to give glory to Him.

Believers who practice these principles will, like Paul, be able to give a positive testimony in the most negative of circumstances.

Paul Before the Sanhedrin (Acts 22:30–23:11)

21

But on the next day, wishing to know for certain why he had been accused by the Jews, he released him and ordered the chief priests and all the Council to assemble, and brought Paul down and set him before them. And Paul, looking intently at the Council, said, "Brethren, I have lived my life with a perfectly good conscience before God up to this day." And the high priest Ananias commanded those standing beside him to strike him on the mouth. Then Paul said to him, "God is going to strike you, you whitewashed wall! And do you sit to try me according to the Law, and in violation of the Law order me to be struck?" But the bystanders said, "Do you revile God's high priest?" And Paul said, "I was not aware, brethren, that he was high priest; for it is written, 'You shall not speak evil of a ruler of your people.'" But perceiving that one part were Sadducees and the other Pharisees, Paul began crying out in the Council, "Brethren, I am a Pharisee, a son of Pharisees; I am on trial for the hope and resurrection of the dead!" And as he said this, there arose a dissension between the Pharisees and Sadducees; and the assembly was divided. For the Sadducees say that there is no resurrection, nor an angel, nor a spirit; but the Pharisees acknowledge them all. And there arose a great uproar; and some of the scribes of

the Pharisaic party stood up and began to argue heatedly, saying, "We find nothing wrong with this man; suppose a spirit or an angel has spoken to him?" And as a great dissension was developing, the commander was afraid Paul would be torn to pieces by them and ordered the troops to go down and take him away from them by force, and bring him into the barracks. But on the night immediately following, the Lord stood at his side and said, "Take courage; for as you have solemnly witnessed to My cause at Jerusalem, so you must witness at Rome also." (22:30–23:11)

A tragic theme running through the thrilling story of the growing church in Acts is the sad reality of Jewish opposition to the church and the gospel. Along with the apostolic preaching of the cross, Luke chronicles the rising tide of Jewish antagonism. Having rejected and executed the long-awaited and hoped-for Messiah, Israel as a nation subsequently rejected those who preached the message of forgiveness and salvation in His name.

The opposition began when the church began—on the Day of Pentecost, after the apostles were baptized in the Holy Spirit and miraculously spoke in other languages. Some in the crowd mocked and ridiculed them, scornfully deriding them as if the apostles were drunk (2:13).

That relatively mild opposition stiffened after Peter's sermon following the healing of a lame man (3:12–26). The Jewish authorities were annoyed "because [the apostles] were teaching the people and proclaiming in Jesus the resurrection from the dead" (4:2). Determined to put an end to this dangerous new teaching, "they laid hands on them, and put them in jail" (4:3). The next day, the Sanhedrin "commanded them not to speak or teach at all in the name of Jesus" (4:18). But refusing to be intimidated, "Peter and John answered and said to them, 'Whether it is right in the sight of God to give heed to you rather than to God, you be the judge; for we cannot stop speaking what we have seen and heard'" (4:19–20).

The opposition from the Jewish leaders continued, as recorded in chapter 5, when the Sanhedrin again arrested and imprisoned the apostles (5:17–18). That frantic attempt to stifle the preaching of the gospel failed when God sent an angel to miraculously release them from prison (5:19–20). They then boldly resumed preaching in the stronghold of the authorities—the temple (5:21). Further threats by the Sanhedrin (5:28), and even a beating (5:40), did not deter the apostles from teaching and preaching the gospel (5:42).

The next outbreak of persecution involved Stephen. That fearless and powerful preacher crushed his Jewish opponents in debate (6:9–10), so frustrating them that they finally arranged for false witnesses to lie about him (6:11). He, too, was then brought before the

Sanhedrin (6:12–15), where he gave a masterful sermon defending both himself and the Christian gospel (7:1–50). He closed that message with a stinging indictment of the Jewish leaders for their hardhearted rejection of the truth (7:51–53). Furious, they drove him out of the city and stoned him to death (7:54–60).

The murder of Stephen was the catalyst for the first widespread persecution of the church (8:1). That persecution, lead by the zealous Pharisee Saul of Tarsus (8:3), scattered the Jerusalem church (8:1) and spread the gospel further (8:4).

Further persecution, this time directed against the church's leaders, came from Herod. Seeking to please the Jewish authorities, he executed James and arrested Peter (12:1–3). Peter was miraculously released from prison (12:7–11) but was forced into seclusion (12:17).

After Paul's encounter with the glorified Christ on the Damascus road, he became Christianity's leading evangelist. Ironically, Paul, once the chief persecutor of Christians, now became the most persecuted of Christians. Jewish opposition first arose against him in Damascus shortly after his conversion (9:23). He met further opposition from unbelieving Jews throughout his missionary journeys. On the island of Cyprus, he confronted a Jewish false prophet (13:6–8). The unbelieving Jews at Pisidian Antioch, filled with jealousy, opposed Paul's teaching (13:45). At Iconium (14:2), Lystra (14:19), Thessalonica (17:5ff.), Berea (17:13), Corinth (18:6, 12–13), Ephesus (19:9), Corinth again as he began his trip to Jerusalem (20:3), and after his arrival in Jerusalem (21:27ff.), Paul faced the hostility of his countrymen.

As chapter 23 opens, Paul again faces Jewish opposition. As seen in the previous section, he had been attacked in the temple grounds by a Jewish mob and savagely beaten. Only the intervention of Roman soldiers saved his life. Claudius Lysias, the commander of the Roman forces in Jerusalem, tried unsuccessfully to find out what Paul had done. He allowed him to address the angry crowd from the steps of Fort Antonia. But Paul's mention of his commission to the Gentiles (22:21) caused the riot to break out afresh. Lysias then decided to use a brutal Roman interrogation method (scourging with a *flagellum*) to extract a confession from him. The discovery that Paul was a Roman citizen halted that proceeding, since it was illegal to so examine a Roman citizen.

By now thoroughly frustrated and perplexed about how to proceed, Lysias decided to summon the Sanhedrin. Accordingly, **on the next day, wishing to know for certain why** Paul **had been accused by the Jews, he released him and ordered the chief priests and all the Council to assemble, and brought** him **down and set him before them.** Whether Lysias at this time **released** Paul from imprisonment or from his chains is not clear. Given his alarm at having put Paul, a Roman citizen, in chains (22:29), probably the former is meant.

Some have questioned whether Lysias had the authority to have **ordered the chief priests and all the Council to assemble.** But this was not a formal convening of the Sanhedrin. Lysias, still **wishing to know for certain why** Paul **had been accused by the Jews,** naturally turned to the highest Jewish court for clarification. He would not have turned a Roman citizen over to the Sanhedrin for trial before determining and evaluating the charges against him. Nor does this hearing have the hallmarks of a formal trial. There were no charges made against Paul, nor did any witnesses testify against him. Further, it does not seem that this meeting took place in the Sanhedrin's normal meeting place on the temple grounds. Lysias **brought Paul down and set him before** the Sanhedrin somewhere outside of Fort Antonia. Roman troops were readily available to rescue Paul (23:10) if things got out of hand again.

Paul's appearance before the Sanhedrin marks the fifth (and last) time that body was called upon to evaluate the claims of Christ. The first was when Jesus Himself stood before it (Mark 14:53–65); the second involved Peter and John (Acts 4:5–22); the third followed their arrest of all the apostles (5:21ff.); and the fourth was the trial of Stephen (Acts 6:12ff.). Five times the peerless communicators of the gospel had proclaimed the truth to the Sanhedrin, and five times its members rejected it. Not only did they condemn themselves (John 3:18), but their rejection also symbolized the nation's rejection of Messiah.

The Sanhedrin (from the Greek word *sunedrion*, "council") was the religious ruling body of the Jews in Roman-occupied Israel. The Sanhedrin's authority was final in matters involving Jewish law, while its authority in civil matters was limited. Roman governors (such as Pilate, Felix, and Festus) and Roman-appointed rulers (such as the Herods) wielded the political clout in Israel.

Although Jewish tradition traces the Sanhedrin's origins to the seventy elders who assisted Moses (Num. 11:16), it actually dates from postexilic times. After the Jewish revolt against Rome (A.D. 66–70), the Sanhedrin lost its remaining vestiges of political power. Driven from Jerusalem, it reconvened at Jamnia but was limited to considering religious questions.

Three main groups composed the Sanhedrin. The High Priests consisted of the president of the Sanhedrin, former presidents (such as Annas, Luke 3:2; Acts 4:6), various officials (such as the captain of the temple guard, Acts 5:24), and others "who were of high-priestly descent" (Acts 4:6). The Elders included members of the priestly aristocracy (such as Nicodemus, John 7:50) and wealthy individuals (such as Joseph of Arimathea, Mark 15:43). The Scribes, mostly drawn from the ranks of the Pharisees, were experts in Jewish law.

Two main religious factions dominated the Sanhedrin: the Sadducees and the Pharisees (cf. 23:6). The Sanhedrin had its own police force (cf. 5:24–26) and could mete out punishment for violations of Jewish law (cf. 5:40). They did not, however, have the right of capital punishment (John 18:31) unless the case involved the desecration of the temple.

Luke presents Paul's appearance before the Sanhedrin in four scenes: the confrontation, the conflict, the conquest, and the consolation.

THE CONFRONTATION

And Paul, looking intently at the Council, said, "Brethren, I have lived my life with a perfectly good conscience before God up to this day." (23:1)

Never one to be intimidated or back away from a confrontation, **Paul** stood for a moment **looking intently at the Council** before beginning to speak. **Looking intently** is from *atenizō*, which means "to gaze upon," "to fix one's eyes on," or "to stare." Some have seen this as further evidence of Paul's poor eyesight; others suggest that he was looking to see whom he could recognize. But more important, Paul's look was one of conscious integrity. He knew he was innocent of any wrongdoing, and he had complete confidence that God was with him. Because of that, he did not cower in fear or guilt.

Paul began by addressing them, surprisingly, as **"brethren"** (the Greek text reads "men, brethren"). The customary way of addressing the Sanhedrin was "Rulers and elders of the people" (Acts 4:8) or "Brethren and fathers" (Acts 7:2). But Paul, unlike Peter or Stephen, had close ties to the Sanhedrin. He undoubtedly knew many of them, having probably once been a member of the Sanhedrin himself (cf. Acts 26:10). Some may have been students of Gamaliel along with him. Certainly many were fellow Pharisees. He had surely worked with some of them to eradicate the Christian church. All this familiarity with the Sanhedrin prompted him to address them as equals.

Even more disconcerting to the Sanhedrin was Paul's bold assertion **"I have lived my life with a perfectly good conscience before God up to this day."** As those who knew him could attest, he had always been motivated by a desire to please God (cf. 24:16; Gal. 1:14; Phil. 3:6). By making this claim, Paul put the members of the Sanhedrin on the defensive. Since he had acted in obedience to God, by opposing him they were actually fighting God.

That Paul had **lived** his **life with a perfectly good conscience before God** does not mean all his actions had always been right. It does mean that Paul felt no guilt for anything he had done, in spite of the

Sanhedrin's accusations. It should be noted that the conscience does not determine whether actions are morally right or wrong—Paul's conscience had once permitted him to persecute Christians. Conscience is the faculty that passes moral judgment on a person's actions (Rom. 2:14–15). But it does so based only on the highest standards of morality and conduct perceived by that individual. It is thus neither the voice of God nor infallible. A conscience uninformed by biblical truth will not necessarily pass accurate judgments (cf. 1 Cor. 4:4). Before his conversion, Paul's had not.

It is possible for the conscience to be damaged, dysfunctional, even destroyed. The Bible speaks of a weak conscience (1 Cor. 8:7, 10), a wounded conscience (1 Cor. 8:12), a defiled conscience (Titus 1:15), an evil conscience (Heb. 10:22), and, worst of all, a seared conscience (1 Tim. 4:2)—one so covered with scar tissue from habitual sin that it no longer responds to the proddings of divine truth. Obviously, a conscience in one of those states will not always assess things properly.

On the other hand, the Bible commends a good conscience (1 Tim. 1:5, 19; Heb. 13:18; 1 Pet. 3:16, 21), a blameless conscience (Acts 24:16), and a clear conscience (1 Tim. 3:9; 2 Tim. 1:3). Such a spiritually healthy conscience results from the forgiveness of sin based on the atoning work of Christ (Heb. 9:14; 10:22). Christians' consciences, informed by the standards of God's Word, are able to assess accurately their actions. Christians thus need to strengthen their consciences by constantly exposing them to the truths of Scripture. Paul had such a fully and rightly informed conscience, and it was not accusing him. (For a biblical study of the conscience, see John MacArthur, *The Vanishing Conscience* [Dallas: Word, 1994].)

THE CONFLICT

And the high priest Ananias commanded those standing beside him to strike him on the mouth. Then Paul said to him, "God is going to strike you, you whitewashed wall! And do you sit to try me according to the Law, and in violation of the Law order me to be struck?" But the bystanders said, "Do you revile God's high priest?" And Paul said, "I was not aware, brethren, that he was high priest; for it is written, 'You shall not speak evil of a ruler of your people.'" (23:2–5)

Outraged by Paul's bold claim to a good conscience, **the high priest Ananias commanded those standing beside him to strike him on the mouth. Ananias,** the son of Nedebaeus, is not to be confused with the former high priest Annas (Luke 3:2). Ananias reigned for eleven or twelve years, beginning in A.D. 47, and was one of the most cruel, evil, corrupt high priests ever to hold office. According to Josephus, he stole from the common priests the tithes that should have gone to them, beating any who resisted (*Antiquities* 20.9.2). He did not hesitate to use violence to further his goals; in fact, a few years earlier the Romans had suspected him of complicity in atrocities committed against the Samaritans. They sent him to Rome to appear before Emperor Claudius, but he was acquitted (*Antiquities* 20.6.2–3). He was hated by the Jewish nationalists because of his staunchly pro-Roman stand. When the Jewish revolt against Rome broke out in A.D. 66, Ananias was promptly killed by the Jewish rebels (*Wars* 2.17.9).

In keeping with his cruel, violent character, Ananias ordered **those standing beside** Paul **to strike him on the mouth.** The verb translated **to strike** (*tuptō*) depicts more than a mere slap to the face. It is the same word used in 21:32 to speak of the crowd's beating of Paul and of the Roman soldiers' beating of Jesus (Matt. 27:30).

Incensed at Ananias's outrageous breach of Jewish law, Paul retorted, **"God is going to strike you, you whitewashed wall!"** He may have remembered Jesus' castigation of the Pharisees as "white-washed tombs" (Matt. 23:27). A more likely allusion, however, is to Ezekiel's denunciation of false prophets as walls plastered over with whitewash, doomed to fall in the flood of divine judgment (Ezek. 13:10–16).

Since Paul had not even been formally charged with a crime, much less convicted of one, he could not legally be beaten. He angrily rebuked Ananias, asking him, **"do you sit to try me according to the Law, and in violation of the Law order me to be struck?"** Paul was more indignant at the flouting of the law than at the pain inflicted by the blow itself.

Some have wondered how to harmonize Paul's strong language with his declaration to the Corinthians that "when we are reviled, we bless" (1 Cor. 4:12). They point out, in contrast, the example of Jesus, who "while being reviled, did not revile in return; while suffering, uttered no threats" (1 Pet. 2:23). When Jesus was struck in violation of the law, He merely asked, "If I have spoken wrongly, bear witness of the wrong; but if rightly, why do you strike Me?" (John 18:23).

The answer is, of course, that Paul was not Jesus. Jesus was the sinless Son of God. Paul, while no doubt the godliest man who ever lived, was still a sinner. He vividly described his battle with indwelling sin in Romans 7:14ff.; this was one time when the flesh prevailed.

Shocked by Paul's stinging rebuke of the high priest, **the bystanders said, "Do you revile God's high priest?"** Revile translates *loidoreō*, which means "to reproach," "to insult," or "to abuse." It is used in John 9:28 when the Jewish leaders insulted and mocked the blind man whom Jesus had healed. Paul used it in 1 Corinthians 4:12 to describe the opposite of blessing. Peter used it to describe the abuse heaped on Jesus (1 Pet. 2:23). The noun form appears twice in the New Testament, both times in lists of vices that characterize unbelievers (1 Cor. 5:11; 6:10). The adjectival form also appears twice in the New Testament. First Timothy 5:14 describes reviling as an activity of Satan, while 1 Peter 3:9 forbids Christians to do it.

The use of *loidoreō* shows that the people felt Paul's strong language was not some calculated legal ploy to take advantage of Ananias's violation of the law but an expression of anger. It was something, as he himself acknowledges in verse 5, that violated God's law. Although an evil man and a disgrace to his office, the high priest still occupied a God-ordained position of authority. He was not to be reviled but respected (cf. Deut. 17:8–12). "The high-priest stands before God. To abuse him, especially in the discharge of his office, is blasphemy" (H. Hanse, "*loidoreō*," in Gerhard Kittel, ed., *Theological Dictionary of the New Testament* [Grand Rapids: Eerdmans, 1967], 4:293–94).

Being the humble man that he was, Paul immediately acknowledged his error, exclaiming, **"I was not aware, brethren, that he was high priest; for it is written, 'You shall not speak evil of a ruler of your people.'"** He offered only the excuse of ignorance for his outburst, although it had been provoked by the high priest's illegally ordering him to be struck. He quickly admitted that he had violated God's express prohibition against slandering a ruler (Ex. 22:28). He even quoted the passage, to show his respect for and submission to the Word of God. Paul's reaction was that of a mature Christian. He saw his sin in relation to how holy God was, not how bad the high priest was. And when he realized his sin, he immediately confessed it and submitted to the authority of Scripture. Christians who thus deal with sin in their lives will save themselves much chastisement (cf. 1 Cor. 11:31).

Skeptics have found it incredible that Paul would not recognize the high priest. Various explanations of his words **"I was not aware, brethren, that he was high priest"** have been offered. Some see in them another manifestation of Paul's poor eyesight, arguing that he could not discern who spoke. Others hold that Paul was so angry that he did not stop to consider to whom he was speaking. Still others believe Paul spoke ironically; since Ananias had not acted like the high priest, how should Paul have recognized him? But the simplest, most straightforward explanation is to take Paul's words at face value. Since he had seldom visited Jerusalem in recent years, he likely did not know Ananias by sight. That this was not a formal convening of the Sanhedrin, but an informal gathering somewhere outside Fort Antonia, offers further support for this view. Paul would have recognized the high priest had he been wearing his high priestly garments and sitting in his official seat.

Whatever the explanation for his failure to recognize the high priest, Paul did not offer it as an excuse. By admitting his error, Paul accepted responsibility for his words. Such a humble, nondefensive attitude is the mark of a spiritual believer.

THE CONQUEST

But perceiving that one part were Sadducees and the other Pharisees, Paul began crying out in the Council, "Brethren, I am a Pharisee, a son of Pharisees; I am on trial for the hope and resurrection of the dead!" And as he said this, there arose a dissension between the Pharisees and Sadducees; and the assembly was divided. For the Sadducees say that there is no resurrection, nor an angel, nor a spirit; but the Pharisees acknowledge them all. And there arose a great uproar; and some of the scribes of the Pharisaic party stood up and began to argue heatedly, saying, "We find nothing wrong with this man; suppose a spirit or an angel has spoken to him?" And as a great dissension was developing, the commander was afraid Paul would be torn to pieces by them and ordered the troops to go down and take him away from them by force, and bring him into the barracks. (23:6–10)

Paul's confrontation with the high priest convinced him that he would not receive a fair hearing from the Sanhedrin. Accordingly, **perceiving that one part were Sadducees and the other Pharisees, Paul began crying out in the Council, "Brethren, I am a Pharisee, a son of Pharisees; I am on trial for the hope and resurrection of the dead!"** As previously noted, two main religious factions dominated the Sanhedrin: the **Sadducees** and the **Pharisees.** Those two factions were socially, politically, and theologically at odds with each other.

Being himself **a son of Pharisees,** Paul appealed to them for support. He cried out, **"I am on trial for the hope and resurrection of the dead!"** The resurrection of Jesus Christ is the central truth of Christianity. Paul asserted that the issue was his belief and proclamation of that truth (cf. 24:21). Belief in resurrection was commonly held by the Christians and Pharisees against the Sadducees.

Paul's appeal fanned into flame the smoldering theological tensions between the Sadducees and Pharisees. Luke notes that **as he said this there arose a dissension between the Pharisees and Sadducees; and the assembly was divided.** For the benefit of his readers who were unaware of the distinctions between the two groups, Luke briefly summarizes them. **The Sadducees,** he explains, **say that there is no resurrection, nor an angel, nor a spirit; but the**

Pharisees acknowledge them all. The Sadducees accepted only the Pentateuch as authoritative. They rejected any concept of an afterlife (cf. Matt. 22:23–33), claiming that it was not found there. The Pharisees, on the other hand, believed in resurrection and the afterlife. Their beliefs were thus more compatible with Christianity than those of the Sadducees. F. F. Bruce notes that "a Sadducee could not become a Christian without abandoning the distinctive theological position of his party; a Pharisee could become a Christian and remain a Pharisee—in the early decades of Christianity, at least" (*The Book of the Acts*, The New International Commentary on the New Testament [Grand Rapids: Eerdmans, 1971], 453). The Scriptures record Pharisees who became Christians, including Nicodemus (John 3:1) and others (Acts 15:5), but no Sadducees.

Paul's appeal threw the meeting into confusion. Rising to the defense of a fellow Pharisee, **some of the scribes of the Pharisaic party stood up and began to argue heatedly, saying, "We find nothing wrong with this man; suppose a spirit or an angel has spoken to him?"** So bitter was the theological dispute between the two parties that the Pharisees were willing to defend Paul against the Sadducees.

Lysias must have watched in growing frustration as the discord grew. Even after bringing Paul before the highest Jewish court, he was no nearer to discovering what crime the apostle had committed. Finally, **as a great dissension was developing, the commander was afraid Paul would be torn to pieces by them and ordered the troops to go down and take him away from them by force, and bring him into the barracks.** Once again the Romans had to rescue Paul from his own people, who hated him as they had hated Christ.

THE CONSOLATION

But on the night immediately following, the Lord stood at his side and said, "Take courage; for as you have solemnly witnessed to My cause at Jerusalem, so you must witness at Rome also." (23:11)

For his own safety, the Romans kept Paul confined in the barracks of Fort Antonia. Alone in his cell, the apostle was physically battered, discouraged, and uncertain of his future. But **on the night immediately following** his abortive hearing before the Sanhedrin, **the Lord stood at his side.** As He had before in times of need (cf. 18:9; 22:17–21), the Lord appeared in person to His servant.

He began by consoling Paul, exhorting him to **take courage.** God graciously comforts His downcast servants, so much so that Scripture calls Him "the God of all comfort" (2 Cor. 1:3). To the Corinthians Paul wrote:

> [God] comforts us in all our affliction so that we may be able to comfort those who are in any affliction with the comfort with which we ourselves are comforted by God. For just as the sufferings of Christ are ours in abundance, so also our comfort is abundant through Christ. (2 Cor. 1:4–5)

Later in Second Corinthians, Paul could write that he was filled with comfort (7:4), because God comforts the depressed (7:6).

The Lord also commended Paul, reminding him **you have solemnly witnessed to My cause at Jerusalem.** Paul had successfully completed the task the Lord had given him in that city.

Finally, the Lord gave Paul hope. He promised him that his life would not end in Jerusalem, but that he would be granted his desire (Rom. 1:9–11; 15:23) to **witness at Rome also.** That gracious promise sustained Paul during the many trials he would endure before he got there.

Providential Protection (Acts 23:12–35)

22

And when it was day, the Jews formed a conspiracy and bound themselves under an oath, saying that they would neither eat nor drink until they had killed Paul. And there were more than forty who formed this plot. And they came to the chief priests and the elders, and said, "We have bound ourselves under a solemn oath to taste nothing until we have killed Paul. Now, therefore, you and the Council notify the commander to bring him down to you, as though you were going to determine his case by a more thorough investigation; and we for our part are ready to slay him before he comes near the place." But the son of Paul's sister heard of their ambush, and he came and entered the barracks and told Paul. And Paul called one of the centurions to him and said, "Lead this young man to the commander, for he has something to report to him." So he took him and led him to the commander and said, "Paul the prisoner called me to him and asked me to lead this young man to you since he has something to tell you." And the commander took him by the hand and stepping aside, began to inquire of him privately, "What is it that you have to report to me?" And he said, "The Jews have agreed to ask you to bring Paul down tomorrow to the Council, as though they were going to inquire somewhat more thoroughly about him. So do not listen to them, for more than forty of them are lying in wait for him who have bound themselves under a curse not to eat or drink until they slay him; and now they are ready and waiting for the promise from you." Therefore the commander let the young man go, instructing him, "Tell no one that you have notified me of these things." And he called to him two of the centurions, and said, "Get two hundred soldiers ready by the third hour of the night to proceed to Caesarea, with seventy horsemen and two hundred spearmen." They were also to provide mounts to put Paul on and bring him safely to Felix the governor. And he wrote a letter having this form:

> "Claudius Lysias, to the most excellent governor Felix, greetings. When this man was arrested by the Jews and was about to be slain by them, I came upon them with the troops and rescued him, having learned that he was a Roman. And wanting to ascertain the charge for which they were accusing him, I brought him down to their Council; and I found him to be accused over questions about their Law, but under no accusation deserving death or imprisonment. And when I was informed that there would be a plot against the man, I sent him to you at once, also instructing his accusers to bring charges against him before you."

So the soldiers, in accordance with their orders, took Paul and brought him by night to Antipatris. But the next day, leaving the horsemen to go on with him, they returned to the barracks. And when these had come to Caesarea and delivered the letter to the governor, they also presented Paul to him. And when he had read it, he asked from what province he was; and when he learned that he was from Cilicia, he said, "I will give you a hearing after your accusers arrive also," giving orders for him to be kept in Herod's Praetorium. (23:12–35)

This passage finds Paul in difficult circumstances. He has been falsely accused, beaten, arrested, imprisoned, and plotted against. Yet God will deliver him—not by a supernatural miracle, but by His providential ordering of circumstances.

Paul's situation closely parallels that of another man of God, David. He, too, was treated unfairly and plotted against—only to repeatedly experience God's providential deliverance.

David first appears in the biblical record in 1 Samuel 16, when he was anointed king in place of the disobedient Saul. Many years would elapse, however, before he began his rule. During much of that time David was a hunted outlaw, pursued by the insanely jealous king whom he had loyally served.

David's association with Saul began when he was providentially chosen as court musician (1 Sam. 16:14–18). His skillful harp playing brought comfort to the tormented king. As a result, Saul loved David greatly and made him his armor bearer (1 Sam. 16:21). Soon afterward, David rescued Saul and Israel from their perennial enemies the Philistines. Fearlessly accepting the challenge of their champion, the giant Goliath, David killed him in single combat (1 Sam. 17:17–51). The dismayed Philistines were then routed by the Israelites (1 Sam. 17:52). Saul rewarded David by making him commander of the army (18:5).

But Saul's admiration for David soon turned to suspicion and jealousy when David received higher acclaim than he did (1 Sam. 18:6–9). For the rest of his life, Saul sought unsuccessfully to kill him. After failing to personally kill him (1 Sam. 18:10–11), Saul demoted him and banished him from the palace. He hoped that David would die in battle against the Philistines (1 Sam. 18:17, 21), but David's skill and triumph in battle won him even higher esteem (1 Sam. 18:30).

Saul then ordered his servants to put David to death (1 Sam. 19:1ff.). Only the intervention of Saul's son Jonathan (1 Sam. 19:1–7), his daughter Michal (1 Sam. 19:11–17), and his mentor Samuel (1 Sam. 19:18–24) saved David's life. But from then until Saul's death in battle against the Philistines, David was a hunted fugitive. Throughout that difficult and dangerous period, David remained loyal to Saul (1 Sam. 24:2ff.; 26:2ff.; cf. 2 Sam. 1:1ff.) and experienced God's providential protection (1 Sam. 23:14, 24–28; 28:1–2; 29:1–11).

Saul's death did not end David's troubles. The northern tribes rejected him as king in favor of Saul's son Ish-bosheth (2 Sam. 2:8–9). It took several years of civil war for David to unite the entire nation under his rule. And even after his ascension to the throne, he faced other severe difficulties. In the most heartbreaking betrayal, his son Absalom led a revolt against him in which his trusted counselor, Ahithophel, and his nephew Amasa were involved. No sooner had that revolt been put down than another broke out (2 Sam. 20:1ff.). Yet, throughout David's difficulties as king, God providentially protected him.

As the apostle Paul sat in his cell, he may have reflected on David's experiences. Perhaps the words of Psalm 56, penned when David fled from Saul to the Philistine city of Gath, came to mind.

> Be gracious to me, O God, for man has trampled upon me; fighting all day long he oppresses me. My foes have trampled upon me all day long, for they are many who fight proudly against me. When I am afraid,

I will put my trust in Thee. In God, whose word I praise, in God I have
put my trust; I shall not be afraid. What can mere man do to me? All day
long they distort my words; all their thoughts are against me for evil.
They attack, they lurk, they watch my steps, as they have waited to take
my life. Because of wickedness, cast them forth, in anger put down the
peoples, O God! Thou hast taken account of my wanderings; put my
tears in Thy bottle; are they not in Thy book? Then my enemies will turn
back in the day when I call; this I know, that God is for me. In God,
whose word I praise, in the Lord, whose word I praise, in God I have put
my trust, I shall not be afraid. What can man do to me? Thy vows are
binding upon me, O God; I will render thank offerings to Thee. For Thou
hast delivered my soul from death, indeed my feet from stumbling, so
that I may walk before God in the light of the living. (Ps. 56:1–13)

That psalm expressed David's confidence in God's care for him,
despite the aggressive oppression of men. Paul, too, had recently experienced difficult circumstances. His attempt to conciliate the Christian
Jews at Jerusalem (21:20ff.) had ended in a riot—one in which he was
nearly killed. His attempt to defend himself before the angry mob who
had seized him in the temple also ended in a riot (21:27ff.). His appearance before the highest Jewish court had ended in chaos. And although
accused of no crime, Paul remained in the custody of the Romans.

As He had in past times of discouragement (18:9; 22:17–21), the
Lord Himself appeared to Paul (23:11) to console him, commend him,
and give him hope. He promised Paul that he would not be killed in
Jerusalem but would live to testify someday in Rome. The Lord further
strengthened Paul's hope in that promise by providentially delivering
him from a plot to murder him.

This narrative passage contains no doctrinal truths or practical
exhortations; it merely recounts an event in Paul's life. Yet no passage of
Scripture could more clearly illustrate the providence of God.

God's providence is His sovereign control over and ordering of
natural circumstances to accomplish His will. It is also illustrated clearly in the Old Testament in the book of Esther, where God providentially
protected His people, Israel, from their destructive enemies. God's providence underlies such familiar and comforting passages as Philippians
4:5–7; Hebrews 13:6; and Luke 12:22–34.

God's dramatic, providential deliverance of Paul plays out in
three scenes: the plot formulated, found out, and frustrated.

THE PLOT FORMULATED

And when it was day, the Jews formed a conspiracy and bound

themselves under an oath, saying that they would neither eat nor drink until they had killed Paul. And there were more than forty who formed this plot. And they came to the chief priests and the elders, and said, "We have bound ourselves under a solemn oath to taste nothing until we have killed Paul. Now, therefore, you and the Council notify the commander to bring him down to you, as though you were going to determine his case by a more thorough investigation; and we for our part are ready to slay him before he comes near the place." (23:12–15)

The **day** after Paul's appearance before the Sanhedrin, some **Jews,** frustrated at seeing Paul escape with his life, formulated a plot to murder him. They **bound themselves under an oath, saying that they would neither eat nor drink until they had killed Paul.** That oath showed the seriousness of their intentions. The Greek text reads, "They anathematized themselves" (cf. Gal. 1:8, 9), thus invoking divine judgment if they failed to carry out their oath. They probably spoke words to the effect of "May God do so to us and more if we eat or drink anything until Paul is dead" (cf. 1 Sam. 14:44; 2 Sam. 3:35; 19:13; 1 Kings 2:23; 2 Kings 6:31).

The scene is tragically reminiscent of Jesus' death. Both Jesus and Paul were Jews, preachers of the gospel to their people, and guilty of no crime. Yet both were plotted against, both stood before a confused Sanhedrin, and both were prisoners in Fort Antonia. Paul truly shared in "the fellowship of His sufferings" (Phil. 3:10; cf. Gal. 6:17).

Why did the Jews react with such violent hostility to someone who had committed no offense against Jewish law, who loved them, and who proclaimed to them salvation through the Messiah, Jesus Christ? Paul gave the answer in 2 Corinthians 4:4: "The god of this world has blinded the minds of the unbelieving, that they might not see the light of the gospel of the glory of Christ, who is the image of God." So deceived were they that they were unable to discern the truth and were swept up into Satan's rebellion. That rebellion began in heaven. Lucifer, not content with being the most exalted of all God's created beings, rebelled against God (Isa. 14:12ff.; Ezek. 28:12ff.; Rev. 12:3–4, 7–9). It continued in the garden, when he tempted Adam and Eve. Their disobedience then led the human race into sin. Determined to thwart God's redemptive plan (cf. Gen. 3:15), Satan tried unsuccessfully to destroy Messiah's nation, His line, and, finally, Messiah Himself. But he was utterly defeated by Christ's saving work on the cross and triumphant resurrection. Since then, he has worked to silence the preachers of the gospel. The plotters were dupes of Satan, willing to be used to stifle the saving gospel by killing the most effective Christian preacher.

Luke relates that **there were more than forty who formed**

this plot. They knew they could not depend on the Romans to execute Paul, since there was no capital crime with which to accuse him. Nor did they dare risk another speech by Paul, fearing he might sway public opinion to his side. Therefore, they decided to take matters into their own hands. **More than forty** men were needed, because Paul would be heavily guarded by Roman soldiers. That many of the conspirators would no doubt be killed in the fracas speaks of their fanaticism (cf. John 16:2). Having many take part in the plot would also serve to deflect any blame away from one individual.

To ensure the plot's success, the conspirators needed the aid of the Sanhedrin. They approached **the chief priests and the elders** who, being Sadducees, would be more eager to help. Significantly, the scribes, who were largely Pharisees like Paul and had recently defended him, were excluded. The conspirators first informed the Sanhedrin of their intentions, saying **"We have bound ourselves under a solemn oath to taste nothing until we have killed Paul."** Then they mentioned the Sanhedrin's part in the plot: **"Now, therefore, you and the Council notify the commander** (the tribune, Claudius Lysias) **to bring him down to you, as though you were going to determine his case by a more thorough investigation; and we for our part are ready to slay him before he comes near the place."** That the conspirators assumed the Sanhedrin's leadership would take part in a murder plot says much about the very apparent corruption of Israel's highest court. Nor did the Sanhedrin disappoint them (v. 20).

THE PLOT FOUND OUT

But the son of Paul's sister heard of their ambush, and he came and entered the barracks and told Paul. And Paul called one of the centurions to him and said, "Lead this young man to the commander, for he has something to report to him." So he took him and led him to the commander and said, "Paul the prisoner called me to him and asked me to lead this young man to you since he has something to tell you." And the commander took him by the hand and stepping aside, began to inquire of him privately, "What is it that you have to report to me?" And he said, "The Jews have agreed to ask you to bring Paul down tomorrow to the Council, as though they were going to inquire somewhat more thoroughly about him. So do not listen to them, for more than forty of them are lying in wait for him who have bound themselves under a curse not to eat or drink until they slay him; and now they are ready and waiting for the promise from you."

Therefore the commander let the young man go, instructing him, "Tell no one that you have notified me of these things." (23:16–22)

With so many conspirators involved, the plot could not be kept secret for long. In God's providence, **the son of Paul's sister heard of their ambush.** This is the only specific reference in Scripture to Paul's family (except for possible references in Rom. 16:7, 11, 21). It raises many questions that cannot be answered with certainty. What was Paul's nephew doing in Jerusalem, since the family home was in Tarsus? Was he following in his uncle's footsteps and studying to be a rabbi? Since Paul's family had apparently disinherited him when he became a believer (Phil. 3:8), why did he care what happened to his uncle? Had Paul's sister or nephew become Christians?

How Paul's nephew heard of the plot is also not known, but when he did, **he came and entered the barracks and told Paul.** Paul had not been charged with a crime, so was merely in protective custody. He was therefore permitted to receive visitors. Knowing the danger of such plots from experience (cf. Acts 9:23, 29; 20:3, 19), **Paul** immediately **called one of the centurions to him and said, "Lead this young man to the commander, for he has something to report to him."**

The centurion **took** Paul's nephew **and led him to the commander and said, "Paul the prisoner** (cf. Eph. 3:1; 2 Tim. 1:8; Philem. 1, 9, 23) **called me to him and asked me to lead this young man to you since he has something to tell you."** Out of respect for Lysias's rank, Paul communicated to him through one of his centurions. That the centurion immediately did what Paul asked shows the respect the apostle's Roman citizenship commanded. In proper military fashion he succinctly informed his commanding officer of the situation.

The **commander** was desperate for any information that would help him decide what to do with Paul. Therefore he gently **took** Paul's nephew **by the hand and stepping aside, began to inquire of him privately, "What is it that you have to report to me?"** The boy was undoubtedly very excited and intimidated by his surroundings, so Lysias took him aside to speak with him privately. He also realized that the information was confidential, since it had not been revealed to the centurion.

The boy then accurately informed Lysias of the details of the plot: **"The Jews have agreed to ask you to bring Paul down tomorrow to the Council, as though they were going to inquire somewhat more thoroughly about him."** Thus, in God's providence, Lysias learned of the plot before the Jews even approached him. Paul's nephew then urged the Roman commander not to give in: **"So do not listen to them, for more than forty of them are lying in wait for him who have bound themselves under a curse not to eat or drink until**

they slay him; and now they are ready and waiting for the promise from you."

Recognizing the seriousness of the situation, Lysias took immediate action. First, he **let the young man go, instructing him, "Tell no one that you have notified me of these things."** If the conspirators realized their plot had been uncovered, they would undoubtedly have abandoned it and formulated another. And if that one were not discovered, Lysias reasoned, Paul might be killed. Further, if the Jews did not know that he knew of the plot, they could not question his motives for sending Paul to Caesarea. Then he took the necessary measures, without imagining he was carrying out God's providential protection of Paul.

THE PLOT FRUSTRATED

And he called to him two of the centurions, and said, "Get two hundred soldiers ready by the third hour of the night to proceed to Caesarea, with seventy horsemen and two hundred spearmen." They were also to provide mounts to put Paul on and bring him safely to Felix the governor. And he wrote a letter having this form:

> **"Claudius Lysias, to the most excellent governor Felix, greetings. When this man was arrested by the Jews and was about to be slain by them, I came upon them with the troops and rescued him, having learned that he was a Roman. And wanting to ascertain the charge for which they were accusing him, I brought him down to their Council; and I found him to be accused over questions about their Law, but under no accusation deserving death or imprisonment. And when I was informed that there would be a plot against the man, I sent him to you at once, also instructing his accusers to bring charges against him before you."**

So the soldiers, in accordance with their orders, took Paul and brought him by night to Antipatris. But the next day, leaving the horsemen to go on with him, they returned to the barracks. And when these had come to Caesarea and delivered the letter to the governor, they also presented Paul to him. And when he had read it, he asked from what province he was; and when he learned that he was from Cilicia, he said, "I will give you a hearing after your accusers arrive also," giving orders for him to be kept in Herod's Praetorium. (23:23–35)

Faced with a difficult and potentially explosive situation, Lysias again proved himself to be an able commander. Realizing things were getting out of hand, he wisely decided to get Paul out of Jerusalem. That would, of course, thwart the plot and keep a prisoner for whom he was responsible from being assassinated. And it would avoid a confrontation with the Jews that could degenerate into a full-scale revolt. Therefore, he decided to pass the problem on to his superior, the Roman governor Felix.

Having made his decision, Lysias wasted no time. **He** immediately **called to him two of the centurions,** and gave them their orders: **"Get two hundred soldiers ready by the third hour of the night to proceed to Caesarea, with seventy horsemen and two hundred spearmen." Caesarea,** some sixty-five miles from Jerusalem, was the seat of the Roman government in Judea. It was there that Felix had his headquarters.

Taking no chances on any further ambush plots, Lysias detailed a strong, heavily armed force of half his thousand-man garrison to escort Paul on the long march to the coast. The **two hundred soldiers** were Roman legionnaires, the most formidable troops of antiquity. **Seventy horsemen** from the cohort's cavalry detachment were also sent, along with **two hundred** lightly armed **spearmen,** or javelin throwers.

Not willing to risk waiting until the next day, Lysias ordered the detachment to leave by **the third hour of the night** (9:00 P.M.). Since speed was important, **they were also to provide mounts to put Paul on**. Their mission was to **bring him safely to Felix the governor,** Lysias's immediate superior.

As was required when a Roman officer sent a prisoner to his superior (Everett F. Harrison, *Interpreting Acts: The Expanding Church* [Grand Rapids: Zondervan, 1986], 373), Lysias **wrote a letter** of explanation to Felix, which Luke summarizes:

> **Claudius Lysias, to the most excellent governor Felix, greetings. When this man was arrested by the Jews and was about to be slain by them, I came upon them with the troops and rescued him, having learned that he was a Roman. And wanting to ascertain the charge for which they were accusing him, I brought him down to their Council; and I found him to be accused over questions about their Law, but under no accusation deserving death or imprisonment. And when I was informed that there would be a plot against the man, I sent him to you at once, also instructing his accusers to bring charges against him before you.** (23:26–30)

Claudius was the Roman name he took (perhaps in honor of Emperor Claudius) when he obtained his citizenship (22:28). Since **Lysias** is a Greek name, it signifies he was probably a free-born Greek by nationality.

He diplomatically addressed the letter **to the most excellent governor Felix.** It gives a reasonably accurate summary of the events leading to his decision to send Paul to Caesarea. Lysias did embellish things to put himself in the best possible light; contrary to what he wrote, he did not discover Paul's Roman citizenship until after he rescued him. And he conveniently failed to mention his order to have Paul scourged and his erroneous assumption that he was the famed Egyptian trouble-maker. Lysias noted his efforts to resolve the case, informing Felix that he tried **to ascertain the charge for which they were accusing him,** and even **brought him down to their Council.** His statement that Paul was **under no accusation deserving death or imprisonment** is tantamount to declaring him innocent. Then Lysias closed by giving his reason for burdening Felix with Paul's case: **"When I was informed that there would be a plot against the man, I sent him to you at once, also instructing his accusers to bring charges against him before you."** Paul's safety required his removal to Caesarea.

Having made all the necessary preparations, **the soldiers, in accordance with their orders, took Paul and brought him by night to Antipatris. Antipatris,** about thirty-five to forty miles away, was a Roman military post often used as a rest stop for travelers between Jerusalem and Caesarea. It had been built by Herod the Great and named in honor of his father, Antipater. To make it there in one night would have required a grueling forced march, especially for the foot soldiers.

After successfully getting past the main danger area around Jerusalem, the troops escorting Paul spent the night in Antipatris. **The next day, leaving the horsemen to go on with** Paul to Caesarea, the foot soldiers **returned to the barracks** in Jerusalem. Antipatris marked the border between Judea and the largely Gentile region of Samaria. The danger of ambush was now greatly reduced, and the cavalry escort would suffice to see Paul safely to Caesarea.

After arriving in **Caesarea,** Paul's escort **delivered the letter to the governor,** and **also presented Paul to him.** When Felix **read** the letter, **he asked from what province** Paul **was.** The answer would determine whether Felix had jurisdiction to hear his case. **When he learned that** Paul **was from Cilicia, he** agreed to hear the case. Since Cilicia, like Judea, was at that time under the Legate of Syria, Felix had the authority to try Paul's case. He so informed the apostle, **"I will give you a hearing after your accusers arrive also"** (cf. v. 30). Meanwhile, he ordered that Paul be kept **in Herod's Praetorium**—the governor's official residence. The stage was thus set for the first in Paul's series of Roman trials.

God's providential protection of His servant demonstrates His faithfulness. Based in part on his own experiences, Paul could declare to the Corinthians that "God is faithful" (1 Cor. 1:9; cf. 10:13; 2 Cor. 1:18; 2 Thess. 3:3). The first step in that direction occurred the day after God's promise to bring Paul to Rome. He also showed His care for Paul by sovereignly providing a safe and comfortable trip to Caesarea and providing the best of accommodations when he arrived there. Paul experienced the truth expressed by Peter: "Casting all your anxiety upon Him, because He cares for you" (1 Pet. 5:7).

Paul on Trial
Phase One:
Before Felix
(Acts 24:1–27)

23

And after five days the high priest Ananias came down with some elders, with a certain attorney named Tertullus; and they brought charges to the governor against Paul. And after Paul had been summoned, Tertullus began to accuse him, saying to the governor, "Since we have through you attained much peace, and since by your providence reforms are being carried out for this nation, we acknowledge this in every way and everywhere, most excellent Felix, with all thankfulness. But, that I may not weary you any further, I beg you to grant us, by your kindness, a brief hearing. For we have found this man a real pest and a fellow who stirs up dissension among all the Jews throughout the world, and a ringleader of the sect of the Nazarenes. And he even tried to desecrate the temple; and then we arrested him. And we wanted to judge him according to our own Law. But Lysias the commander came along, and with much violence took him out of our hands, ordering his accusers to come before you. And by examining him yourself concerning all these matters, you will be able to ascertain the things of which we accuse him." And the Jews also joined in the attack, asserting that these things were so. And when the governor had nodded for him to speak, Paul responded: "Knowing that for many years you have been a judge to this nation, I cheerfully make my defense, since you can take note of the fact that no more than twelve days ago I went up to Jerusalem to worship. And neither in the temple, nor in the synagogues, nor in the city itself did they find me carrying on a discussion with anyone or causing a riot. Nor can they prove to you the charges of which they now accuse me. But this I admit to you, that according to the Way which they call a sect I do serve the God of our fathers, believing everything that is in accordance with the Law, and that is written in the Prophets; having a hope in God, which these men cherish themselves, that there shall certainly be a resurrection of both the righteous and the wicked. In view of this, I also do my best to maintain always a blameless conscience both before God and before men. Now after several years I came to bring alms to my nation and to present offerings; in which they found me occupied in the temple, having been purified, without any crowd or uproar. But there were certain Jews from Asia—who ought to have been present before you, and to make accusation, if they should have anything against me. Or else let these men themselves tell what misdeed they found when I stood before the Council, other than for this one statement which I shouted out while standing among them, 'For the resurrection of the dead I am on trial before you today.'" But Felix, having a more exact knowledge about the Way, put them off, saying, "When Lysias the commander comes down, I will decide your case." And he gave orders to the centurion for him to be kept in custody and yet have some freedom, and not to prevent any of his friends from ministering to him. But some days later, Felix arrived with Drusilla, his wife who was a Jewess, and sent for Paul, and heard him speak about faith in Christ Jesus. And as he was discussing righteousness, self-control and the judgment to come, Felix became frightened and said, "Go away for the present, and when I find time, I will summon you." At the same time too, he was hoping that money would be given him by Paul; therefore he also used to send for him quite often and converse with him. But after two years had passed, Felix was succeeded by Porcius Festus; and wishing to do the Jews a favor, Felix left Paul imprisoned. (24:1–27)

This chapter presents one of the most tragic examples of missed opportunity in all of Scripture. Felix, the Roman governor of Judea, had the privilege of spending much time with the apostle Paul. Yet, sadly, he let the opportunity slip away, and there is no evidence to indicate he was not eternally lost.

The Bible gives many examples of missed opportunity concerning salvation. Some pagan philosophers, after hearing Paul's able defense of Christianity on Mars Hill in Athens, dismissed him with the words "We shall hear you again concerning this" (Acts 17:32). But Paul soon left Athens, never to return, and the philosophers never heard him again.

Luke 9:57–62 records the lost opportunities of some would-be disciples of the Lord:

> And as they were going along the road, someone said to Him, "I will follow You wherever You go." And Jesus said to him, "The foxes have holes, and the birds of the air have nests, but the Son of Man has nowhere to lay His head." And He said to another, "Follow Me." But he said, "Permit me first to go and bury my father." But He said to him, "Allow the dead to bury their own dead; but as for you, go and proclaim everywhere the kingdom of God." And another also said, "I will follow You, Lord; but first permit me to say good-bye to those at home." But Jesus said to him, "No one, after putting his hand to the plow and looking back, is fit for the kingdom of God."

The parable of the wise and foolish virgins (Matt. 25:1–12) also illustrates the tragedy of missed opportunity. So does the story of the rebellious Israelites who died in the wilderness and failed to enter the Promised Land (Heb. 3:7ff.).

But the most striking example of lost opportunity is Judas. Judas was graciously granted an opportunity given to only eleven others—to live and minister with the Lord Jesus Christ during His earthly ministry. He could have sat on one of the twelve thrones in the kingdom, judging the twelve tribes of Israel (Matt. 19:28). His name could have been on one of the twelve foundation stones of the celestial Jerusalem (Rev. 21:14). He could have been one of the most honored saints in all of redemptive history. Instead, Judas became a thief, hypocrite, and traitor. He threw away his opportunity for a paltry thirty pieces of silver, committed suicide, and was condemned to eternal damnation. Our Lord summed up Judas's life in the fearful words of Matthew 26:24: "Woe to that man by whom the Son of Man is betrayed! It would have been good for that man if he had not been born."

Felix was tragically similar to Judas. Judas lived with the Lord Jesus for more than three years; Felix had Paul in his palace for two. Judas had many opportunities to talk with Jesus; Felix "used to send for [Paul] quite often and converse with him" (v. 26). Judas betrayed the Son of God for money; Felix "was hoping that money would be given him by Paul" (v. 26). Judas betrayed the Lord to the Jewish authorities; Felix, fearing those same authorities, betrayed Paul by refusing to release him despite his innocence.

Paul's hearing before Felix, like any trial, consisted of three parts: the prosecution, the defense, and the verdict.

THE PROSECUTION

And after five days the high priest Ananias came down with some elders, with a certain attorney named Tertullus; and they brought charges to the governor against Paul. And after Paul had been summoned, Tertullus began to accuse him, saying to the governor, "Since we have through you attained much peace, and since by your providence reforms are being carried out for this nation, we acknowledge this in every way and everywhere, most excellent Felix, with all thankfulness. But, that I may not weary you any further, I beg you to grant us, by your kindness, a brief hearing. For we have found this man a real pest and a fellow who stirs up dissension among all the Jews throughout the world, and a ringleader of the sect of the Nazarenes. And he even tried to desecrate the temple; and then we arrested him. And we wanted to judge him according to our own Law. But Lysias the commander came along, and with much violence took him out of our hands, ordering his accusers to come before you. And by examining him yourself concerning all these matters, you will be able to ascertain the things of which we accuse him." And the Jews also joined in the attack, asserting that these things were so. (24:1–9)

Five days after Paul arrived at Caesarea, **the high priest Ananias came down** from Jerusalem **with some** of the **elders** from the Sanhedrin. Not content with merely running Paul out of Jerusalem, they continued to seek his life. To put their case together, find an attorney, travel the sixty-five miles to Caesarea, and do it all in only five days required fast action on their part. Perhaps they feared Felix would release Paul if they did not move swiftly to bring charges against him.

Ananias was one of the most corrupt high priests in Israel's history. He viewed Paul as a threat to his position, and someone who must be eliminated. Also in the entourage were several **elders,** key leaders of the Sanhedrin. That the religious and political leaders of Israel came in person to accuse Paul shows how serious a threat he posed to them.

The high priest and the elders themselves did not argue the case against Paul, however. For that they hired **a certain attorney named Tertullus** and through him **brought charges to the governor**

against Paul. Whether he was a Roman or a Hellenistic Jew is not known, but he was likely chosen because he was well versed in Roman law. It was not unusual for Jews to hire such experts to represent them in Roman legal proceedings.

The hearing began **after Paul had been summoned.** Before **Tertullus began to accuse him,** he addressed Felix with the type of flowery, flattering, complimentary speech (known as the *captatio benevolentiae*) customary in such situations. Unfortunately, there was not much good that could be said about Felix, procurator (governor) of Judea from A.D. 52 to 59. A former slave, Felix owed his position to the influence of his brother Pallas, a favorite of Emperor Claudius. The Roman historian Tacitus disdainfully dismissed him with the comment "He exercised the power of a king with the mind of a slave" (F. F. Bruce, *Paul: Apostle of the Heart Set Free* [Grand Rapids: Eerdmans, 1977], 355).

Tertullus's opening statement to Felix, **"Since we have through you attained much peace, and since by your providence reforms are being carried out for this nation, we acknowledge this in every way and everywhere, most excellent Felix, with all thankfulness,"** stretched the truth to the breaking point. Felix did manage to suppress some of the roving bands of *sicarii* ("assassins")—fiercely nationalistic anti-Roman terrorists (cf. chapter 20 of this volume). He also defeated the Egyptian false messiah whom Lysias wrongly assumed Paul to be (cf. chapter 20 of this volume). But his methods were so brutal that he outraged and alienated the Jews, causing even more unrest. If he carried out any reforms, history does not record them. His inept rule led to his removal from office by Nero two years after this hearing (24:27). Despite Tertullus's flattering words, the Jewish people would not have felt much thankfulness toward Felix. Tertullus closed his introductory remarks with the customary promise to be brief: **"that I may not weary you any further, I beg you to grant us, by your kindness, a brief hearing."** While such promises were often broken, Tertullus was forced to keep his—since there was little good he could say about Felix and little bad he could say about Paul.

Turning then to the case against Paul, Tertullus brought three charges: sedition (violation of Roman law), sectarianism (violation of Jewish law), and sacrilege (violation of God's law).

The first charge, of sedition (insurrection, rebellion), was the most serious to bring against Paul in a Roman court and was the only one that actually involved a crime against Rome. The Romans dealt firmly and severely with disturbers of the *Pax Romana*. Many of the Jewish leaders present would experience that truth firsthand a few years later, when the Romans brutally crushed the Jewish revolt of A.D. 66–70. Before introducing the charge of sedition, Tertullus declared to Felix, **"we have found this man a real pest."** That description of Paul accurately reflects the Sanhedrin's hatred for him but was not a specific charge.

Tertullus then presented the specific allegation by denouncing the "pest," Paul, as **"a fellow who stirs up dissension** against Rome **among all the Jews throughout the world"** (cf. Acts 17:7). If the hypocritical Sanhedrin, which itself desired Rome's overthrow, could have substantiated this grossly exaggerated charge, Paul would have been in serious trouble. Rome did not tolerate those who stirred up public dissension. But while it is true that Paul had been involved in riots, he had been the riots' victim, not their instigator.

Tertullus cleverly avoided naming any specific instance. Had he done so, Felix could have transferred Paul's case to the jurisdiction in which that riot occurred. Not wanting Paul tried by a governor over whom they had no influence, the Jewish leaders contented themselves with the vague general charge of seditious insurrection. But as is the case throughout Acts when Christianity is the issue in a Roman court, that charge could not be proven. The Holy Spirit recorded those trials, in part, to refute the charge that Christians were political revolutionaries and to make clear that they did not violate Roman civil law (cf. Rom. 13:1–7; Titus 3:1–7; 1 Pet. 2:13–17). The real issue, as Gallio correctly perceived (18:12–16), was Jewish hostility to the gospel. Because of his "more exact knowledge about the Way" (v. 22), and Lysias's evaluation (23:29), Felix was aware of the motives behind the Sanhedrin's specious charges, and he found its vague, unsubstantiated charges inadmissible as evidence.

The second charge leveled against Paul was sectarianism, or heresy. Paul was, according to Tertullus, **a ringleader of the sect of the Nazarenes.** *Prōtostatēs* (**ringleader**) is a military term meaning "one who stands in the front rank." Although Tertullus certainly did not mean it as a compliment, it was true of Paul. **Nazarenes** was a derisive term for the followers of Jesus, who was from Nazareth and was called the Nazarene (cf. 6:14; John 1:46; 7:41, 52). Although it appears only in Acts, that title must have been commonly used, since Tertullus did not explain it to Felix. The implication of such a sectarian identity was that Paul was the leader of a messianic sect troublesome to Israel and thus to Rome.

The third charge, the one that had originally led to Paul's arrest, was that he **tried to desecrate the temple.** Attempting to give a veneer of legality to the savage attack of the mob, the Jews whitewashed their effort to kill him by claiming to have **arrested** Paul themselves (though the Romans had actually done that to protect him from the mob). Unlike the hotheaded mob that had accused him of several blasphemies (21:28), however, the Sanhedrin was careful to accuse Paul only of attempting to desecrate the temple. There was no evidence that he had actually done so; if he had, the Jews had the right to handle the matter themselves, without hauling Paul before a Roman court (cf. the discussion of 21:28–29 in chapter 20 of this volume). Again, since they had no evidence to present to Felix, they contented themselves with a general accusation.

The further twisting of the facts by the lawyer, given in the last phrase of verse 6, all of verse 7, and the first part of verse 8 (**And we wanted to judge him according to our own Law. But Lysias the commander came along, and with much violence took him out of our hands, ordering his accusers to come before you.**), is omitted by many ancient manuscripts. If the passage is not in the original text, then Tertullus is urging Felix to examine Paul. His recital of events would then end abruptly with the statement **and then we arrested him**. But since it is not likely that Paul would have confirmed Tertullus's false accusations under examination, but rather would have denied them, it would have been counterproductive to ask Felix to examine him (v. 8). The Sanhedrin's only hope in doing that would have been, given enough rope, Paul would hang himself—an extremely unlikely event.

On the other hand, if the passage is included in the text, the representatives of the Sanhedrin would be saying they had already done all the examining and evidence-gathering and were there to present a completed case. They would be falsely accusing Lysias of subverting proper Jewish legal procedure (**"we wanted to judge him according to our own Law"**) and abusing his authority. (Although Paul was the one who was beaten, the Sanhedrin's representatives ignored the truth and complained that **"Lysias the commander came along, and with much violence took him out of our hands."**) They were confident that **by examining him** (Lysias, not Paul) **concerning all these matters,** Felix would **be able to ascertain the things of which** they accused **him**. That would help explain Felix's decision to postpone a verdict until he heard from Lysias (v. 22). **The Jews also joined in the attack, asserting that the** charges brought by their attorney were true. On that note, the prosecution's case ended.

THE DEFENSE

And when the governor had nodded for him to speak, Paul responded: "Knowing that for many years you have been a judge to this nation, I cheerfully make my defense, since you can take note of the fact that no more than twelve days ago I went up to Jerusalem to worship. And neither in the temple, nor in the synagogues, nor in the city itself did they find me carrying on a discussion with anyone or causing a riot. Nor can they prove to you the charges of which they now accuse me. But this I admit to you,

that according to the Way which they call a sect I do serve the God of our fathers, believing everything that is in accordance with the Law, and that is written in the Prophets; having a hope in God, which these men cherish themselves, that there shall certainly be a resurrection of both the righteous and the wicked. In view of this, I also do my best to maintain always a blameless conscience both before God and before men. Now after several years I came to bring alms to my nation and to present offerings; in which they found me occupied in the temple, having been purified, without any crowd or uproar. But there were certain Jews from Asia—who ought to have been present before you, and to make accusation, if they should have anything against me. Or else let these men themselves tell what misdeed they found when I stood before the Council, other than for this one statement which I shouted out while standing among them, 'For the resurrection of the dead I am on trial before you today.'** (24:10–21)

Paul began his defense after **the governor nodded for him to speak.** Not having a lawyer to represent him, he **responded** for himself to Felix: **"Knowing that for many years you have been a judge to this nation, I cheerfully make my defense."** Felix had been governor for about five years and had served under Cumanus, governor of Samaria, for several years before that. Unlike Tertullus, however, Paul's intent was not to flatter Felix (cf. Ps. 12:3; Prov. 26:28; 29:5). Paul merely reminded Felix that he had served long enough in Palestine to be acquainted with Jewish beliefs and customs. He was thus obligated to render a fair decision.

Paul's masterful defense calmly and categorically refuted the charges one by one. First, he pointed out the absurdity of the charge of sedition, urging Felix to **"take note of the fact that no more than twelve days ago I went up to Jerusalem to worship."** Five of those **twelve days** had been spent in Caesarea, and much of his time in Jerusalem had been taken up with his purification rites (21:23–27). Even if Paul had been so inclined, he had not had time to stir up a rebellion. His goal in coming to Jerusalem, however, had not been to incite a revolt but **to worship.**

Paul offered further proof of his innocence (cf. 25:8; 28:17–18) by pointing out that **"neither in the temple, nor in the synagogues, nor in the city itself did they find me carrying on a discussion with anyone or causing a riot."** He had engaged in no public debates, nor was he guilty of **causing a riot.** In fact, he had not gone to Jerusalem on an evangelistic mission but to bring an offering for the poor (v. 17; cf. Rom. 15:25–28; 1 Cor. 16:1–4; 2 Cor. 8:1ff.).

As the above evidence shows, the charge of sedition was totally false. Paul pointed that out to Felix, insisting that the Sanhedrin could not **prove the charges of which they now** accused him. Since the two remaining charges were religious in nature, they were outside the competence of a Roman court to judge. Felix should have dismissed the case at that point for lack of evidence.

In reply to the second charge, of sectarianism, Paul acknowledged being a Christian but denied that Christianity was heretical. He said to Felix, **"But this I admit to you, that according to the Way which they call a sect I do serve the God of our fathers."** Tertullus had derisively referred to Christians as Nazarenes (v. 5), but Paul called Christianity **the Way** (cf. v. 22; Acts 9:2; 19:9, 23). Although the Jewish leaders denounced Christianity as a dangerous **sect,** Paul emphatically declared, **"I do serve the God of our fathers"** (the historic title for the God of Israel, Gen. 48:15; Ex. 3:15; Deut. 26:7; 1 Chron. 12:17; 29:18; 2 Chron. 20:6; Ezra 7:27; Dan. 2:23; Acts 3:13; 5:30). To be a Christian, Paul insisted, was not to forsake worshiping the true God but to be devoted to Him.

In contrast to his Jewish accusers (who were mostly Sadducees), Paul believed **everything that is in accordance with the Law, and that is written in the Prophets.** He turned the tables on his adversaries, pointing out that they were the real heretics. They did not truly worship God, since they rejected His Son (John 5:23). Paul accepted the plenary (full) inspiration of the Old Testament Scriptures, believing **everything** written in them. The Sadducees accepted only the Pentateuch as divinely inspired, while the Pharisees accepted the entire Old Testament. But both rejected the clear testimony of the Law and the Prophets to Jesus Christ (John 5:39, 46; cf. Luke 24:27, 44; John 1:45). Far from being a heretic, Paul was more orthodox than his accusers, since he served the God of his fathers, believed in the inspiration of the entire Old Testament, and accepted everything it taught.

Paul's belief in the Old Testament led him to have **a hope in God, which these men cherish themselves, that there shall certainly be a resurrection of both the righteous and the wicked.** The resurrection was the **hope** of the Jewish people, being taught in the Old Testament (Job 19:25–27; Isa. 26:19; Dan. 12:2). Here Paul placed himself, in contrast to the skeptical Sadducees, firmly within mainstream Jewish theology. Since the Sadducees did not believe in resurrection, Paul's reference to **men** who **cherish** that hope includes the Pharisees in the delegation. This is the only time, either in Acts or the epistles, that Paul explicitly refers to **a resurrection of both the righteous and the wicked** (cf. Matt. 25:31ff.; John 5:28–29; Rev. 20:11–15).

Paul's belief in the resurrection and coming judgment was not mere doctrinal orthodoxy without impact on his life. It caused him to **do** his **best to maintain always a blameless conscience both before God and before men.** In a similar vein, John wrote:

> Beloved, now we are children of God, and it has not appeared as yet what we shall be. We know that, when He appears, we shall be like Him, because we shall see Him just as He is. And everyone who has this hope fixed on Him purifies himself, just as He is pure. (1 John 3:2–3)

To rebut the final allegation against him (sacrilege, attempting to profane the temple), Paul recounted for Felix the circumstances of his visit to Jerusalem: **"Now after several years I came to bring alms to my nation and to present offerings."** Far from seeking to stir up trouble, Paul came to Jerusalem on a mission of mercy. He brought an offering for the needy Jewish Christians, collected from the Gentile churches.

After delivering the offering to the Jerusalem church, Paul agreed to sponsor four Jewish Christians who were taking Nazirite vows (cf. chapter 19 of this volume). As their sponsor, Paul would participate in the ceremony marking the end of their vows. Having recently returned to Israel from Gentile regions, he needed first to undergo ritual purification. It was while doing that, Paul informed Felix, that **"they found me occupied in the temple, having been purified, without any crowd or uproar."** Again Paul emphasized that he had not caused any disturbance; he was merely doing what any devout Jew would do.

Paul then turned to the real cause of the disturbance—**certain Jews from** the Roman province of **Asia.** Their false charge that Paul desecrated the temple provoked the ensuing riot. Accordingly, as Paul reminded Felix, those Asian Jews **"ought to have been present before you, and to make accusation, if they should have anything against me"** (cf. 25:16). This was a telling point in Paul's favor, because "Roman law was very strong against accusers who abandoned their charges" (A. N. Sherwin-White, *Roman Society and Roman Law in the New Testament* [Oxford: Oxford University Press, 1963], 52). That the eyewitnesses of Paul's alleged desecration of the temple failed to show up undermined the Sanhedrin's case.

Pressing home the point, Paul boldly challenged the Sanhedrin to **"tell what misdeed they found when I stood before the Council, other than for this one statement which I shouted out while standing among them, 'For the resurrection of the dead I am on trial before you today.'"** Since the Sanhedrin's witnesses had failed to show up, let them tell Felix what they found Paul guilty of when he stood before them (23:1–10). The only "crime" they could accuse him of was the **statement** he **shouted out while standing among them,**

'For the resurrection of the dead I am on trial before you today.' But belief in resurrection was not a crime, even under Jewish law (the Pharisees accepted it), much less Roman law. So Paul successfully refuted all charges against him. The issues were theological, not civil or criminal, and therefore did not belong in a Roman court.

THE VERDICT

But Felix, having a more exact knowledge about the Way, put them off, saying, "When Lysias the commander comes down, I will decide your case." And he gave orders to the centurion for him to be kept in custody and yet have some freedom, and not to prevent any of his friends from ministering to him. But some days later, Felix arrived with Drusilla, his wife who was a Jewess, and sent for Paul, and heard him speak about faith in Christ Jesus. And as he was discussing righteousness, self-control and the judgment to come, Felix became frightened and said, "Go away for the present, and when I find time, I will summon you." At the same time too, he was hoping that money would be given him by Paul; therefore he also used to send for him quite often and converse with him. But after two years had passed, Felix was succeeded by Porcius Festus; and wishing to do the Jews a favor, Felix left Paul imprisoned. (24:22–27)

Felix faced a difficult decision. His prisoner was a Roman citizen, against whom no eyewitnesses had come forward to verify any of the alleged crimes. Nor had the Sanhedrin, the highest Jewish court, found him guilty of anything specific. And **Felix** himself had **a more exact knowledge about the Way** (possibly from his Jewish wife, Drusilla). He knew that Christians were not political revolutionaries and that the charges against Paul were baseless. Therefore, the only verdict possible under Roman law was innocent. Yet such a verdict would infuriate the Jewish leaders and possibly lead to further unrest. Felix could not afford to have that happen.

Like many politicians before and since who have been trapped between justice and popularity, Felix decided his wisest course was to avoid making a decision. **Put them off** translates a form of the verb *anaballō*, the legal term for adjourning a hearing. He justified the delay on the pretext of needing further information from Claudius Lysias (which the Jews had urged him to seek, vv. 7–8). Therefore he informed the parties, **"When Lysias the commander comes down, I will decide your case."** Lysias had already given Felix a written report stating that the matter was a question of Jewish law (23:29). He had also plainly stated his belief that Paul was not guilty of any crime (23:29). It is unlikely that Lysias had any further information to add, and there is no evidence that Felix ever did summon him. Felix simply used that intention as an excuse for stalling.

Meanwhile, Felix **gave orders to the centurion for** Paul **to be kept in custody.** By so doing, Felix hoped to placate the Jewish authorities, since he had refused to rule in their favor. Since Paul was a Roman citizen who had not been convicted of a crime, Felix ordered the centurion to let the apostle **have some freedom, and not to prevent any of his friends from ministering to him.** He was kept under guard but not in close confinement.

His prisoner evidently intrigued him, however, for **some days later, Felix arrived with Drusilla, his wife who was a Jewess, and sent for Paul, and heard him speak about faith in Christ Jesus**. **Drusilla,** the youngest daughter of Herod Agrippa I (the Herod of Acts 12), was Felix's third wife (his first had been a granddaughter of Antony and Cleopatra). While still in her teens, Drusilla had been given in marriage to the king of Emesa (located in the province of Syria). Struck by her renowned beauty, Felix contrived (with the help of a Cypriot magician) to lure her away from her husband. At age sixteen she became his wife and bore him a son, who was killed in the eruption of Mount Vesuvius (A.D. 79). At this time, she was not yet twenty years old. According to some manuscripts, it was at her urging that Felix sent for Paul. And as noted above, it was possibly through her that Felix obtained his knowledge of Christianity.

Paul spoke to them **about** the **faith in Christ Jesus** (the definite article appears in the Greek text; cf. Jude 3). In other words, he discussed the gospel and Christian beliefs with them. Zeroing in on every sinner's dilemma, Paul specifically **was discussing righteousness, self-control and the judgment to come. Righteousness** is the absolute standard demanded by God's holy nature (cf. Matt. 5:48; 1 Pet. 1:15–16). **Self-control** is man's required response to bring him into conformity with God's law. **Judgment** is the inevitable result (apart from saving faith in Christ) of failing to control oneself so as to live up to God's standards. Since Felix was living with a woman he had lured away from her husband, it is understandable that **Felix became frightened**. Because he lacked the first two virtues, he faced inevitable divine judgment.

Felix's fear did not lead him to repentance, however. Merely alarmed, he dismissed Paul, telling him, **"Go away for the present, and when I find time, I will summon you."** He let the opportunity pass, heedless of the truth that "now is the acceptable time, behold, now is the day of salvation" (2 Cor. 6:2).

The moment of conviction and opportunity passed. Felix (though apparently without Drusilla) was able **to send for** Paul **quite often** during the next two years **and converse with him,** without again becoming alarmed. His motives were not spiritual but materialistic. No doubt inspired by Paul's comment in verse 17, Felix **was hoping that money would be given him by Paul.** Although Roman law strictly prohibited the taking of bribes, it was nonetheless common practice. Felix hoped Paul would try to bribe his way out of custody.

But no bribe was ever forthcoming, and **after two years had passed, Felix was succeeded by Porcius Festus.** Felix's brutal suppression of a riot in Caesarea so infuriated the Jews that they managed to get him removed from office. Emperor Nero recalled him to Rome, where he would have faced severe punishment had his influential brother Pallas not interceded for him. After his recall, Felix vanished from history. Although he knew Paul was innocent, he refused to the end to release him. Luke notes that **wishing to do the Jews a favor, Felix left Paul imprisoned.** Seeking the Sanhedrin's goodwill was expedient for his personal success, considering the circumstances of his recall.

Felix stands for all time as a tragic example of missed opportunity. In the words of the writer of Hebrews,

> for if we go on sinning willfully after receiving the knowledge of the truth, there no longer remains a sacrifice for sins, but a certain terrifying expectation of judgment, and the fury of a fire which will consume the adversaries. (Heb. 10:26–27)

All who are tempted, like Felix, to postpone a decision about Jesus Christ would do well to heed the sobering warning of Hebrews 3:7-8*a:* "Therefore, just as the Holy Spirit says, 'Today if you hear His voice, do not harden your hearts.'"

Paul on Trial Phase Two: Before Festus (Acts 25:1–12)

24

Festus therefore, having arrived in the province, three days later went up to Jerusalem from Caesarea. And the chief priests and the leading men of the Jews brought charges against Paul; and they were urging him, requesting a concession against Paul, that he might have him brought to Jerusalem (at the same time, setting an ambush to kill him on the way). Festus then answered that Paul was being kept in custody at Caesarea and that he himself was about to leave shortly. "Therefore," he said, "let the influential men among you go there with me, and if there is anything wrong about the man, let them prosecute him." And after he had spent not more than eight or ten days among them, he went down to Caesarea; and on the next day he took his seat on the tribunal and ordered Paul to be brought. And after he had arrived, the Jews who had come down from Jerusalem stood around him, bringing many and serious charges against him which they could not prove; while Paul said in his own defense, "I have committed no offense either against the Law of the Jews or against the temple or against Caesar." But Festus, wishing to do the Jews a favor, answered Paul and said, "Are you willing to go up to Jerusalem and stand trial before me on these charges?" But Paul said, "I am standing before Caesar's tribunal, where I

ought to be tried. I have done no wrong to the Jews, as you also very well know. If then I am a wrongdoer, and have committed anything worthy of death, I do not refuse to die; but if none of those things is true of which these men accuse me, no one can hand me over to them. I appeal to Caesar." Then when Festus had conferred with his council, he answered, "You have appealed to Caesar, to Caesar you shall go." (25:1–12)

The latter part of Acts finds Paul a prisoner of Rome. Because of his faithfulness, he had made an unparalleled impact for Jesus Christ on the world. He had evangelized the lost, boldly confronted false religion, founded churches, and discipled faithful men for the task of spreading the gospel.

But Paul's diligent, faithful, tireless efforts stirred up a wake of hatred and opposition from the enemies of the gospel. Shortly after his conversion, he "kept increasing in strength and confounding the Jews who lived at Damascus by proving that this Jesus is the Christ" (Acts 9:22). Shocked and outraged by his startling change from persecutor to evangelist (9:21), "the Jews plotted together to do away with him" (9:23). But Paul discovered their plot and managed to escape (9:24).

That early incident set the pattern for Paul's ministry; it started that way and stayed that way. Seemingly everywhere he went, he faced hostility, opposition, even outright persecution. Most of that opposition came from unbelieving Jews—a fact that deeply grieved him (Rom. 9:1–3). Other times, as in Ephesus (19:21–41), it came from Gentile followers of false religion.

We have already learned that Paul's Jewish enemies managed to have him arrested by the Romans on trumped-up charges (21:27–33). For the next several years, he remained a prisoner, first in Jerusalem, then in Caesarea, finally in Rome. During that time, he repeatedly defended himself against the false charges brought against him. Shortly after Roman troops rescued him from the angry mob on the temple grounds, Paul defended himself from the steps of Fort Antonia (21:37–22:21). Unable to determine Paul's crime, Claudius Lysias, the Roman commander at Jerusalem, brought him before the Sanhedrin (22:30–23:11). But the highest court in Israel failed to convict him of any wrongdoing. Learning of a plot against Paul's life, Lysias sent him to Caesarea, the Roman headquarters in Judea (23:12–33). There he stood trial before the governor, Felix, and again was exonerated (24:1–27). Felix, however, fearing the Jewish authorities (and hoping for a bribe from Paul), rendered no verdict but instead kept Paul imprisoned for the remaining two years of his term as governor.

This text records Paul's fourth defense, before Porcius Festus, Felix's successor as governor. Felix's brutal term in office had culminated in the ruthless subduing of a riot in Caesarea. When the outraged Jews sent a delegation to Rome to protest Felix's actions, Emperor Nero recalled the governor to Rome in disgrace. Festus soon arrived in Judea to replace him.

Unlike Felix, who was a former slave, Festus was a member of the Roman nobility. Little is known of his brief term as governor (he died about two years after taking office). Since the first-century Jewish historian Josephus described him as better than his predecessor (Felix) and his successor (Albinus), he appears to have been an able leader.

Paul's trial before Festus unfolds in four scenes: the assassination plotted, the accusations presented, the absence of proof, and the appeal proposed.

THE ASSASSINATION PLOTTED

Festus therefore, having arrived in the province, three days later went up to Jerusalem from Caesarea. And the chief priests and the leading men of the Jews brought charges against Paul; and they were urging him, requesting a concession against Paul, that he might have him brought to Jerusalem (at the same time, setting an ambush to kill him on the way). Festus then answered that Paul was being kept in custody at Caesarea and that he himself was about to leave shortly. "Therefore," he said, "let the influential men among you go there with me, and if there is anything wrong about the man, let them prosecute him." (25:1–5)

When **Festus,** the new governor, **arrived in the province** of Judea, he inherited the political problems left by his predecessor's inept rule. Felix's callousness and cruelty had left a legacy of profound hatred toward Rome by the Jews. Their hostility and suspicion now focused on Festus, their new Roman overlord in occupied Palestine.

Unlike Felix, Festus was not a procrastinator. He moved swiftly to acquaint himself with the situation; a mere **three days** after arriving in Judea, he **went up to Jerusalem from Caesarea.** His first goal was to meet the Jewish leaders (the high priest and the Sanhedrin) and, as much as possible, conciliate them. Those leaders, Festus knew, were the key to establishing peace in Judea. And maintaining peace was the highest priority of a Roman provincial governor.

Festus faced a difficult challenge, as the Jews had proven to be adept at manipulating their governors. Capitalizing on Pilate's blunders, they had blackmailed him into executing Jesus. And although they had failed to pressure Felix into executing Paul, they had forced him to keep the innocent apostle imprisoned and out of circulation.

Adding to that challenge was the constant threat of revolution. Two centuries earlier, under the Maccabees, the Jews had thrown off the yoke of Greece. More recent times had seen the rise of ultranationalistic movements such as the Zealots. The revolt that was always smoldering would finally erupt in A.D. 66. Festus, like his predecessors, faced the dilemma of maintaining control without sparking a revolt.

Not only did Festus inherit Felix's political problems, he also inherited his most celebrated prisoner. Although Paul had been imprisoned in Caesarea for the past two years, the Jewish authorities in Jerusalem had not forgotten about him. One of the first things **the chief priests and the leading men of the Jews** did after Festus arrived in Jerusalem was to revive the **charges against Paul.** Perhaps they feared that the new governor would, as often happened, quickly dispose of the cases left by his predecessor and release Paul. Hoping to capitalize on Festus's inexperience and desire to placate them, **they were** repeatedly **urging him, requesting a concession against Paul.**

Their request seemed innocent enough—merely that Festus **might** order Paul to be **brought to Jerusalem** for trial. But **at the same time,** Luke notes, they intended **setting an ambush to kill him on the way.** The old ambush plot, foiled two years earlier by Claudius Lysias, was revived—this time by the Sanhedrin itself.

Festus was not to be so easily duped, however. To the Jewish leaders' request he cautiously **answered that Paul was being kept in custody at Caesarea and that he himself was about to leave shortly** to return there. Accordingly, he saw no reason to transport the prisoner to Jerusalem. He maintained that the proper place for Paul, a Roman citizen, to be tried was at Caesarea, seat of Roman rule in Judea. If **the influential men** of the Jewish nation believed **there** was **anything wrong about** Paul, they could **prosecute him** there. Though Festus was inexperienced, had an obvious desire to conciliate the Jewish authorities, and lacked personal knowledge of Paul, God used him, as He had others, to providentially protect Paul from another plot against his life.

THE ACCUSATIONS PRESENTED

And after he had spent not more than eight or ten days among them, he went down to Caesarea; and on the next day he took his seat on the tribunal and ordered Paul to be brought. And after he had arrived, the Jews who had come down from Jerusalem stood around him, bringing many and serious charges against him (25:6–7a)

True to his word, Festus, **after he had spent not more than**

eight or ten days among them, went down from Jerusalem **to Caesarea.** Proving himself again to be a man of action, **on the next day he took his seat on the tribunal** (the *bēma*, or judgment seat, cf. Matt. 27:19; John 19:13; Acts 18:12; 25:10, 17), thus making it an official Roman trial, **and ordered Paul to be brought** before him.

After the defendant **had arrived, the Jews who had come down from Jerusalem stood around him, bringing many and serious charges against him.** They swarmed around Paul like a pack of wolves attacking a sheep. But these wolves were toothless; the **many serious charges** they brought were the same ones (sedition, sectarianism, and sacrilege, cf. 24:5–6) that they had been unable to prove two years earlier before Felix. Those unsubstantiated charges were no more likely to convince Festus than they had Felix.

THE ABSENCE OF PROOF

which they could not prove; while Paul said in his own defense, "I have committed no offense either against the Law of the Jews or against the temple or against Caesar." But Festus, wishing to do the Jews a favor, answered Paul and said, "Are you willing to go up to Jerusalem and stand trial before me on these charges?" But Paul said, "I am standing before Caesar's tribunal, where I ought to be tried. I have done no wrong to the Jews, as you also very well know. If then I am a wrongdoer, and have committed anything worthy of death, I do not refuse to die; but if none of those things is true of which these men accuse me, no one can hand me over to them." (25:7b–11a)

Although the Sanhedrin had made very serious charges against Paul **they could not prove** them. Two years had passed since Paul's trial before Felix, but they still had no witnesses, no evidence, and therefore no case. That argues convincingly for the apostle's innocence and for their biased hatred of Jesus and the gospel.

Here, as he does throughout Acts, Luke stresses that Christians are innocent, law-abiding people. The town clerk at Ephesus acknowledged that (19:37), as did Gallio, proconsul of Achaia (18:12ff.). The frequent allegations by unbelieving Jews that Christians were political revolutionaries were untrue. Ironically, it was those same Jews, not the Christians, who finally rose in open revolt against Rome. When Rome ultimately did take action against the Christians, it was not because they were revolutionaries. The Romans persecuted and killed them for refusing, on religious grounds, to participate in the empire-unifying ritual of emperor worship.

Since the Jews had presented no evidence against him, **Paul** merely **said in his own defense, "I have committed no offense either against the Law of the Jews** (sectarianism) **or against the temple** (sacrilege) **or against Caesar** (sedition)**."** He thus denied point by point the charges against him.

Festus found himself on the horns of the same dilemma that had impaled Felix. Paul was a Roman citizen, falsely accused and obviously innocent. But to release him would antagonize the Jewish leaders—the same leaders Festus desperately needed to conciliate to keep the peace.

To his credit, Festus, unlike Felix, did not sweep the problem under the rug. Seeking a way out of his dilemma, he proposed a compromise. **Wishing to do the Jews a favor,** Festus asked **Paul, "Are you willing to go up to Jerusalem and stand trial before me on these charges?"** That the trial was to be before Festus, not the Sanhedrin, was no doubt intended to reassure Paul that his rights as a Roman citizen would be protected.

To the inexperienced Festus, that no doubt seemed like an acceptable compromise. But Paul knew the Jewish leaders far better than he did. The "compromise" actually gave them everything they wanted. The members of the Sanhedrin did not care who presided over Paul's trial—they never intended there to be one. They planned to murder him on the way to Jerusalem (v. 3).

By now understandably frustrated at his failure to obtain justice, **Paul** immediately rejected Festus's compromise. Since, as governor, Festus was the emperor's representative, Paul could rightly claim, **I am standing before Caesar's tribunal.** As a Roman citizen, that was **where** he ought **to be tried;** there was no reason to go to Jerusalem. The reference to **Caesar's tribunal** also served as a subtle reminder to Festus of his duty as the emperor's official agent.

Paul again affirmed his innocence, asserting, **"I have done no wrong to the Jews."** Because they had presented no evidence against him, the Jewish leaders could not successfully dispute that claim. Paul's bold words to Festus **"as you also very well know"** served as a rebuke and a call to integrity, since he did know that Paul was innocent (vv. 18–19). The high standards of Roman justice, and his duty as a Roman judge, demanded that he release the apostle.

Paul then clarified his motives. **"If then I am a wrongdoer,"** he said to Festus, **"and have committed anything worthy of death, I do not refuse to die."** He was not attempting to evade justice; instead, he demanded it by declaring, **"but if none of those things is true of which these men accuse me, no one can hand me over to them."** As a Roman citizen, Paul had the right to expect justice from a Roman court. Since there was no case against him, he was under no obligation to put himself into the hands of the Jewish authorities (cf. v. 16).

Festus's obvious readiness to appease the Jews put Paul in a difficult and dangerous situation. He had no illusions (even if Festus did) about what his fate would be if he did survive a murder plot and stand trial in Jerusalem. He knew how adroitly the Jewish leaders would capitalize on Festus's inexperience. To return to Jerusalem meant almost certain death. Paul therefore chose a bold course of action.

THE APPEAL PROPOSED

"I appeal to Caesar." Then when Festus had conferred with his council, he answered, "You have appealed to Caesar, to Caesar you shall go." (25:11*b*–12)

Festus's willingness to compromise did not bode well for Paul's getting a fair trial in Jerusalem. Exercising his right as a Roman citizen, Paul announced his decision to **appeal** his case **to Caesar**. Such appeals could come after the verdict (*appellatio*) or, as in Paul's case, before it (*provocatio*). Once granted, the appeal took the case out of the governor's hands and transferred it to the emperor. Paul's appeal seems at first glance to be sheer madness, since the emperor at the time was the infamous Nero. However, the early years of Nero's reign (during which Paul's appeal took place) were not marked by the cruelty and insanity of his later years.

Paul's appeal offered Festus a convenient way out of the impasse. Thus it comes as no surprise that after **Festus had conferred with his council** and obtained its legal advice, he granted Paul's appeal. Undoubtedly relieved to have this thorny problem taken out of his hands, he informed the apostle, **"You have appealed to Caesar, to Caesar you shall go."**

When Festus announced that his appeal had been granted, Paul must have felt a sense of exhilaration. The Lord had kept His promise (23:11), and Paul was at last going to Rome.

From this passage several important lessons emerge. First, it is another tragic example of Jewish hostility to the gospel—a theme running throughout Acts (4:1–31; 5:17–42; 6:9–15; 8:1–4; 9:23; 13:6, 45; 14:2, 19; 17:1–9, 13; 18:5–17; 19:8–9; 20:3; 21:27ff.; 23:12ff.). Jesus predicted that opposition in His words to His disciples recorded in John 15:18–25:

If the world hates you, you know that it has hated Me before it hated you. If you were of the world, the world would love its own; but because you are not of the world, but I chose you out of the world, therefore the world hates you. Remember the word that I said to you, "A slave is not greater than his master." If they persecuted Me, they will also persecute you; if they kept My word, they will keep yours also. But all these things they will do to you for My name's sake, because they do not know the One who sent Me. If I had not come and spoken to them, they would not have sin, but now they have no excuse for their sin. He who hates Me hates My Father also. If I had not done among them the works which no one else did, they would not have sin; but now they have both seen and hated Me and My Father as well. But they have done this in order that the word may be fulfilled that is written in their Law, "They hated Me without a cause."

The Lord's reference to "their Law" shows that He had the unbelieving Jews (particularly their leaders) in mind.

No religion is neutral about Jesus Christ; all non-Christian religions are openly or subtly opposed to Him. As He Himself put it, "He who is not with Me is against Me" (Matt. 12:30). Persecution of Christians by false religion is always based on two premises: it is based on false accusations, and it is for Christ's sake. Believers are to live blameless lives and so reveal their critics' accusations to be false (Titus 2:2–8; 1 Pet. 2:12, 15; 3:16).

A second truth this text illustrates is the binding power of sin. Although he had been out of the mainstream, incarcerated at Caesarea for two years, the Sanhedrin's hatred of Paul had not abated. "Truly, truly, I say to you," Jesus said in John 8:34, "everyone who commits sin is the slave of sin." In Romans 6:16, Paul asked rhetorically, "Do you not know that when you present yourselves to someone as slaves for obedience, you are slaves of the one whom you obey, either of sin resulting in death, or of obedience resulting in righteousness?" Peter wrote in 2 Peter 2:19, "By what a man is overcome, by this he is enslaved." The Jewish leaders were enslaved by their venomous hatred of Paul, an innocent man.

Third, this passage reveals the sovereignty of God in human affairs (cf. Gen. 45:7–8; Dan. 4:17; Luke 22:53; John 7:30; 19:10–11; Acts 2:23). The Sanhedrin's request to bring Paul to Jerusalem to stand trial seemed innocent enough. Festus needed the Jewish leaders' support, so it was essential for him to conciliate them. Granting that seemingly innocuous request would have been, from Festus's perspective, an easy concession. But God providentially intervened to protect His servant.

Fourth, the believer's proper relation to government also appears in this passage. Paul willingly submitted to the Roman government— even as embodied in the person of Nero. He practiced the principle he set forth in Romans 13:1–5:

Let every person be in subjection to the governing authorities. For there is no authority except from God, and those which exist are established by God. Therefore he who resists authority has opposed the ordinance of God; and they who have opposed will receive condemnation upon themselves. For rulers are not a cause of fear for good behavior, but for evil. Do you want to have no fear of authority? Do what is good, and you will have praise from the same; for it is a minister of God to you for good. But if you do what is evil, be afraid; for it does not bear the sword for nothing; for it is a minister of God, an avenger who brings wrath upon the one who practices evil. Wherefore it is necessary to be in subjection, not only because of wrath, but also for conscience' sake.

Understanding and applying these principles helped Paul's life have the powerful impact on the world that it did.

Paul on Trial Phase Three: Before Agrippa (Acts 25:13–26:32)

Now when several days had elapsed, King Agrippa and Bernice arrived at Caesarea, and paid their respects to Festus. And while they were spending many days there, Festus laid Paul's case before the king, saying, "There is a certain man left a prisoner by Felix; and when I was at Jerusalem, the chief priests and the elders of the Jews brought charges against him, asking for a sentence of condemnation upon him. And I answered them that it is not the custom of the Romans to hand over any man before the accused meets his accusers face to face, and has an opportunity to make his defense against the charges. And so after they had assembled here, I made no delay, but on the next day took my seat on the tribunal, and ordered the man to be brought. And when the accusers stood up, they began bringing charges against him not of such crimes as I was expecting; but they simply had some points of disagreement with him about their own religion and about a certain dead man, Jesus, whom Paul asserted to be alive. And being at a loss how to investigate such matters, I asked whether he was willing to go to Jerusalem and there stand trial on these matters. But when Paul appealed to be held in custody for the Emperor's decision, I ordered him to be kept in custody until I send him to Caesar." And Agrippa said to Festus, "I also would like to hear the man myself." "Tomorrow," he said, "you shall hear him." And so, on the next day when Agrippa had come together with Bernice, amid great pomp, and had entered the auditorium accompanied by the commanders and the prominent men of the city, at the command of Festus, Paul was brought in. And Festus said, "King Agrippa, and all you gentlemen here present with us, you behold this man about whom all the people of the Jews appealed to me, both at Jerusalem and here, loudly declaring that he ought not to live any longer. But I found that he had committed nothing worthy of death; and since he himself appealed to the Emperor, I decided to send him. Yet I have nothing definite about him to write to my lord. Therefore I have brought him before you all and especially before you, King Agrippa, so that after the investigation has taken place, I may have something to write. For it seems absurd to me in sending a prisoner, not to indicate also the charges against him." And Agrippa said to Paul, "You are permitted to speak for yourself." Then Paul stretched out his hand and proceeded to make his defense: "In regard to all the things of which I am accused by the Jews, I consider myself fortunate, King Agrippa, that I am about to make my defense before you today; especially because you are an expert in all customs and questions among the Jews; therefore I beg you to listen to me patiently. So then, all Jews know my manner of life from my youth up, which from the beginning was spent among my own nation and at Jerusalem; since they have known about me for a long time previously, if they are willing to testify, that I lived as a Pharisee according to the strictest sect of our religion. And now I am standing trial for the hope of the promise made by God to our fathers; the promise to which our twelve tribes hope to attain, as they earnestly serve God night and day. And for this hope, O King, I am being accused by Jews. Why is it considered incredible among you people if God does raise the dead? So then, I thought to myself that I had to do many things hostile to the name of Jesus of Nazareth. And this is just what I did in Jerusalem; not only did I lock up many of the saints in prisons, having received authority from the chief priests, but also when they were being put to death I cast my vote against them. And as I punished them often in all the synagogues, I tried to force them to blaspheme; and being furiously enraged at them, I kept pursuing them even to foreign cities. While thus engaged as I was journeying to Damascus with the authority and commission of the chief priests, at midday, O King, I saw on the way a light from heaven, brighter than the sun, shining all around me and those who were journeying with me. And when we had all fallen to the ground, I heard a voice saying to me in the Hebrew dialect, 'Saul, Saul, why are you persecuting Me? It is hard for you to kick against the goads.' And I said, 'Who art Thou, Lord?' And the Lord said, 'I am Jesus whom you are persecuting. But arise, and stand on your feet; for this purpose I have appeared to you, to appoint you a minister and a witness not only to the things which you have seen, but also to the things in which I will appear to you; delivering you from the Jewish people and from the Gentiles, to whom I am sending you, to open their eyes so that they may turn from darkness to light and from the dominion of Satan to God, in order that they may receive forgiveness of sins and an inheritance among those who have been sanctified by faith in Me.' Consequently, King Agrippa, I did not prove disobedient to the heavenly vision, but kept declaring both to those of Damascus first, and also at Jerusalem and then throughout all the region of Judea, and even to the Gentiles, that they should repent and turn to God, performing deeds appropriate to repentance. For this reason some Jews seized me in the temple and tried to put me to death. And so, having obtained help from God, I stand to this day testifying both to small and great, stating nothing but what the Prophets and Moses said was going to take place; that the Christ was to suffer, and that by reason of His resurrection from the dead He should be the first to proclaim light both to the Jewish people and to the Gentiles." And while Paul was saying this in his defense, Festus said in a loud voice, "Paul, you are out of your mind! Your great learning is driving you mad." But Paul said, "I am not out of my mind, most excellent Festus, but I utter words of sober truth. For the king knows about these matters, and I speak to him also with confidence, since I am persuaded that none of these things escape his notice; for this has not been done in a corner. King Agrippa, do you believe the Prophets? I know that you do." And Agrippa replied to Paul, "In a short time you will persuade me to become a Christian." And Paul said, "I would to God, that whether in a short or long time, not only you, but also all who hear me this day, might become such as I am, except for these chains." And the king arose and the governor and Bernice, and those who were sitting with them, and when they had drawn aside, they began talking to one another, saying, "This man is not doing anything worthy of death or imprisonment." And Agrippa said to Festus, "This man might have been set free if he had not appealed to Caesar." (25:13–26:32)

Paul's appeal of his case to the emperor (25:11) had resolved a difficult impasse for Festus. Like his predecessor, Felix, he knew Paul was innocent of the charges leveled against him by the Jewish leaders. But to release the apostle would anger those leaders and possibly provoke riots among the Jews. Seeking above all to keep peace in Judea, Felix and Festus realized they needed the Jewish leaders' cooperation.

Felix's solution was to avoid making a decision, instead allowing Paul to languish in prison for two years (24:22–27). Inheriting Paul's case from Felix, Festus attempted to compromise by placating the Jewish authorities. He proposed a hearing in Jerusalem, promising Paul he would preside over it (25:9). Realizing that he would not get a fair hearing under any circumstances, Paul exercised his right as a Roman citizen to appeal his case to the emperor.

That appeal, though resolving an impasse, presented Festus with a fresh difficulty. As governor he was required to send a report along with Paul to Rome, detailing the charges against him. But in Paul's case, those charges were theological and general in nature. Festus, only two weeks into his term as governor, was unfamiliar with the nuances of Jewish theology. Since he did not understand the charges (cf. vv. 18–19), he could not write a coherent report explaining them to the emperor. Fortunately, aid arrived in the person of Herod Agrippa.

THE CONSULTATION REGARDING PAUL'S TESTIMONY

Now when several days had elapsed, King Agrippa and Bernice arrived at Caesarea, and paid their respects to Festus. And while they were spending many days there, Festus laid Paul's case before the king, saying, "There is a certain man left a prisoner by Felix; and when I was at Jerusalem, the chief priests and the elders of the Jews brought charges against him, asking for a sentence of condemnation upon him. And I answered them that it is not the custom of the Romans to hand over any man before the accused meets his accusers face to face, and has an opportunity to make his defense against the charges. And so after they had assembled here, I made no delay, but on the next day took my seat on the tribunal, and ordered the man to be brought. And when the accusers stood up, they began bringing charges against him not of such crimes as I was expecting; but they simply had some points of disagreement with him about their own religion and about a certain dead man, Jesus, whom Paul asserted to be alive. And being at a loss how to investigate such matters, I asked whether he was willing to go to Jerusalem and there stand trial on these matters. But when Paul appealed to be held in custody for the Emperor's decision, I ordered him to be kept in custody

until I send him to Caesar." And Agrippa said to Festus, "I also would like to hear the man myself." "Tomorrow," he said, "you shall hear him." (25:13–22)

Several days after Paul's appeal to Caesar, **King Agrippa** (Herod Agrippa II) **and** his consort **Bernice arrived at Caesarea.** They had come to pay **their respects to** the new governor, **Festus.** The last in the line of Herods who figured prominently in New Testament history, Agrippa II ruled the northern part of Palestine during the Roman occupation. His father, Agrippa I, was the Herod who killed James, arrested Peter, and met an untimely end, being eaten by worms after failing to give God glory (Acts 12:1–23). His great-uncle, Herod Antipas, figured prominently in the gospels (Luke 3:1) as the ruler who executed John the Baptist (Mark 6:14–29), sought Jesus' life (Luke 13:31–33), and later tried Him (Luke 23:7–12). His great-grandfather was Herod the Great, who ruled at the time of Jesus' birth (Matt. 2:1–19; Luke 1:5) and murdered the children of Bethlehem in an effort to kill the newborn King.

Agrippa's private life was scandalous; **Bernice** was not only his consort but also his sister. (Their sister, Drusilla, was the wife of the former governor, Felix.) Their incestuous relationship was the subject of gossip in Rome (where Agrippa had grown up). Bernice would occasionally leave her brother and lover for another man (she had been the mistress of Emperor Vespasian and later of his son Titus), but she always returned. They are inseparable in the Acts narrative (cf. 25:13, 23; 26:30); she is, as some have suggested, the symbol of Agrippa's vice.

Although he did not rule Judea, Agrippa had been granted control of the temple treasury and the right to appoint the high priest. The Romans considered him an expert on Jewish affairs, as did Paul (26:3). Agrippa tried to prevent the Jewish revolt, but when it broke out in A.D. 66, he sided with the Romans and thus became a traitor to his people.

The nature of the royal couple's state visit required their **spending many days** in Caesarea. That gave Festus opportunity to seek Agrippa's experience and expert advice. He **laid Paul's case before the king, saying** to him, **"There is a certain man left a prisoner by Felix."** Felix had left Paul in prison to placate the Jewish leaders. Festus then reviewed for Agrippa Paul's situation: **When I was at Jerusalem, the chief priests and the elders of the Jews brought charges against him, asking for a sentence of condemnation upon him.** Festus's words throw new light on the Jews' request (25:3). From his perspective, they did not want a fair trial for Paul but a summary judgment of condemnation. Steeped in the proud tradition of Roman justice, Festus properly **answered them that it is not the custom of the Romans to hand over any man before the accused meets his accusers face to face, and has an opportunity to make his defense**

against the charges. Although Paul had already faced his accusers before Felix (and was not convicted of any crime), Festus wanted to discharge his duty and hear the case himself before rendering a verdict.

Refusing to accede to the Sanhedrin's demands to have the trial in Jerusalem (so that Jews could ambush Paul on the way, 25:3), Festus decided to hold the hearing in Caesarea (25:4–5). **"And so,** he continued, **"after they had assembled here, I made no delay, but on the next day took my seat on the tribunal, and ordered the man to be brought"** (25:6). After his return to Caesarea, Festus moved swiftly to try the case. To his surprise, **"when the accusers stood up, they began bringing charges against him not of such crimes as I was expecting."** Festus had naturally assumed that charges brought against Paul in a Roman court would involve serious violations of Roman law. Instead, he told Agrippa, **"they simply had some points of disagreement with him about their own religion and about a certain dead man, Jesus, whom Paul asserted to be alive."** Festus did not understand the issue or its implications and so was not qualified to rule on such matters, which in any case did not belong in a Roman court. The refusal of Gallio, the Roman governor of Achaia, to hear a similar case had established a legal precedent that could have been applied (18:12–16).

Knowing that an obviously intelligent, educated man such as Paul would claim that a **dead man** had come **alive** must have especially baffled Festus (cf. 26:24). Yet it was precisely the issue of the resurrection of Jesus Christ that most clearly set Christianity apart from Judaism and was the cornerstone of the gospel. Festus could not understand the implications of Christ's resurrection because he was ignorant of His life and ministry, and of Scripture.

Perplexed, **and being at a loss how to investigate such matters,** Festus had **asked** Paul **whether he was willing to go to Jerusalem and there stand trial on these matters.** Paul, of course, refused. He knew, even if Festus did not, that he would never get a fair trial in Jerusalem (even if he got there alive). As a Roman citizen, he had the right to be tried before the emperor's representative in a Roman court (25:10). And since the Jews had presented to Festus no evidence of wrongdoing on Paul's part (25:10), why bother with another hearing before them?

Having no other recourse, Paul appealed his case to Caesar's court (25:11). Festus explained to Agrippa that **"when Paul appealed to be held in custody for the Emperor's decision, I ordered him to be kept in custody until I send him to Caesar."** Festus's words put the blame for the present dilemma on Paul; the implication is that had the apostle been willing to go to Jerusalem, the matter could have been settled. Yet it was Festus's obvious desire to do the Jews a favor (25:9) that forced Paul's appeal. Had the governor done what justice demanded and released the obviously innocent apostle, no appeal would have been necessary. In God's providence, Paul was kept in Roman custody as a protection against being assassinated.

The term **Emperor** is an adjective, *Sebastos*, and literally means "the revered or worshiped one." It is the Greek equivalent of the Latin title *Augustus*, which was commonly applied to the emperor. Because of Paul's appeal, Festus was duty-bound to order him **to be kept in custody until** he could **send him to Caesar.** Festus needed Agrippa's help to come up with a valid charge against Paul for his report to the emperor.

No doubt flattered by the appeal to his expertise—and curious—**Agrippa said to Festus, "I also would like to hear the man myself."** The imperfect tense of *boulomai* (**I would like**) suggests Agrippa had been wanting to hear Paul for a long time. He undoubtedly knew of Paul and looked forward to hearing the leading spokesman for Christianity in person. **"Tomorrow,"** Festus assured him, **"you shall hear him."**

THE CIRCUMSTANCES OF PAUL'S TESTIMONY

And so, on the next day when Agrippa had come together with Bernice, amid great pomp, and had entered the auditorium accompanied by the commanders and the prominent men of the city, at the command of Festus, Paul was brought in. And Festus said, "King Agrippa, and all you gentlemen here present with us, you behold this man about whom all the people of the Jews appealed to me, both at Jerusalem and here, loudly declaring that he ought not to live any longer. But I found that he had committed nothing worthy of death; and since he himself appealed to the Emperor, I decided to send him. Yet I have nothing definite about him to write to my lord. Therefore I have brought him before you all and especially before you, King Agrippa, so that after the investigation has taken place, I may have something to write. For it seems absurd to me in sending a prisoner, not to indicate also the charges against him." (25:23–27)

This scene is one of the most riveting in the New Testament. **On the next day,** the day after Festus's consultation with Agrippa about Paul, **Agrippa** came, **together with Bernice, amid great pomp** and **entered the auditorium**. *Phantasia* (**pomp**) appears only here in the New Testament and denotes a grand, showy pageant. Festus turned Paul's hearing into an occasion to honor Agrippa. Accordingly, Agrippa and Bernice were **accompanied by the commanders** (the five tribunes commanding the five cohorts stationed at Caesarea) **and the prominent men of the city.**

The spectacle must have been breathtaking. Agrippa would have been decked out in all the trappings of royalty, including a purple robe, golden crown, rings, and perhaps a scepter. Bernice, though not technically Agrippa's queen, would have been similarly attired. The five tribunes would have been wearing their full-dress uniforms, **the prominent men of the city** wearing their finest clothes. An immaculately dressed honor guard of soldiers undoubtedly escorted the dignitaries into the auditorium.

When everyone was seated, **Festus** gave the **command,** and **Paul was brought in.** The contrast could not have been more striking. Into the midst of the assembly hall, crowded with the most important people in Caesarea, walked a Jew who has been described as short, bald, and physically unimposing (cf. 2 Cor. 10:10). Murmurs of surprise must have greeted his appearance; many in the crowd probably found it hard to believe that this seemingly unimpressive man was the cause of so much controversy. But appearances can be deceiving. History has judged Paul to be one of the most noble and powerful men who ever lived—and the crowd to be a collection of pompous fools.

The stage was set, and **Festus** opened the proceedings by introducing Paul: **"King Agrippa, and all you gentlemen here present with us, you behold this man about whom all the people of the Jews appealed to me, both at Jerusalem and here, loudly declaring that he ought not to live any longer."** He then honestly admitted his problem. Festus had heard the Jews' accusations against Paul and concluded that **he had committed nothing worthy of death.** Thus again, this Roman official affirmed Paul's innocence. But Paul, for the reasons noted earlier, had **appealed to the Emperor,** and Festus had **decided to send him.** The governor then got to the crux of his dilemma, admitting, **"I have nothing definite about him to write to my lord."** Festus did not understand the religious issues at stake. He hoped that the results of this **investigation** would provide him with **something** coherent **to write** in his official report. It was obviously **absurd** (if not dangerous) to send a **prisoner** to Caesar for trial and **not indicate the charges against him.** The emperor would not look favorably on a provincial governor who so wasted his court's time.

Paul was probably not legally bound to attend the inquiry. He had already appealed his case to the emperor, thus taking it out of Festus's jurisdiction. But Paul would not think of passing up an opportunity to preach the gospel in such an important setting. Here is still another example of his courageous commitment to serve the Lord Jesus Christ in every circumstance. The vehicle for his gospel proclamation was to be the powerful, dramatic testimony of his conversion on the road to Damascus.

THE COMMENCEMENT OF PAUL'S TESTIMONY

And Agrippa said to Paul, "You are permitted to speak for yourself." Then Paul stretched out his hand and proceeded to make his defense: "In regard to all the things of which I am accused by the Jews, I consider myself fortunate, King Agrippa, that I am about to make my defense before you today; especially because you are an expert in all customs and questions among the Jews; therefore I beg you to listen to me patiently. So then, all Jews know my manner of life from my youth up, which from the beginning was spent among my own nation and at Jerusalem; since they have known about me for a long time previously, if they are willing to testify, that I lived as a Pharisee according to the strictest sect of our religion. And now I am standing trial for the hope of the promise made by God to our fathers; the promise to which our twelve tribes hope to attain, as they earnestly serve God night and day. And for this hope, O King, I am being accused by Jews. Why is it considered incredible among you people if God does raise the dead? So then, I thought to myself that I had to do many things hostile to the name of Jesus of Nazareth. And this is just what I did in Jerusalem; not only did I lock up many of the saints in prisons, having received authority from the chief priests, but also when they were being put to death I cast my vote against them. And as I punished them often in all the synagogues, I tried to force them to blaspheme; and being furiously enraged at them, I kept pursuing them even to foreign cities. While thus engaged as I was journeying to Damascus with the authority and commission of the chief priests, at midday, O King, I saw on the way a light from heaven, brighter than the sun, shining all around me and those who were journeying with me. And when we had all fallen to the ground, I heard a voice saying to me in the Hebrew dialect, 'Saul, Saul, why are you persecuting Me? It is hard for you to kick against the goads.' And I said, 'Who art Thou, Lord?' And the Lord said, 'I am Jesus whom you are persecuting. But arise, and stand on your feet; for this purpose I have appeared to you, to appoint you a minister and a witness not only to the things which you have seen, but also to the things in which I will appear to you; delivering you from the Jewish people and from the Gentiles, to whom I am sending you, to open their eyes so that they may turn from darkness to light and from

the dominion of Satan to God, in order that they may receive forgiveness of sins and an inheritance among those who have been sanctified by faith in Me.'" (26:1–18)

Agrippa took charge of the proceedings, and, since there were no accusers or accusations, informed **Paul, "You are permitted to speak for yourself."** Taking his cue, **Paul stretched out his hand and proceeded to make his defense.** Because Agrippa was the key figure, Paul addressed his remarks to him, beginning with the courteous statement **"In regard to all the things of which I am accused by the Jews, I consider myself fortunate, King Agrippa, that I am about to make my defense before you today."** That was not flattery; Paul believed that Agrippa, because of his Roman orientation, was not likely to be sympathetic to the Sanhedrin. And his Jewish background made him **an expert in all customs and questions among the Jews,** so that he could grasp the issues. To Paul, then, Agrippa was both objective and knowledgeable—perhaps a prime candidate for conversion.

The primary goal of Paul's testimony was not to exonerate himself, but to convert Agrippa (cf. 26:28). The apostle **therefore** did not hesitate to **beg** Agrippa **to listen to** him **patiently.** Paul saw himself as an ambassador, representing Jesus Christ to the world, begging people to be reconciled to God. That was the goal of his ministry, as he wrote to the Corinthians:

> Therefore if any man is in Christ, he is a new creature; the old things passed away; behold, new things have come. Now all these things are from God, who reconciled us to Himself through Christ, and gave us the ministry of reconciliation, namely, that God was in Christ reconciling the world to Himself, not counting their trespasses against them, and He has committed to us the word of reconciliation. Therefore, we are ambassadors for Christ, as though God were entreating through us; we beg you on behalf of Christ, be reconciled to God. (2 Cor. 5:17–20)

Paul understood his calling from the very first. In Damascus, shortly after his conversion, Ananias told him, "For you will be a witness for Him to all men of what you have seen and heard" (Acts 22:15). No matter what his circumstances were, Paul always saw himself as an ambassador for Jesus Christ. Writing from prison in Rome, he could still call himself "an ambassador in chains" (Eph. 6:20). Paul cared nothing for his own life; he cared only that Jesus Christ be exalted (Acts 21:13; Phil. 1:21).

Paul's testimony contains two main themes: Jesus Christ's resurrection proves Him to be the Messiah, and Paul's transformed life proves the reality of Christ's resurrection. He masterfully weaves the saving gospel through this first-person account.

To show how startling and complete the divine transformation of his life was, Paul began his testimony by describing his life before his conversion. He reminded Agrippa that **"all Jews know my manner of life from my youth up, which from the beginning was spent among my own nation and at Jerusalem."** Paul was well known to the Jewish authorities; he had been educated in Jerusalem (Acts 22:3) and later he became the chief persecutor of the Christian faith (cf. Acts 8:1–3; 9:1–2). The Jewish leaders thus had **known about** him **for a long time.** Further, **if they** were **willing to testify** to it, they knew **that** Paul had **lived as a Pharisee according to the strictest sect of** their **religion.** Josephus described the Pharisees as "a certain sect of the Jews that appear more religious than others, and seem to interpret the laws more accurately" (*Wars* 1.5.2). When Paul wanted to describe his zeal for the law, it was enough for him to say, "As to the Law, a Pharisee" (Phil. 3:5). Paul stressed that point to show how remarkable his conversion to the Christian faith was. He had been as zealous and committed as any Jew of his day (cf. Gal. 1:13-14) and was an unlikely prospect for such a conversion.

As he had in his trial before Felix (cf. 24:14–15), Paul affirmed his commitment to the teaching of the Old Testament. He declared to Agrippa, **"I am standing trial for the hope of the promise made by God to our fathers; the promise to which our twelve tribes hope to attain, as they earnestly serve God night and day. And for this hope, O King, I am being accused by Jews."** This zealous, orthodox Jew was at that moment **standing trial for** believing in **the hope of the promise made by God to** the Jewish **fathers.** That **hope** was the coming of the Messiah and His kingdom (cf. 1:6; 3:22–24; 13:23–33; Gal. 3:17–18; 4:4; Titus 2:13; 1 Pet. 1:11–12) and, specifically, the resurrection connected with His coming. It was that **promise** that was **made by God** throughout the Old Testament: Messiah would come to take away sin and establish His kingdom of righteousness. And it was that very **promise to which** the **twelve tribes** of Israel hoped **to attain as they earnestly** served **God night and day**. (Paul's mention of the **twelve tribes** shows that the ten northern tribes are not lost [cf. Matt. 19:28; Luke 22:30; James 1:1; Rev. 21:12].) Yet, incredibly, it was for proclaiming that very **hope** fulfilled in Jesus Christ that Paul was **being accused by** these apostate **Jews.**

The incongruity of his being condemned for believing what the Jewish people had always believed caused Paul to exclaim, **"Why is it considered incredible among you people if God does raise the dead?"** By raising Jesus from the dead, God validated the Old Testament promise of resurrection, at the same time demonstrating that Jesus was Israel's long-awaited Messiah.

But it was just this point that Agrippa, along with many other Jews, was not willing to concede. Most Jews (except for the Sadducees, Matt. 22:23) accepted the general concept of resurrection (cf. John 5:28–29; 11:24). What they did not accept was that Jesus Christ rose from the dead and was their Messiah. When confronted with the undeniable fact of His resurrection, the Jewish leaders had concocted the story that the disciples stole His body. They even bribed the Roman guards to confirm their lie. So while Agrippa no doubt accepted the general Jewish belief in resurrection, he, like the other leaders and the nation, did not accept the resurrection of Christ or His messiahship.

Paul understood that perfectly, having once believed the same way himself. He had once **thought that** he **had to do many things hostile to the name of Jesus of Nazareth.** And that is **just what** he **did in Jerusalem. Not only did** he proceed to **lock up many of the saints in prisons, having received authority from the chief priests, but also**, he notes, referring to incidents like the murder of Stephen (7:58), **"when they were being put to death I cast my vote against them."** The Greek phrase translated **I cast my vote** literally reads "I threw my pebble." The reference is to the ancient custom of recording votes—a black pebble for conviction and a white one for acquittal. Paul's reference to voting against Christians may indicate he had once been a member of the Sanhedrin.

Paul also **punished** Christians **often in all the synagogues,** attempting by torture **to force them to blaspheme.** If he could not kill them, he at least wanted to force them to recant. Viewing Christians as dangerous and blasphemous heretics caused Paul to be **furiously enraged at them** (cf. 9:1; Gal. 1:13–14). Not content to cleanse Jerusalem of Christians, he **kept pursuing them even to foreign cities.**

It was **while thus engaged** that the event took place which transformed his life (and marked a major turning point in history). Paul was **journeying to Damascus with the authority and commission of the chief priests** to arrest any Christians he might find there. Suddenly, **at midday,** he reports, he **saw on the way a light from heaven, brighter** even **than the** brilliant Middle Eastern **sun, shining all around** him **and those who were journeying with** him. After Paul and his fellow persecutors **had all fallen to the ground,** he **heard the voice** of the risen, ascended, and glorified Lord Jesus Christ **saying to** him **in the Hebrew dialect** (Aramaic), **"Saul, Saul, why are you persecuting Me? It is hard for you to kick against the goads."** To fight God, as Saul was doing, was to fight a losing battle. It was as stupid as an ox kicking **against the goads** (sharpened rods used to herd cattle).

Stunned, blinded, and terrified, Saul of Tarsus, the erstwhile persecutor of Christians, says he could only stammer out, **"Who art Thou, Lord?"** The reply **"I am Jesus whom you are persecuting,"** rocked him to the core of his being. The One Saul had hated and despised as a blasphemer and a false teacher threatening the sacredness of Judaism was indeed who He had claimed to be—Israel's Messiah. A murmur of surprised disbelief must have gone through the people in the crowd as Paul related Jesus' words. They believed Jesus to be dead and that His zealous disciples had stolen His body to fake His resurrection. How then could Paul claim to have spoken with Him?

Paul further explains that Jesus **appeared** to him **for** a specific **purpose: to appoint** him **a minister and a witness not only to the things which** he had **seen, but also to the things in which** Jesus would **appear to** him (cf. Acts 18:9–10; 22:17–21; 23:11; 2 Cor. 12:1–7; Gal. 1:11–12). Knowing Paul would face fierce opposition as he preached the One he had persecuted, the Lord promised to be faithful in **delivering** him **from the Jewish people and from the Gentiles**. It was they **to whom** the Lord was **sending** (*apostellō*, from which the noun *apostolos* ["apostle"] derives) Paul. This was Paul's commissioning as an apostle. An apostle had to have been an eyewitness of the resurrected Christ (Acts 1:21–22), and Paul was (cf. 1 Cor. 9:1; 15:8).

As an apostle, Paul was called to proclaim the good news of salvation from judgment through the work of Jesus Christ. That life-giving message would first **open** people's **eyes.** Jesus characterized unbelievers as blind, led by blind leaders (Matt. 15:14), of whom 2 Corinthians 4:4 says, "The god of this world has blinded the minds of the unbelieving." The Holy Spirit uses the Word of God to open the eyes of the spiritually blind, Jesus taught, by

> [convicting] the world concerning sin, and righteousness, and judgment; concerning sin, because they do not believe in Me; and concerning righteousness, because I go to the Father, and you no longer behold Me; and concerning judgment, because the ruler of this world has been judged. (John 16:8–11)

Genuine conviction will result in transformation of life, as those convicted **turn from darkness to light and from the dominion of Satan to God.** The Bible teaches that unbelievers live in spiritual darkness. Paul described them as

> being darkened in their understanding, excluded from the life of God, because of the ignorance that is in them, because of the hardness of their heart; and they, having become callous, have given themselves over to sensuality, for the practice of every kind of impurity with greediness. (Eph. 4:18–19)

Scripture frequently uses light as a metaphor for salvation (Matt. 4:16; John 1:4, 5, 7–9; 3:19–21; 8:12; 9:5; 12:36, 46; Acts 13:47; 26:23; 2 Cor. 4:4; 6:14; Eph. 5:8–9, 14; 1 Thess. 5:5; 1 John 1:7; 2:8–10). Because of that, salvation can be described as being called "out of darkness into His marvelous light" (1 Pet. 2:9), and believers can be described as sharers "in the inheritance of the saints in light," who have been "delivered . . . from the domain of darkness, and transferred . . . to the kingdom of His beloved Son" (Col. 1:12–13).

The blessed result of salvation is **forgiveness of sins** (Matt. 1:21; 26:28; Luke 1:77; 24:47; Acts 3:19; 5:31; 10:43; 13:38; 1 Cor. 15:3; Gal. 1:4; Col. 1:14; Heb. 8:12; 9:28; 10:12; 1 Pet. 2:24; 3:18; 1 John 2:1–2; 3:5; 4:10; Rev. 1:5). In Romans 4:7–8, Paul wrote, "Blessed are those whose lawless deeds have been forgiven, and whose sins have been covered. Blessed is the man whose sin the Lord will not take into account." Later in that same epistle, he described the complete forgiveness believers experience by asking rhetorically,

> Who will bring a charge against God's elect? God is the one who justifies; who is the one who condemns? Christ Jesus is He who died, yes, rather who was raised, who is at the right hand of God, who also intercedes for us. (Rom. 8:33–34)

The apostle John said simply, "I am writing to you, little children, because your sins are forgiven you for His name's sake" (1 John 2:12).

A final gospel blessing Paul mentions is that believers receive **an inheritance among those who have been sanctified** (cf. Acts 20:32; Eph. 1:11, 14, 18; Col. 1:12; 3:24; Heb. 9:15). Peter described that inheritance as one that is "imperishable and undefiled and will not fade away, reserved in heaven for you" (1 Pet. 1:4). That inheritance is the riches of eternal heaven.

The clear teaching of Scripture is that this salvation comes to a person only **by faith in** Jesus Christ apart from any human works (John 3:14–17; 6:69; Acts 13:39; 15:9; 16:31; Rom. 3:21–28; 4:5; 5:1; 9:30; 10:9–11; Gal. 2:16; 3:11, 24; Phil. 3:9). Writing to the Ephesians, Paul stated that truth clearly and succinctly when he wrote, "For by grace you have been saved through faith; and that not of yourselves, it is the gift of God; not as a result of works, that no one should boast" (Eph. 2:8–9).

Paul's dramatic testimony provides powerful evidence for Christ's resurrection, especially because he had formerly been such a hostile and violent opponent of the Christian faith. Paul was not seeking to discover whether or not Jesus was the Messiah; he had already decided He was not. Nor had he been persuaded by talking with Christians. Paul did not talk to Christians—he arrested them and sought their imprisonment and execution. Only the direct, miraculous, supernatural intervention of the risen, living Jesus Himself turned Paul from persecutor of Christians to apostle of Jesus Christ.

THE CULMINATION OF PAUL'S TESTIMONY

Consequently, King Agrippa, I did not prove disobedient to the heavenly vision, but kept declaring both to those of Damascus first, and also at Jerusalem and then throughout all the region of Judea, and even to the Gentiles, that they should repent and turn to God, performing deeds appropriate to repentance. For this reason some Jews seized me in the temple and tried to put me to death. And so, having obtained help from God, I stand to this day testifying both to small and great, stating nothing but what the Prophets and Moses said was going to take place; that the Christ was to suffer, and that by reason of His resurrection from the dead He should be the first to proclaim light both to the Jewish people and to the Gentiles." (26:19–23)

The call to the ministry, like the call to salvation, is a sovereign act of God that demands and incorporates human response. **Consequently,** Paul **did not prove disobedient to the heavenly vision** he had received of the Lord Jesus Christ.

Obedience is the sine qua non of the Christian life. It accompanies true salvation (Rom. 6:16; 1 Pet. 1:14), acknowledges God's authority (Acts 5:29), is an expression of trust in God (Heb. 11:8), and is the proof of believers' love for Him (John 14:15, 21).

Paul expressed his obedience by **declaring both to those of Damascus first, and also at Jerusalem and then throughout all the region of Judea, and even to the Gentiles, that they should repent and turn to God, performing deeds appropriate to repentance.** That sentence summarizes Paul's ministry, which began in **Damascus** (Acts 9:20–22), spread to **Jerusalem** (9:26–29), from which it influenced **Judea,** then finally extended **even to the Gentiles.** Everywhere he preached, his message was the same: people **should repent and turn to God, performing deeds appropriate to repentance.** *Metanoia* (**repentance**) involves a change of mind that results in a change of behavior. Paul's use of *epistrephō* (**turn**), which frequently describes sinners turning to God (Luke 1:16–17; Acts 9:35; 11:21; 14:15; 15:19; 2 Cor. 3:16; 1 Thess. 1:9; 1 Pet. 2:25), reinforces that meaning. Those who truly **repent and turn to God** will perform **deeds appropriate to repentance** (Matt. 3:8; 7:16, 20; James 2:18).

It was **for this reason,** because of Paul's faithful preaching of the gospel, that **some Jews seized** him **in the temple and tried to put** him **to death** (21:27ff.). That set all the events in motion that had led to this very moment of encounter with Agrippa. They were especially irate that he proclaimed the spiritual equality of Jews and Gentiles (cf. 22:21–23). But Paul **obtained help from God,** who had recently delivered him from two plots against his life (23:12ff.; 25:2–5) and who had helped him throughout his ministry (2 Cor. 1:8–10; 2 Tim. 3:11; 4:17–18). Because of God's help, Paul could declare to Agrippa, **"I stand to this day testifying both to small and great, stating nothing but what the Prophets and Moses said was going to take place."** By placing himself in the line of Moses and the other Old Testament writers, Paul again stressed that Christianity is not heretical but the fulfillment of Scripture. The Old Testament predicted **"that the Christ was to suffer** (Ps. 22; Isa. 53) **and that by reason of His resurrection from the dead** (Ps. 16:10; cf. Acts 13:30–37), **He should be the first** (*prōtos*; first in preeminence, not chronology) **to proclaim light both to the Jewish people and to the Gentiles"** (cf. Isa. 42:6; 49:6).

Paul's testimony may be summarized as follows. He was a devout, zealous Jew—even to the extreme of persecuting Christians, whom he believed perverted Judaism. Jesus Christ, whose appearance to Paul proves His resurrection, sovereignly changed his life and called him both to salvation and to the ministry. Paul thereafter preached the gospel of grace to the Gentiles, thus placing them on a spiritual par with the Jews. Because of that, some jealous Jews tried to kill him, and that is why he stood before Agrippa that day.

THE CONSEQUENCES OF PAUL'S TESTIMONY

And while Paul was saying this in his defense, Festus said in a loud voice, "Paul, you are out of your mind! Your great learning is driving you mad." But Paul said, "I am not out of my mind, most excellent Festus, but I utter words of sober truth. For the king knows about these matters, and I speak to him also with confidence, since I am persuaded that none of these things escape his notice; for this has not been done in a corner. King Agrippa, do you believe the Prophets? I know that you do." And Agrippa replied to Paul, "In a short time you will persuade me to become a Christian." And Paul said, "I would to God, that whether in a short or long time, not only you, but also all who hear me this day, might become such as I am, except for these chains." And the king arose and the governor and Bernice, and those who were sitting with them, and when they had drawn aside, they began talking to one another, saying, "This man is not doing any-

thing worthy of death or imprisonment." And Agrippa said to Festus, "This man might have been set free if he had not appealed to Caesar." (26:24–32)

Festus had listened with growing bewilderment as **Paul** continued speaking in **his** own **defense.** Paul was obviously a learned and brilliant man, so how could he believe what he was saying was really true? Did he really think that Jesus of Nazareth, a man executed under one of Festus's predecessors as governor, Pilate, was alive and had spoken to him? Finally, Paul's explicit declaration of Christ's resurrection was too much for Festus's rational sensibilities. Interrupting Paul's speech, he blurted out **in a loud voice, "Paul, you are out of your mind! Your great learning is driving you mad."** Every intelligent Roman knew that dead men do not come back to life and talk to people; therefore, Paul's mental musings must have caused him to lose touch with reality.

It is not surprising that Paul was accused of being insane; so was Jesus (Mark 3:21; John 8:48, 52; 10:20). The reason for the accusations against both is found in 1 Corinthians 1:18: "For the word of the cross is to those who are perishing foolishness, but to us who are being saved it is the power of God." **But Paul** was definitely **not out of** his **mind.** On the contrary, he spoke **words of sober truth,** from a sound mind, with total control of his senses.

Paul took advantage of Festus's interruption to focus on Agrippa, first speaking of him in the third person, then addressing him directly. Continuing to address Festus, Paul said, **"the king (Agrippa) knows about these matters, and I speak to him also with confidence, since I am persuaded that none of these things escape his notice; for this has not been done in a corner."** Paul called Agrippa as a witness to his sanity, since the Jews believed in resurrection, and the matters of which the apostle spoke (the death of Jesus, and the claim of the Christians that He rose from the dead) were common knowledge in Palestine. By remaining silent, Agrippa confirmed the truth of what Paul said.

Then Paul boldly confronted Agrippa directly. **"King Agrippa, do you believe the Prophets? I know that you do."** The implication was that if he did, he would have to concede that Jesus was the Messiah. Agrippa was stuck in a quandary. Admitting his belief in the prophets was tantamount to acknowledging Jesus as Messiah. That would make him look foolish before his Roman friends and outrage his Jewish subjects. Yet a Jewish king could hardly disavow the revered prophets of his people. Consequently, he avoided the question, mockingly replying instead **to Paul, "In a short time you will persuade me to become a Christian."** The phrase is better translated as a question: "Do you think you can persuade me to become a Christian in such a short time?"

Paul's response was gracious and dignified: **"I would to God, that whether in a short or long time, not only you, but also all who hear me this day, might become such as I am, except for these chains."** No matter how long it took, it was Paul's heartfelt desire that all who heard him would come to know the Lord Jesus Christ. The scene is again one of startling incongruity. A lowly prisoner in chains tells the gathered political and military leaders and other important figures that he wishes they could be like him. Their fading, fleeting treasure was here on earth; Paul had "an unfailing treasure in heaven, where no thief comes near, nor moth destroys" (Luke 12:33).

With these words by Paul, the inquiry ended. Agrippa **the king arose,** along with **the governor and** the wicked **Bernice, and those** advisers **who were sitting with them**. After **they had drawn aside, they began talking to one another** about Paul's case. Whatever their view of Paul's sanity, they all agreed that he was **not doing anything worthy of death or imprisonment,** yet they lacked the courage to release him. Agrippa summed up the view of all when he **said to Festus, "This man might have been set free if he had not appealed to Caesar."**

The question arises as to why Paul could not be released, since both Festus and Agrippa had found him innocent of wrongdoing. Noted expert on Roman law A. N. Sherwin-White explains:

> When Agrippa remarked: "this man could have been released if he had not appealed to Caesar," this does not mean that in strict law the governor could not pronounce an acquittal after the act of appeal. It is not a question of law, but of the relations between the emperor and his subordinates, and of that element of non-constitutional power which the Romans called *auctoritas*, "prestige," on which the supremacy of the Princeps so largely depended. No sensible man with hopes of promotion would dream of short-circuiting the appeal to Caesar unless he had specific authority to do so. (*Roman Society and Roman Law in the New Testament* [Oxford: Oxford University Press, 1963], 65)

Once again, Paul had been found innocent of any wrongdoing. He had boldly proclaimed the gospel to some of the most important people in Palestine. Now, after two years of waiting, it was time for the Lord's promise to Paul to be fulfilled: "Take courage; for as you have solemnly witnessed to My cause at Jerusalem, so you must witness at Rome also" (Acts 23:11).

Paul's Journey to Rome, Part 1 The Storm and Shipwreck (Acts 27:1–44)

26

And when it was decided that we should sail for Italy, they proceeded to deliver Paul and some other prisoners to a centurion of the Augustan cohort named Julius. And embarking in an Adramyttian ship, which was about to sail to the regions along the coast of Asia, we put out to sea, accompanied by Aristarchus, a Macedonian of Thessalonica. And the next day we put in at Sidon; and Julius treated Paul with consideration and allowed him to go to his friends and receive care. And from there we put out to sea and sailed under the shelter of Cyprus because the winds were contrary. And when we had sailed through the sea along the coast of Cilicia and Pamphylia, we landed at Myra in Lycia. And there the centurion found an Alexandrian ship sailing for Italy, and he put us aboard it. And when we had sailed slowly for a good many days, and with difficulty had arrived off Cnidus, since the wind did not permit us to go farther, we sailed under the shelter of Crete, off Salmone; and with difficulty sailing past it we came to a certain place called Fair Havens, near which was the city of Lasea. And when considerable time had passed and the voyage was now dangerous, since even the fast was already over, Paul began to admonish them, and said to them, "Men, I perceive that the voyage will certainly be attended with damage and great loss, not only of the cargo and the ship, but also of our lives." But the centurion was more persuaded by the pilot and the captain of the ship, than by what was being said by Paul. And because the harbor was not suitable for wintering, the majority reached a decision to put out to sea from there, if somehow they could reach Phoenix, a harbor of Crete, facing southwest and northwest, and spend the winter there. And when a moderate south wind came up, supposing that they had gained their purpose, they weighed anchor and began sailing along Crete, close inshore. But before very long there rushed down from the land a violent wind, called Euraquilo; and when the ship was caught in it, and could not face the wind, we gave way to it, and let ourselves be driven along. And running under the shelter of a small island called Clauda, we were scarcely able to get the ship's boat under control. And after they had hoisted it up, they used supporting cables in undergirding the ship; and fearing that they might run aground on the shallows of Syrtis, they let down the sea anchor, and so let themselves be driven along. The next day as we were being violently storm-tossed, they began to jettison the cargo; and on the third day they threw the ship's tackle overboard with their own hands. And since neither sun nor stars appeared for many days, and no small storm was assailing us, from then on all hope of our being saved was gradually abandoned. And when they had gone a long time without food, then Paul stood up in their midst and said, "Men, you ought to have followed my advice and not to have set sail from Crete, and incurred this damage and loss. And yet now I urge you to keep up your courage, for there shall be no loss of life among you, but only of the ship. For this very night an angel of the God to whom I belong and whom I serve stood before me, saying, 'Do not be afraid, Paul; you must stand before Caesar; and behold, God has granted you all those who are sailing with you.' Therefore, keep up your courage, men, for I believe God, that it will turn out exactly as I have been told. But we must run aground on a certain island." But when the fourteenth night had come, as we were being driven about in the Adriatic Sea, about midnight the sailors began to surmise that they were approaching some land. And they took soundings, and found it to be twenty fathoms; and a little farther on they took another sounding and found it to be fifteen fathoms. And fearing that we might run aground somewhere on the rocks, they cast four anchors from the stern and wished for daybreak. And as the sailors were trying to escape from the ship, and had let down the ship's boat into the sea, on the pretense of intending to lay out anchors from the bow, Paul said to the centurion and to the soldiers, "Unless these men remain in the ship, you yourselves cannot be saved." Then the soldiers cut away the ropes of the ship's boat, and let it fall away. And until the day was about to dawn, Paul was encouraging them all to take some food, saying, "Today is the fourteenth day that you have been constantly watching and going without eating, having taken nothing. Therefore I encourage you to take some food, for this is for your preservation; for not a hair from the head of any of you shall perish." And having said this, he took bread and gave thanks to God in the presence of all; and he broke it and began to eat. And all of them were encouraged, and they themselves also took food. And all of us in the ship were two hundred and seventy-six persons. And when they had eaten enough, they began to lighten the ship by throwing out the wheat into the sea. And when day came, they could not recognize the land; but they did observe a certain bay with a beach, and they resolved to drive the ship onto it if they could. And casting off the anchors, they left them in the sea while at the same time they were loosening the ropes of the rudders, and hoisting the foresail to the wind, they were heading for the beach. But striking a reef where two seas met, they ran the vessel aground; and the prow stuck fast and remained immovable, but the stern began to be broken up by the force of the waves. And the soldiers' plan was to kill the prisoners, that none of them should swim away and escape; but the centurion, wanting to bring Paul safely through, kept them from their intention, and commanded that those who could swim should jump overboard first and get to land, and the rest should follow, some on planks, and others on various things from the ship. And thus it happened that they all were brought safely to land. (27:1–44)

Our society places a premium on leadership. Government, the military, business, education, even sports teams, are all desperately seeking qualified leaders. Books, seminars, tape albums, and training courses on leadership abound. Some people even make their living traveling around lecturing corporate executives on the fine points of leadership.

The world's traditional model of a leader has been labeled the Strong Natural Leader. The profile of such leaders might include the following characteristics. They are visionary. Their goals and plans reach far into the future. They are action-oriented and are always on the move; they are never content with the status quo. They are marked by courage (or the willingness to take risks because they believe in their plans). Such leaders have the nerve to make the tough decisions. They are usually energetic, capable of working long hours. They tend to be objective-oriented, not people-oriented. Their focus is usually more on the task than the persons involved in the task. Like overprotective parents, they have to control those under them. They are egocentric. Their whole world revolves around themselves, their plans, and their objectives. They possess resolute self-confidence. They are intolerant of incompetence in others. People who do not meet their expectations or fail to perform at a high level are not retained. Finally, they are seen by others (and themselves) as indispensable. Without them, the enterprise is doomed to failure.

It was such natural leaders, dominating dictators who use charismatic control, that our Lord described in Mark 10:42: "You know that those who are recognized as rulers of the Gentiles lord it over them; and their great men exercise authority over them." As common as such leadership is in the world, it is not an acceptable role model for leadership in Christ's kingdom:

> But it is not so among you, but whoever wishes to become great among you shall be your servant; and whoever wishes to be first among you shall be slave of all. For even the Son of Man did not come to be served, but to serve, and to give His life a ransom for many." (Mark 10:43–45)

Several factors combine to make leadership difficult. The first is fear of failure. Leaders' failures are out in the open for all to see; there is no place for them to hide. Such fear, often resulting from leaders' underestimating themselves, can paralyze them into inaction.

Relatedly, sometimes leaders struggle with mistrusting their own judgment. They fear making a decision, lest it turn out to be the wrong one. So to avoid saying the wrong thing, they say nothing.

Some insecure leaders find it difficult to trust others enough to delegate tasks. Their motto is "If you want a job done right, do it yourself." And when they do give a task to someone else, their perfectionism drives them to be constantly peering over that person's shoulder.

Leaders who take firm, authoritative stands run the risk of alienating others. For leaders in the church, commitment to the Word must never be compromised. Yet that commitment must be expressed in humility and love.

A final tension in leadership is defensiveness. Some leaders feel the need for explaining and justifying their actions, which can lead to weak, indecisive expressions.

It is times of challenge and crisis that reveal the qualities of true leaders. Winston Churchill had been in and out of the British government for many years before becoming prime minister. He assumed that position at one of the lowest points of the Second World War (he took office on May 10, 1940—the day the Germans invaded France and the Low Countries). His indomitable courage as he led his nation through the crisis days that lay ahead has caused many to regard him as the greatest leader of the twentieth century.

Acts 27 opens with Paul as a prisoner, not in charge of anyone or anything. All that was altered, however, when a severe crisis hit the party he was traveling with. By the end of the chapter, Paul, the prisoner, had become the acknowledged leader over all. His ability to deal with a crisis elevated him to that role.

Among other emphases manifest through this unique chapter, it is helpful to note the issue of the greatness of Paul's leadership. The story of his emerging leadership during a storm-filled journey across the Mediterranean Sea, and the resulting shipwreck, unfolds in four stages: the start, the stay, the storm, and the shipwreck.

THE START

And when it was decided that we should sail for Italy, they proceeded to deliver Paul and some other prisoners to a centurion of the Augustan cohort named Julius. And embarking in an Adramyttian ship, which was about to sail to the regions along the coast of Asia, we put out to sea, accompanied by Aristarchus, a Macedonian of Thessalonica. And the next day we put in at Sidon; and Julius treated Paul with consideration and allowed him to go to his friends and receive care. And from there we put out to sea and sailed under the shelter of Cyprus because the winds were contrary. And when we had sailed through the sea along the coast of Cilicia and Pamphylia, we landed at Myra in Lycia. And there the centurion found an Alexandrian ship sailing for Italy, and he put us aboard it. And when we had sailed slowly for a good many days, and with difficulty had arrived off Cnidus, since the wind did not permit us to go farther, we sailed under the shelter of Crete, off Salmone; and with difficulty sailing past it we came to a certain place called Fair Havens, near which was the city of Lasea. (27:1–8)

The use of the first person plural pronoun **we** indicates the return of Paul's physician and beloved friend, Luke. Absent from the narrative since 21:18, he had probably been living in Caesarea, or nearby, during the two years of Paul's imprisonment there. Now he was on hand to **sail** with Paul **for Italy.** They were **accompanied by** another of Paul's beloved fellow workers, **Aristarchus, a Macedonian of Thessalonica.** Aristarchus first appeared in Acts when he was seized by the angry rioters at Ephesus (19:29). He accompanied the apostle on his journey to Jerusalem with the offering from the Gentile churches (20:4). He later ministered to Paul during the apostle's imprisonment at Rome (Col. 4:10). According to tradition, Aristarchus, like Paul, suffered martyrdom under Nero. That he and Luke were willing to accompany Paul on a hazardous, uncomfortable voyage shows their love for the apostle and his ministry. In addition, some have speculated that they may have identified themselves as Paul's slaves so that they could accompany him (cf. Sir William M. Ramsay, *St. Paul the Traveller and the Roman Citizen* [reprint; Grand Rapids: Baker, 1975], 316).

The journey began when **Paul and some other prisoners** bound for Rome from Caesarea were placed in the custody of **a centurion of the Augustan cohort named Julius.** There is evidence that such an Augustan cohort was stationed in Palestine during the reign of Agrippa II. It is possible that Julius represented the emperor by undertaking special duties, such as escorting important prisoners. Like other centurions mentioned in the New Testament (cf. Matt. 8:5ff., 27:54; Acts 10:1ff.), he was a man of integrity.

Julius put his party of soldiers, prisoners, and servants on board an **Adramyttian ship, which was about to sail to the regions along the coast of Asia.** Adramyttium, its home port, was located on the northwest coast of Asia Minor, near Troas. From Asia Minor they would have little trouble finding passage to Italy. They **put out to sea,** making port **the next day** at **Sidon,** seventy miles to the north.

In Sidon, **Julius treated Paul with consideration and,** surprisingly, **allowed him to go to his friends and receive care.** Paul was a very important prisoner to allow to run around loose. He was a Roman citizen, on his way to Rome to have his appeal heard by the emperor. More significant, he was hated by the Jewish leaders at Jerusalem. His presence could have sparked a riot among Sidon's Jewish population, exacerbating the volatile relations between the Jews and Rome. Further, Paul's life may have been at risk, and Julius would have paid with his own life if he lost such an important prisoner. Yet, Julius had grown to trust Paul and believed the apostle would not do anything to bring harm to him. How fast Paul developed this trust is a rich lesson in leadership. People will trust one whom they believe has others' best interests at heart, not merely their own. Paul cared about people like Julius, and Julius knew it.

The church at Sidon, whose members Luke describes as Paul's **friends** (cf. 3 John 14), was likely founded by Christians fleeing Jerusalem after Stephen's martyrdom (Acts 8:1–4). Paul undoubtedly spent time teaching the Sidonian believers and enjoying fellowship with them (which had been impossible during his imprisonment at Caesarea).

Through their kindness and love, Paul was able to **receive care,** probably in the form of provisions for his journey.

Leaving Sidon, Paul and his traveling companions **put out to sea and sailed under the shelter of Cyprus because the winds were contrary.** They passed between Cyprus and the mainland, keeping to the lee side of the island for shelter from the prevailing westerly winds. Smaller coastal vessels (like theirs) avoided crossing long stretches of open ocean, preferring to stay as close to shore as possible.

The ship continued its voyage across the northeastern Mediterranean, sailing **along the coast of Cilicia and Pamphylia.** Those regions were very familiar to Paul; he was originally from Cilicia (Acts 22:3) and had traveled extensively in those areas on his missionary journeys. Helped by local offshore winds and a west-flowing current, the ship worked its way west along the southern shore of Asia Minor, making port **at Myra in Lycia** and disembarking.

Myra was a chief port for the Imperial grain fleet, whose ships made the circuit between Egypt and Rome. **There the centurion,** needing to find transportation for the rest of the way, **found an Alexandrian** grain **ship sailing for Italy, and he put** his party **aboard it.** Leaving **Myra,** the ship **sailed slowly for a good many days** against the strong northwest wind **and with difficulty arrived off Cnidus.** Located on a peninsula at the southwest tip of Asia Minor, **Cnidus** was another harbor frequented by Egyptian merchant ships. When the travelers **arrived off Cnidus,** they left the shelter of the mainland and the strong, contrary **wind did not permit** them **to go farther** west. The ship was forced to turn south toward the island of Crete.

Reaching **the shelter of Crete off Salmone** (a promontory on Crete's northeast shore), the ship again **with difficulty** sailed along the coast. Rounding the southeast corner of the island, it finally arrived at **a certain place called Fair Havens, near which was the city of Lasea.** There, weary from fighting the weather, the travelers entered the bay. The first foreboding sign of what was to come had manifested itself.

THE STAY

And when considerable time had passed and the voyage was now dangerous, since even the fast was already over, Paul began to admonish them, and said to them, "Men, I perceive that the voyage will certainly be attended with damage and great loss, not only of the cargo and the ship, but also of our lives." But the centurion was more persuaded by the pilot and the captain of the ship, than by what was being said by Paul. And because the harbor was not suitable for wintering, the majority reached a deci-

**sion to put out to sea from there, if somehow they could reach
Phoenix, a harbor of Crete, facing southwest and northwest, and
spend the winter there.** (27:9–12)

The ship was delayed for a **considerable time** in Fair Havens,
apparently waiting for a change in the winds. To continue **the voyage
was now dangerous,** since it was late in the sailing season. Luke notes
that **even the fast** (the Day of Atonement) **was already over.** For
ancient sailing vessels, travel was problematic and dangerous from mid-
September to mid-November. All sailing in the open sea ceased from
mid-November until at least February. Inasmuch as the Day of
Atonement fell in late September or early October, Paul's ship was
already well into the danger period.

Apparently the sailors and Julius had a discussion to plan their
course of action. Paul, an experienced traveler, was allowed to speak. At
the meeting, **Paul began to admonish them, and said to them,
"Men, I perceive that the voyage will certainly be attended with
damage and great loss, not only of the cargo and the ship, but
also of our lives."** The apostle wisely counseled them not to gamble;
he had already experienced three shipwrecks (2 Cor. 11:25) and was not
anxious for a fourth. Since it was late in the season, and they had already
had problems with the winds, Paul warned that the ship should winter
right there in Fair Havens. Here again is another feature of good leadership—wisdom and care in taking risks (in this case with the travelers'
lives and the ship's valuable cargo).

Regrettably (but understandably), **the centurion was more
persuaded by the pilot and the captain of the ship, than by what
was being said by Paul.** (Because the ship belonged to the imperial
grain fleet, the centurion—not the pilot or the captain—was the ranking
officer on board.) Julius obviously had grown to respect Paul and value
his experience as a traveler. The advice of the professional seamen, however, carried more weight with the centurion. Therefore, **because the
harbor** at Fair Havens **was not suitable for wintering, the majority**
involved in the discussion **reached a decision to put out to sea from
there.** Their plan was to **reach Phoenix, a harbor of Crete, facing
southwest and northwest, and spend the winter there.** Since the
harbor at Fair Havens was exposed to winds from half the compass
points (though small islands did provide some shelter), it was a less
desirable place to spend the winter. Because the harbor at **Phoenix**
(about forty miles away) faced **southwest and northwest,** it provided
much better shelter from the winter storms.

The decision was made for comfort—one the sailors and Julius
would soon regret. They would realize that Paul's counsel had been
wise—thus strengthening his place in their minds as a leader.

The Storm

And when a moderate south wind came up, supposing that they had gained their purpose, they weighed anchor and began sailing along Crete, close inshore. But before very long there rushed down from the land a violent wind, called Euraquilo; and when the ship was caught in it, and could not face the wind, we gave way to it, and let ourselves be driven along. And running under the shelter of a small island called Clauda, we were scarcely able to get the ship's boat under control. And after they had hoisted it up, they used supporting cables in undergirding the ship; and fearing that they might run aground on the shallows of Syrtis, they let down the sea anchor, and so let themselves be driven along. The next day as we were being violently storm-tossed, they began to jettison the cargo; and on the third day they threw the ship's tackle overboard with their own hands. And since neither sun nor stars appeared for many days, and no small storm was assailing us, from then on all hope of our being saved was gradually abandoned. And when they had gone a long time without food, then Paul stood up in their midst and said, "Men, you ought to have followed my advice and not to have set sail from Crete, and incurred this damage and loss. And yet now I urge you to keep up your courage, for there shall be no loss of life among you, but only of the ship. For this very night an angel of the God to whom I belong and whom I serve stood before me, saying, 'Do not be afraid, Paul; you must stand before Caesar; and behold, God has granted you all those who are sailing with you.' Therefore, keep up your courage, men, for I believe God, that it will turn out exactly as I have been told. But we must run aground on a certain island." (27:13–26)

Not long afterward, **when a moderate south wind came up,** the sailors decided they had received the conditions they were looking for. **They weighed anchor,** left Fair Havens, **and began sailing along** the south shore of **Crete, close inshore.** With any luck, they hoped to reach Phoenix in a few hours.

But before very long, the disaster Paul had predicted struck. Roaring **down from the** mountains of Crete came the dreaded, **violent,** east-northeast **wind, called Euraquilo** (a hybrid word from the Greek word *euros*; "east wind," and the Latin word *aquilo*; "north wind"). This powerful, dangerous windstorm was dreaded by all who sailed the Mediterranean. When **the ship was caught in it, and could not face into the wind,** the sailors had no choice but to give **way to it, and let**

themselves **be driven along.** Out of control, the ship was just being pushed by the wind.

The travelers gained a brief respite from the fierce storm **under the shelter of a small island called Clauda,** about twenty-three miles southwest of Crete. Making good use of the temporary shelter Clauda provided, the sailors took what steps they could to rig the ship to bear the storm. First, with difficulty they managed to get **the ship's boat under control.** This lifeboat and tender, usually towed behind, was taken on board in bad weather. By now it undoubtedly was filled with water, which accounts for the difficulty in hauling it aboard. Luke's use of the plural pronoun **we** may indicate that even the passengers helped secure the boat. Social distinctions began to disappear in the fight for survival.

After they had hoisted the dingy on board, the crew members **used supporting cables in undergirding the ship.** This procedure, known as frapping, involved wrapping cables around the ship's hull and then winching them tight. Thus supported, the ship would be better able to withstand the severe pounding of wind and sea.

What the third precaution taken by the sailors was is not clear. The NASB reads, **fearing that they might run aground on the shallows of Syrtis, they let down the sea anchor, and so let themselves be driven along.** The **Syrtis** was the dreaded graveyard of ships off the North African coast. Although the Syrtis was still far away, the sailors did not know how far, nor how far the storm might blow the ship. Lowering **the sea anchor** would act as a drag and help prevent the ship from drifting that far south. Alternatively, the phrase translated **let down the sea anchor** may be translated "lowered the gear." In that case, the reference would be to lowering the mainsail, which otherwise would be torn to shreds by the violent wind. However the phrase is translated, the sailors obviously did both—it would have been self-defeating to put out an anchor with the mainsail still rigged.

During the following days, the crew took further steps to help the ship ride out the storm. On **the next day,** with the ship still **being violently storm-tossed, they began to jettison the cargo** (though not all of it—cf. v. 38)**; and on the third day they threw the ship's tackle overboard with their own hands.** The **ship's tackle** refers to miscellaneous equipment not crucial to sailing the ship. That probably included the massive spar to which the mainsail had been attached. Luke notes that **they threw** it overboard **with their own hands** (some Greek manuscripts read "we threw," indicating again that the passengers helped); the crew would likely have had no equipment on board able to lift the heavy spar.

All the sailors' efforts were to no avail, however. When **neither sun nor stars appeared for many days** (thus rendering navigation impossible), it became apparent that **no small storm was assailing them. From then on all hope of being saved was gradually abandoned.** Only those who have been in a violent storm at sea can fully appreciate the terror the passengers and crew must have felt. The towering, white-capped seas; the roaring of the wind; the violent rocking of the ship as first the bow, then the stern rose high in the air, only to plunge quickly down again; the constant motion, inducing seasickness and making it difficult to stand, let alone walk; the wind-driven salt spray stinging and blinding those exposed on deck; and, worst of all, the looming reality of an awful death by drowning—all those factors combined to unnerve even the most experienced sailor.

It was at this dark moment that Paul's leadership skills shone most brightly. **And when they had gone a long time without food** (due to seasickness, the difficulty of preparing food in the storm, and perhaps the spoilage of some of their provisions), **then Paul stood up in their midst.** They had not listened to him when they were safely anchored at Fair Havens. But these were no professional sailors and amateurs now, just a group of desperate men fighting for their lives. Firmly establishing his credibility, Paul reminded them, **"Men, you ought to have followed my advice and not to have set sail from Crete, and incurred this damage and loss."** Had they heeded his sound advice, they would not have been in this difficulty. The apostle's purpose, however, was not only to chide them but to encourage them. "Therefore," he urged them, **"keep up your courage, for there shall be no loss of life among you, but only of the ship."** That may have seemed wishful thinking and small comfort to passengers and crew, who certainly did not see any hope. But Paul had received divine revelation!

To confirm his words (and encourage the others on board), Paul confidently continued, **"For this very night an angel of the God to whom I belong and whom I serve stood before me, saying, 'Do not be afraid, Paul; you must stand before Caesar; and behold, God has granted you all those who are sailing with you.'"** The others were to benefit from the Lord's protection of Paul (cf. Gen. 39:5, 23; 1 Cor. 7:14). Unbelievers have no idea how much they owe, in the mercy of God, to the presence of righteous men among them. **"Therefore,"** he urged them, **"keep up your courage, men, for I believe God, that it will turn out exactly as I have been told."** Then, perhaps for the benefit of any skeptics who might have wondered how they were going to escape drowning if the ship were lost, the apostle added, **"But we must run aground on a certain island."**

The stage was set for the dramatic conclusion to this ill-fated voyage and the fulfillment of God's promises.

THE SHIPWRECK

But when the fourteenth night had come, as we were being driven about in the Adriatic Sea, about midnight the sailors began to surmise that they were approaching some land. And they took soundings, and found it to be twenty fathoms; and a little farther on they took another sounding and found it to be fifteen fathoms. And fearing that we might run aground somewhere on the rocks, they cast four anchors from the stern and wished for daybreak. And as the sailors were trying to escape from the ship, and had let down the ship's boat into the sea, on the pretense of intending to lay out anchors from the bow, Paul said to the centurion and to the soldiers, "Unless these men remain in the ship, you yourselves cannot be saved." Then the soldiers cut away the ropes of the ship's boat, and let it fall away. And until the day was about to dawn, Paul was encouraging them all to take some food, saying, "Today is the fourteenth day that you have been constantly watching and going without eating, having taken nothing. Therefore I encourage you to take some food, for this is for your preservation; for not a hair from the head of any of you shall perish." And having said this, he took bread and gave thanks to God in the presence of all; and he broke it and began to eat. And all of them were encouraged, and they themselves also took food. And all of us in the ship were two hundred and seventy-six persons. And when they had eaten enough, they began to lighten the ship by throwing out the wheat into the sea. And when day came, they could not recognize the land; but they did observe a certain bay with a beach, and they resolved to drive the ship onto it if they could. And casting off the anchors, they left them in the sea while at the same time they were loosening the ropes of the rudders, and hoisting the foresail to the wind, they were heading for the beach. But striking a reef where two seas met, they ran the vessel aground; and the prow stuck fast and remained immovable, but the stern began to be broken up by the force of the waves. And the soldiers' plan was to kill the prisoners, that none of them should swim away and escape; but the centurion, wanting to bring Paul safely through, kept them from their intention, and commanded that those who could swim should jump overboard first and get to land, and the rest should follow, some on planks, and others on various things from the ship. And thus it happened that they all were brought safely to land. (27:27–44)

By now Paul had earned the leadership over all on the vessel. He alone remained calm, wise, and in control, because he had absolute trust in God's promise (through the angel) to save all those on the ship.

The fourteenth night since their departure from Fair Havens found Paul and his fellow travelers still **being driven about in the Adriatic Sea.** The **Adriatic Sea** mentioned here is not to be confused with the modern Adriatic Sea, located between Italy and Croatia. In Paul's day, that body of water was known as the Gulf of Adria. The Sea of Adria (**Adriatic Sea**) referred to the central Mediterranean. With storm clouds obscuring the sun by day and the stars by night, the sailors could not navigate. Thus, they could only guess that they were somewhere in the central Mediterranean.

Finally, after two weeks of effort and terror, their ordeal showed signs of ending. **About midnight** on that fourteenth night, **the sailors began to surmise that they were approaching some land,** presumably because they heard the crashing of surf on a shore. Though they did not recognize it in the dark, they were approaching the island of Malta, south of Sicily. In fact, they were only about three miles from the entrance of what is known today (for obvious reasons) as St. Paul's Bay. Remarkably, in the providence of God, the storm had driven them across the Mediterranean to a small dot of land in the middle of the sea.

The nineteenth-century British yachtsman James Smith made a detailed study of the voyage recorded in this chapter. His research, published in his classic book *The Voyage and Shipwreck of St. Paul*, confirms the remarkable accuracy of Luke's account. F. F. Bruce relates Smith's findings:

> Smith relates how he made careful enquiries of experienced Mediterranean navigators in order to ascertain the mean rate of drift of a ship of this kind laid-to in such a gale. The conclusion which he reached was a mean drift of about thirty-six miles in twenty-four hours. The soundings recorded in v. 28 indicate that the ship was passing Koura, a point on the east coast of Malta, on her way into St. Paul's Bay. "But the distance from Clauda to the point of Koura . . . is 476.6 miles, which, at the rate as deduced from the information . . . , would take exactly thirteen days, one hour, and twenty-one minutes." And not only so: "The coincidence of the actual bearing of St. Paul's Bay from Clauda, and the direction in which a ship must have driven in order to avoid the Syrtis, is if possible still more striking than that of the time actually consumed, and the calculated time." Then, after carefully reckoning the direction of the ship's course from the direction of the wind, from the angle of the ship's head with the wind, and from the lee-way, he goes on: "Hence according to these calculations, a ship starting late in the evening from Clauda would, by midnight on the 14th [day], be less than three miles from the entrance of St. Paul's Bay. I admit that a

coincidence so very close as this, is to a certain extent accidental, but it is an accident which could not have happened had there been any inaccuracy on the part of the author of the narrative with regard to the numerous incidents upon which the calculations are founded, or had the ship been wrecked anywhere but at Malta, for there is no other place agreeing, either in name or description, within the limits to which we are tied down by calculations founded upon the narrative." (*The Book of the Acts*, The New International Commentary on the New Testament [Grand Rapids: Eerdmans, 1971], 514–15)

Scripture is accurate, and God is true to His word.

To confirm their suspicions, the sailors **took soundings** (using a weight attached to a length of rope) **and found** the water's depth **to be twenty fathoms** (120 feet); **and a little farther on they took another sounding and found it to be fifteen fathoms** (ninety feet). The decreasing depth of the water showed that they were, in fact, approaching land.

Since hitting a strange shore in the dark in a violent storm was not what the sailors had in mind, **they cast four anchors from the stern** (to hold the ship in place and keep the bow pointed toward the shore) **and wished for daybreak.** It soon became evident, however, that **the sailors** were not content with mere wishing. Panicking and shirking their responsibilities, they foolishly abandoned the relative safety of the larger vessel and **were trying to escape from the ship.** They actually **let down the ship's boat into the** stormy **sea,** while **on the pretense of intending to lay out anchors from the bow**, intending to try to escape to shore.

Ever alert, **Paul** noticed what they were doing. He again exercised leadership by warning **the centurion and the soldiers, "Unless these men remain in the ship, you yourselves cannot be saved."** God's promise that all would be saved (v. 24) assumed they would stay together; the sailors' treachery threatened that unity. Nor did God's promise negate human responsibility. God uses natural means, and He was there using Paul, the centurion and his soldiers, as well as those wicked sailors. The sailors' skills would be sorely needed the next day (cf. vv. 39–41), when escape from the ship actually took place. Not about to repeat their earlier mistake of failing to listen to Paul (which by now they deeply regretted), **the soldiers cut away the ropes of the ship's boat, and let it fall away.** That probably was not what the apostle intended; the dingy could have been useful the next day in bringing some ashore. Getting rid of the dingy did, however, prevent any further escape attempts.

Finally, the long night of anxious waiting ended. As **day was about to dawn, Paul** began **encouraging them all to take some** food, saying, **"Today is the fourteenth day that you have been constantly watching and going without eating, having taken nothing. Therefore I encourage you to take some food, for this is for your preservation; for not a hair from the head of any of you shall perish."** For the reasons noted earlier, the passengers and crew had eaten little or nothing since leaving Fair Havens. Now they needed to strengthen themselves for the last hurdle, getting from the ship to the beach. Using a familiar Jewish proverb (cf. 1 Sam. 14:45; 2 Sam. 14:11; 1 Kings 1:52; Luke 21:18), Paul again reminded them of God's promise to deliver them, declaring **"not a hair from the head of any of you shall perish."**

Then, leading by example, **he took bread and gave thanks to God in the presence of all; and he broke it and began to eat.** Inspired by Paul's calm, reassuring attitude, the rest **were encouraged, and they themselves also took food**—all **two hundred and seventy-six persons** on board.

After **they had eaten enough,** they began to make preparations to beach the vessel. The first step was **to lighten the ship** (so it would ride higher in the water and go farther up the beach) **by throwing out the** remaining **wheat into the sea.** The next step was to find a spot to run the ship on shore. But **when day came, they could not recognize the land.** However, **they did observe a certain bay with a beach, and they resolved to drive the ship onto it if they could.** Having chosen their spot, the sailors began making preparations to beach the ship. They began by **casting off the anchors,** leaving **them in the sea.** They were no longer needed, and the sailors did not want their extra weight on board. **At the same time they were loosening the ropes** that bound the **rudders** to the sides of the ship. Then, **hoisting the foresail to the wind, they** headed **for the beach.** The crew intended to beach the ship much like a modern landing craft.

But then the final disaster of this ill-fated voyage took place. **Striking a reef where two seas met, they ran the vessel aground; and the prow stuck fast and remained immovable, but the stern began to be broken up by the force of the waves.** The ship was hopelessly caught; the bow could not be freed from the reef, and the stern was being battered to pieces by the thunderous breakers.

Clearly, the end had come, and it was time to abandon ship. Fearing the punishment they would face if the prisoners escaped (cf. Acts 12:19; 16:27), **the soldiers' plan was to kill** them, so **that none of them should swim away and escape** in the confusion. However, **the centurion, wanting to bring Paul safely through, kept them from their intention.** Paul had repeatedly proved his value, and Julius had grown to respect him as the voyage progressed. Instead of allowing his men to slaughter the prisoners, he ordered all soldiers, prisoners, crew, and passengers to abandon ship. Julius **commanded that those who could swim should jump overboard first and get to land, and the rest should follow, some on planks, and others on various things from the ship. And thus it happened that all** 276 people on board **were brought safely to land**—just as God had promised. God's power and providence had triumphed, and His glory had been displayed.

Looking back over this dramatic episode in Paul's life, several key principles of true biblical leadership can be clearly seen.

First, a leader is trusted. Paul was an important prisoner, whose escape or death would have meant serious trouble for Julius. Yet somehow during the brief journey from Caesarea to Sidon, Paul convinced the centurion that he could be trusted. Julius therefore let him leave the ship to be ministered to by the Christians there.

Second, a leader takes the initiative. At the council at Fair Havens, Paul, although a prisoner, did not hesitate to give his advice.

Third, a leader uses good judgment. Had the centurion and sailors heeded Paul's sound advice, they would have been spared a terrible ordeal—and the loss of the ship.

Fourth, a leader speaks with authority. In the midst of the raging storm, Paul's confident assertion that all on board would be saved must have seemed like madness. But his unshakable confidence in God's Word caused him to speak out boldly. Paul also called others to obedience; he was the one who prevented the sailors from abandoning the rest of the passengers (v. 31).

Fifth, a leader strengthens others. Paul three times encouraged the terrified passengers and crew (vv. 22, 25, 34)—twice not to lose hope and once to eat. His calmness, confidence, and optimistic trust in God also reassured the others.

Sixth, a leader never compromises his absolutes. Paul prevented the crew from prematurely abandoning the ship. God had said that all would be saved, but all must remain together, and Paul refused to compromise on that instruction.

Seventh, and most important, a leader leads by example. Believing God would do exactly as He said, Paul set an example for the others by remaining calm and confident. Realizing they needed to eat before attempting to get ashore, Paul "took bread and gave thanks to God in the presence of all; and he broke it and began to eat" (v. 35). His example motivated the others, "and they themselves also took food" (v. 36). Leaders do not push people from behind; they lead them from the front.

These timeless principles of leadership, manifested in the midst of appalling circumstances, reveal Paul as the godly leader he was. They must characterize every leader who wishes to effectively lead God's people.

Paul's Journey to Rome, Part 2 The Last Lap: Malta to Rome (Acts 28:1–16)

And when they had been brought safely through, then we found out that the island was called Malta. And the natives showed us extraordinary kindness; for because of the rain that had set in and because of the cold, they kindled a fire and received us all. But when Paul had gathered a bundle of sticks and laid them on the fire, a viper came out because of the heat, and fastened on his hand. And when the natives saw the creature hanging from his hand, they began saying to one another, "Undoubtedly this man is a murderer, and though he has been saved from the sea, justice has not allowed him to live." However he shook the creature off into the fire and suffered no harm. But they were expecting that he was about to swell up or suddenly fall down dead. But after they had waited a long time and had seen nothing unusual happen to him, they changed their minds and began to say that he was a god. Now in the neighborhood of that place were lands belonging to the leading man of the island, named Publius, who welcomed us and entertained us courteously three days. And it came about that the father of Publius was lying in bed afflicted with recurrent fever and dysentery; and Paul went in to see him and after he had prayed, he laid his hands on him and healed him. And after this had happened, the rest of the people on the

island who had diseases were coming to him and getting cured. And they also honored us with many marks of respect; and when we were setting sail, they supplied us with all we needed. And at the end of three months we set sail on an Alexandrian ship which had wintered at the island, and which had the Twin Brothers for its figurehead. And after we put in at Syracuse, we stayed there for three days. And from there we sailed around and arrived at Rhegium, and a day later a south wind sprang up, and on the second day we came to Puteoli. There we found some brethren, and were invited to stay with them for seven days; and thus we came to Rome. And the brethren, when they heard about us, came from there as far as the Market of Appius and Three Inns to meet us; and when Paul saw them, he thanked God and took courage. And when we entered Rome, Paul was allowed to stay by himself, with the soldier who was guarding him. (28:1–16)

It is a foundational biblical truth that obedience brings God's blessing, disobedience His chastening. In Luke 11:28, Jesus said, "Blessed are those who hear the word of God, and observe it." James reveals that it is the "effectual doer" who "shall be blessed in what he does" (James 1:25). In Deuteronomy 11:26–28, Moses exhorted the Israelites:

> See, I am setting before you today a blessing and a curse: the blessing, if you listen to the commandments of the Lord your God, which I am commanding you today; and the curse, if you do not listen to the commandments of the Lord your God, but turn aside from the way which I am commanding you today, by following other gods which you have not known. (cf. Deut. 28:1ff.)

Because of his obedience, King Uzziah "was marvelously helped until he was strong" (2 Chron. 26:15). "But when he became strong, his heart was so proud that he acted corruptly, and he was unfaithful to the Lord his God, for he entered the temple of the Lord to burn incense on the altar of incense" (v. 16). For that act of disobedience God struck him with leprosy, and he lived in disgrace the rest of his life.

One way God blesses those who obey Him is by granting their desires. In Psalm 21:1–2, David wrote, "O Lord, in Thy strength the king will be glad, and in Thy salvation how greatly he will rejoice! Thou hast given him his heart's desire, and Thou hast not withheld the request of his lips." Psalm 37:4 promises, "Delight yourself in the Lord; and He will give you the desires of your heart," while Psalm 145:19 declares, "He will fulfill the desire of those who fear Him." Proverbs 10:24 contrasts the disobedient with the obedient: "What the wicked fears will come upon him," but "the desire of the righteous will be granted."

The apostle Paul had desired for many years to visit Rome. In Acts 19:21 he said, "After I have been there [Jerusalem], I must also see Rome." He repeatedly expressed that desire to the Roman Christians:

> For I long to see you in order that I may impart some spiritual gift to you, that you may be established . . . Thus, for my part, I am eager to preach the gospel to you also who are in Rome. . . . I have had for many years a longing to come to you. (Rom. 1:11, 15; 15:23)

At long last, the time had come for God to grant His faithful servant's desire. After years of waiting, two years in a Roman prison, a terrifying two-week-long storm at sea, and his fourth shipwreck (cf. 2 Cor. 11:25), Paul would at last see Rome. This climactic passage records the story of the apostle's arrival in the imperial capital.

Acts 28 opens with Paul on the Mediterranean island of Malta. He had left Caesarea more than two months earlier, bound for Rome to have his appeal heard by the emperor. In a risky attempt to reach a more favorable harbor on Crete to winter in, the apostle's ship had been caught in the dreaded Euraquilo. That violent storm had driven the vessel for fourteen terror-filled days across the Mediterranean to Malta. There the crew attempted to beach the ship, but it ran aground and was destroyed by the pounding surf. Miraculously, all 276 persons on board managed to reach the shore safely. God had promised Paul that although the ship would be destroyed, no lives would be lost (27:22). He had also promised that the ship would run aground on an island (27:26). Both promises were fulfilled when the ship reached Malta.

The events of Acts 28:1–16 unfold in five scenes: pagan hospitality, potential harm, public healing, the promise honored, and private housing.

PAGAN HOSPITALITY

And when they had been brought safely through, then we found out that the island was called Malta. And the natives showed us extraordinary kindness; for because of the rain that had set in and because of the cold, they kindled a fire and received us all. (28:1–2)

Having made it **safely through** the breakers to the beach, the people from the wrecked freighter huddled wet and exhausted on the shore. It was only **then** that **they found out that the island** they were on **was Malta.** Although some of the crew had probably been to Malta before, they had never seen St. Paul's Bay. They would have stopped at the main port, called Valletta.

Malta, located fifty-eight miles south of Sicily, is about seventeen miles long and nine miles wide. Since it is not a large island, it would not have taken the sailors long to discover where they were. They may have found out from the nearby inhabitants. Those inhabitants were of Phoenician descent, and the name Malta meant, appropriately, "a place of refuge" in the Phoenician language. Malta became a British possession early in the nineteenth century and gained its independence in 1964.

Luke's use of the term **natives** to describe the people of Malta does not mean they were primitive or uncivilized. *Barbaroi* (**natives**) denotes people whose native language was not Greek or Latin; it is not necessarily a derogatory term.

The reaction of the Maltese to their unexpected visitors proves that they were anything but uncivilized. Luke records that they **showed extraordinary kindness,** beyond what would normally be expected. They did not murder or enslave the victims of the shipwreck, as sometimes happened in the ancient world. Instead, Luke says, **because of the rain that had set in and because of the cold, they kindled a fire and received us all.** Exhausted from their long ordeal, soaked from their swim to shore, drenched by the driving rain, and chilled by the cold November wind, they welcomed a fire to warm themselves.

God requires Christians, both church leaders (1 Tim. 3:2; Titus 1:8) and all believers (Rom. 12:13; Heb. 13:2; 1 Pet. 4:9), to show hospitality. That the pagan Maltese exhibited it illustrates an important theological truth. One aspect of God's general revelation to all people is the moral law written on their hearts. Although the specifics may vary, every culture holds some things to be right and other things to be wrong. Paul sets forth that truth in his letter to the Romans:

> For when Gentiles who do not have the Law do instinctively the things of the Law, these, not having the Law, are a law to themselves, in that they show the work of the Law written in their hearts, their conscience bearing witness, and their thoughts alternately accusing or else defending them . . . And will not he who is physically uncircumcised, if he keeps the Law, will he not judge you who though having the letter of the Law and circumcision are a transgressor of the Law? (Rom. 2:14–15, 27)

Because God has so revealed Himself, all men are without excuse:

Therefore you are without excuse, every man of you who passes judgment, for in that you judge another, you condemn yourself; for you who judge practice the same things. And we know that the judgment of God rightly falls upon those who practice such things. And do you suppose this, O man, when you pass judgment upon those who practice such things and do the same yourself, that you will escape the judgment of God? (Rom. 2:1–3)

God can justly condemn those who never hear the gospel because they fail to keep the moral standards they impose on others. Because "there is no partiality with God, . . . all who have sinned without the Law [who have only general revelation] will also perish without the Law; and all who have sinned under the Law will be judged by the Law" (Rom. 2:11–12).

POTENTIAL HARM

But when Paul had gathered a bundle of sticks and laid them on the fire, a viper came out because of the heat, and fastened on his hand. And when the natives saw the creature hanging from his hand, they began saying to one another, "Undoubtedly this man is a murderer, and though he has been saved from the sea, justice has not allowed him to live." However he shook the creature off into the fire and suffered no harm. But they were expecting that he was about to swell up or suddenly fall down dead. But after they had waited a long time and had seen nothing unusual happen to him, they changed their minds and began to say that he was a god. (28:3–6)

Wood needed to be added continually to the bonfire to keep it from going out. It is a measure of Paul's character that he humbly stooped to perform such a menial task. Humility is essential to true leadership. "Even the Son of Man," Jesus said, "did not come to be served, but to serve, and to give His life a ransom for many" (Mark 10:45). He gave the classic illustration of humble service by washing the quarrelsome disciples' feet (John 13:3ff.).

Having **gathered a bundle of sticks,** Paul **laid them on the fire.** Unfortunately, one of the "sticks" was alive, and **a viper came out because of the heat, and fastened on his hand.** Startled from its lethargy by the sudden heat, the venomous reptile immediately bit Paul on the hand.

Critics have charged that this is a fictional attempt by Luke to glorify Paul, or that Luke mistook a harmless snake for a poisonous one.

They raise those objections because Malta today has no poisonous snakes. But that does not prove that there were none there nineteen centuries ago. They have disappeared due to the progress of civilization on Malta since Paul's day.

As a trained physician, Luke would be unlikely to mistake a harmless snake for a poisonous one. Sir William Ramsay notes that "a trained medical man in ancient times was usually a good authority about serpents, to which great respect was paid in ancient medicine and custom" (*Luke the Physician* [Grand Rapids: Baker, 1996], 63–64). But the most convincing proof that this was in fact a poisonous snake comes from the reaction of the islanders, who fully expected Paul to die after being bitten. **When the natives saw the creature** (*thērion*—"Aristotle and the medical writers apply the word to venomous serpents, the viper in particular" [A. T. Robertson, *Word Pictures in the New Testament* (Grand Rapids: Baker's reprint of the 1930 edition), 3:479]) **hanging from his hand, they began saying to one another, "Undoubtedly this man is a murderer, and though he has been saved from the sea, justice has not allowed him to live."**

Here is another illustration of the truth that all cultures have a sense of justice. The islanders had no doubt from the presence of Roman soldiers that Paul was a serious criminal, likely a **murderer,** and as such would not escape his fate. Although he had **been saved from the sea, justice** (probably a reference to *Dikē*, the goddess of justice) would not allow **him to live.** The pagan Maltese had a clear sense of right and wrong; they "show[ed] the work of the Law written in their hearts" (Rom. 2:15).

Although once disposed to killing Christians, Paul, since his conversion, was no murderer. He merely **shook the creature off into the fire and suffered no harm.** The apostle's calmness was conspicuous; most people bitten by poisonous snakes panic. But Paul had absolute faith in God's repeated promises that he would see Rome (Acts 23:11; 27:24). Therefore, he knew he would not die on Malta. As always in Acts, God used this miracle to authenticate His message and His messenger.

The islanders, however, **were** still **expecting** Paul's hand **to swell up** from the bite, **or** that he would **suddenly fall down dead.** But when they **had waited a long time and had seen nothing unusual happen to him, they changed their minds and began to say that he was a god.** Obviously they had been mistaken; this was no victim of their goddess but a god himself, they thought. Such divine beings were, they believed, impervious to such trivialities as snakebite. This was not the first time Paul had been mistaken for a god (Acts 14:6ff.), and he no doubt quickly set the islanders straight.

PUBLIC HEALING

Now in the neighborhood of that place were lands belonging to the leading man of the island, named Publius, who welcomed us and entertained us courteously three days. And it came about that the father of Publius was lying in bed afflicted with recurrent fever and dysentery; and Paul went in to see him and after he had prayed, he laid his hands on him and healed him. And after this had happened, the rest of the people on the island who had diseases were coming to him and getting cured. And they also honored us with many marks of respect; and when we were setting sail, they supplied us with all we needed. And at the end of three months we set sail on an Alexandrian ship which had wintered at the island, and which had the Twin Brothers for its figurehead. (28:7–11)

Not far from St. Paul's Bay **were lands belonging to the leading man of the island, named Publius.** As his title **the leading man of the island** (*tō prōtō tēs nēsou*) indicates, he was the Roman governor of Malta. Inscriptional evidence confirms Luke's use of that title (cf. Bruce, *Acts*, 523). Publius graciously **welcomed** all 276 persons **and entertained** them **courteously** for **three days** until they could make arrangements for winter quarters.

Publius extended hospitality even though his **father was lying in bed afflicted with recurrent fever and dysentery.** The **recurrent fever** was likely the gastric fever, caused by a microbe found in goat's milk, which was common on Malta. **Dysentery,** often resulting from poor sanitation, was also common in the ancient world.

God often rewards acts of kindness to His people (cf. Gen. 12:3; Matt. 10:40–42; 25:31ff.), and Paul was able to repay Publius for his hospitality. He **went in to see** Publius's father, **and after he had prayed, he laid his hands on him and healed him.** Paul's prayer acknowledged his dependence on God's power; his laying on of hands affirmed that God was working through him.

Not surprisingly, **after this had happened, the rest of the people on the island who had diseases were coming to** Paul **and getting cured.** Although Luke does not mention it, Paul undoubtedly preached the gospel to the Maltese, since the purpose of miracles was to authenticate Paul as God's messenger. Given Julius's lenient treatment of him, and their three-month stay (v. 11), Paul would have had many opportunities to preach. According to tradition, the church on Malta dates from this time, with Publius as its first pastor.

Verse 10 also implies that a church was founded at this time on

Malta. Luke records that the islanders **honored** Paul and the others **with many marks of respect; and when** they **were setting sail, supplied** them **with all** they **needed.** That outpouring of love suggests that at least some of the Maltese were receptive to the preaching of the gospel.

After spending the **three months** of winter on Malta, Paul and his companions were finally able to leave. With sea travel beginning again, Julius was able to arrange transport to Italy for his soldiers and prisoners **on an Alexandrian ship which had wintered at the island, and which had the Twin Brothers for its figurehead.** The **Alexandrian ship** was probably another in the imperial grain fleet. Luke's note that it **had the Twin Brothers for its figurehead** serves to identify the specific ship on which they traveled. The **Twin Brothers** were Castor and Pollux, sons of Zeus in Greek mythology and viewed as the gods who protected sailors.

THE PROMISE HONORED

And after we put in at Syracuse, we stayed there for three days. And from there we sailed around and arrived at Rhegium, and a day later a south wind sprang up, and on the second day we came to Puteoli. There we found some brethren, and were invited to stay with them for seven days; and thus we came to Rome. And the brethren, when they heard about us, came from there as far as the Market of Appius and Three Inns to meet us; and when Paul saw them, he thanked God and took courage. (28:12–15)

Leaving Malta, the ship **put in at Syracuse,** 100 miles away on the southeastern shore of Sicily. According to tradition, Paul founded a church in Syracuse during the **three days** the ship stopped there. After their short visit, the travelers **sailed around** (tacked against the wind) **and arrived at Rhegium,** on the southern tip of the Italian peninsula. There they waited for a favorable wind to take the ship through the Straits of Messina (which separate Sicily from the Italian mainland). The next **day a south wind sprang up, and on the second day** after leaving Rhegium, the ship arrived at **Puteoli. Puteoli,** modern Pozzuoli, was the most important commercial port in Italy. Although almost 150 miles from Rome, it was the capital's chief seaport. (Ostia, an artificial harbor near Rome, had already been built. It would not significantly affect Puteoli's trade, however, until early in the second century.) Located on the bay of Naples near Neapolis (modern Naples) and the doomed city of Pompeii, Puteoli in Paul's day was a city of 100,000 people. It is thought to have been the chief port for the Egyptian grain fleet.

Not unexpectedly in a city of that size, Paul and his companions **found some brethren** (Christians) in Puteoli. Those believers **invited** the travelers **to stay with them,** and, with Julius's permission (cf. 27:3), they stayed **for seven days**. From there, Luke notes with dramatic understatement, **we came to Rome.**

Luke then fills in, briefly, the details of their journey along the Appian Way from Puteoli to Rome. **The brethren** (Christians) **of Rome, when they heard about us** (undoubtedly from the Christians of Puteoli)**, came from there as far as the Market of Appius and Three Inns to meet us.** Some walked as far south as **the Market of Appius,** forty-three miles from Rome; others, possibly getting a later start, met Paul ten miles closer to Rome at the **Three Inns.** Deeply moved by their visible demonstration of love for him, **Paul thanked God and took courage.**

THE PRISONER HOUSED

And when we entered Rome, Paul was allowed to stay by himself, with the soldier who was guarding him. (28:16)

Paul's lenient treatment by Roman officials continued. After the apostle and his party **entered Rome, Paul was allowed to stay by himself with** a **soldier guarding him.** That soldier (probably several in turn) was chained to Paul's wrist (v. 20).

This passage reveals several ways in which God blesses His faithful servants.

First, He surrounds them with kindness. Julius showed Paul kindness by allowing him to go ashore in Sidon (27:3). The Maltese also showed him kindness after the shipwreck (28:1–2, 10).

Second, God meets their needs. Publius provided Paul with a place to stay on Malta (28:7), as did the Christians at Puteoli (28:14).

Third, God encourages them. During the terrifying ordeal of the storm at sea, God sent an angel to hearten Paul (27:23–24). And the apostle was greatly encouraged by the Roman Christians, who eagerly met him well outside the city (28:15).

Fourth, God delivers them from harm. He delivered Paul from a storm, a shipwreck, and a snakebite.

Fifth, God blesses their influence. Paul greatly affected those who survived the storm and shipwreck. And through his ministry, a church was most likely begun on Malta and possibly at Syracuse.

Finally, God fulfills their desires. Paul had yearned for many years to see Rome; now that desire had been granted.

Proverbs 28:20 sums it up in the promise "a faithful man will abound with blessing."

The Story
That Never Ends
(Acts 28:17–31)

28

And it happened that after three days he called together those who were the leading men of the Jews, and when they had come together, he began saying to them, "Brethren, though I had done nothing against our people, or the customs of our fathers, yet I was delivered prisoner from Jerusalem into the hands of the Romans. And when they had examined me, they were willing to release me because there was no ground for putting me to death. But when the Jews objected, I was forced to appeal to Caesar; not that I had any accusation against my nation. For this reason therefore, I requested to see you and to speak with you, for I am wearing this chain for the sake of the hope of Israel." And they said to him, "We have neither received letters from Judea concerning you, nor have any of the brethren come here and reported or spoken anything bad about you. But we desire to hear from you what your views are; for concerning this sect, it is known to us that it is spoken against everywhere." And when they had set a day for him, they came to him at his lodging in large numbers; and he was explaining to them by solemnly testifying about the kingdom of God, and trying to persuade them concerning Jesus, from both the Law of Moses and from the Prophets, from morning until evening. And some were being persuaded by the things

spoken, but others would not believe. And when they did not agree with one another, they began leaving after Paul had spoken one parting word, "The Holy Spirit rightly spoke through Isaiah the prophet to your fathers, saying, 'Go to this people and say, "You will keep on hearing, but will not understand; and you will keep on seeing, but will not perceive; for the heart of this people has become dull, and with their ears they scarcely hear, and they have closed their eyes; lest they should see with their eyes, and hear with their ears, and understand with their heart and return, and I should heal them."' Let it be known to you therefore, that this salvation of God has been sent to the Gentiles; they will also listen." And he stayed two full years in his own rented quarters, and was welcoming all who came to him, preaching the kingdom of God, and teaching concerning the Lord Jesus Christ with all openness, unhindered. (28:17–31)

The final chapter of Acts is both an end and a beginning. In it Luke brings his narrative of the beginnings and early history of the church to a close. That narrative covers the expansion of the church geographically, from its birth in Jerusalem on the Day of Pentecost, to Judea, Samaria, and much of the Roman world (cf. 1:8). Acts also records the expansion of the church ethnically. What began as an exclusively Jewish institution grew to embrace the Samaritans and the Gentiles.

Through the tireless efforts of the apostle Paul, churches were founded, strengthened, given leaders, and protected from false teachers. But his bold, uncompromising preaching earned him many enemies. Finally, they managed to have him arrested and imprisoned by the Romans. After three hearings before Roman judges had failed to resolve his case, Paul had been forced to appeal to the emperor. Following a harrowing sea voyage and shipwreck, the apostle finally reached the imperial capital. It is at that point that Luke's account ends.

But the story does not end there. Released from the Roman imprisonment recorded in Acts 28, Paul resumed his missionary efforts—probably even reaching Spain (Rom. 15:24). Arrested a second time a few years later, he was finally executed. (For a defense of the view that Paul was twice imprisoned at Rome, see John MacArthur, *1 Timothy*, MacArthur New Testament Commentary [Chicago: Moody, 1995], x–xi.) But the story of the church did not end with Paul's death or that of the last surviving apostle, John, near the end of the first century. The apostles handed the baton to a second generation of leaders, who in turn handed it to others. As a result, the church's history is still being written today.

Although Acts ends abruptly, it is not incomplete. It reveals the church's source of power—the Holy Spirit; the pattern of blessing for the church—walking in the Spirit; the church's message—the saving gospel of Jesus Christ; the perils to the church—sin from within, false teachers from without; and the church's priorities—teach the Word to those who know Christ, and preach the gospel to those who do not.

Acts ends with Paul in Rome. Proud capital of the greatest empire the world had ever known, Rome was a center of decadent paganism. Paul thus found himself a prisoner in the middle of a vast mission field. It is fitting that Acts, which has focused so much on evangelism, closes with the account of Paul's first (but not last, cf. Phil. 1:13; 4:22) evangelistic effort in Rome. That effort unfolds in five stages: Paul's introduction, the Jewish leaders' interest, the gospel's presentation, Israel's rejection, and the story's incompleteness.

PAUL'S INTRODUCTION

And it happened that after three days he called together those who were the leading men of the Jews, and when they had come together, he began saying to them, "Brethren, though I had done nothing against our people, or the customs of our fathers, yet I was delivered prisoner from Jerusalem into the hands of the Romans. And when they had examined me, they were willing to release me because there was no ground for putting me to death. But when the Jews objected, I was forced to appeal to Caesar; not that I had any accusation against my nation. For this reason therefore, I requested to see you and to speak with you, for I am wearing this chain for the sake of the hope of Israel." (28:17–20)

Never one to waste time, **three days** after arriving **in Rome** Paul **called together those who were the leading men of the Jews.** The **leading men** of Rome's Jewish community included the prominent men from the synagogues. It had always been Paul's pattern, when he evangelized a city, to go first to the Jewish community (cf. Rom. 1:16). And though Paul had been accused of being anti-Semitic, that was opposite the truth (cf. Rom. 9:1–3; 10:1). Despite the abuse and persecution he had experienced from the Jewish people throughout his ministry, he bore his countrymen no animosity. Therefore, he went directly to them after arriving in Rome. It is likely that Paul assumed they had heard about him from the Jews at Jerusalem.

The apostle faced a delicate task. He needed to explain why he was a prisoner, and to defend his innocence, without alienating the members of Rome's Jewish community. His brief defense before them is the sixth and final one recorded in Acts (cf. 21:27ff.; 22:30ff.; 24:1ff.; 25:1–12; 25:13ff.). After the leaders **had come** to his lodging, **he began saying to them, "Brethren, though I had done nothing against**

our people, or the customs of our fathers, yet I was delivered prisoner from Jerusalem into the hands of the Romans." The Sanhedrin had falsely accused him of sedition against Rome, of being the leader of a heretical sect, and of violating the Temple (cf. 24:5–6). Rome's Jewish leaders would not have been too concerned with the first charge, and Paul did not even mention it. The second two charges he categorically denied, declaring **"I have done nothing against our people, or the customs of our fathers."** It was only the Sanhedrin's hostility to the gospel that caused the apostle to be **delivered prisoner from Jerusalem into the hands of the Romans.**

To support his claim of innocence, Paul pointed out that **"when the Romans had examined me, they were willing to release me because there was no ground for putting me to death."** Three Roman officials, the tribune Claudius Lysias (23:28–29), and the governors Felix (24:22–27) and Festus (25:18–19), as well as Herod Agrippa (26:31–32), had affirmed Paul's innocence. The Sanhedrin could not prove its case despite three separate hearings.

The only reason the Romans did not free Paul was that **the Jews objected,** making it politically imprudent for either Felix or Festus to release him. It was because of those objections that Paul **was forced to appeal to Caesar;** it was **not,** he hastened to add, **"that I had any accusation against my nation."** The political intriguing of the Sanhedrin left him no recourse but to appeal to the emperor, thus transferring his case out of Palestine. Paul did not want anything he had done to be interpreted as an attack on the Jewish people. His actions were strictly defensive, not offensive; he was the accused, not the accuser.

So the Jewish leaders of Rome could hear everything from him firsthand, Paul **requested to see** them **and to speak with** them. Then he brought up the real issue behind his arrest and imprisonment. He declared, **"I am wearing this chain** (cf. Eph. 6:20; 2 Tim. 1:16) **for the sake of the hope of Israel."** The glorious hope of Israel was the coming of the Messiah and the resurrection and kingdom associated with His coming. It was Paul's preaching of Jesus as the resurrected King that antagonized the Jewish authorities.

That he was on trial for his belief in Israel's hope was a recurring theme in Paul's defenses. At his hearing before the Sanhedrin, Paul "perceiving that one part were Sadducees and the other Pharisees, began crying out in the Council, 'Brethren, I am a Pharisee, a son of Pharisees; I am on trial for the hope and resurrection of the dead'" (23:6)! On trial before Felix, Paul declared to the governor:

> But this I admit to you, that according to the Way which they call a sect I do serve the God of our fathers, believing everything that is in accor-

dance with the Law, and that is written in the Prophets; having a hope in God, which these men cherish themselves, that there shall certainly be a resurrection of both the righteous and the wicked. (24:14–15)

Paul insisted to Agrippa that "I am standing trial for the hope of the promise made by God to our fathers" (26:6).

That hope was firmly grounded in the Old Testament. It is expressed in the ancient book of Job: "Even after my skin is destroyed, yet from my flesh I shall see God; whom I myself shall behold, and whom my eyes shall see and not another" (Job 19:26–27). Isaiah prophesied, "Your dead will live; their corpses will rise. You who lie in the dust, awake and shout for joy, for your dew is as the dew of the dawn, and the earth will give birth to the departed spirits" (Isa. 26:19). In Daniel 12:2, Daniel was told, "Many of those who sleep in the dust of the ground will awake, these to everlasting life, but the others to disgrace and everlasting contempt."

The Jewish Leaders' Interest

And they said to him, "We have neither received letters from Judea concerning you, nor have any of the brethren come here and reported or spoken anything bad about you. But we desire to hear from you what your views are; for concerning this sect, it is known to us that it is spoken against everywhere." (28:21–22)

The Jewish leaders denied any knowledge of Paul's case. They had heard nothing officially, having **received** no **letters from Judea concerning** Paul, or unofficially, since none **of the brethren** had **come** to Rome **and reported or spoken anything bad about** him.

Some have found it incredible that no word about Paul had reached Rome's Jewish community. But Paul left Palestine on one of the last ships of the previous sailing season, and he arrived in Italy on one of the first ships of the present one. It would have been difficult for someone from Palestine to have arrived in Rome before he did. It may also be true, as some have suggested, that there was little interaction between the Jews of Rome and those of Judea.

Despite any information the Roman Jews may have had, they most likely were deliberately turning a blind eye legally to Paul's case. After having been temporarily expelled from Rome about ten years earlier for clashing with the Christians, they were not anxious for any more controversy. Besides, the Sanhedrin had not asked them to get involved. And they undoubtedly realized the weakness of the case against the apostle. Paul had already been exonerated by two Roman provincial governors; now his case was to be heard by the emperor. Not wishing to look foolish in front of Nero (or face the penalties Roman law meted out for frivolous prosecution—cf. A. N. Sherwin-White, *Roman Society and Roman Law in the New Testament* [Oxford: Oxford University Press, 1963], 52)—they decided their wisest course of action was to disassociate themselves from Paul's case.

Diplomatically they assured Paul of their **desire to hear from** him **what** his **views** were. Cautiously, noncommittally, they acknowledged the obvious: **"concerning this sect, it is known to us that it is spoken against everywhere."** They were not completely ignorant of Christianity, which had been established in Rome for many years.

The Gospel's Presentation

And when they had set a day for him, they came to him at his lodging in large numbers; and he was explaining to them by solemnly testifying about the kingdom of God, and trying to persuade them concerning Jesus, from both the Law of Moses and from the Prophets, from morning until evening. And some were being persuaded by the things spoken, but others would not believe. (28:23–24)

Consistent with their expressed willingness to hear more about Christianity from Paul, the Jewish leaders **had set a day** to return and hear **him.** On the appointed day, **they came to him at his lodging in large numbers.** Paul spent the entire day, **from morning until evening**, proclaiming the way of salvation to them. Luke records that he **was explaining to them by solemnly testifying about the kingdom of God, and trying to persuade them concerning Jesus, from both the Law of Moses and from the Prophets.**

The **kingdom of God** encompasses God's rule in the sphere of salvation, not just the future millennial reign of Jesus Christ. **Testifying about the kingdom** meant preaching the gospel, the good news that God sovereignly calls sinners hopelessly caught in the realm of Satan, death, and destruction to enter the realm of salvation, life, and glory. Paul proclaimed the truths concerning Christ, the way of salvation, and righteous living (Rom. 14:17). He pointed the way for them to enter the sphere of salvation and enjoy fellowship with God.

The vehicle Paul used in **trying to persuade them concerning Jesus** was the **Law of Moses and the Prophets** (the common designation of the Old Testament—cf. Matt. 7:12; Luke 16:16; Acts 13:15; Rom. 3:21). This was Paul's pattern throughout Acts for evangelizing Jews (for a sample of one of his sermons, see Acts 13:16ff.).

As always, the gospel proved divisive. By the end of the day, **some were being persuaded by the things spoken** by Paul, **but others would not believe.** Belief in Jesus as the Messiah, whose atoning sacrifice is the only acceptable payment for sins, coupled with repentance, is man's responsibility. To refuse to do so is to disobey God (cf. John 16:9; Acts 17:31; 2 Cor. 6:1–2; Heb. 3:7–12). As before in Acts, Paul's hearers were divided into those who believed and those who did not:

> But the multitude of the city was divided; and some sided with the Jews, and some with the apostles. (14:4)

> And some of them were persuaded and joined Paul and Silas, along with a great multitude of the God-fearing Greeks and a number of the leading women. But the Jews, becoming jealous and taking along some wicked men from the market place, formed a mob and set the city in an uproar; and coming upon the house of Jason, they were seeking to bring them out to the people. (17:4–5)

> And when they resisted and blasphemed, he shook out his garments and said to them, "Your blood be upon your own heads! I am clean. From now on I shall go to the Gentiles." And he departed from there and went to the house of a certain man named Titius Justus, a worshiper of God, whose house was next to the synagogue. And Crispus, the leader of the synagogue, believed in the Lord with all his household, and many of the Corinthians when they heard were believing and being baptized. (18:6–8)

> And he entered the synagogue and continued speaking out boldly for three months, reasoning and persuading them about the kingdom of God. But when some were becoming hardened and disobedient, speaking evil of the Way before the multitude, he withdrew from them and took away the disciples, reasoning daily in the school of Tyrannus. (19:8–9)

While there was always a believing remnant, most of the Jewish people rejected their Messiah.

Israel's Rejection

And when they did not agree with one another, they began leaving after Paul had spoken one parting word, "The Holy Spirit rightly spoke through Isaiah the prophet to your fathers, saying,

'Go to this people and say, "You will keep on hearing, but will not
understand; and you will keep on seeing, but will not perceive;
for the heart of this people has become dull, and with their ears
they scarcely hear, and they have closed their eyes; lest they
should see with their eyes, and hear with their ears, and understand with their heart and return, and I should heal them."' Let
it be known to you therefore, that this salvation of God has been
sent to the Gentiles; they will also listen. And when he had said
these words, the Jews departed, and had great reasoning among
themselves." (28:25–29)**

Those Jews in Rome who refused to believe Paul were continuing their nation's sad history of rejecting God's messengers. Several times
in Jeremiah, God lamented that fact. In Jeremiah 7:25–26, for example,
God said to wayward, rebellious Israel:

> Since the day that your fathers came out of the land of Egypt until this
> day, I have sent you all My servants the prophets, daily rising early and
> sending them. Yet they did not listen to Me or incline their ear, but stiff-
> ened their neck; they did evil more than their fathers. (cf. 29:19; 35:15;
> 44:4)

Rejecting God's messengers led to disaster for Israel (2 Kings 17:13). Like
the wicked vine growers in Jesus' parable (Matt. 21:33–41), their ultimate
rejection of God came when they killed His Son.

Unable to **agree with one another,** the Jewish leaders **began
leaving after Paul had spoken one parting word** of warning from
the Holy Spirit, who **rightly spoke through Isaiah the prophet** (a
concise definition of the divine inspiration of Scripture; cf. 2 Pet. 1:21) **to**
their **fathers.** The apostle's solemn warning that broke up the meeting
was a quote from Isaiah 6:9–10:

> **Go to this people and say, "You will keep on hearing, but will
> not understand; and you will keep on seeing, but will not per-
> ceive; for the heart of this people has become dull, and with
> their ears they scarcely hear, and they have closed their eyes;
> lest they should see with their eyes, and hear with their ears,
> and understand with their heart and return, and I should heal
> them." (28:26–27)**

That passage was also quoted by the Lord Jesus Christ as a rebuke of
Israel's hardhearted rejection of the gospel (cf. Matt. 13:14–15; John
12:39–40). Israel's willful act of rejection was sovereignly confirmed by

God; because of continual unbelief, she became unable to believe (cf. John 12:37, 39–40).

As he had on other occasions (Acts 13:46–47; 18:6; 19:8–10; cf. 11:18; 14:27; 15:14–18), Paul **let it be known to** his Jewish hearers **that this salvation of God has been sent to the Gentiles; they will also listen.** He expanded that truth in his letter to the Roman Christians:

> But if some of the branches were broken off, and you, being a wild olive, were grafted in among them and became partaker with them of the rich root of the olive tree, . . . You [Gentiles] will say then, "Branches were broken off so that I might be grafted in." Quite right, they were broken off for their unbelief, but you stand by your faith. Do not be conceited, but fear; for if God did not spare the natural branches, neither will He spare you. Behold then the kindness and severity of God; to those who fell, severity, but to you, God's kindness, if you continue in His kindness; otherwise you also will be cut off. (Rom. 11:17, 19–22)

Is Israel's rejection final? Paul answered that question in Romans 11:1–2: "I say then, God has not rejected His people, has He? May it never be! For I too am an Israelite, a descendant of Abraham, of the tribe of Benjamin. God has not rejected His people whom He foreknew." In verse 23 he added, "They also, if they do not continue in their unbelief, will be grafted in; for God is able to graft them in again." The day is coming when "all Israel will be saved" (v. 26). Israel's rejection will not cancel God's promises to bless her believing remnant. The day of Israel's faith in Jesus Christ is yet to come (Zech. 12:10).

THE STORY'S INCOMPLETENESS

And he stayed two full years in his own rented quarters, and was welcoming all who came to him, preaching the kingdom of God, and teaching concerning the Lord Jesus Christ with all openness, unhindered. (28:30–31)

For **two full years,** Paul remained a prisoner **in his own rented quarters** in Rome. He had the freedom to welcome **all who came to him,** although presumably he was not free to leave his quarters. The conditions of his imprisonment did not keep him from **preaching the kingdom of God, and teaching concerning the Lord Jesus Christ with all openness, unhindered** by the Romans.

What happened during those two years? Paul carried out an extensive evangelistic campaign (cf. Phil. 1:13; 4:22), aided by some of his dear fellow workers (cf. Col. 4:10–12, 14; Philem. 24). He also wrote four New Testament epistles: Ephesians, Philippians, Colossians, and Philemon.

What happened when the two years were over? Paul was released (cf. *1 Timothy*, MacArthur New Testament Commentary, x–xi). Since two provincial governors had found him innocent of wrongdoing, it is reasonable to assume the emperor would have too. But a more likely scenario is that the Jewish leaders from Palestine never showed up in Rome to prosecute the case, and Paul won by default. As noted above, Roman law took a dim view of poorly substantiated cases. And the Jews had achieved their goal by getting Paul out of Palestine and into Roman custody. Commentators differ over whether there was a two-year statute of limitations in Paul's day. But even if there were not, Paul's case would likely have been dismissed when it came to trial if no one was there to press charges.

What was the reason for the two-year delay? First, delays were not uncommon due to the backlog of cases. Second, the records pertaining to Paul's case were probably lost in the shipwreck. It would have taken some time to have had them resent from Caesarea. Third, the authorities awaited the arrival of the Jewish leaders, who probably failed to show up. Since Roman law gave Paul the right to face his accusers (25:16), no trial was likely in their absence.

Because Acts is preeminently a book about evangelism, it is appropriate to conclude by drawing several principles of evangelism from Paul's example.

First, Paul preached the gospel whenever and wherever he had opportunity. Under house arrest (vv. 16, 20, 23, 30), he nevertheless continued "preaching the kingdom of God, and teaching concerning the Lord Jesus Christ with all openness" (v. 31).

Second, Paul's message was clothed in humility and graciousness. In vv. 17–20, he was tactful, respectful, and conciliatory to the Jewish leaders at Rome.

Third, Paul preached biblically (v. 23) and doctrinally (v. 31).

Fourth, Paul never wasted opportunity. He began his evangelistic outreach only three days after arriving in Rome (v. 17).

Fifth, Paul preached tirelessly (v. 23) and incessantly (vv. 30–31).

Sixth, Paul preached to everyone—both Jews (vv. 23–27) and Gentiles (v. 28).

Finally, and most important, Paul preached Jesus Christ as Lord, Savior, and Messiah (v. 23).

The church in Acts faithfully carried out Christ's charge "Be My witnesses both in Jerusalem, and in all Judea and Samaria, and even to the remotest part of the earth" (Acts 1:8). The church has passed the baton through many hands down through the centuries to us. Will future generations find that we ran our segment of the race faithfully?

Bibliography

Abbott-Smith, G. *A Manual Greek Lexicon of the New Testament.* Edinburgh: T.& T. Clark, 1977.

Barnes, Albert. *Notes on the New Testament: Acts-Romans.* Grand Rapids: Baker. Reprint of the 1884–85 edition.

Blaiklock, E. M. *The Acts of the Apostles.* Grand Rapids: Eerdmans, 1975.

Blaiklock, E. M., and R. K. Harrison, eds. *The New International Dictionary of Biblical Archaeology.* Grand Rapids: Zondervan, 1983.

Bruce, F. F. "Acts of the Apostles." In *The International Standard Bible Encyclopedia.* Edited by Geoffrey W. Bromiley. Volume 1. Grand Rapids: Eerdmans, 1989.

_____. "The Acts of the Apostles." In *The New Bible Commentary: Revised.* Edited by D. Guthrie and J. A. Motyer. Grand Rapids: Eerdmans, 1978.

_____. *The Book of the Acts.* The New International Commentary on the New Testament. Grand Rapids: Eerdmans, 1971.

_____. *Paul: Apostle of the Heart Set Free.* Grand Rapids: Eerdmans, 1977.

Dana, H. E., and Julius R. Mantey. *A Manual Grammar of the Greek New Testament.* New York, Macmillan, 1957.

Erdman, Charles R. *The Acts*. Philadelphia: Westminster, 1977.

Gundry, Robert H. *A Survey of the New Testament*. Grand Rapids: Zondervan, 1970.

Guthrie, Donald. *New Testament Introduction*. Downers Grove, Ill.: InterVarsity, 1978.

Harrison, Everett F. *Interpreting Acts: The Expanding Church*. Grand Rapids: Zondervan, 1986.

Hiebert, D. Edmond. *An Introduction to the New Testament: Volume 1: The Gospels and Acts*. Chicago: Moody, 1979.

Kent, Homer A., Jr. *Jerusalem to Rome*. Grand Rapids: Baker, 1992.

Kistemaker, Simon J. *New Testament Commentary: Acts*. Grand Rapids: Baker, 1990.

Lenski, R. C. H. *The Interpretation of the Acts of the Apostles*. Minneapolis: Augsburg, 1961.

Linnemann, Eta. *Is There a Synoptic Problem?* Grand Rapids: Baker, 1992.

Longenecker, Richard N. "The Acts of the Apostles." In *The Expositor's Bible Commentary*. Edited by Frank E. Gaebelein. Volume 9. Grand Rapids: Zondervan: 1981.

Marshall, I. Howard. *The Acts of the Apostles*. Grand Rapids: Eerdmans, 1984.

Morgan, G. Campbell. *The Acts of the Apostles*. New York: Revell, 1924.

Munck, Johannes. *The Acts of the Apostles*. Garden City, N.Y.: Doubleday, 1973.

Pfeiffer, Charles F., and Howard F. Vos. *The Wycliffe Historical Geography of Bible Lands*. Chicago: Moody, 1967.

Polhill, John B. *The New American Commentary: Acts*. Nashville: Broadman, 1992.

Rackham, Richard B. *The Acts of the Apostles*. Grand Rapids: Baker, 1978.

Ramsay, W. M. *St. Paul the Traveller and the Roman Citizen*. Reprint. Grand Rapids: Baker, 1975.

Robertson, A. T. *Word Pictures in the New Testament*. Reprint. Grand Rapids: Baker, 1930.

Sherwin-White, A. N. *Roman Society and Roman Law in the New Testament*. Oxford: Oxford University Press, 1963.

Smith, James. *The Voyage and Shipwreck of St. Paul*. Reprint. Grand Rapids: Baker, 1978.

Stokes, G. T. "The Acts of the Apostles." In *The Expositor's Bible*. Edited by W. Robertson Nicoll. New York: A. C. Armstrong and Son, 1903.

Stott, John. *The Spirit, the Church, and The World: The Message of Acts.* Downers Grove, Ill.: InterVarsity, 1990.

Thomas, Robert L., and Stanley N. Gundry, eds. *A Harmony of the Gospels.* Chicago: Moody, 1978.

Vincent, Marvin R. *Word Studies in the New Testament.* Grand Rapids: Eerdmans, 1946.

Vine, W. E. *An Expository Dictionary of New Testament Words.* Old Tappan, N.J.: Revell, 1966.

Williams, David J. *Acts.* The New International Biblical Commentary. Peabody, Mass.: Hendrickson, 1990.

Indexes

Index of Greek Words

Makedonas, 186
mathētēs, 164
metanoia, 216, 337
muriades, 249
nomizō, 53
noutheteō, 228
pais, 204
paroxunō, 130
paroxusmos, 82
parrēsiazomai, 172
peithō, 173
phantasia, 329
pisteusantes, 164
poimainō, 224
politarchs, 124
praxeis, 177
prōtos, 338
prōtostatēs, 304
radiourgias, 10

Sebastos, 329
sicarii, 303
sikariōn, 263
skēnopoios, 148
sklērunō, 173
spermologos, 131
stratēgos, 103
sunbibazō, 188
sunedrion, 278
suntrophos, 4
tarassō, 72
tassō, 39
theōreō, 249
thērion, 362
thorubeō, 204
thorubos, 194
tō prōtō tēs nēsou, 363
tuptō, 281

Index of Scripture

Index of Subjects

Moody Press, a ministry of Moody Bible Institute,
is designed for education, evangelization, and edification.
If we may assist you in knowing more about Christ
and the Christian life, please write us without obligation:
Moody Press, c/o MLM, Chicago, Illinois 60610.